P9-CFT-484

Kitchen Cures

Homemade Remedies for Your Health

Reader's Digest

The Reader's Digest Association, Inc.
New York, NY | Montreal

Project Staff

EDITOR
Neil Wertheimer

SENIOR ART DIRECTOR
Rich Kershner

COVER DESIGN
George McKeon

PRINCIPAL WRITER
Sara Altshul

CONTRIBUTING WRITER
Denise Foley

MEDICAL ADVISOR AND REVIEWER
Dr. Pamela Hops

COPY EDITOR
Marcia Mangum Cronin

PHOTOGRAPHER
Frances Janisch

STYLISTS
Paul Lowe, Don Gilder

INDEXER
Cohen Carruth Indexes

Reader's Digest Content Creation Studio

VP, EDITOR IN CHIEF
Neil Wertheimer

CREATIVE DIRECTOR
Michele Laseau

EXECUTIVE MANAGING EDITOR
Donna Ruvituso

ASSOCIATE DIRECTOR, NORTH AMERICA PREPRESS
Douglas A. Croll

MANUFACTURING MANAGER
John L. Cassidy

MARKETING DIRECTOR
Dawn Nelson

The Reader's Digest Association, Inc.

PRESIDENT AND CHIEF EXECUTIVE OFFICER
Mary G. Berner

PRESIDENT, READER'S DIGEST COMMUNITY
Lisa Sharples

PRESIDENT, RD MEDIA
Dan Lagani

NORTH AMERICAN CHIEF MARKETING OFFICER
Lisa Karpinski

A READER'S DIGEST BOOK

Copyright © 2011 The Reader's Digest Association, Inc.

All rights reserved. Unauthorized reproduction, in any manner, is prohibited.

Reader's Digest is a registered trademark of The Reader's Digest Association, Inc.

Library of Congress Cataloging in Publication Data is available upon request.

ISBN 13: 978-1-60652-330-8

We are committed to both the quality of our products and the service we provide to our customers. We value your comments, so please feel free to contact us.

The Reader's Digest Association, Inc.
Adult Trade Publishing
44 S. Broadway
White Plains, NY 10601

For more Reader's Digest products and information, visit our website:
www.rd.com (in the United States)

Printed in China

1 3 5 7 9 10 8 6 4 2

NOTE TO READERS
The information in this book should not be substituted for, or used to alter, medical therapy without your doctor's advice. For a specific health problem, consult your physician for guidance. The mention of any products, retail businesses, or websites in this book does not imply or constitute an endorsement by the authors or by The Reader's Digest Association, Inc.

Cures That Work

The proof is in! Home remedies often rival or even exceed the healing power of drugstore medicines. Recent studies have shown that . . .

Aloe gel improves psoriasis better than prescription cream

Baking soda slows the progress of chronic kidney disease

Clove oil is a powerful fungus killer

Green tea can help you lose weight

Walnuts and canned fish lower cholesterol levels

Honey truly does enhance wound healing

Smelling lavender and rosemary oil reduces anxiety

And that's just a taste! *Kitchen Cures* is your comprehensive guide to natural healing at home. Here are more than 1,000 remedies for the most common health ailments and conditions. Save money, save time, heal faster and safer . . . just turn the page!

contents

{ PART TWO }

looking & feeling great 88

Use your kitchen pantry to boost your appearance and your health

{ PART THREE }

easing what ails you 130

Proven kitchen-cabinet remedies for 74 of the most common health concerns

{ PART FOUR }

practical home healing 356

Tips and lists to help you get started

index 371

folk healing the modern way

Welcome to a whole new world of natural home rememdies

When grandparents reminisce about the good ol' days, they probably don't talk much about how clever they were at remedying things like colds, scrapes, or toothaches. But a mere 40 years ago—and for thousands of years before that—the majority of healing was pretty much a do-it-yourself enterprise. Except for serious emergencies, everyone needed to have at least a smattering of healing ability to pre-serve and protect their family's health.

That meant learning to heal with whatever staples they had on hand. And, strange as some of those old cures sound today (imagine plastering your chest with mustard paste), it turns out that our fore-bears knew what they were doing. Home remedies really did work, and still do.

So why are they used so infrequently today? Over time, as researchers discov-ered effective new drugs, treatments and "procedures" for remedying diseases and injuries, we lost the need—and the know-how and confidence—for using home remedies to treat common health problems. Instead, we've come to rely much more heavily on pills, doctors, and store-bought cures for all that ails us.

But times are changing again. In labo-ratories around the world, researchers in recent years have explored and confirmed the healing power of many of our favorite pantry items. In these costly and compli-cated times, it's just good common sense to rediscover time-honored home remedies for treating simple but annoying woes—before you pay for an expensive doctor's visit.

Inexpensive health solutions

This book provides over a thousand ways to cure yourself and your family safely and inexpensively. Got athlete's foot? Instead of losing half a day seeing a doctor, and then writing a check for an expensive antifungal lotion, you can try a homemade tea-tree oil remedy for just pennies. Got a hacking cough? A tea made from your supply of dried thyme may clear it up in a day or two, without the need for a prescription drug or an over-the-counter cough syrup—which research has recently shown, doesn't work very well, if at all.

That said, not every remedy in this book will work for everyone. That's true for store-bought medicine, and it's true for homemade remedies. But unlike some prescription drugs, these simple, natural recipes are less likely to cost you significant money or to have unpleasant side effects.

Consider the satisfaction you'll derive from learning how to make delicious, soothing teas from herbs and spices you probably already have in your pantry. You'll discover healing creams and ointments you can whip up from ingredients like olive oil and honey, and digestive aids that require nothing more than a little baking soda, a bit of ginger, or a dash of hot sauce. No matter what minor ills or accidents befall your family members, just turn to the index where you'll find a cheap, effective, easy-to-make remedy to fix them right up.

Remedies worth sharing

In compiling this collection, we reached back through time to find the most effective, time-tested home remedies we could get our hands on. We discovered herbal recipes from traditional Chinese and Indian medicine. We unearthed healing wisdom, born of necessity, that Native Americans and North American pioneers handed down from generation to generation. We sorted through books on regional folk medicine from all over Europe, South America, and beyond. Our search for these remedies carried us through history, from the era of Hippocrates to the battlefields of World War I to the backyard gardens of 21st century herbal healers.

Though we cast a wide net, our final criteria for the best home remedies were determined using a highly selective process.

• First, remedies had to come from common ingredients found in kitchen pantries. Occasionally, we stretched our notion of "pantry" a bit to accommodate a few refrigerated items (eggs and yogurt, for example) or the aloe plant, which you can grow on a windowsill.

• Second, remedies had to be simple to whip up and easy to use. And naturally, they all had to be safe. We put the remedies to a test: Is this something we might actually use ourselves? Or would recommend to a loved one? Or use on our own children? They made the cut when we could answer, "Yes, these are remedies we would absolutely use."

• Third, the remedies had to stand the test of time. For example, when we saw an herb that was used to treat nervous conditions from the time of the Romans to the 19th century, we knew we were on to something. We then searched the scientific literature to make sure that there was a medical rationale for its effectiveness and safety.

One thing home remedies have going for them is that they harness the power of ritual—in itself a potent healing tool. The very act of making a remedy from scratch, applying it with love, and believing that it will help your loved one get better has healing powers that may enhance or even trump ingredients in the "cure." So we've often included time-tested remedies that combine safe, gentle, healing ingredients and a soothing application, even if they haven't been scientifically proven.

After we rejected all the odd, less-credible, more-complicated, and slightly risky remedies, what remained were the wonderful (and sometimes wondrous) remedies you'll find in this book—more than 1,000 that have helped heal millions of people over hundreds, if not thousands, of years. Finally, every single one of these remedies was carefully vetted by our medical reviewer to ensure that all are safe for you to use as recommended.

Use kitchen cures wisely

If traditional cures were used daily for thousands of years, they probably work or else people wouldn't have used them. But there are always risks—of side effects, of interactions with drugs, or of simply being the wrong remedy. The home remedies in this book are supported by strong anecdotal evidence of their effectiveness—and in many cases by scientific studies—and they have been carefully screened for safety by our medical advisor. But there are times when you'll want to exercise extra caution, such as:

If you are pregnant. Do not take any herbs, supplements, or over-the-counter medications without first checking with your doctor. Even innocuous remedies might have unwanted effects on your pregnancy or your baby.

If you are taking prescription medication. Talk to your doctor about possible interactions between your prescribed medication and any remedies recommended in this book. And tell your doctor about any other supplements or medications that you take at the same time—particularly if you have a chronic condition such as diabetes or heart disease.

If you know you are allergic to a food or medication. Exercise caution or consult your doctor before you eat or drink any remedy that might contain the allergen.

If you have a serious health condition. Pay special attention to "When to Call the Doctor" at the beginning of each chapter. The purpose of these home remedies is to help you deal with everyday ailments and improve your overall health—not to mask serious conditions that require medical treatment.

If you are treating a child or infant. Some home remedies just aren't appropriate for children or babies. Unless a remedy is specifically recommended for children, ask your pediatrician for advice before treating your kids.

If you are experiencing unwanted effects. Although side effects from using safe home remedies are uncommon, allergic reactions can occur, even if you've never been allergic to something before. If you have a reaction, immediately stop using the product.

When using essential oils. These products are highly concentrated natural chemicals, and so pose some risks. Most essential oils must be diluted in carrier oil before being applied to the skin. Some oils, particularly citrus ones, can make your skin extra-sensitive to the sun, and should be applied with caution or not at all before sun exposure. Never swallow or even taste essential oils; most are toxic when taken internally. Keep bottles and jars sealed and out of the reach of children. Finally, if an essential oil is accidentally swallowed, do not induce vomiting. Call a poison hotline or get the person to an emergency room immediately.

Winning combinations

No matter how much we believe in home remedies, few of us are willing to completely turn our backs on conventional medicine. What most of us want is the best of both worlds—the cutting-edge tools of modern medicine combined with the natural, at-home treatments that earlier generations depended on. As more than one expert has noted, if you get hit by a car, or have a heart attack or stroke, you want the best, newest, state-of-the-art treatments medical science has to offer. But if you have a chronic condition, such as diabetes, arthritis, or irritable bowel syndrome, you might want treatments that blend natural remedies with the latest up-to-date methods.

This approach, known as integrative medicine, makes wonderful sense. If you have heart disease or diabetes, for example, you want the most advanced care available. Yet there's so much you can do yourself at the same time—not only to relieve symptoms and feel better, but also to give nature a hand and help your body recover more quickly or even reverse the condition. Be sure to let your doctor know that you're interested in using as many natural approaches as makes sense for your condition.

It might surprise you to hear your endocrinologist suggest, for example, that you switch breakfast cereals. That's because she's seen the studies that suggest cinnamon can help lower your blood-sugar levels. And your cardiologist might have a positive take on herbs like garlic, which is proven to help reduce blood pressure and lower cholesterol.

One thing about home remedies is that they are often more art than science. Many of the traditional formulas we found for teas, creams, steams and baths called for measurements that, truth be told, weren't well defined. For instance, a grandmother may have written, a "spoonful" of honey, a "handful" of garlic, or a "few pinches" of baking soda. Happily, in many cases the exact amounts aren't critical to the remedy's effectiveness. Still, for best results, follow the recipes as written. We've edited them to include ingredients most likely to provide some direct health benefits, while omitting those that are ineffective, hard to come by, or might cause problems.

Few of the remedies in this book require special supplies—just the diverse items you'll find on the shelves in your kitchen cabinets. Occasionally, we'll include ingredients you probably don't have (such as beeswax), which are easy to find and are essential to some very useful remedies.

Temporary relief, or even a cure, may be just a few steps away. If one remedy doesn't work for you, try another. If it does work, be sure to tell a loved one or friend so that they might one day benefit from it, too.

Happy healing!

top pantry healers

An A-to-Z guide to the natural medicines sitting on your kitchen shelves

You probably don't look inside your kitchen cabinet and think *drugstore*. But for untold generations, that's exactly the role kitchen pantries have performed. You'd be surprised how many everyday staples have a successful second career as natural medicine. After all, it's a lot quicker, simpler, and cheaper to make a paste of baking soda and water and dab it on a bug bite than it is to drive to the drugstore for an expensive anti-itch cream.

In the pages ahead, you'll discover the remarkable healing benefits of many familiar, inexpensive items that are already sitting right there on your pantry shelves. You'll learn how to harness the healing power of time-tested staples like honey, vinegar, baking soda, and plain old salt. The antinausea power of ginger. The heart protection of canned salmon and sardines. Mustard's unique ability to fight athlete's foot, and turmeric's potential for preventing serious chronic diseases—and even cancer.

And don't miss the special features posted in each entry, including shopping tips, safety information, and indispensable advice about how to buy and store your pantry healing ingredients to retain their maximum potency and effectiveness.

aloe

Aloe is one of the most versatile kitchen healers around—but please don't keep this one in your pantry. Instead, you'll want to grow the spiny succulent plant on your windowsill, because its stalky leaves contain a gel-like substance that healers think of as Mother Nature's first aid kit. This lily cousin thrives on neglect and is so hardy that you'll be able to harvest its wound-repairing, skin-moisturizing, ulcer-soothing magic for years to come.

rooted in history

Aloe (*Aloe vera* and *Aloe barbadensis*) has been used medicinally for at least 5,500 years. The first documentation of its healing uses are on an Egyptian papyrus dating back to 3500 BC. Legend has it that Aristotle convinced Alexander the Great to invade the island of Socotra in the Indian Ocean just for its aloe supply, which healed his warriors' wounds and got them back on the battlefield faster. In a very different use, Cleopatra—and other gorgeous leading ladies of history—reportedly relied on aloe for beautifying their complexions.

Aloe plants migrated from Africa to America in the 17th and 18th centuries, where they were soon adopted by healers in the New World.

what's in it?

Though aloe is 99 percent water, the clear gel inside the leaves contains a handy assortment of potent healing

USE FOR

Acne

Age spots

Athlete's foot

Blisters

Burns (minor)

Canker sores

Cold sores

Dandruff

Eczema

Dry hair

Fine lines/
    light wrinkles

Gum problems

Heat rash

Hemorrhoids

Nosebleed

Psoriasis

Razor burn

Shingles

Stings and bites

Sunburn

Ulcers

Warts

compounds. Take glycoproteins and polysaccharides, for example. Glycoproteins speed healing by stopping pain and inflammation. Polysaccharides moisturize skin, stimulate its growth and repair, and enhance wound healing. What's more, aloe gel contains a pain-relieving substance called bradykininase that helps reduce swelling. The mineral magnesium lactate, another aloe gel component, soothes itching and eases allergic rashes.

what science says

In 2009, Iranian researchers reviewed 40 studies published about aloe's effectiveness as a skin treatment. They reported that there is scientific evidence to back using aloe gel for treating genital herpes, psoriasis, human papillomavirus, seborrheic dermatitis, frostbite, and burns.

The same year, a different team of Iranian scientists examined aloe's ability to heal second-degree skin burns. (Second-degree burns affect both the top and the second layers of the skin, causing painful blisters and inflammation.) The researchers compared aloe to a tried-and-true burn ointment called silver sulfadiazine, which prevents infection of second- and third-degree burns. As it turns out, the burns treated with aloe healed three days faster than those receiving the more standard medicine.

And in Thailand, researchers studying psoriasis treatments published a study that compared aloe to a conventional steroid cream. Eighty people with mild to moderate psoriasis were randomly treated with aloe vera or the steroid cream for eight weeks. The results were about the same, though the aloe treatment had a slight edge over the steroid treatment.

on the horizon

The same compounds that make aloe a smart treatment for skin problems intrigue scientists focused on finding solutions for problems like colitis and ulcers. As their thinking goes, if aloe can heal external wounds, it might just heal internal wounds. Turns out, they could be right. Studies conducted in the mid-1990s suggest that drinking pure aloe gel may help ease ulcerative colitis by reducing inflammation in the GI tract.

Good to Know

Aloe plants produce another substance called aloe latex, which comes from the skin of the aloe leaf. It's a bitter yellow liquid that performs as a powerful laxative. Too powerful, in fact. Classified as a stimulant laxative, it can cause severe cramping and diarrhea and can even affect your electrolyte balance, minerals that play a critical role in the body. Trust us, this is not good medicine for irregularity or constipation.

Aloe gel contains a pain-relieving substance that helps reduce swelling.

In one United Kingdom study, 44 people with ulcerative colitis were either given about 3 ounces of aloe vera gel twice a day or a sham juice for a month. Of the 30 people who took aloe, 9 people experienced symptom relief, compared to 1 person in the group of 14 people who took the fake treatment. The researchers noted that aloe was a safe treatment that needs more study.

Korean researchers put aloe to the test on rats with stomach ulcers and observed that taking aloe seemed to regenerate tissue cells. However, what works on a rat might not work on a human, so these results need confirmation via clinical trials conducted on people.

Finally, back in 2003, leading researchers from Harvard Medical School reviewed 109 studies that tested supplements for helping people control their blood sugar. They concluded that the results for aloe studies were promising but preliminary. Discuss aloe with your doctor if you're taking medications to lower your blood sugar.

BUYER's tip

The best aloe gel comes directly from a living plant. Just chop off a nice, thick stalk, slice it lengthwise, and squeeze the gel directly onto your skin. Be sure not to get the goo on your clothes; it will leave an ugly stain. You can find aloe plants at most places live plants are sold. They respond very well to almost no attention and grow nicely on a sunny windowsill.

No aloe plant? No problem. You can find pure aloe gel at most health food stores. Just read the label carefully to make sure the product is 100 percent pure aloe gel with no additional ingredients.

baking soda

Baking soda is without question the hardest working multitasker on your pantry shelf. It's an essential baking ingredient—it's what makes cakes, cookies, and other treats rise. It's also an effective and "green" household cleaner and a deodorizer that de-stinks cat pans, garbage cans, refrigerator interiors, and other smelly things—even feet and underarms. And as it turns out, baking soda is also a gentle, fast-acting remedy for a plethora of annoying health conditions, from diaper rash to sunburn pain.

what's in it?

Baking soda is a mildly alkaline salt that reacts easily with acids, releasing carbon dioxide and creating effervescence. Most baking soda—that is, sodium bicarbonate—is derived from soda ash that occurs naturally as an ore called trona. Trona is mined in the Green River Basin in Wyoming.

what science says

Good old-fashioned baking soda has recently captured the attention of kidney disease researchers. This cheap pantry item may slow the decline of kidney function in some people who have advanced chronic kidney disease. When people with advanced kidney disease took a small daily dose of baking soda in addition to their usual care, kidney function declined about two-thirds slower than it did in patients who didn't take baking soda. Kidney disease

USE FOR

Anal itching

Asthma

Athlete's foot

Bad breath

Bladder infections

Body odor

Canker sores

Diaper rash

Flatulence

Foot and
  underarm odor

Healthy teeth

Heartburn

Hives

Indigestion

Poison ivy/oak

Sore throat

Stings and bites

Sunburn

BUYER'S tip

Find baking soda in the baking supply aisle of the supermarket. Store it in a cool, dry pantry. Since it's a very stable compound, baking soda has an almost limitless shelf life. For topical use, it can be mixed with water to form a paste, but it must be totally dissolved before it is taken internally.

Good to Know

Baking soda meets standards as a safe food additive and can be used freely, with two critical caveats. First, anyone on a sodium-restricted diet should consult a physician before taking it internally, because it could increase sodium levels. Second, because baking soda contains sodium, don't use it regularly if you have high blood pressure or heart failure.

progressed rapidly in just 9 percent of people who took baking soda, compared to 45 percent of people who didn't take it. The people taking baking soda were also less likely to develop end-stage renal disease, a life-threatening condition that causes people to require dialysis. However, critics of the 2009 study take its results with a grain of salt. Here's why: The treatment wasn't compared to a placebo, and the researchers knew which patients were getting the baking soda and which weren't.

neutralize acid, soothe the itch

Baking soda's ability to take the itch and sting out of a variety of skin problems comes from its alkaline nature. Chemicals with pH values of 6 and lower are acids. Those with a pH of 8 or above are alkaline. (Water, which comes in at 7, is neutral.) With a pH of 9, baking soda is alkaline enough to take the edge off potentially harsh acids. This is how it eases heartburn, by neutralizing the stomach acid (hydrochloric acid) that causes heartburn's uncomfortable burning sensation.

That action also comes into play for relieving the itch and sting of bug bites, poison ivy, and poison oak. The same holds true for diaper rash: Baking soda lessens itching and helps irritated skin heal more quickly.

a box full of healing

Because baking soda lowers the bacteria-friendly acidic environment inside the bladder, it can be a useful home remedy for easing the discomfort of bladder infections. As a gargle for sore throats, it reduces pain-causing acids, and mixed with a little water as a tooth polish, it whitens teeth and combats the acids that gnaw away at tooth enamel. And it has the advantage of being less abrasive than most toothpaste. The baking soda paste will also help fight acne: Rubbing a blackhead gently with the paste for two to three minutes will loosen it. A dusting of baking soda under the arms or on the feet serves as an inexpensive deodorant.

cayenne pepper

People who don't like spicy foods often think that hot-pepper lovers are savaging their mouths and digestive systems. But nothing could be further from the truth. That burning sensation in your mouth when you eat foods spiced with cayenne pepper (*Capsicum annuum*) and its many hot-pepper cousins comes from capsaicin, the oily compound responsible for its many health benefits. Turns out that eating spicy foods does wonders for you—everything from managing pain to opening up clogged airways to potentially even managing diabetes.

what's in it?

The hotter a chili pepper is, the more capsaicin it contains. Capsaicin short-circuits pain by depleting nerve cells of a chemical called substance P, which helps transfer pain signals along nerve endings to the brain. Because of that pain-depleting action, you'll find capsaicin in many prescription and over-the-counter creams, ointments, and patches for arthritis and muscle pain. It's also used for treating postsurgical pain, shingles pain, and diabetes-related nerve pain.

But that's not all. Capsaicin also is a metabolism booster, speeding up your calorie-burning furnace for a couple of hours after eating. Plus hot peppers work as an anti-inflammatory. Finally, hot peppers contain plenty of vitamins A and C along with flavonoids and carotenoids, plant pigments that act as antioxidants.

USE FOR

Arthritis
Carpal tunnel
  syndrome
Colds and flu
Fever
Foot problems
Laryngitis
Nasal congestion
Nausea and
  vomiting
Nosebleed
Pain relief
Shingles
Sore throat
Toothache
Weight management

BUYER'S tip

Cayenne pepper is available in the spice section at the supermarket. It is also known as ground red pepper.

Fresh cayenne peppers can burn or irritate skin. Wear rubber gloves when handling fresh hot peppers, don't touch your eyes or nose, and wash hands after preparing them. Same goes for the spice—use a utensil to measure and add to recipes, not your fingers. If you use topical capsaicin creams, be sure to follow label directions.

Good to Know

Because cayenne shrinks blood vessels in your nose and throat, it helps relieve congestion when you sprinkle some into hot soup. Or shake in as much as you can tolerate of hot sauce or other fiery condiments for the same congestion-busting effects.

rooted in history

All these benefits of cayenne pepper—not to mention the wonderful flavor it can add to our food—have been well known for a *very* long time. There's evidence that Native Americans have used cayenne as both a food and a medicine for at least 9,000 years. Traditional healers in India, China, Japan, and Korea use it to remedy digestive problems, poor appetite, and circulatory problems.

what science says

In one study, published in the *American Journal of Clinical Nutrition*, researchers found that people with diabetes who ate a meal laced liberally with chile pepper needed less insulin after eating to reduce their blood sugar, suggesting the spice may have antidiabetes benefits. Those results were backed by Thai researchers in 2009. Trouble is, you have to use at least a teaspoon of the stuff before you get the glucose-lowering benefit—which might be too much heat for people whose palates aren't fireproof.

on the horizon

Researchers are hard at work in labs all over the world, trying to figure out how to harness capsaicin's tumor-busting potential. At the Massachusetts Institute of Technology, scientists are studying capsaicin's effects on colon cancer cells. In a recent study, they learned that capsaicin can make cancer cells self-destruct because it affects levels of nitric oxide. Meanwhile, at Cedars-Sinai Medical Center at UCLA School of Medicine, scientists looked at capsaicin's effect on breast cancer cells. In a new study, they revealed that capsaicin slowed breast cancer cell growth in test tube models. In their animal studies, they reported that capsaicin decreased experimentally induced tumors in mice by 50 percent and inhibited the development of precancerous lesions by up to 80 percent.

Finally, in lab tests published in 2009, Taiwanese researchers showed that capsaicin makes stomach cancer cells self-destruct. It will likely take years of research before we know whether or not eating cayenne can prevent or treat cancer in humans. However, there's certainly no downside to eating the hot stuff regularly just in case.

chamomile

When the day has frazzled your nerves to the extent that you feel like pulling your hair out, it's time to sit down and have a nice cup of chamomile tea. And your nerves aren't the only thing chamomile tea is good at soothing: This herb is wonderful for easing digestive distress, skin irritations, and occasional mild insomnia.

rooted in history

Chamomile (*Matricaria recutita*) tea is made from the tiny daisy-like flowers of a lacy-leafed plant that now grows all over the world. This delicate, apple-scented beverage has been soothing folks for thousands of years, dating back to the ancient Romans, Egyptians, and Greeks. The world's first great healers—Hippocrates, Asclepius, Dioscorides, and Galen—all documented its use.

Back in the day, chamomile tea provided a medicine chest's worth of useful remedies. Its list of treatable conditions included cold-related symptoms, stomach and gastrointestinal problems, toothaches, convulsions, and insomnia. People used chamomile as a gargle or antiseptic wash and inhaled the tea's steam to reduce congestion and clear up irritations throughout the respiratory tract.

Historically, midwives treated pregnancy and childbirth issues with chamomile tea. Today, despite reservations that chamomile's effect on uterine muscles could stimulate uterine contractions, the tea is generally considered safe for

USE FOR

Acne
Anal itching
Arthritis
Belching
Blisters
Body odor
Colic
Diarrhea
Digestive problems
Gum problems
Headache
Healthy skin
Hives
Insomnia
Menstrual cramps
Morning sickness
Nausea
Shingles
Sore throat
Stings and bites
Ulcers

Chamomile may cause an allergic reaction among those sensitive to ragweed and other members of the aster family, including chrysanthemums. To be on the safe side, avoid taking chamomile if you have asthma. The flowers contain pollen and may cause dermatitis, although allergic skin reactions are rare. Chamomile may increase the effects of sedating drugs and blood-thinning drugs.

pregnant women. Healers also soaked poultices in a hot chamomile infusion to soothe back pain, gout, earaches, skin inflammations, bruises, and arthritis.

what's in it?

Chamomile contains a handful of major healing components. Among them are chamazulene and alpha-bisabolol. Chamazulene, formed during the heating of the tea or extract, has proven anti-inflammatory activity. Alpha-bisabolol is antibacterial, antifungal, and anti-inflammatory, and can promote the healing of ulcers, burns, and eczema. Chamomile's volatile oils help expel digestive gas, relax muscles, kill bacteria, and have a sedative effect.

what science says

Recently, science proved that the ancients were right on target when they prescribed chamomile tea to calm frayed nerves. In 2009, researchers from the University of Pennsylvania conducted a gold standard clinical trial (meaning that it was placebo-controlled and neither the researchers nor the participants knew whether they were getting a real or a sham treatment) to study chamomile's effects on people with generalized anxiety disorder. Fifty-seven people with mild to moderate anxiety disorder took either chamomile as an extract or a fake treatment daily for eight weeks. The researchers reported that folks in the chamomile group had significantly improved scores—meaning

A soothing bedtime story

Chamomile tea's ability to calm jangled nerves was immortalized in Beatrix Potter's famous children's story *The Tale of Peter Rabbit*, treasured by children for more than 100 years. Against his mother's wishes, little Peter sneaks into Mr. McGregor's garden, eats too much, is chased by McGregor, and catches a chill while hiding in a watering can. When Peter arrives home, he doesn't feel well. His mother puts him to bed early with a dose of chamomile tea—"one tablespoonful to be taken at bedtime"—which is still a common remedy for ailing and anxious children.

they were less anxious—on standardized tests than those who took the sham treatment.

enjoy a cup (or three) of comfort

When you drink chamomile tea regularly (two or three cups every day), it can protect against peptic ulcers; ease irritable bowel syndrome, indigestion, and stomach cramps; and act as a gentle, natural tranquilizer. What's more, chamomile tea can prevent muscle spasms and relax the smooth muscles that line the internal organs, such as the stomach and the uterus, making it a good remedy for easing stomach upsets and menstrual cramps.

Even though chamomile flowers contain pollen and may cause an allergic reaction when ingested or applied externally, researchers have found that chamomile may have antiallergenic properties. The potential effect is attributed to the as-yet-unconfirmed histamine-blocking action of chemical compounds called azulenes.

BUYER'S tip

Find chamomile tea bags in the tea section of the supermarket or in health food stores. Look for tiny daisy-like flowers inside the bags and a pleasant, apple aroma. Discard tea bags that aren't fragrant—they've likely lost their healing power. Pour boiling water over one to three tea bags, cover the cup, steep for 10 minutes, then enjoy. Traditionally, the recommended medicinal dosage calls for drinking one cup three or four times a day to heal digestive complaints. One strong cup before bedtime can ease mild insomnia.

chocolate (dark)

You've got to love modern science, especially when it comes up with excellent reasons for people to indulge in delectable dark chocolate. Now we know that chocolate, once considered a "sinful" indulgence, actually contains the same disease-fighting antioxidants found in red wine and in many fruits and vegetables that are linked to a decreased risk of heart disease.

USE FOR

Added antioxidants

Anxiety

Back pain

Boosting mood

Heart health

High blood pressure

Mood enhancement

Stress

rooted in history

Both the Mayans and the Aztecs believed that chocolate was magical, even divine, and used it in their sacred rituals. The Aztec king, Montezuma, may have been the first to serve chocolate to Spanish conquistadors, who at first sneered at the unsweetened drink, calling it "a bitter drink for pigs." But once the conquistadors mixed it with sugar, they were hooked. Chocolate was among the treasures the Spanish brought back from the New World, and after its introduction in 1528, its source and preparation were kept secret for over 90 years. But by the 17th century, chocolate was popular all over Europe and was considered nutritious, medicinal, and even a libido enhancer. Legend has it that the libertine Casanova was a big fan. Chocolate then made its way back across the Atlantic as Europeans settled in North America. It became such a desirable and valuable commodity that Revolutionary War soldiers were given chocolate as part of their standard rations, and sometimes it was even used in lieu of cash wages.

what's in it?

The cacao beans used to make the chocolate liquor, cocoa butter, and cocoa powder found in chocolate products are chock full of flavonoids. These powerful antioxidants neutralize the free radicals that damage cells and cause disease. Dark chocolate contains far more flavonoid-rich cocoa particles than milk chocolate—so if you're eating chocolate for your health, forgo the sweet stuff and choose chocolate that contains at least 60 percent cacao. The higher the percentage of cacao, the more good stuff the chocolate contains. Chocolate's flavonoids increase the body's levels of nitric oxide, a gas that causes blood vessels to relax and expand, which in turn promotes healthy circulation and blood pressure. Chocolate is made up of three kinds of fats in roughly equal amounts. One is oleic acid, a heart-healthy fat also found in olive oil. The others are stearic and palmitic acids, which are forms of saturated fats. Unlike the saturated fats that increase unhealthy cholesterol, stearic acid appears to have a neutral effect on it. Palmitic acid, on the other hand, does raise cholesterol levels, but it only makes up about a third of chocolate's fat calories.

what science says

Chocolate is a gift of love on Valentine's Day and a fabled reliever of romantic encounters gone wrong. Women, in particular, are known to reach for chocolate when nursing a case of the blues. Now, scientists are a baby step closer to figuring out the reason for chocolate's happy-making reputation. In a recent study, scientists from the Nestlé Research Center in Switzerland examined chocolate's effects on stress hormone levels. They enrolled 30 people in the study and tested their anxiety levels. Thirteen people tested as high anxiety; 17 tested as low anxiety. Everyone got 20 grams of dark chocolate (about an ounce) twice a day. After two weeks, researchers performed blood and urine tests and discovered that chocolate lowered levels of stress hormones in all the volunteers but there was a bigger drop for the high-anxiety people than for the low-anxiety people.

As to matters of the heart: The American Heart Association recently summarized years of chocolate research in a report published in its journal, *Circulation*. The conclusion? "Cocoa does indeed exert beneficial cardiovascular

The calorie issue

The amount of dark chocolate, 3.5 ounces (100 g), used in some studies contains a whopping 550 calories. That's just too much of a good thing for most people to eat regularly. If you're going to indulge daily, settle for 1.5 ounces (40 g), which contains 220 calories. But be sure to trim 220 less healthful calories elsewhere in your diet, or risk packing on 23 pounds over a year's time.

Good to Know

Chocolate is rich in phenylethylamine (PEA), a naturally occurring compound that has effects similar to amphetamine. It can trigger migraine headaches in susceptible people.

effects." The reason for the benefits, the report said, are chocolate's concentration of polyphenols, which are also found in fruits and vegetables.

For example, in 2008, researchers at Johns Hopkins University and Sinai Hospital in Baltimore concluded that eating 3.5 ounces of dark chocolate (70 percent cocoa) every day for a week can lower unhealthy LDL cholesterol by 6 percent and raise healthy HDL cholesterol by 8 percent. Finally, Italian researchers, in collaboration with the USDA Human Nutrition Research Center on Aging at Tufts University, studied 19 people with high blood pressure and blood sugar control problems. They gave them a daily serving of either 3.5 ounces of dark or white chocolate. After 15 days, the groups switched chocolates. Turns out that eating dark chocolate—but not white—lowers systolic pressure (the first number in a blood pressure reading) by 12 points and diastolic pressure by 9 points. What's more, eating dark chocolate reduced inflammation, another risk factor for heart disease, and increased insulin sensitivity, an important factor in treating type 2 diabetes.

BUYER'S tip

Choose dark chocolate over milk chocolate—look for cocoa content of at least 60 to 75 percent. The higher the percentage, the more bitter the chocolate will taste, but the richer it will be in antioxidants. Milk chocolate hasn't been proven to have similar health benefits, and it contains milk fat, which is highly saturated. Processing removes most of the flavonoids from cocoa and chocolate syrup. White chocolate contains no cocoa and has no health benefits.

cinnamon

Cinnamon (*Cinnamomum verum*) comes from the bark of a small tree native to Asia, and it's been revered for its healing power for nearly 5,000 years, making it one of the world's oldest natural remedies. Chefs around the world rely on cinnamon for the distinctive flavor that enhances dishes, both sweet and savory. Today, cinnamon has captured the attention of researchers who've learned that it can be a powerful tool for helping balance blood sugar.

rooted in history

The first healer to write about cinnamon back in 2800 BC or so was Shen Nung, known as the father of Chinese medicine. In Egypt, cinnamon was among the several spices used for mummification. The Phoenicians and Hebrews called it "qinamon," and it was mentioned in the Hebrew Bible in Exodus (chapter 30, verse 23).

By the time the Europeans discovered cinnamon around the first century, it was so prized that 350 grams of the stuff cost 15 times more than silver. In the Middle Ages, cinnamon was used as a remedy for coughs and indigestion, though only by the wealthy—it was still wildly expensive. Historically, healers have recommended the spice for an amazing and diverse collection of human ills, including kidney trouble, bed-wetting, morning sickness, rheumatism, heart pain, warts, and toothaches.

USE FOR

Anti-inflammatory

Antiseptic

Bad breath

Blood sugar regulation

Fever

Flatulence

High cholesterol

Indigestion

Memory problems

Nausea and vomiting

Yeast infections

Good to Know

Some people can be allergic to cinnamon, but the amounts used in cooking are generally considered safe. In large doses, cinnamon can cause gastrointestinal problems and kidney damage.

Cinnamon essential oil can cause redness and burning when it comes in contact with the skin. Never take the oil internally—it can cause nausea, vomiting, and kidney damage. Pregnant women and people with stomach or intestinal ulcers should not use cinnamon medicinally.

what's in it?

Cinnamon is rich in essential oils that contain active medicinal compounds, including cinnamaldehyde, cinnamyl acetate, and cinnamyl alcohol. Collectively, these have significant antibacterial and antifungal action—so much so that research shows that cinnamon can be as effective as chemical food preservatives. Cinnamaldehyde prevents blood platelets from clumping, which means that cinnamon can help protect you against strokes and heart attacks. Cinnamon is also known as a powerful antioxidant that helps lessen inflammation.

what science says

Recently, scientists discovered that cinnamon lowers blood sugar levels in people who have type 2 diabetes and reduces heart disease risks for overweight people. In 2009, the American College of Nutrition published a study that helped clarify how cinnamon accomplishes this. In the study, conducted by a researcher from the U.S. Department of Agriculture, 22 overweight and obese people were given either 250 milligrams of cinnamon or a placebo twice a day for 12 weeks. The fasting blood sugar of those in the cinnamon group dropped from 114 to 102 mg/dL—a very healthy decline. The fasting blood sugar of the people in the placebo group increased a bit, from 112 to 113 mg/dL.

Many of cinnamon's traditional uses have been put to the test of science. Recent studies, for example, demonstrate its ability to stimulate the gastrointestinal tract, lending support to folk healers' long-held belief that the spice eases gas, nausea, vomiting, and other forms of gastrointestinal distress. That cinnamon is also a powerful antiseptic is no longer simply a matter of folk wisdom. A Japanese study demonstrated its ability to kill fungi, bacteria, and other microorganisms, including the bacteria that cause botulism and staph infections.

cloves

Cloves (*Syzygium aromaticum, Eugenia caryophyllus*), the very spice you use to spike hams and enliven cookies, muffins, and other treats, can also be a handy, temporary stand-in for your dentist and can ease sore throats. Cloves are the unopened pink flower buds of an evergreen tree. They are handpicked and dried until they turn brown.

rooted in history

Cloves originated in the Moluccas, formerly known as the Spice Islands of Indonesia. It's said that back in 200 BC, Chinese courtiers would nibble cloves when addressing the emperor so as not to offend him with their bad breath.

As with other aromatic spices, cloves became popular in Europe during the Middle Ages, when aristocrats relied on cloves' sharp flavor to mask the taste of poorly preserved foods.

Later, as cloves became more available, healers used them to remedy such complaints as nausea, vomiting, indigestion, diarrhea, toothache, warts, and worms. The 17th-century British herbalist Nicholas Culpeper, whose wisdom the early settlers often relied upon, advised that cloves would "help digestion, stop looseness and quicken the sight."

what's in it?

Cloves contain an anti-inflammatory chemical called eugenol. In animal studies, it inhibited COX-2, an enzyme that spurs inflammation (the same enzyme that so-called

USE FOR

Arthritis

Athlete's foot

Headache

Menstrual cramps

Motion sickness

Mouth inflammation

Smoking cessation

Sore throat

Toothache

COX-2 inhibitor drugs such as Celebrex quash). Cloves also contain a variety of flavonoids, including kaempferol and rhamnetin, which helps explain why their antioxidant properties rank so high. The combination of cloves' anti-inflammatory and antioxidant properties spells heaps of health benefits, from boosting protection from heart disease to helping stave off cancer, as well as slowing the cartilage and bone damage caused by arthritis. Compounds in cloves, like those found in cinnamon, also appear to improve insulin function. Trouble is, there's no science suggesting the amounts of cloves needed to achieve these benefits.

what science says

Current science doesn't have much to say on the subject of using cloves medicinally as far as humans are concerned. But clinical studies have been performed on lab animals and in test tubes, with some pretty interesting results.

Most recently, in 2009, Indian researchers learned that eugenol reduced the incidence of experimentally induced stomach tumors in mice and speculated that cloves could one day play a role in cancer prevention and treatment.

In another study published in 2009, Portuguese scientists tested clove oil and discovered that it inhibited a variety of fungi responsible for infections in humans, including *Candida* and *Aspergillus*. The results led the researchers to recommend more studies to develop clove oil as a treatment for fungal infections. Finally, in a 2004 study, Indian scientists decided to see whether there was any scientific basis behind cloves' legendary reputation as an aphrodisiac. They gave male rats various doses of clove extract every day for a week and teamed them up with receptive female rats. Turned out, the highest doses made the male rats especially frisky and romantic, so the researchers concluded that cloves "enhanced their sexual behavior."

pain-killing toothache treatment

American 19th-century Eclectic physicians, who upheld a philosophy of "alignment with nature," were the first to extract the volatile oil from clove buds. Soon, its pain-

BUYER'S tip

Find whole cloves in the spice aisle of your supermarket. It's best to purchase cloves and other spices from stores with a high turnover, to assure freshness. When squeezed with a fingernail, fresh cloves will release some of their oil.

To use cloves for a toothache: Put a couple of whole cloves in your mouth. Let them soften a bit, then bite on them gently with good molars to release their oil. Then move them next to the painful tooth and keep them there for up to half an hour. Clove oil has a numbing effect.

killing effects made it the top home remedy for toothaches. In the days when dentists were few and far between, people would soak a cotton ball in the oil and apply it to an aching tooth. The oil had a nasty sting, but it did numb the ache—at least for a little while.

Clove oil is not only an effective painkiller but also a potent antiseptic. Even today, dentists use it to disinfect root canals and mix it with zinc oxide to make temporary fillings.

smokers, take note

Sucking on cloves has been said to help smokers kick the habit because it replaces nicotine's lingering taste, which increases the craving for tobacco, with the piquant taste of cloves. The slight numbing sensation it imparts may also help numb the urge to light up.

Good to Know

Pure clove oil can irritate the skin. Never use it internally, except to dab on teeth or gums to ease toothache pain.

coffee

People have been drinking coffee as an eye-opener for thousands of years. For nearly as long, its health benefits have been debated—often vigorously. Now, emerging research suggests coffee is loaded with antioxidants that may actually protect you against cancer and diabetes.

USE FOR

Added antioxidants

Alertness

Asthma

Blood sugar regulation

Constipation

Gallstone prevention

Gout

Hangover

Memory

Stroke risk reduction

rooted in history

Legend has it that coffee was discovered in the Kaffa region of Ethiopia, when a herder connected the dots between his especially energetic goats and the berries they'd been munching. Though we can't vouch for the story, we do know that coffee has brewed up controversy throughout its history. It became popular in the Mideast in the 16th century and was promptly banned for its stimulating effects by conservative clerics. Later, coffee made its way to England, and by 1675, coffeehouses were springing up all over the country. Its popularity soon spread throughout Europe and to North America.

what's in it?

To some extent, what's in that cup of coffee you're drinking depends on the type of coffee, where it was grown, and how it was roasted and brewed. But caffeine, an alkaloid, is common to all coffees (with the obvious exception of decaf) and is responsible for its energizing effects. Coffee also contains chlorogenic acid, which supports a healthy liver.

what science says

Research suggests that a cup of joe may do more for you than keep you alert during that mind-numbing meeting or endless car trip. Coffee contains potentially valuable compounds, including disease-fighting antioxidants that mop up dangerous free radicals in the body and help lessen inflammation.

Scientists who study health trends in broad populations say that coffee drinkers appear to gain protection against several diseases. For example, when Harvard University researchers studied the link between women's coffee consumption and stroke risk among the 83,000 women enrolled in the Nurses' Health Study, they discovered that years of coffee drinking didn't increase their risk, and in fact, may have slightly reduced the women's chances of having a stroke.

What's more, despite the fact that caffeine raises blood sugar levels, which ratchets up the risk of type 2 diabetes, several large studies have found that consuming coffee appears to *protect* against this increasingly common disease. One analysis of studies involving more than 193,000 people and published in the *Journal of the American Medical Association* found that heavy coffee drinkers—people who drink up to seven cups per day—seemed to cut their risk of type 2 diabetes by up to 35 percent. In a few studies, people who drank decaffeinated coffee seemed to lower their risk even more.

In a study of more than 47,000 men, researchers learned that downing several cups of coffee a day may cut the risk of developing Parkinson's disease, a devastating neurological condition, by 58 percent. And in more good news for men, researchers from Harvard Medical School found out that men who drank the most coffee had a 60 percent lower risk of developing aggressive prostate cancer than non-coffee drinkers. Though the researchers aren't sure why this link occurs, they suspect that coffee's antioxidants and minerals may play a role. They presented their findings at a cancer conference in December 2009.

Finally, an unusual 2009 study conducted in Hong Kong reported that coffee seems to enhance cooperative behavior and improve social support—which sounds like a good excuse to enjoy a coffee break with your colleagues.

BUYER'S tip

For the best flavor and maximum health benefits, buy whole coffee beans and grind at home right before using. Coffee loses its freshness quickly; you should buy enough beans just for a week or two. Store in a dry, dark place at room temperature. Though you can store an unopened coffee package in the freezer, once opened, keep in a cupboard. Refreezing hurts the beans.

Good to Know

Though drinking coffee or other caffeinated beverages produces a rise in blood pressure, the effect is mild and fades quickly. Several major studies have failed to find any link between a coffee habit and chronically elevated blood pressure. One large study of more than 155,000 women found no connection between coffee drinking and the risk of developing high blood pressure.

Can coffee fight cancer?

Although preliminary research back in the 1970s and 1980s linked coffee drinking and caffeine consumption to breast and pancreatic cancers, larger and more sensitive studies failed to find an association between the brew and any form of cancer. In fact, recent research suggests that coffee may actually protect against certain cancers.

A review of studies determined that people who drink coffee (regular or decaf) or tea regularly reduce their risk of colon cancer by 24 percent. What's more, studies involving more than 241,000 subjects show that people who sip just two cups a day slash their risk of liver cancer by 43 percent. Most scientists who study coffee today have dismissed concerns about cancer and have begun to focus on how this popular drink might promote health.

remember this!

Cognitive problems are sometimes a symptom of dementia, but let's face it: Many otherwise healthy people become a bit forgetful after middle age. Coffee may help. In one French study, women over 80 who drank three cups or more per day were 70 percent less likely to have memory decline than those who drank one cup or less.

There's also preliminary research to suggest that coffee may even protect against Alzheimer's disease. A 2007 analysis of four studies found that coffee drinkers had a 30 percent reduced risk for the most common form of dementia. That research was supplemented in 2009, when two studies were published in the *Journal of Alzheimer's Disease*. Researchers at the Florida Alzheimer's Disease Center gave caffeine to elderly mice bred to develop symptoms of the disease. The caffeine significantly decreased abnormal levels of the protein linked to Alzheimer's. The researchers said that their findings provided evidence that caffeine could not only protect the brain from the disease process, but could actually treat it. They hope to conduct similar studies in humans.

lose the gallstones

If you're prone to gallstones, drinking coffee may help prevent an attack, says a 1999 study, which found that men who drink two or three cups of java per day reduce their risk of developing gallstones by 40 percent. Some scientists believe caffeine blocks development of these painful masses, which form in the gallbladder and bile ducts. In 2002, researchers at Harvard reported that women could expect similar results. Those who drank three or four cups of coffee reduced their chances of gallstones by 22 to 28 percent.

coriander seed

If a jar of coriander seeds isn't already on your spice rack, consider adding it to your shopping list. Not only do the seeds lend an interesting savor to foods (it's reminiscent of citrus peel and thyme), but this historic remedy for troubled digestion may even help balance your cholesterol.

rooted in history

Traditional Chinese physicians began using coriander (*Coriandrum sativum*) in 600 AD. They recommended it, as did Indian and European healers, as a digestive aid and often combined it with other stomach-soothing seeds like anise, caraway, and fennel. In Germany, coriander tea is still used medicinally for digestive complaints and is added to formulas for laxatives because it helps counteract their stomach-upsetting effects. It is approved by Commission E, the German equivalent of the U.S. Food and Drug Administration or Health Canada, for loss of appetite and digestive complaints, including mild cramping, flatulence, and bloating.

what's in it?

Like most spices, coriander seed is a complex blend of chemicals, including linalool, anethole, and camphor. It also contains the antioxidants quercetin and rutin—which may be why it's been studied for its ability to quell inflammation and balance blood sugar. Coriander is reported to have strong lipolytic activity—meaning, it helps break

USE FOR

Body odor
Digestive distress
Fever
High cholesterol
Loss of appetite

down fats. A coriander compound called dodecenal, which is found in the seeds and the fresh leaves of the plant, was found to be twice as potent as the antibiotic drug gentamicin for killing the bacteria *Salmonella*.

Even without these powerful healing micronutrients, coriander seeds abound with health. They are high in fiber and protein, and rich as well in many vitamins and minerals you need for everyday health. Among them are calcium, iron, phosphorus, carotene, thiamine, riboflavin, and niacin.

Good to Know

Coriander contains many antibacterial compounds. And bacteria are what creates body odor. So some herbalists recommend making a strong tea from crushed coriander, soaking a cloth in it, and applying the tea compress under your arms for a few minutes for a lovely smelling treatment for body odor.

what science says

Frankly, science doesn't say all that much about this spice—yet. But recently, Indian scientists studied coriander seeds' potential for lowering cholesterol. In research published in 2008, the scientists added the seeds to high-fat rat chow that contained added cholesterol—a rat version of the fast-food diet. The coriander-fed rats had lower "bad" LDL cholesterol and higher "good" HDL cholesterol than the rats that didn't eat coriander. Obviously, more study is needed before we know whether coriander seeds might lower human cholesterol.

Coriander or cilantro?

Confused about what coriander is exactly? It's no wonder if you are. The leaves of the coriander plant are almost always referred to as cilantro, which is the Spanish word for coriander. But the seeds are always called coriander. And cilantro herb tastes vastly different than coriander spice; it is strong, slightly bitter, and usually generates a love-it-or-hate-it response. Also called Chinese parsley, cilantro is a staple in Mexican, Thai, Vietnamese, and Indian cooking.

cranberry juice

Don't exile cranberries to the holiday relish plate—enjoy them year-round as juice, a dried snack fruit, and a tasty toss-in for cereals, muffins, and other baked goods. Cranberries belong to the same family as blueberries, and like them, are packed to the brim with antioxidants. As a home remedy, you can rely on cranberry juice to fight bladder infections.

rooted in history

If ever there was an all-American fruit, it's the cranberry. Native Americans cooked them and ate them sweetened with honey and maple syrup, a dish that certainly could have been served at the Pilgrim's first Thanksgiving dinner. Healers used them medicinally in poultices for wounds, and it probably was fairly effective. Cranberries are rich in tannins, which would have helped stop bleeding, and they contain compounds with antibiotic effects that would have prevented wounds from becoming infected.

what's in it?

Cranberries contain antioxidants, some of which come from proanthocyanidins (which give the berries their vivid color). These neutralize the particles in the body called free radicals. Like tiny Pac-Man characters, free radicals careen through the body and damage cell membranes and DNA—and can even cause cell death. Eating a variety of brightly colored fruits and vegetables ensures that you get a broad

USE FOR

Added antioxidants

Bladder infections

Cystitis prevention

Fatigue

Gout

Kidney and
  bladder stones

Urinary tract
  infections

Alas, the majority of cranberry juice products on
a grocery store shelf are
actually "cocktail" blends
that contain precious few
cranberries and more
sweeteners than in soda.
To get the health ben-
efits of cranberries, get
100 percent pure cran-
berry juice.

spectrum of antioxidants, which cut your risks for developing a host of chronic diseases, including cancer, heart disease, and diabetes.

what science says

Studies have shown that drinking cranberry juice regularly can decrease the number of urinary tract infections in women who are prone to them, by inhibiting the ability of the *E. coli* bacteria to adhere to bladder walls. Interestingly, a study conducted at Harvard Medical School showed that eating a 1.5-ounce serving of sweetened dried cranberries might also be able to inhibit bacterial adherence and could potentially also help prevent UTIs.

top remedy for bladder problems

Cranberry juice has long been used as a home remedy for cystitis and to prevent kidney and bladder stones. Originally, this benefit was attributed to quinic acid, a cranberry substance that increases urine acidity and prevents the formation of calcium stones. Researchers thought that this acidity helped prevent cystitis. Studies show, however, that cranberries also contain a natural antibiotic substance that makes the bladder walls inhospitable to the organisms responsible for urinary tract infections. This prevents the bacteria from forming colonies; instead, they are washed out of the body in the urine. (Blueberry juice has a similar protective effect.)

BUYER'S tip

Most commercial cranberry juice is too diluted to be effective in preventing or treating urinary tract infections. It also contains large amounts of sugar or other sweeteners. Use a juicer to make your own cranberry juice. To reduce the amount of sugar needed, dilute a cup of freshly squeezed juice with 2 to 3 cups of apple juice, then sweeten to taste if necessary. You can buy organic, unsweetened cranberry juice in health food stores. Mix a little with club soda for a tart, refreshing drink.

fish (canned)

You probably never thought of canned fish as a home remedy, but that's a mindset we hope to change. Eating fish just a few times a week will make your heart stronger and healthier—and that's only one of the considerable health benefits you'll gain as a fish eater. Discover the virtues of canned fish, and a sharper memory, a happier mood, and potentially, a longer, healthier life will be as close as your can opener.

what's in it?
Certain kinds of canned fish, especially salmon, sardines, herring, and, to a lesser extent, tuna, are loaded with omega-3 fatty acids. These help your body manufacture compounds called series 3 prostaglandins, which are helpful hormone-like substances that make platelets less sticky, reduce inflammation, and improve blood flow.

what science says
Some studies suggest that people who eat omega-3–rich fish are less likely to suffer from a decline in age-related thinking skills and memory. Other studies link low levels of omega-3s to higher rates of depression.

In the landmark, 25-plus-year-old Physicians' Health Study, which is still producing data about health, the men who ate fish at least once a week were 52 percent less likely to die of a heart attack than men who ate fish once a month or less. It's not yet known whether the effect is

USE FOR

Acne

Anxiety

Arthritis

Asthma

Bone loss

Carpal tunnel
 syndrome

Depression

Eye irritation

Healthy nails

Heart health

High blood pressure

Hot flashes

Improved immunity

Inflammatory
 conditions

Memory and
 cognition

Menstrual cramps

Psoriasis

Stroke prevention

Ulcers

High levels of mercury are a concern for fish eaters. In general, smaller-sized fish like wild salmon and herring contain less mercury than large fish, like tuna. Of the canned tunas, choose light tuna, because it's lower in mercury than albacore. Some consumer groups recommend that pregnant women eat no more than 6 ounces (170 g) of light tuna every 4 days; every 10 days for albacore.

Wild-caught salmon has the lowest mercury content and the highest omega-3 levels; almost all canned salmon is wild-caught. Pacific Northwest salmon is the best choice because of the purity of those waters.

due to one factor or many, but evidence so far points to the ability of omega-3s to decrease the stickiness of blood platelets, making it less likely that they will clump together to form clots. They also increase the flexibility of red blood cells, enabling them to pass more readily through tiny vessels, reduce inflammation of the artery walls, and lower levels of triglycerides in your blood.

A study of more than 43,000 men, published in 2003, showed that men who ate about 3 to 5 ounces (85–140 g) of fish one to three times a month were 43 percent less likely to have an ischemic stroke, the most common type of stroke, which is caused by blood clots.

Good to Know

A cup of tuna that's canned in water is 179 calories. The same amount of tuna canned in oil is 289 calories. So if flavor isn't an issue, choose water-packed varieties. One suggested exception: tuna packed in olive oil is so delectable on salads, that except for a spritz of lemon, you'll need no other dressing. Enjoy this as an occasional treat, since oil-packed tuna contains more mercury than water-packed.

Do keep an eye on your omega-3 intake, especially if you're taking blood-thinning medications. More than 3 grams of omega-3 a day may increase your risk for bleeding.

flaxseed

Flaxseed (*Linum usitatissimum*) has been called a super-food—and with good reason. It's amazing how powerfully healthy these tiny seeds are. Harvested from the same plant that has supplied the fiber for linen since the dawn of time, flaxseed should be thought of as your strong-armed ally against high cholesterol, heart disease, symptoms of menopause, and even some forms of cancer. Make sure it has a permanent place in your pantry.

rooted in history

Flax is one of the world's oldest cultivated plants; people have grown it for its fiber, oil, and seeds for something like 10,000 years. The first record of its food use dates back to 3000 BC in Babylonia. Its medicinal use was first recorded, so far as we know, by Hippocrates, the father of medicine, who used flax to relieve intestinal discomfort. Roman healers relied on flax to ease coughs, urinary tract problems, and constipation.

North American healers, back in the day, used crushed flaxseed as a poultice for abscesses, ulcers, and inflammations. Linseed oil, a flaxseed product, was a popular cough syrup ingredient. And flaxseed tea, with a little lemon and honey, was often recommended for coughs and colds.

what's in it?

Flaxseed is a bountiful source of phytoestrogens called lignans, which act like a weak form of estrogen in the

USE FOR

Acne

Anxiety

Back pain

Carpal tunnel
   syndrome

Conjunctivitis

Constipation

Coughs

Depression

Eczema

Eye Irritation

Gout

Healthy skin

Heart health

Hemorrhoids

High cholesterol

Lower stroke risk

Menopausal
   symptoms

Psoriasis

Stable blood sugar

Ulcers

Weight loss

body. Lignans block estrogen receptors on cells—which means they prevent the uptake of stronger, pro-cancer estrogen—and may contribute to reduced rates of certain hormone-related cancers, including ovarian, breast, and prostate cancer. Other anticancer benefits have been attributed to lignans' ability to lower tumor necrosis factor, a protein compound involved in the inflammatory process.

And that's not all. Flax is an abundant source of alpha-linolenic acid (ALA), an essential fatty acid the body uses to make omega-3 fatty acids. ALA thins the blood and makes it less sticky, thus reducing the risk of heart attack and stroke. The little seeds also lower cholesterol, thanks to their big stores of soluble fiber: A tablespoon of ground flaxseed sprinkled over cereal or yogurt provides an easy 2.3 grams of fiber. Flaxseed's anti-inflammatory power may also help keep various conditions, from acne to asthma, at bay.

what science says

According to a 2009 study published in the *American Journal of Clinical Nutrition*, postmenopausal women and people who have high cholesterol could lower their cholesterol significantly simply by adding flaxseed to their diets. The researchers reviewed 28 studies on flax published between 1990 and 2008 before arriving at their conclusion.

on the horizon

When researchers study flaxseed and its potential for reducing the incidence of cancer, intriguing—and hopeful— evidence often emerges. For example, studies suggest that flaxseed and other foods rich in lignans (which include barley, oatmeal, and wheat bran) are potent cancer fighters. A flax-supplemented diet prevented breast cancer and slowed the growth and spread of malignant tumors in animal studies.

What's more, animal research shows that flaxseed also appears to increase the effectiveness of tamoxifen, a drug that reduces the risk of breast cancer by interfering with estrogen. Some studies suggest that flaxseed may prevent other forms of cancer that are fed by hormones, including prostate cancer.

While the research is exciting, little of it involves humans. A few studies have found that women who consume the most lignans have a lower-than-expected risk of

BUYER'S tip

To add flaxseed to your diet, buy it in bulk at a natural foods store, and keep it in an airtight container in the pantry. Pick up a coffee grinder and grind the amount you need every day, because ground flaxseed is highly perishable. If you grind too much, refrigerate the excess in a plastic bag and use promptly.

breast cancer, though the benefit may be limited to women who have not reached menopause. Until more studies are completed, it's too soon to call flaxseed a cancer-fighter. However, its other benefits make it a smart food to eat regularly, so if flax does turn out to fight cancer, you can consider it a bonus.

flaxseed oil

Just as olives are different than olive oil, so is flaxseed different than flaxseed oil. In particular, flaxseed oil doesn't contain the lignans that appear so useful on the cancer front. However, flaxseed oil is 50 to 60 percent alpha-linolenic acid (ALA), an essential omega-3 fatty acid. Unlike other well-known omega-3 oils—like eicosapentaenoic acid (EPA) and docosahexaenoic acid (DHA), which are found in fish—ALA comes strictly from plants.

Buy flaxseed oil at health-food stores. The best products are made with fresh-pressed seeds, bottled in opaque containers, and processed at low temperatures. The oil is highly perishable and needs to be refrigerated. Don't cook with flaxseed oil; use it raw as a salad dressing or veggie drizzle or an ingredient in smoothies and other recipes that don't require heating.

Researchers see hopeful evidence that flaxseed can help reduce the incidence of cancer.

Good to Know

If you're a woman past menopause or have diabetes, read on. News about flaxseed oil that emerged in 2009 offers hope about avoiding osteoporosis. Researchers at the National Research Center in Cairo, Egypt, studied the effect of diabetes on bone health to see whether flaxseed oil could delay the onset of the bone-weakening disease. One key finding: that diabetes puts post-menopausal women at increased risk for osteoporosis. The researchers concluded that flaxseed oil improves bone health and could prevent osteoporosis. The study was conducted on lab rats, so human studies need to confirm this effect in women. Bottom line: Since flaxseed oil's other health benefits are well-proven, it certainly makes sense to add a spoonful or two to veggies and salads in hopes of preventing osteoporosis, especially if you're at risk for the disease.

garlic

More health benefits have been ascribed to garlic (*Allium sativum*) than to just about any other food—and with good reason. The short list of reasons why it's smart to be a frequent garlic eater include its antibiotic action, its ability to foil respiratory ailments in the making, and its potential for boosting the health of your heart and protecting you against certain cancers.

rooted in history

Could garlic be the secret that helped raise the great pyramids? It's possible: The Egyptians rationed it to pyramid builders to boost their strength (and to help prevent dysentery). Meanwhile, across the Red Sea, a garlic prescription written in cuneiform was discovered on a Sumerian clay tablet dating back to 3000 BC. Chinese and Indian healers wrote of using garlic as a blood thinner back in 1500 BC. Hippocrates reportedly used garlic to treat cervical cancer. In the early 1700s, French gravediggers drank a brew of crushed garlic and wine in hopes of warding off the plague.

Garlic's first investigator was none other than Louis Pasteur, the great French scientist. He discovered its antibacterial and antifungal powers in the mid-1800s. Later, at his hospital in Africa, Albert Schweitzer used garlic to treat dysentery.

Finally, garlic played a helpful patriotic role during World Wars I and II, when soldiers were given the stuff to prevent gangrene.

USE FOR

Athlete's foot

Cancer protection

Colds and flu

Earache

Gastrointestinal ailments

High blood pressure

High cholesterol

Improved immunity

Respiratory infections

Ringworm

Sinusitis

Swimmer's ear

Ulcers

Urinary tract infections

Warts

Yeast infections

what's in it?

A garlic bulb is a virtual chemical factory full of substances that are highly volatile. Because they're so unstable, their health benefits depend on how fresh the garlic is, and whether it's been crushed, chopped, chewed, or cooked. Among these are sulfur compounds including thiosulfinates, which are responsible for garlic's distinctive aroma and for many of its effects. Garlic's heart-protective ability has recently been attributed to a chemical called S-allylcysteine.

Another active component is a substance called alliin. When a clove is crushed, bruised, or chewed, the alliin is converted into allicin, which cannot survive the heat of cooking or the acid in your stomach. But when you chew fresh garlic, the allicin (and its benefits) is quickly absorbed in your mouth.

Garlic has antibacterial, antimicrobial, and antifungal activity, which in addition to its other benefits, makes it a great home remedy for healing wounds and athlete's foot and for expelling worms.

what science says

Garlic studies published in 2008 and 2009 confirm that garlic lowers cholesterol and blood pressure and helps prevent the common cold, and that a diet rich in the pungent stuff can reduce the risk for prostate and other cancers.

Also recently, researchers from the University of Connecticut ended confusion about the best way to use garlic. They discovered that freshly crushed garlic, rather than garlic that's been processed or cooked, is best for helping protect against heart attacks.

the heart-protecting bulb

When eaten daily, garlic can help lower heart disease risk by as much as 76 percent. It performs this miraculous feat by moderately reducing cholesterol levels (by between 5 and 10 percent in some studies), by thinning the blood and thereby staving off dangerous clots, and by acting as an antioxidant. Garlic's sulfur compounds also appear to ward off cancer, especially stomach and colorectal cancer. The compounds flush out carcinogens before they can damage cell DNA, and they force cancer cells that do develop to self-destruct.

BUYER'S tip

Garlic bulbs should be plump, with smooth, firm cloves. Store in an open container in a cool, well-ventilated pantry for up to two months; don't refrigerate. Cloves that have sprouted are fine to use, though they're less pungent. Mince the sprout and cook along with the garlic.

Good to Know

Eating five or more cloves a day can result in heartburn, flatulence, and intestinal distress. Because garlic is a blood thinner, people taking aspirin or anticoagulant drugs, as well as people with clotting disorders, should check with their doctors before taking medicinal amounts of garlic. In rare cases, garlic may cause an allergic reaction.

Since drying alters the active ingredients of fresh garlic, don't substitute dried powdered garlic when using garlic medicinally.

ginger

Inexpensive, fast acting, scientifically proven, and delicious are terrific attributes for a home remedy to have. And when it comes to easing motion sickness and nausea, ginger is all of those—and more. Ginger (*Zingiber officinale*) has a track record for attacking inflammation and easing pain, both excellent reasons to make sure this rhizome has a dedicated space in your kitchen medicine cabinet.

rooted in history

People have been spicing up their foods with ginger for over 4,000 years. One of its first fans, in fact, was Confucius, who legendarily added it to everything he ate. Ancient Chinese, Indian, Roman, and Grecian healers wrote about the gnarly root's medicinal value, and the list of ills they pitted it against is a long one. Once early North American medics discovered ginger, they used it in warm baths to soothe bruises and tired muscles. As a home remedy, folks chewed gingerroot to soothe sore throats and grated it into olive oil as an antidandruff potion. Warm ginger compresses were an old-time treatment for soothing sinus congestion, menstrual cramps, and general aches and fatigue.

what's in it?

Researchers have identified more than 400 chemicals in gingerroot, though we know about the medicinal properties of only a handful of them. Ginger's antinausea and anti-vomiting properties are likely due to the compounds

USE FOR

Arthritis

Back pain

Belching

Bursitis and
   tendinitis

Colds and flu

Coughs

Dandruff

Fever

Flatulence

Hangover

Indigestion

Migraines

Menstrual cramps

Morning sickness

Motion sickness

Nausea and
   vomiting

Sinusitis

Stomachaches

Toothache

Ulcers

6-gingerol, 6-shogaol, and galanolactone. Scientists believe that they may act on the brain's "vomiting center" to subdue the urge to vomit. They also work in the digestive tract to ease the sensation of nausea.

Gingerols, shogaols, and another compound, paradols, are behind ginger's anti-inflammatory actions. The powerful antioxidant, 6-gingerol, inhibits production of nitric oxide, which forms a really nasty free radical called peroxynitrite that's known to cause cell death. Inhibiting this free radical is proven to ease inflammation and pain and to improve diseases that affect blood vessels. In fact, gingerols act like the COX-II selective, nonsteroidal anti-inflammatory drugs (NSAIDs) such as Celebrex, which explains why ginger has been clinically proven to ease osteoarthritis pain. Unlike NSAIDs, however, ginger has no toxic side effects.

what science says

Recently, scientists have learned more about ginger's ability to suppress cancer cells, an action researchers have been studying for years. In one 2009 study, researchers from the University of Minnesota discovered that 6-gingerol, one of the herb's active compounds, suppressed the growth of colorectal tumors in lab mice. And on a test of human breast cancer cells conducted in the lab, researchers in Korea demonstrated that 6-gingerol inhibited the cells' ability to metastasize, or spread, to other parts of the body.

Iranian researchers recently studied ginger's ability to lower cholesterol. When they gave ginger or a placebo to people with high cholesterol for 45 days, those who took the ginger had lower levels of LDL (unhealthy) cholesterol and higher levels of HDL (healthy) cholesterol than did the people who took the placebo.

Research has also proven that ginger reduces pain and swelling in people with arthritis. It may work against migraines by blocking inflammatory substances called prostaglandins.

And then there are the digestive benefits. In the early 1980s, American scientists began reporting that ginger prevents motion sickness better than popular commercial products. Subsequent research in the United States, Sweden, Germany, and Britain confirms that ginger reduces dizziness, anesthesia-related nausea, and the vomiting and cold sweats associated with seasickness.

BUYER's tip

Buy clean, plump, firm rhizomes (actually, ginger's an underground stem, not the roots), then wrap them tightly in foil and store in the vegetable crisper of the refrigerator for several weeks. Buy powdered ginger in the spice aisle.

Good to Know

Don't give ginger to children under the age of two. Check with your pediatrician before giving ginger to older children.

honey

Honey is truly one of nature's sweetest miracles. Tiny bees, zipping along at up to 15 miles an hour, zoom as far as nine miles away to search for nectar. During just one nectar foray, bees may visit 100 flowers. Sweeter than sugar, honey's thick, syrupy texture makes it the perfect home remedy for easing coughs and sore throats, while its high sugar content makes it a natural antibiotic.

rooted in history

Honey just might be the world's oldest home remedy; bees have been producing the stuff for at least 100 million years. Written references to honey date back 7,500 years or so to Egypt and Sumeria. Of the 900 known remedies in ancient Egyptian medicine, 500 contained honey. In the first century, Pliny the Elder recorded his cure for dropsy and bladder stones in a recipe that included honey and powdered bees. It's been written that ancient Olympians dined on honey and figs to enhance their athletic performance.

By medieval times, honey's medicinal use was mostly limited to its ability to make medicines taste a little less terrible, and it was also used externally to heal wounds. Hundreds of years later, honey found its way into recipes for patent medicines all over the world.

what science says

Science has focused its attention on honey's wound-healing ability. A small study conducted in the United Kingdom

USE FOR

Acne

Allergies

Anxiety

Chapped lips

Colds and flu

Conjunctivitis

Constipation

Coughs

Cuts and scrapes

Eczema

Hangovers

Healthy skin

Heartburn

Hiccups

Indigestion

Laryngitis

Psoriasis

Shingles

Ulcers

showed that Manuka honey (a New Zealand variety) healed wounds from radiation therapy that had not responded to conventional treatments. In another recent study conducted in the United Kingdom, the wounds of 105 patients were treated either with honey or a conventional dressing. After 12 weeks, the honey treatment healed wounds 12 percent faster than did the conventional dressing.

Turns out that honey is more than a sweet addition to cough syrups. In one study, conducted by researchers at Pennsylvania State University, honey improved coughs better than dextromethorphan (DM), a common ingredient in many cough suppressants.

what's in it?

You won't be surprised to learn that honey is mostly made up of sugars—38.2 percent fructose, 31 percent glucose; disaccharides such as sucrose and maltose and oligosaccharides made up the rest. That honey is laced with beneficial substances is clear: In a new study, some of the phytonutrients found in raw honey were shown to prevent colon cancer in lab animals.

Honey also contains antioxidants, including one called pinocembrin. Chinese test-tube and animal studies showed that pinocembrin seems to protect brain cells. Whether it has a similar effect in humans is as yet unknown. Other honey antioxidants include quercetin, kaempferol, and apigenin.

gentle wound healer

Honey's high sugar content, combined with its hydrogen peroxide and propolis (a compound in nectar that kills bacteria) content, pulls moisture from wounds, denies bacteria the moisture they need to survive, and locks out harmful external contaminants—actions that help wounds heal faster.

In the days before antibiotics, infection was the greatest health threat. Even small wounds could turn deadly, which is why doctors often carried honey in their black bags. Even now that triple-antibiotic creams are in every medicine chest, some doctors believe that honey might be a superior wound dressing in some cases. It works so well that a number of manufacturers sell honey-impregnated dressings for hard-to-heal wounds.

Good to Know

Spores of *Clostridium botulinum* have been found in about 10 percent of honeys sampled by the Centers for Disease Control and Prevention (CDC) in the United States. So don't give honey to infants under the age of 12 months, because *C. botulinum* can cause serious illness during the first year of life.

BUYER'S tip

In general, the darker the honey, the more antioxidants it contains. Honeys from buckwheat flowers, sage, and tupelo have more antioxidants, and raw, unprocessed honey contains the most health-boosting properties. What's more, darker honeys have more intense flavors. Store honey in a well-sealed container in a dark, dry kitchen cabinet.

horseradish

You might stir horseradish into seafood cocktail sauces or use it as a roast beef garnish, but you probably never think about the stuff as a potent remedy for bad chest colds. Reach for horseradish (*Armoracia rusticana*) the next time someone in your care comes down with a respiratory infection, and you'll be amazed at how effectively this eye-watering root helps break up stubborn congestion.

rooted in history

Horseradish, cultivated for its root for more than 3,500 years, has served double duty as a pungent condiment and a medicine throughout its history. By the 18th century, horseradish was included in the Materia Medica of the *London Pharmacopoeias*, making it an official medicine. Physicians treated coughs, including whooping cough, and hoarseness with horseradish. Healers pounded the root into plasters or rubs, which they applied to the skin to ease rheumatism, sciatica, facial pain, gout, and other achy, painful conditions. Cosmetically, horseradish was used as a freckle remover and to clear and freshen the complexion.

what's in it?

Horseradish contains mustard oil glycosides, which are sharp-tasting compounds found in several plant species, including mustard. These act as irritants when applied to the skin and cause blood vessels to dilate. The combined effect can serve as a counter-irritant that can ease pain and help break up chest congestion.

Horseradish is also antimicrobial and acts as a nasal, sinus, and bronchial decongestant, which is how it helps clear up colds and respiratory tract infections. Its antiseptic properties and a diuretic effect have also been used to treat urinary tract infections.

what science says

Search the scientific literature on horseradish, and you'll come up all but empty-handed. One study in 2007 found some evidence that a product containing horseradish and nasturtium might prevent new bladder infections in people with a history of chronic bladder infections. However, experts considered the study weak.

Despite the lack of scientific evidence, its centuries of traditional use prompted German officials to include horseradish as an approved herbal medicine in its influential Commission E report. Its recommended uses are for respiratory illnesses and urinary tract infections when taken internally, and for treating minor muscle aches and chest congestion when used externally as a poultice.

BUYER'S tip

If you're lucky enough to find fresh horseradish at a farmers' market, or if you grow your own, just peel and grate it as needed—it loses its pungency soon after grating or when heated. To make prepared horseradish: Grate the root (in a well-aired place to dissipate the fumes), and add ½ cup white wine vinegar and ¼ teaspoon salt to each cup of pulp. Store, covered, in the refrigerator. Or buy prepared horseradish (the kind that's sold from a refrigerated case), and store it in the refrigerator.

Good to Know

Wasabi is the green paste served with Japanese dishes like sushi. It comes from the plant *Wasabia japonica* and has similar congestion-clearing properties as horseradish. But you may never have tasted the real stuff, no matter how big a sushi lover you are. That's because most of the wasabi you get in Japanese restaurants is made from a cheap blend of regular horseradish powder, mustard powder, cornstarch, and food coloring. Real wasabi, available in powders or pastes, is fairly expensive. Make sure to read the labels carefully to ensure you're getting pure wasabi.

lemon

You get more than a tart blast when you suck on a slice of lemon or sip lemonade. Lemons are an extraordinarily rich source of healing compounds that improve immunity, strengthen blood vessels, and help skin heal. They may even block cell changes that can lead to cancer. A generous squeeze or two of lemon and a spoonful of honey in a cup of hot water is the perfect sore throat elixir. Lemon is also an indispensable ingredient for concocting homemade cough syrups and DIY beauty treatments.

rooted in history

Originally developed as a cross between a fruit called the citron and the lime, lemons probably originated in China or India some 2,500 years ago. Arabs introduced them to Spain and North Africa around the 11th century, and the Crusaders helped spread them through the rest of Europe. Christopher Columbus brought them to the Americas on his second voyage in 1493, and they've been grown in Florida since the 1500s. Centuries ago, British sailors ate lemons by the boatload to prevent scurvy, a deadly disease caused by vitamin C deficiency. A single lemon packs 39 milligrams of vitamin C, more than half the Recommended Dietary Allowance.

Miners and pioneers also relied on lemons to fight scurvy during the California gold rush, and valued them so highly that they'd pay as much as one dollar a lemon back in 1849, a huge sum back then for a tiny fruit—in today's money, that's about $25.58.

USE FOR

Acne

Allergies

Age spots

Antiseptic

Body odor

Calluses and corns

Colds and flu

Constipation

Coughs

Energy

Fever

Indigestion

Healthy skin

Heartburn

Kidney stones

Mood enhancement

Morning sickness

Motion sickness

Sinusitis

Sore throat

Varicose veins

what's in it?

The vitamin C in lemons lowers levels of histamine, the chemical that contributes to stuffy noses and runny eyes. The vitamin is a powerful antioxidant that also reduces levels of free radicals, those nasty cell-damaging molecules, and helps guard against heart disease. (Several studies have shown that low levels of vitamin C increase the risk for heart attacks. When cholesterol becomes oxidized—attacked by free radicals—it's more likely to turn into artery-clogging plaque.) The body uses vitamin C to boost the activity of immune cells and manufacture collagen, the tissue-building substance that assists in wound healing.

Lemons are also loaded with citric acid, a chemical that reduces calcium excretion and helps prevent the formation of kidney stones. If kidney stones are an issue for you, consider drinking eight 8-ounce glasses of lemonade made with fresh lemon juice daily (sweetened with as little sugar as possible). This refreshing drink prevents the formation of kidney stones as effectively as do prescription citrate drugs, such as potassium citrate.

Finally, lemon zest is rich in a bioflavonoid (a group of antioxidant plant chemicals) called rutin, which strengthens the walls of the veins and capillaries and reduces the pain—and even the occurrence—of varicose veins.

BUYER'S tip

Look for unblemished lemons with a rich yellow color and smooth skin. Coarse or rough texture often indicates the skin is thick, meaning less flesh and juice inside. Another buyer's trick is sensing the weight: the heavier it feels, the better. Before you juice them, roll them on a flat surface with the palm of your hand. This helps them yield more juice.

Good to Know

There are more than one variety of lemon on sale at your local market. The Eureka lemon contains seeds, tends to be more pebbly, and has a short neck. Lisbon lemons are smoother and usually seedless. Both are quite sour. Meyer lemons, on the other hand, are sweeter and wonderful in drinks and desserts. It's far harder to find Meyer lemons, but they are becoming trendy. Believed to have originated in China as a cross between a lemon and an orange, they are rounder than a typical lemon and might have a slightly orange shade to their skin.

mustard

The tiny seeds of this leafy broccoli and cabbage relative make one of the most popular condiments of all time. But mustard is much more than a taste bud perker-upper. Healers have known for ages that mustard's pungent heat thins mucus and makes it easier to breathe when you have a cold or flu. What's more, mustard contains a variety of chemical compounds with impressive healing credentials.

rooted in history

To the ancients, mustard was practically a panacea. Egyptian, Sumerian, and Chinese healers all used mustard seeds as medicine. The famous Greek physician, Dioscorides, counted on mustard to treat conditions as diverse as epilepsy and tonsillitis, and the early Romans chewed the seeds to ease toothache pain and used mustard ointments to treat stings. But the most famous mustard remedy is the mustard plaster, which dates back to Hippocrates, the father of medicine, as a treatment for lung problems and rheumatism. It's a testament to its success that healers in countries all over the world have relied on mustard plasters for a long list of ailments. However, we cringe at one of its uses: In 18th-century Russia, mustard plasters were administered as a treatment for mental illness.

what's in it?

Mustard seeds are loaded with phytonutrients called glucosinolates, which are responsible for mustard's spiciness. They help protect against colon and rectal cancer. What's

USE FOR

Athlete's foot

Arthritis pain

Back pain

Belching

Bursitis and
  tendinitis

Chest congestion

Colds and flu

Fever

Headache

Ringworm

more, mustard seeds rank as good sources of omega-3 fatty acids, tryptophan, selenium, and magnesium—but you'd have to eat a two-teaspoon sized serving of mustard seeds to reap those nutritional benefits. Finally, mustard seeds contain hefty doses of myrosin and sinigrin, chemicals that make mucus watery and easier to expel from the body.

the warming remedy

Herbalists call mustard a rubefacient, meaning that it stimulates circulation, which creates soothing warmth when you apply it to the skin. Like cayenne pepper, it also appears to deplete nerve cells of substance P, a chemical that transmits pain signals back to the brain. Soaking your feet in hot water with a little mustard powder is the ultimate multitasking remedy: It can unblock a stuffed head, help ease fever, and soothe a headache—all by drawing blood to the feet. This eases the pressure on the blood vessels in your head, helps disperse congestion, and increases circulation.

A traditional congestion remedy is to apply a mustard plaster—made by crushing a few tablespoonfuls of mustard seeds and adding them to a cup of flour or cornmeal along with a little water to make a paste—to your chest. The aroma unclogs nasal stuffiness, while the "heat" increases blood circulation in the chest and makes it easier to breathe. Just don't leave the plaster on too long (usually no more than 15 minutes) or it will burn the skin. You can protect the skin before you put the plaster on by applying a coating of petroleum jelly. Be sure to wash your hands thoroughly after handling a mustard plaster and before touching your eyes, nose, or mouth.

Good to Know

If you eat mustard seeds, beware: They have a laxative effect and can make you vomit if you eat enough of them—about a teaspoonful or so.

Other warnings: Mustard plasters can burn and blister sensitive skin after only 15 minutes. Prolonged external use can result in skin and nerve damage, so don't use for longer than two weeks. Mustard fumes may irritate the eyes, nose, and lungs (in fact, mustard derivatives are used as chemical weapons). Do not give mustard seeds or mustard oil to children under the age of six or people with kidney problems.

BUYER'S tip

Three kinds of mustard seeds are available: those from the black (*Brassica nigra*), white (*Brassica alba*) and brown (*Brassica juncea*) mustard plants. Black mustard seeds have the sharpest flavor. White mustard seeds are actually yellow and are used to make American mustard and yellow mustard powder. Brown seeds are used to make Dijon and other brown mustards. For the remedies in this book, buy white (yellow) mustard seeds and grind them in a coffee grinder or buy mustard power, such as Coleman's.

nuts & seeds

No matter what kind of nuts or seeds may be lurking in your pantry, it's a safe bet that they're loaded with vitamins, minerals, fiber, essential fatty acids, antioxidants, and plant sterols. These healthful compounds make nuts a tasty way to help ease or prevent a variety of conditions— including diabetes, heart disease, cancer, and gallstones. Though you probably think of nuts as a high-calorie item, there's new science to prove they even have a place in your battle against weight gain.

rooted in history

Nuts are among mankind's oldest food sources. Evidence found in Israeli archeological digs reveal that at least seven different nuts were on the human menu some 780,000 years ago. Among them: pistachios, water chestnuts, and wild almonds. The oldest walnut remains come from Iraq, dated at 50,000 years old; early Romans considered walnuts as "food for the gods." Pecans have been found in Texas excavations dating back to 6100 BC. And the almond, mentioned in the Old Testament of the Bible, was one of man's earliest cultivated foods.

what's in them?

Though different kinds of nuts contain different types and levels of healthful substances, researchers tell us that most nuts contain compounds such as tocopherols, folic acid, selenium, magnesium, phosphorus, zinc, fiber, and sev-

USE FOR

Acne

Anxiety

Asthma

Back pain

Blood sugar control

Breast tenderness

Cancer prevention

Extra energy

Eye irritation

Gallstones

Healthy skin
 and nails

Heart disease
 prevention

High cholesterol

Immunity

Menopausal and
 menstrual
 symptoms

Morning sickness

Stress

Weight management

eral phytochemicals. Studies indicate that these are likely responsible for nuts' antioxidant, anti-inflammatory, and anticancer properties.

That said, some are more nutritious than others. A half-cup serving of almonds, peanuts, pine nuts, pistachios, or sunflower seeds, for instance, provides more than 500 milligrams of potassium, more than you'll get from eating a whole banana.

A 1-ounce (30 g) serving of almonds provides almost 50 percent of the Recommended Dietary Allowance (RDA) of vitamin E and a similar serving of hazelnuts, about 30 percent. In fact, nuts and seeds are one of the best food sources of vitamin E, an important antioxidant that enhances the immune system, protects cell membranes, and helps make red blood cells.

We're just getting started. A half-cup of almonds contains an impressive 3 milligrams of iron; pistachios have 2 milligrams. Pumpkin and sesame seeds are also good sources of iron. Likewise, a cup of almonds has 400 milligrams of calcium, more than is found in a cup of milk.

Most nuts and seeds contain B vitamins such as niacin, thiamin, and folate. Just a half-cup of peanuts contains 25 percent of the RDA.

Brazil nuts? They're high in the antioxidant selenium. A quarter ounce (7 g) provides more than twice the RDA for this mineral.

Walnuts are especially rich in ellagic acid, an antioxidant that may inhibit the growth of cancer cells. Walnuts also are rich in omega-3 fatty acids. In one study, men and women with high cholesterol levels added walnuts to a healthy Mediterranean diet. Their LDL cholesterol and heart disease risk both dropped.

Hazelnuts are rich in vitamin E, fiber, and copper and contain the same amount of potassium as half a banana.

Finally, 1 ounce (30 g) of sunflower seed kernels contains about 75 percent of the RDA of vitamin E. Sunflower seeds are also rich in selenium, copper, fiber, iron, zinc, folate, and vitamin B_6.

what science says

Two studies published in 2009 attest to the powerful impact nuts can have on your health when you eat them regularly.

BUYER'S tip

Nut production generally involves pesticides. If this concerns you, seek out organically grown nuts or nut butters, which you can find in health or natural food stores. Nuts bought in their shells last the longest; sliced or crushed nuts lose flavor and nutrients faster.

Researchers at Purdue University tested the impact on hunger of various snack foods, including unsalted peanuts, other nuts, and rice cakes. They found that following a peanut or peanut butter snack, people's hunger was reduced for two and a half hours. With other snacks, hunger returned within a half hour. Interestingly, the peanut snackers adjusted their calorie intake spontaneously and did not add extra calories to their daily diet. Further, there was a positive change in the fatty-acid profile of the diet reflecting the good-quality (monounsaturated) fats found in the peanuts.

In a study conducted at Loma Linda University in California, researchers discovered that eating a walnut-enriched diet lowered triglyceride and cholesterol levels a shade better than did eating a diet that included heart-healthy salmon. Harvard University researchers agreed with those findings and published a study concluding that walnut-rich diets lower total cholesterol as well as LDL (unhealthy) cholesterol.

Meanwhile, Yale University researchers learned that when people with type 2 diabetes ate diets supplemented with 2 ounces of walnuts for eight weeks, their blood vessel health improved significantly. The researchers said that eating walnuts had the potential to lower the overall cardiac risks for people with type 2 diabetes. What's more, eating walnuts reduced participants' blood sugar and total cholesterol levels.

just say "nuts"

Those recent findings are confirmed by large-scale studies that looked at the diets and lifestyles of thousands of men and women.

The Nurses' Health Study, for example, found that women who ate more than 5 ounces (140 g) of nuts per week had a 35 percent lower risk of heart attack and death from heart disease than those who never ate nuts or ate them less than once a month.

Likewise, the Physicians' Health Study found that men who ate nuts two or three times per week had a 47 percent reduced risk of sudden death from cardiac arrest compared with those who rarely or never ate nuts. And a third study showed that almonds significantly lowered LDL cholesterol in those who already had elevated cholesterol levels.

nuts and weight loss

You'd think that eating nuts—which are high in fat and calories—would lead to weight gain. But you'd be wrong.

In one 2009 study, Harvard University researchers evaluated the Nurses' Health Study II, which included 51,188 women, to see what impact eating nuts had on weight changes over an eight-year period. Turns out, the women whose diets included nuts didn't gain weight. The researchers even suggested that eating nuts could be a weight control tool.

And in a 2007 Spanish study, researchers followed the diets of 8,865 men and women for a little more than two years. They also found that nuts weren't responsible for weight gain.

Still, you can't add nuts to an otherwise unhealthy diet and expect to lose weight. In most research, nuts and seeds have had the best effect when used as a substitute for, not an addition to, highly saturated fats. So enjoy nuts regularly—but in moderation. And remember that calories do count when it comes to weight loss. Macadamia nuts have more than 1,000 calories per cup; Brazil nuts are a close second. Other nuts and seeds contain about 700 to 850 calories per cup. When it comes to a healthy serving of nuts, think "handful."

allergy alert

Some nuts, especially peanuts (technically, peanuts are legumes), provoke allergic reactions in many people. Symptoms range from a tingling sensation in the mouth to hives and, in extreme cases, to anaphylaxis, a life-threatening emergency. But because the different varieties are not closely related, a person who is allergic to walnuts, for example, may be able to eat another type of nut or seed.

Watch the calories

Nuts can break your calorie budget if you're not careful. Nuts listed in bold type are relatively low in saturated fat and high in healthy monounsaturated fat or omega-3 fatty acids.

NUT	CALORIES*	NUTS	FIBER*
Almonds	169	22	3.3 g
Brazil nuts	186	6	2.1 g
Cashews	163	18	0.9 g
Hazelnuts	178	21	2.7 g
Macadamia nuts	204	10–12	2.3 g
Peanuts	166	35	2.3 g
Pecans	201	15 halves	2.7 g
Pine nuts	191	167	1.0 g
Pistachios	169	49	2.4 g
Walnuts	185	14 halves	1.9 g

*per 1-ounce serving
Sources: *American Journal of Clinical Nutrition*; USDA Nutrient Database; *Nutrition Reviews*.

oats

Few breakfast foods are as heart-warming as a steaming bowl of oatmeal, especially on a chilly morning. Heart-warming—and heart-healthy, as it turns out. That's because oats are richly laced with polyphenols and saponins, which are powerful antioxidants with disease-fighting properties. Oats also contain potent skin-soothing components, which make this grain an indispensable ingredient for DIY beauty recipes.

rooted in history

Though ancient Egyptians used oats as a soothing skin treatment, it's unlikely that they actually ate them. Oats have been found in Egyptian tombs and in Bronze Age caves dating back between 3000 and 4000 BC, but whether they were used for human or animal consumption is lost to the mists of time. Either way, this is one food whose medicinal properties the ancient Greeks and Romans simply didn't understand. The Romans used it only for horse feed and looked down their noses at the "oat-eating barbarians" to their north. It's been suggested that if the Romans ate their oatmeal, maybe they would have had more of a shot at repelling the oat-eating Picts of Scotland (among other barbarians) who eventually brought down the Roman Empire.

what's in it?

Oats contain beta-glucan, a special type of fiber with immune-enhancing, blood-sugar stabilizing, and

USE FOR

Acne

Anal itching

Blood sugar
  regulation

Breast tenderness

Cancer prevention

Chicken pox

Depression

Foot odor

Healthy skin

Heart health

High blood pressure

High cholesterol

Improved immunity

Itching

Poison ivy/oak

Psoriasis

Shingles

Stress

Sunburn

Warts

Weight
  management

cholesterol-lowering properties. Antioxidants called ave-nanthramides, found only in oats, destroy free radicals. These antioxidants also help prevent atherosclerosis (also known as "hardening of the arteries"). Combined, these two actions can give your heart's health a powerful boost. Further, oats are a good source of selenium, a powerful antioxidant involved in repairing DNA. Selenium is also linked to a reduced risk for cancer, especially colon cancer. Finally, studies show that oats' avenanthramides reduce itching and inflammation when applied to the skin.

Good to Know

To make oatmeal less healthful, just add lots of butter or sugar. But we recommend going the other direction: Mix-ins like blueberries, cinnamon, cranberries, chopped nuts, ground flaxseeds, or raisins add extra nutrition to an already wonderful food.

what science says

A 2009 study conducted at the Athens University Medical School and Diabetes Center in Greece confirmed that eating oats lowers harmful LDL cholesterol and can improve insulin resistance in people with type 2 diabetes. In the study, 46 people were given either a daily serving of bread enriched with 3 grams of beta glucan (about the amount you'd get in a cup and a half of cooked oatmeal) or plain white bread. After three weeks, people in the beta glucan group lowered their LDL by almost 16 percent and lowered their total cholesterol by almost 13 percent. But in the white bread group, people's LDL levels decreased by about 3 percent and their total cholesterol increased by about 2 percent. People in the beta glucan group experienced an insulin resistance drop, but insulin resistance increased slightly in the white bread group.

stay fuller longer

Since oats take a long time to digest, they tend to keep you feeling full longer. It's likely that oats' protein and fiber content contribute to this effect. In one study comparing oatmeal to a sugared flaked cereal for breakfast, researchers found that subjects who ate oatmeal at breakfast consumed one-third fewer calories for lunch, thus helping with weight management.

shrink your numbers

To substantially lower your cholesterol and insulin resistance, aim for 3 grams of beta glucan every day. You'll find that in one cup of cooked oat bran, one and a half cups of cooked oatmeal, or three pouches of instant oatmeal.

Oats contain a special type of fiber with immune-enhancing properties.

Eating oatmeal regularly may reduce the risk of heart disease in women—beyond lowering cholesterol. The Nurses' Health Study found that those who ate oatmeal five or more times per week had a heart disease risk reduction of 29 percent. The authors think there's more to this effect than just oats' soluble fiber—it could be the result of antioxidants like the avenanthramides. Other studies have shown that oats may boost levels of the protective HDL cholesterol.

Another number oats can help reduce is your blood pressure. A study conducted in Minnesota looked at people who were taking medication for high blood pressure. Half of them were asked to eat a cup and a half of oatmeal along with an oat-based snack, while the other half ate low-fiber cereals and snacks. The people who were consuming the oats showed a significant drop in blood pressure.

BUYER'S tip

Let your taste buds be your guide when it comes to choosing oatmeal. Nutritionally, all varieties are about the same (but watch the sugar and salt content of instant oatmeal).

• Oat groats, also known as whole-oat groats or whole oats, are minimally processed—only the outer hull is removed. They are very nutritious but are chewy and must be soaked and cooked a long time. They can be used as a substitute for barley or rice.

• Rolled oats, also called oatmeal, rolled oatmeal, or old-fashioned oats, are oat groats that are steamed, rolled, and flaked so they cook quickly.

• Instant oatmeal consists of very thin, precooked oat flakes that need only to be mixed with a hot liquid. They often have flavorings, sugar, and salt added.

• Steel-cut oats, also called Irish oats, Irish oatmeal, Scotch oats, or Scotch oatmeal, are groats that have been chopped into small pieces but not rolled into flakes. They are chewier than rolled oats and are often used for hot oatmeal cereals and muesli.

Whichever type you choose, store oats in a tightly sealed container for up to six months.

olive oil

Nutritionists have sung the praises of the Mediterranean diet for so long that it's easy to forget how radical the idea was that certain fats, like olive oil, could actually be good for your heart. But the evidence was strong: In the mid-1980s, a long-term study comparing rates of cardiovascular disease in seven countries revealed that heart attacks were relatively uncommon in countries where the people consumed lots of olive oil, including Italy and Greece. Since then, scores of clinical studies have left little doubt that olive oil protects the cardiovascular system.

rooted in history

Olives grow where little else survives—hot, dry climates suit olive trees just fine. So it's no surprise that the first olive oil probably came from a Mediterranean country like Syria, Lebanon, Palestine, or Israel. The ancients put a high price on their olive oil—in ancient Syria, around 2000 BC, its value was five times that of wine. But that probably had to do with its use as a lamp oil.

Olive oil figured prominently into religious rites and rituals. It was used to consecrate the dead and to anoint royalty and warriors. In fact, the word Messiah means "the anointed one." The ancients used olive oil for medicinal ointments, in beauty concoctions, to give skin and hair a healthy glow, and to make soap. In the world's first cookbook, *De Re Coquinaria* (Cooking Matters), by the Roman gourmet Apicius, olive oil is among the 10 most common ingredients in the book's 468 recipes.

USE FOR

Allergies

Asthma

Back pain

Brittle nails

Cancer risk reduction

Chapped lips

Clear skin

Eczema

Head lice

Heart health

High blood pressure

High cholesterol

Infection prevention

Menstrual symptoms

Moisturizer

Nosebleed

Psoriasis

Sore feet

Scientists have long known that a diet rich in olive oil protects the heart. Now they are finally discovering how.

what science says

Scientists have known for decades that people whose diets are rich in olive oil have low rates of heart disease. Now they've figured out more about how the golden green liquid works its magic.

In a recent study, Spanish researchers reported that when people ate olive oil-enriched Mediterranean-style diets for a year, their blood pressure dropped significantly. People in the study whose Mediterranean-style diets were enriched with nuts also dropped a bit, but people in a third group, on a basic low-fat diet, experienced no blood pressure changes. People in the olive oil group also experienced a substantial drop in their levels of C-reactive protein (an inflammation marker linked to heart disease) compared to people in the other two groups. (The C-reactive protein levels of those in the low-fat group actually rose.) The most fascinating thing to come out of this study? Olive oil seems to change the structure of red blood cells, which the researchers speculated could account for its ability to lower cholesterol and blood pressure.

Also recently, Italian researchers compared over 20,000 cases of people with cancer to 18,000 healthy people. They discovered that people whose diets included olive oil and other healthy fats had a lower cancer risk.

Finally, Spanish researchers in 2009 followed men with severely high cholesterol, all of whom were taking the cholesterol-lowering drug simvastatin, for six months. There were two groups: men whose diets contained olive oil or men who used sunflower oil. Men in the olive oil group

Good to Know

Yes, olives are great for you, too, and make a fine snack in moderation. Most olives are inedible straight from the tree; they need to be cured to remove certain bitter chemicals. The variations between olives all relate to their ripeness at harvest, the curing process used, and their exposure to air during the curing process (air is one way to turn an olive dark). The only health caveat for olives is saltiness: Some types are overloaded with the stuff. If you love olives but can't handle the salt, give them a rinse before eating.

lowered their total cholesterol more than did the men in the sunflower oil group, leading the researchers to advise that people with high cholesterol use olive oil instead of sunflower oil, even if they're taking effective cholesterol-lowering medications.

oil that acts like heart medicine

Still other studies show that olive oil acts a bit like aspirin, reducing levels of chronic low-grade inflammation, another culprit behind heart attacks. Finally, olive oil is teeming with antioxidants, which act on cholesterol to make it less likely to stick to artery walls. Olive oil is rich in unique disease-fighting phytochemicals, vitamin E, and mono-unsaturated fat, which all help to clear cholesterol from arteries. The antioxidant phytochemicals hydroxytyrosol and oleuropein may work together, according to laboratory studies, to help protect against breast cancer, high blood pressure, infection-causing bacteria, and heart disease. Lignans, present in extra-virgin olive oil, may protect against cancer by suppressing early cancer changes in cells.

the best press

The heat and chemicals used in processing olive oil can diminish its nutrient content, which is why it's best to choose minimally processed oils, such as extra-virgin, cold-pressed oil.

Virgin olive oil is the oily juice pressed from the olive. It is unrefined. The term virgin refers to oils that are slightly more acidic than the extra-virgin ones; they must contain no more than 3 grams of free oleic acid per 100 grams.

Extra-virgin olive oil is the least acidic and has a maximum acid level of 1 gram of free oleic acid per 100 grams of oil. It's the choice of chefs because it offers the widest variety of flavors and aromas and has a "fruity" flavor.

The flavor differences are due to the regions where the olives are cultivated, the climate, the variety of olive, and to some degree the manner in which the olives are harvested. Steer clear of bottles labeled "extra light" and "light." These olive oils are the most refined, yet are no lower in calories or fat. They lack the flavor and many of the benefits of the extra-virgin olive oils.

BUYER'S tip

As we noted, cold-pressed extra-virgin olive oil is the best choice, both for flavor and health. It contains far more antioxidants than other olive oils. To preserve those antioxidants, keep your oil away from heat, light, and air. They not only turn the oil rancid but also lower anti-oxidant content. Store your oil in a cool, dark place in an airtight opaque container. Use extra-virgin for dipping and salad dressings; use virgin olive oil for sautéing.

peppermint

Count on sprightly peppermint (*Mentha piperita*) as your go-to herb for easing upset stomachs and minor digestive woes. The oils it contains, especially menthol and menthone, relax the smooth muscles that line the intestinal tract, helping to relieve cramping. Menthol's decongestant, mucus-thinning action makes it a smart addition to remedies for colds and coughs. Mint is also a wonderful ingredient in home remedies for soothing itchy skin irritations.

rooted in history

As Greek myth has it, when the god Pluto fell in love with the nymph, Menthe, his wife, Proserpine, fell into a fit of jealous rage and—poof! She changed Menthe into the plant we now call mint. Based on the myth's romance, the ancient Greek philosopher Theophrastus officially gave mint its botanical name, Menthe.

Early Romans cooked with mint, and the Greeks used it as a restorative, much like smelling salts. England's great 17th-century herbalist, Nicholas Culpeper, called mint "singularly good" for some 40 different health problems. Among them, he recommended it for headaches, a use that one small 1994 study has confirmed.

what's in it?

More than 100 components have been identified in mint. As with all medicinal plants, their exact composition

USE FOR

Acne

Arthritis

Belching

Body odor

Colds and flu

Coughs

Extra energy

Fatigue

Flatulence

Foot problems

Headache

Indigestion

Irritable bowel
  syndrome

Morning sickness

Nausea and
  vomiting

Pain relief

Sinusitis

Skin care

Sore throat

Stings and bites

varies somewhat, depending on where and how the plant was grown and its particular variety—there are hundreds of mints. In general, mints contain the volatile oil menthol, which relaxes intestinal spasms, eases abdominal pain, and acts as a decongestant and topical pain reliever. It also contains the flavonoids rutin, luteolin, hesperidin, and eriocitrin, which have antiviral and antioxidant properties.

what science says

As a digestive aid, mint is hard to beat—even though relatively few clinical studies have been conducted on the herb. Instead of looking at the herb itself, most studies have focused on peppermint oil and its ability to ease symptoms of irritable bowel syndrome, or IBS.

Most recently, researchers at the Tehran University of Medical Sciences gave 90 people with IBS a placebo or a specially coated, delayed-release peppermint oil capsule three times a day for eight weeks. At the end of the study, 14 people who took the peppermint oil reported that they were free of pain or discomfort.

And in a Taiwanese study, IBS patients given peppermint-oil capsules 15 to 30 minutes before meals experienced significantly less bloating, stomach rumbling, and gas. Abdominal pain was reduced or disappeared entirely in some cases.

Good to Know

Peppermint is easy to grow—in fact, it's *too* easy. Experts recommend growing it in pots rather than in a bed because the plant often takes over a garden. Peppermint plants prefer full or partial sun and loamy soil. Use the leaves to make tea, flavor ice water, top ice cream, or add zest to vegetables and stir-fries.

BUYER'S tip

Find peppermint tea bags in supermarkets and health food stores; peppermint essential oil is sold in health food stores.

red wine

USE FOR

Allergies

Blood sugar control

Cold sores

High blood pressure

High cholesterol

Heart and
  artery health

Longevity

The traditional French diet flies in the face of current nutritional wisdom. It's liberally laced with cheese, butter, rich meats, patés, and other artery-clogging delicacies doctors tell us to avoid like the plague. Yet the French have a much lower death rate from heart disease than you'd expect. Researchers called the mystery the French Paradox, and as far back as the early 1990s, they began to suspect that wine could be the reason for the anomaly. Turns out, they were on the right track, and ever since, research has been pouring in about red wine's health benefits.

rooted in history

The first written record of wine is in the Old Testament. One of Noah's first tasks after the ark landed and the floodwaters cleared was to plant a vineyard and make wine.

The first physical proof of wine's ancient usage came when archeologists unearthed pottery containing wine residue in present-day Iran. They were able to date their find back to around 5000 BC. From that time on, wine spread throughout the Middle East to the Mediterranean. The Greeks so loved their wine that they dedicated the god Dionysus to it. The Romans loved their wine, too. The great Roman physician Galen documented his findings about wine's medicinal value.

With the fall of the Roman Empire, wine making slid into a decline, but monks revived the art during the Dark Ages. In fact, as monasteries spread, monks planted some of the finest vineyards in Europe, many of which are still producing grapes.

what's in it?

Wine's heart-healthy benefits come from its antioxidants, which include resveratrol, catechin, epicatechin, and proanthocyanidins. Resveratrol is found in the grape skins, making red wine healthier for your heart than white wine because grape skins are removed from the process before they can color the white wine. No grape skins, no resveratrol.

Grape seeds contain proanthocyanidins, potent antioxidants that have anti-inflammatory effects. These decrease DNA damage and appear to be better at scavenging free radicals and preventing oxidative cell damage to brain and liver tissues than other antioxidants.

what science says

Recent studies have revealed that resveratrol may be a key to longevity. At the University of Connecticut School of Medicine, researchers discovered that resveratrol extends the lifespan in yeast by activating a longevity gene known as SirT1. That's the same gene involved in the increased lifespan of people on calorie-restricted diets.

This finding builds on years of substantial wine research, including the INTERHEART study, conducted in 52 countries around the world. Researchers examined 15,152 people who had suffered heart attacks and compared their cases to those of 14,820 healthy people. They learned that drinking wine regularly, in moderation, protects against heart attacks, especially for women.

wine or grape juice?

Wine has an edge over grape juice for one key reason: Without alcohol, the body can't absorb resveratrol. Still, grape juice protects you in other important ways.

In a 2009 study, Korean researchers gave about 12.5 ounces of grape juice (more or less, depending on the person's weight) or a placebo juice to 40 healthy people. After eight weeks, people in the grape juice group lowered their blood pressure and had positive changes in their blood level of antioxidants. The researchers concluded that drinking grape juice could lower the risk of age-related diseases.

BUYER'S tip

Never drink (or cook with) cheap "cooking wines." These are often sold in the condiments section of supermarkets. They're generally made with low-quality wine, and they're loaded with sodium. Good rule of thumb: If you wouldn't drink it, don't cook with it.

Good to Know

On average, pinot noir has twice the resveratrol of other red wines. In one study of nutrients in California wines, merlot and cabernet sauvignon came in second and third place, respectively.

rosemary

If the only time you pull out your spice bottle of rosemary is when you're cooking lamb, you're missing out on a wonderful remedy for soothing nerves, boosting energy, and even enhancing memory. Rosemary (*Rosmarinus officinalis*) contains flavonoids with potent antioxidant action. These compounds may also strengthen blood vessels, can lessen inflammation, and may reduce the risk of cancers, arteriosclerosis, and other chronic diseases.

rooted in history

Rosemary's reputation as a memory-booster dates back to ancient Greece, when students would stick sprigs of it in their hair while studying for exams. And Grecian mourners would toss rosemary into graves as a symbol of remembrance. Thousands of years later, during the time of the Tudors, Sir Thomas More would write that he planted rosemary in his garden because it was "the herb sacred to remembrance." Even Shakespeare knew about rosemary's memory powers when he wrote these words for Hamlet's Ophelia: "There's rosemary, that's for remembrance."

Cosmetically, rosemary has been used to restore thinning hair. It was also a key ingredient in a concoction called "Queen of Hungary" water. History is a little murky about its actual creation, but for centuries, women used this rosemary-scented potion as a beauty lotion and perfume. An herbal book written in 1525 recommends rosemary boiled in wine as a facial wash.

what's in it?

Rosemary contains several flavonoids, including diosmin, diosmetin, genkwanin, and apigenin. Odd names aside, these white and yellow plant pigments have all been linked to beneficial actions in test tube studies. What we don't yet know, however, is how much rosemary you'd have to ingest to achieve those benefits. Still, the benefits are impressive. For example, apigenin can inhibit the growth of pancreatic cancer cells. Diosmin strengthens blood vessel walls. And genkwanin may help prevent wrinkles by triggering collagen production.

Other rosemary compounds include rosmarinic acid, which has anti-inflammatory and antioxidant properties. Rosemary extracts are also known to be antiviral.

Good to Know

Do not use rosemary medicinally if you are pregnant or breastfeeding.

what science says

In a recent study, researchers from Florida Atlantic University College of Nursing designed a method to test the effects of inhaling rosemary or lavender essential oil on anxiety and stress levels. They recruited 40 graduate nursing students and gave them an exam, and then measured their stress levels, pulse, and blood pressure. Then the volunteers took a second exam using a lavender inhaler, which they were instructed to sniff before and during the test. The students took a third test, using a rosemary inhaler.

The students said that when it came to test taking, rosemary was more helpful than lavender. It improved their recall and helped them stay alert during the test, the researchers reported. The lavender relaxed the students so well that it actually lessened their test-taking ability. The researchers concluded that rosemary heightens your awareness, improves concentration, and generally makes you more alert.

In a study conducted in 2007, Taiwanese scientists analyzed an extract of rosemary leaves and identified its five major compounds, which they then tested. Their findings led them to conclude that rosemary can be considered an "herbal anti-inflammatory and anti-tumor agent."

BUYER'S *tip*

Find dried rosemary leaves in the spice aisle of the supermarket. You can also buy it fresh in many markets, and it's a wonderful herb to grow in your garden.

sage

The herb you lace your Thanksgiving turkey stuffing with was prized for its medicinal power long before the Pilgrims landed at Plymouth Rock. Sage (*Salvia officinalis*) takes its scientific name from the Latin word *salvere*, which means "to be saved." That name is apt indeed: In pre-refrigeration days, sage was used to preserve meat. Healers consider it a handy remedy for digestive upsets, sore throats, colds, and sinusitis. And women transitioning through menopause often bless sage for its ability to reduce the dreaded night sweats.

rooted in history

Sage was sacred to the Romans, so much so that they even created a special ceremony for gathering it. In 1597, Gerard, the great British herbalist, wrote that sage was "singularly" good for the head and brain, quickened senses and memory, strengthened the sinews, and healed shaking and trembling. At least two old proverbs celebrate sage's medicinal value: "Why should a man die whilst sage grows in his garden," and, "He that would live for aye (forever) must eat sage in May."

what's in it?

Sage contains a complex blend of compounds, including diterpenes, which help give the herb its flavor and its health benefits. Of these, carnosic acid and carnosol (also found in rosemary) are antioxidants with anti-inflammatory properties. In lab studies, these two compounds appear to

USE FOR

Anxiety

Body odor

Canker sores

Colds and
    congestion

Concentration

Digestive problems

Foot problems

Healthy skin

High cholesterol

Laryngitis

Memory

Night sweats

Perspiration

Ringworm

Sinusitis

Sore throat

be able to lower blood sugar, though studies on humans are needed to confirm this action. Camphor is an antioxidant that kills fungi and bacteria, which explains sage's old use as a meat preservative. Other sage compounds are known to kill viruses.

what science says

In 2009, Portuguese researchers published a pilot study to see whether sage could lower blood glucose or cholesterol levels in healthy women. They gave six women 10 ounces of sage tea twice a day for four weeks. Though there were no effects on glucose levels, after eight weeks, the tea lowered the women's LDL (unhealthy) cholesterol by 12.4 percent, and increased their levels of HDL (healthy) cholesterol by 50.6 percent. What's more, drinking sage tea also raised blood levels of antioxidants. The researchers said that their study proves that sage tea is a safe and healthful beverage.

Sage reduces excess secretions from the sinuses and upper respiratory tract and also has a drying effect on excessive sweating—especially night sweats associated with menopause. Though there's only one study that supports this phenomenon, traditional herbalists frequently recommend sage for excess perspiration and night sweats.

Sage also improves memory, concentration, and anxiety. The results of a recent clinical trial, conducted on older adults, suggest that sage enhances attention as well as memory. In a 2006 study on healthy young adults, sage reduced anxiety and improved their performance when they took a test requiring them to "multitask."

Good to Know

Don't use sage medicinally when you're pregnant or breastfeeding, and don't give medicinal amounts to children.

BUYER'S tip

Find dried sage in the spice aisle of your supermarket. Give it a sniff to make sure it's aromatic before you use it—that indicates freshness and potency. You can also find it fresh in many markets or easily grow it in your garden.

salt

You could say that as humans, all of us are "the salt of the earth"—not only the extra-good folks. That's because humans require from 5 to 10 grams of salt every day. Over a lifetime, a person might take in as much as 644 pounds of the stuff. Our bodies use salt, or sodium chloride, as an electrolyte, which is an electrically charged solution. This regulates the functioning of muscles and nerves and maintains our blood pressure, among many other critical operations.

rooted in history

Salt began to influence humans before the dawn of time. Neolithic settlements were founded at salt springs, and ever since our earliest days, salt has been an essential part of culture. In fact, controlling salt gave rise to three of the world's greatest civilizations: China, Egypt, and the Roman Empire. The Romans built one of their major roads, Via Salaria, or "salt road," from Rome to the Adriatic Sea to make it easier to transport the stuff. Roman soldiers were often paid in salt, and that's where the word "salary" comes from.

The earliest known book about drugs, published nearly 5,000 years ago in China, described over 40 kinds of salt, along with two methods for extracting and converting it—methods that are stunningly similar to modern-day techniques.

Since ancient times, salt helped people preserve and transport foods. Not only did salted foods keep longer,

USE FOR

Acne

Boils

Calluses

Canker sores

Chicken pox

Colds and congestion

Constipation

Dry skin

Earache

Foot odor

Gum problems

Hemorrhoids

Ingrown toenails

Menstrual problems

Muscle cramps

Psoriasis

Ringworm

Skin infections

Sore throat

Splinters

Toothache

Yeast infections

but salt dehydrated fish and meats and made them easier to ship. Finally, salt has played a key role in historic events, from the French Revolution to the Indian drive for independence from British rule.

the healing power of salt

It's no surprise that a substance linked so closely to life, both biologically and culturally, should have so many uses as a home remedy. Take simple salt water, for example. Because higher concentrations of sodium chloride draw water from surrounding tissues by osmosis, salt water helps soothe swollen gums and heal abscesses. Today, your dentist will tell you to rinse with warm salt water to ease gum irritation and speed healing. For generations, people suffering from head colds have relied on warm, diluted salt water, sniffed gently up the nostrils, to clear mucus from the nasal passages. And a salt-water gargle is a classic sore throat remedy.

Two teaspoons of salt in a pint of lukewarm water make a footbath that helps curb fungal infections by softening and cleansing the skin. Similarly, a salt-water soak makes it easier to remove a stubborn splinter. Salt water heated to body temperature may relieve earaches by loosening wax.

BUYER'S tip

When it comes to using salt in remedies, there's no difference between kosher salt, sea salt, or table salt. However, table salt will dissolve quicker.

Good to Know

Salt may make a terrific home remedy on occasion, but don't interpret that to mean it's healthy to add lots to your food. Most North Americans get two to three times as much salt in their diet as they should, and for many people, that contributes to high blood pressure. The vast majority of us would benefit from lowering our salt intake. The best way to achieve that? Eat fewer processed foods.

tea

Think of those tea bags stashed in your kitchen cabinet as the ultimate life-extending home remedy. In particular, green tea has so many scientifically proven benefits that we wonder why everyone isn't drinking several cups a day. Though the word "tea" refers to all brews made with hot water and herbs, true tea is made from the leaves of an evergreen shrub, *Camellia sinensis*. Differences in the way the leaves are processed account for black, green, white, and oolong varieties. People who drink green tea lower their risk of dying from heart disease or stroke and have lower rates of heart disease, stroke, cancer, and even tooth decay. But don't neglect black or oolong teas. These hearty brews are also abundantly laced with disease-hindering antioxidants.

rooted in history

People have been brewing tea leaves for half a million years. The Chinese were among the first to cultivate the tea plant, which was considered medicinal as far back as 1046 BC. Chinese Taoists hailed tea as an "elixir of immortality," and artists and poets celebrated tea in their work. Utterly democratic in its appeal, tea was both an imperial tribute and a drink sold on street corners.

A Buddhist priest introduced the Japanese to a powdered green tea called matcha, which he'd discovered in China. Tea drinking then spread like wildfire throughout 12th-century Japan, and became essential to Japanese culture. It took Westerners hundreds of years to discover tea,

USE FOR

Acne

Anal itching

Arthritis

Boils

Cancer protection

Chicken pox

Cold sores

Colds and flu

Conjunctivitis

Coughs

Cuts

Diarrhea

Fatigue

Foot odor

Heart health

Hemorrhoids

Memory

Poison ivy/oak

Stings and bites

Stress

Sunburn

Toothache

Ulcers

but when they brought it back home from their first visits to Japan in the 1850s, it didn't create much interest, except in the Netherlands.

The Dutch eventually introduced tea to America, much to the delight of American colonists. Tea became such a hot colonial commodity that the British decided to tax and control it, a practice that inspired the historic act of defiance known as the Boston Tea Party.

what's in it?

Tea contains compounds called catechins. According to the National Cancer Institute, these profoundly healthy plant chemicals are potent antioxidants with antiviral and potential anti-cancer benefits. One tea catechin, known as EGCG, is 100 times more powerful than vitamin C—and it protects the DNA in cells from cancer-inducing changes. Although the highest concentration of catechins is found in green tea, black tea is also a good source. Brand-name teas are mixtures of as many as 20 different varieties of leaves, blended to ensure a consistent flavor.

what science says

The science doesn't get much clearer than this: Drinking black tea beats water when it comes to health benefits, say British nutrition researchers who reviewed 14 years of black tea studies. Not only does black tea hydrate you as well as water does, but it keeps your heart and teeth healthy and improves your mood and alertness.

Research also makes clear the antioxidant power of tea. Scientists at Tufts University in Boston compared the "ORAC" capacity of tea with 22 vegetables. ORAC refers to the Oxygen Radical Absorbance Capacity, a measurement of the total antioxidant power of foods and other chemical substances: The higher the ORAC score, the greater its antioxidant capacity. Although there was variation among various teas, the highest scoring teas were green tea and black tea, brewed for 5 minutes. They outranked the best fruits and vegetables.

And Greek researchers concluded in a recent study that drinking tea is linked to lower blood sugar among healthy senior citizens.

||||||||||||||||||||||||||||||||

Tea 101

All non-herbal tea is made from the same plant. So what makes for the different types of tea? How it is processed.

To make **black** tea, the dried leaves are crushed to liberate enzymes, which react with the catechins over a few hours to produce changes in color and flavor. This is often referred to as "fermentation." **Green** tea is not fermented; the leaves are first steamed to halt any enzyme activity. **Oolong** tea is partially fermented.

on the horizon

In late 2009, scientists from the Boston Biomedical Research Institute and the University of Pennsylvania announced a breakthrough that could potentially change the prognosis of fatal brain disorders like Alzheimer's, Huntington's, and Parkinson's diseases. They found that when they combined the green tea component EGCG with another chemical called DAPH-12, the combo destroyed amyloids, the protein structures that cause these diseases.

Amyloids wrap around brain tissues or fill nerve cells. Eventually, they suffocate the cells and cause loss of memory, language, motor function, and premature death. This study marks the first time scientists have successfully destroyed amyloids, which are notoriously impenetrable structures, the researchers said. Though the findings are cause for hope, they

Herbal teas

These are teas made from the dried leaves of flowers and herbs. While they have entirely different chemical profiles from black or green tea, they still offer many health benefits. Here's a rundown:

Lavender. This tea with a floral bouquet is brewed from dried lavender flowers and can calm you at the end of the day.

Lemon balm. This minty, lemony tea helps soothe jittery nerves.

Nettle. Made from the same plant that causes stinging skin irritation, nettle tea is rich in vitamin C and several minerals. Herbalists recommend it to treat arthritis, allergic rhinitis, and gout and to increase milk production in nursing mothers. Avoid it during pregnancy because it may cause uterine contractions.

Peppermint. Tea from this mint plant is refreshing (especially iced in the summer). It stimulates digestion and dispels gas. Avoid it if you have a hiatal hernia because peppermint promotes reflux of the stomach contents into the esophagus.

Raspberry leaf. Herbalists recommend raspberry tea to ease menstrual cramps.

Rose hips. Rich in vitamin C, rose hips tea can serve as an alternative to orange juice.

Rosemary. Tea from this popular garden herb can boost memory and alertness, but drinking more than two or three cups a day may irritate the stomach.

Rooibos. The leaves of Southern Africa's rooibos (pronounced roy-boss) plant (*Aspalathus linearis*) have been brewed as a refreshing beverage for centuries. Its delicious flavor and remarkable antioxidant capacity gives it the potential to improve general health and well-being.

Sage. A cup of sage tea before bedtime may prevent menopausal night sweats.

Thyme. Herbalists recommend thyme tea for gastrointestinal complaints and especially to treat lung congestion and coughs.

are still extremely preliminary. Next steps for the researchers will be to further explore the EGCG combination and its potential against these dreaded diseases.

green tea and cancer

Researchers suspect that polyphenols in green tea may play a play an important role in cancer prevention—they believe that polyphenols help kill cancer cells and stop their progression.

Recent studies examining green tea's ability to slow prostate, esophageal, and colorectal cancers have posted positive results. In a study of 472 women with breast cancer, those who drank the most green tea experienced the least spread of the disease. They also found that women in the early stages of breast cancer who drank at least five cups of green tea every day before their diagnoses, were less likely to have the disease recur after they completed treatment. However, drinking green tea had no effect on women in the late stages of breast cancer.

In skin-cancer studies, lab animals that were given tea developed one-tenth as many tumors as animals that were given water.

While tea is mainly valued for its cancer-preventing powers, there's some evidence that it many help people who already have cancer. The EGCG in green tea inhibits the production of urokinase, an enzyme that cancer cells need in order to grow. It also seems to stimulate the process of programmed cell death, or apoptosis, in cancer cells.

BUYER's tip

For the freshest tea, shop at a store that has a good turnover rate and buy only as much as you can use in a month. Tea is best stored in a cool, dry pantry. Refrigerating or freezing can ruin its flavor. Green tea has less caffeine than black tea, but otherwise has a similar chemical profile.

Good to Know

Two to three cups of tea a day is probably enough to provide most of the health benefits. One caveat: If you usually take your tea with milk, you might be missing out on some of the health protection. Proteins in milk may bind to tea's polyphenols and block their beneficial effects. If you're sensitive to caffeine, stick with decaf varieties.

thyme

The same herb that adds savor to sauces, soups, stuffings, stews, and salads also makes a handy and effective home remedy for coughs. Thyme is a potent germ-killer that's been approved in Germany for bronchitis, whooping cough, and upper respiratory infections. When diluted, its essential oil can help prevent gum disease and athlete's foot. And here's something we bet you didn't know: Thyme tea can neutralize foul-smelling flatulence.

rooted in history

Ancient Sumerians and Egyptians used thyme (*Thymus vulgaris*) as a medicine and also to embalm the dead, which we hope says more about thyme's preservative powers than its medicinal ones. The Romans believed that bathing in thyme would provide vigor; they also burned it to repel venomous creatures and made thyme-infused cheese and even alcoholic beverages. As early as the 1600s, British herbalist Nicholas Culpeper recognized thyme's ability to treat coughs and called it "a noble strengthener of the lungs." He wrote that thyme was the best treatment for "hooping cough," purging phlegm, and relieving shortness of breath.

Thyme was one of the first herbs European settlers brought to the New World, and colonists grew it in their gardens. They brewed thyme tea to relieve cold symptoms, including fever, congestion, cough, and disturbed sleep.

USE FOR

Allergies

Arthritis

Athlete's foot

Boils

Bronchitis

Chest congestion

Coughs

Colds and flu

Dandruff

Flatulence

Foot problems

Gout

Gum disease

Headache

Healthy skin

Jock itch

Mouthwash

Periodontal disease

Sinusitis

Upper respiratory
  infections

Whooping cough

Thyme's main constituent, thymol, is a strong antiseptic, which prompted Missourian Joseph Lawrence to include it in the mouthwash he invented in 1879, which he called Listerine.

what's in it?

Thymol, thyme's most abundant medicinal constituent, kills *Porphyromomas gingivalis*, *Selenomonas artemidis*, and *Streptococcus sobrinus*, which are common germs associated with periodontal disease, tooth decay, and oral infections. Thyme also contains flavonoids that prevent muscle spasms as well as rosmarinic acid, an antioxidant that helps reduce inflammation.

thyme fights coughs

Thyme's expectorant, antiseptic, and antispasmodic properties suppress coughs, loosen congestion, and fight infections in the throat and lungs. Another reason for thyme's effectiveness as a cough and congestion remedy is that thyme oil, when ingested, is removed from the body through the lungs. As a result, its healing constituents can work directly where they are most needed.

BUYER'S tip

Find dried thyme leaves in the spice section of the supermarket. Thyme comes in many varieties and makes a wonderful, low-growing garden herb. Lemon thyme is especially attractive and tasty.

Good to Know

While all culinary usages of thyme are perfectly healthy and safe, don't take thyme medicinally during pregnancy (culinary amounts are fine). Never take pure thyme oil internally. Dilute thyme essential oil in a carrier oil such as olive oil before using it externally because pure thyme oil can irritate skin.

turmeric

Turmeric (*Curcuma longa*) might well be the most promising of all the medicinal herbs. You know it as the citrusy-sharp spice that gives a golden glow to curry. But over the last decade or so, medical researchers have focused serious attention on turmeric. In particular, they're interested in a component of the herb called curcumin, a potent antioxidant that dramatically reduces inflammation. Studies also show that curcumin has a protective effect on the liver. What's more, recent research reveals it has a remarkable range of potential anticancer effects.

USE FOR

Alzheimer's disease

Arthritis

Asthma

Boils

Bursitis and tendinitis

Cancer prevention

Eczema

High cholesterol

Memory

Psoriasis

Ringworm

rooted in history

Indians have used turmeric for at least 2,500 years, first as a dye and later as a seasoning. By 700 AD, traders carried it to China and later to Africa. Marco Polo wrote about turmeric in the 13th century, amazed by the common plant whose rhizome flavored and colored food almost as well as saffron, which was wildly expensive in comparison. An ointment containing turmeric, which was recommended for food poisoning, was mentioned in an Ayurvedic medicine book dating back to 250 BC.

what's in it?

Turmeric's medicinal properties come largely from curcumin and a volatile oil called turmerone. Turmeric also contains more than two dozen anti-inflammatory compounds, including six different COX-2 inhibitors. These compounds inhibit the COX-2 enzyme, which speeds up the formation of substances that cause inflammation and pain and may also cause tumor cells to grow. Turmeric also contains compounds that block the formation of beta-amyloid, the substance responsible for the plaques that diminish brain function and cause Alzheimer's disease.

what science says

Biochemists at the University of Illinois at Urbana-Champaign recently made a landmark discovery about how the body regulates inflammation. In a nutshell, they deciphered a molecular code that controls the function of a protein called NF-kappa B. This protein acts like a molecular "switch" that flips on when the cell is under attack and off when the attack has been cleared. When switched on, NF-kappa B moves into the cell's nucleus and triggers the proteins that cause inflammation. When the switch doesn't get turned off, which can happen when the cell is under stress, "things can go crazy in the body," said the researchers.

What does all this biochemistry have to do with turmeric? Good question. Turns out, turmeric plays a role in turning off NF-kappa B, says a leading researcher from the University of Texas MD Anderson Cancer Center in Houston. Taking 1 teaspoon (2 g) of turmeric a day can lessen the effects of inflammatory conditions, such as rheumatoid arthritis, osteoarthritis, asthma, and, potentially, cancer, heart disease, diabetes, and depression.

Separately, turmeric has been shown to reduce harmful cholesterol levels in the blood and reduce the development of hardened and blocked arteries. Clinical trials also have shown turmeric is effective in reducing the symptoms of rheumatoid arthritis and postoperative inflammation.

on the horizon

Researchers began investigating turmeric's potential against cancer when they noticed that some studies showed that people living in India, where turmeric is a key ingredient in many recipes, had up to a 50 percent lower incidence of cancer. Subsequent test tube and animal studies have confirmed that curcumin kills cancer cells and slows tumor growth. But much more study is needed before we know whether or not curcumin can become an effective cancer treatment.

BUYER'S tip

India produces nearly all the world's turmeric, and as it turns out, also consumes 80 percent of the crop, according to reports. That said, turmeric is easy to find: It will be in the spice aisle of any major supermarket. It should be a bright marigold color and have lots of fragrance. Keep it well sealed and store in a cool, dry, dark pantry.

Good to Know

Use in culinary amounts only during pregnancy. High medicinal doses may inhibit fertility. Don't take large doses if you take anticoagulants or non-steroidal anti-inflammatory drugs (NSAIDs).

vinegar

Its name comes from the French word *vinaigre*, or "sour wine," and it's a mouth-puckering liquid that not only puts the zing in your salad but is also the bane of bacteria, the foe of fungi, the solution to jellyfish stings, and the soother of sunburns. In fact, over the past 5,000 years, vinegar has taken aim against everything from headaches and sore muscles to the Black Death. Used correctly, it can settle your stomach, stave off swimmer's ear, make hair more lustrous, and soften skin. Some people swear that vinegar mixed with honey and warm water can take the pain out of leg cramps. Others use vinegar to dry up cold sores. What's more, it's an antiseptic "green cleaner" that shines glass as well as high-priced cleaning sprays. Hard to believe that something so sour can be so sweet for your health!

rooted in history

Back in 5000 BC, the Babylonians turned date palm fruit into vinegar and used it to pickle and preserve foods. From residue found in ancient urns, we know that the Egyptians were also using vinegar, probably for similar reasons, around 3000 BC. Vinegar is mentioned in both the Old and New Testaments of the Bible: In Ruth 2:14 is a passage about Ruth dipping bread into vinegar to refresh herself after slaving in the barley fields. Hippocrates, the Greek father of medicine, prescribed vinegar mixed with honey to treat ills including coughs and colds.

In World War I, soldiers' wounds were bathed in vinegar, and even today, if you can stand the sting, it's an adequate disinfectant if you have a scratch or sore.

what's in it?

Vinegar can be made from a huge number of plants, but all have one thing in common. Put a drop of vinegar—any type—on your tongue, and you'll know immediately what gives the tangy liquid its puckery nature. Vinegar is acidic, thanks to a high concentration of acetic acid, formed when bacteria feast on a fermented liquid. Acetic acid kills bacteria and fungi and is the active ingredient in some drugs that treat ear infections.

vinegar for weight loss

Japanese scientists reported in a recently completed study that when mice were fed a high-fat diet and given vinegar supplements, they developed about 10 percent less body fat than mice that got only the fatty food. They discovered that vinegar worked at a genetic level by influencing genes linked to fatty acid oxidation and energy-burning proteins. The scientists believe that vinegar suppresses body fat accumulation, though more studies are needed to see whether vinegar can have the same effect in people.

Good to Know

Too much vinegar may cause stomach upset. People who are allergic to molds may develop a reaction to non-distilled vinegar.

BUYER'S tip

Healers tend to prefer apple cider vinegar for use in home remedies. Here's why: Fermented apples are rich in pectin, a type of fiber that's excellent for digestion. Apples also contain malic acid, which combines with magnesium in your body to help fight aches and pains. So unless told otherwise, use cider vinegar for healing.

Around the world with vinegar

Wherever you travel, you'll find native varieties of vinegar brewed from whatever is locally handy. In the Philippines, it's sugarcane; in Thailand, it's coconut; and in China, red, white, and black rice wine vinegars have flavored stir-fries for more than 5,000 years.

Elsewhere you'll find vinegar made from honey, potatoes, dates, nuts, and berries. And in the Mediterranean, it's grapes that become red and white wine vinegars. Americans are most familiar with cider vinegar (from apples) or plain, distilled white vinegar that's the product of grain.

wheat germ

Wheat germ is the nutritional heart of the wheat kernel. When white flour is processed, this "germ" is milled out; that's why white flour contains so little nutritive value. Although it's the smallest part of the grain, the germ is chock-full of nutrients, including vitamin E, thiamine, folate, magnesium, and zinc. It's also one of the few plant parts in nature that contains the entire vitamin B-complex.

rooted in history

Wheat is one of man's longest-cultivated grains and has been farmed for as long as 9,000 years. Wheat became an ancient symbol of prosperity, fertility, abundance, and life. The fertility gods of Greece, Egypt, and Rome shared wheat as one of their symbols. Native Americans cultivated wheat, baking it into breads, tortillas, and cakes, and brewing it into beverages.

In Ayurveda, the traditional medical system of India, wheat is used to treat stress and mental problems and is said to strengthen the muscles.

what's in it?

The vitamin E in wheat germ contains a powerful anti-oxidant that is linked to heart health as well as a strong immune system. The fat in wheat germ (1.5 g in 2 table-spoons) is predominantly polyunsaturated fat, which can help lower LDL cholesterol levels when it replaces saturated fat in the diet. Wheat germ is also a source of plant sterols that help lower cholesterol levels.

And because it is a complex carb that is slow to digest, wheat germ has a low glycemic index (GI) number and may reduce the risk of type-2 diabetes. According to a recent study by Harvard Medical School, eating more whole-grain foods, such as wheat germ, reduces the risk of type 2 diabetes for women.

BUYER'S tip

Find wheat germ in the cereal aisle of your supermarket and in health food stores. Wheat germ is sold in both toasted and natural forms. Once it has been opened, keep the wheat germ jar tightly sealed and refrigerated to prevent it from going rancid. Defatted wheat germ contains much less vitamin E and does not need refrigeration. It can be kept in the cupboard.

Good to Know

Whenever you can, include a little of this delicious whole grain when you're cooking or baking. Its nutty flavor enhances banana or zucchini bread, rice pudding, coffee cake, apple crisp, pizza dough, bread dough, savory pie dough, and even homemade cookies. You can sprinkle it over cereals or on top of salads, mix it into meat loaf, hamburgers, or veggie burgers, or use it as a substitute for some or all of the bread crumbs when coating fish, chicken, or vegetables.

looking & feeling great

Use your kitchen pantry to boost your appearance and your health

Take a good look around a drugstore, and you quickly realize that medicine takes up only a small amount of the shelf space. Gobbling up much of the real estate are shampoos, skin creams, cosmetics, and other products that aren't meant to make you *feel* better, but rather *look* better.

There's nothing vain about that. Looking your best is a crucial part of being happy, which in turn is a crucial part of good health. Only trouble is, a multibillion-dollar "personal care" industry has us convinced that it takes costly concoctions to achieve that look-good, feel-good balance we all want.

Don't be deceived. Long before the rise of supermodels and mega-beauty brands, our grandparents and their forebears took care of themselves just fine with everyday pantry items. In the pages ahead, you'll find surprising yet effective ways to harness your kitchen pantry to achieve all that you dream of for your health and appearance. And you'll save a fortune achieving it. Now *that's* a beautiful thing.

healthy, smooth skin

You know what healthy skin looks like. It sparkles, no matter how old you are. Even if you haven't inherited a flawless complexion, you can make the most of what you've got without resorting to beauty products whose prices make you weak in the knees. Here's a little secret about some of those expensive products: Many contain ingredients whose effective stand-ins already live on the shelves of your kitchen cabinet.

Skin care basics

Before you embark on a do-it-yourself skin care regimen, it's important to know your skin type and how best to care for it. Skin experts classify complexions into four general types: normal, dry, oily, and sensitive. They also recognize that mature skin requires special care as women transition through menopause and beyond.

Normal skin is clear, supple, and soft, neither too dry nor too oily. It is not overly sensitive to sun, climate, or the environment.

Dry skin looks dull, feels tight after washing, and needs constant protection and moisturizing to avoid flaking and peeling.

Oily skin might feel soft and supple, but it looks shiny and needs to be cleansed several times a day. Pores are larger than those of either normal or dry skin. This type of skin is often prone to blackheads and pimples.

Pantry HEALERS

Almonds

Aloe vera gel

Bay leaves

Chamomile tea

Cinnamon

Cloves

Flaxseeds

Ginger

Green tea

Honey

Lavender
  essential oil

Oats

Olive oil

Peppermint

Rice

Rosemary

Salts

Tea tree oil

Wheat germ

Witch hazel

Sensitive skin reacts badly to sunlight or irritants. It burns easily and may develop rashes, blotches, or spots when exposed to new substances, such as the chemicals often found in commercial skin-cleansing products.

Most people have a combination of skin types—for example, basically normal with some oily areas on the forehead, around the nose, and on the chin, and maybe some dryness around the eyes.

All skin types benefit when you cleanse, tone, and moisturize twice a day—once in the morning and again before bedtime. In addition, two simple DIY treatments—steaming and exfoliating—can help make your skin look spa-pampered.

• *Cleansing:* Choose a cleanser based on your skin type, and perform this essential daily ritual gently to remove makeup and grime.

• *Toning:* After cleansing, use a toner to remove cleanser residue and close the pores.

• *Moisturizing:* Based on your skin type, choose an appropriate moisturizer and smooth over face, neck, and décolletage twice a day.

• *Steaming:* Once or twice a week, give your face a 10-minute steam cleaning. Steaming works naturally to improve microcirculation to the skin's surface. It also flushes out toxins and debris by opening pores and makes

Pantry foods for clear skin

Tweaking an unhealthy diet is the first step to enhancing your skin's health and radiance. First move: Cut way back on fatty and sugary foods. These contribute to the inflammation that can worsen any skin condition. Replace unhealthy junk foods with delicious foods rich in antioxidants and other nutrients that are proven to improve skin health. When you keep your larder full of foods like these, you can whip up a healthy snack or meal in less time than it takes to zip through the drive-through. Enjoy them regularly as noted, and your skin will soon reap the rewards.

FOOD	HOW MUCH
Canned salmon	3.5 ounces twice a week
Green tea	2 or more cups a day, hot or iced
Flaxseeds	2 tablespoons freshly ground seeds a day
Olive oil	1 tablespoon a day
Canned sardines	2 ounces once or twice a week
Canola oil	1 tablespoon a day
Brazil nuts	Small handful two or three a times week

it easier for your skin to absorb the essential oils and aromatic herbs in the water.

- *Exfoliating:* Once a week, go over the skin with a simple, homemade scrub blend. This will remove dead skin cells, promote circulation, and improve clarity and radiance.

recipes for cleansing

Fragrant Facial Cleanser

This beautifully scented cleanser is a gentle way to remove makeup and cleanse your skin. It's suitable for all skin types. Almond, jojoba, and avocado oils are light and especially suited for complexion care. You can find them at health and natural food stores. If you don't use them, you can substitute olive or canola oil.

¼ cup olive oil
¼ cup almond, jojoba, or avocado oil (optional)
10 drops lavender essential oil

Place the olive oil, almond oil, and lavender oil in a 4-ounce sterilized glass jar with a tight-fitting lid and shake until blended. Store in a cool, dark place. To use, saturate a cotton ball with oil and sweep over your face to remove makeup. Rinse well with warm water and follow with a toner.

Canola–Tea Tree Oil Cleanser

Use this cleanser on normal to dry skin that's prone to the occasional blemish.

¼ cup canola oil
10 drops tea tree oil

Place the canola oil and tea tree oil in a 4-ounce sterilized glass jar with a tight-fitting lid and shake until blended. Store in a cool, dark place. To use, saturate a cotton ball with oil and sweep over your face to remove makeup. Rinse well with warm water and follow with a toner.

recipes for toning

Clarifying Green Tea Toner

This gently astringent blend contains vinegar to restore the skin's pH balance. The anti-oxidant-rich green tea helps counter sun damage, while the fennel seeds are said to be cleansing and hydrating. You can find vegetable glycerin at health food stores and online.

> 1 tablespoon green tea leaves (cut open a tea bag or two)
> 1 teaspoon crushed fennel seeds
> ½ cup boiling water
> 2 tablespoons apple cider vinegar
> 1 teaspoon vegetable glycerin

1. Place the tea leaves and fennel seeds in a bowl and cover with the boiling water. Cover the bowl and allow the herbs to steep until the water cools. Strain. Combine the fennel water, vinegar, and glycerin in a bottle.

2. To use, shake well. Saturate a cotton ball with the liquid and wipe over your skin after cleansing. Store the toner in the refrigerator and use within 10 days.

Minty Astringent

Barley water is a good source of zinc and sulfur, two minerals that help balance oil production. Peppermint is refreshing and stimulating, and rosemary calms inflammation.

> 1 tablespoon dried peppermint
> 1 tablespoon dried rosemary
> ½ cup witch hazel
> 2 tablespoons vodka
> 1 tablespoon pearl barley
> ½ cup water
> 5 drops peppermint essential oil (optional)

1. Grind the peppermint and rosemary in a blender or clean coffee grinder. Transfer to a jar with a tight-fitting lid.

2. Add the witch hazel and vodka. Cover the jar tightly and shake vigorously for a few minutes. Put the jar in the pantry and steep for 10 days. After 10 days, strain the liquid into a sterilized canning jar with a tight-fitting lid.

3. Put the barley in a saucepan with the water. Bring to a boil, then reduce the heat and simmer, covered, for 15 minutes. Cool, then strain, reserving liquid.

4. Combine the barley water and herbal liquid in a bottle. Add the peppermint oil, if using.

5. Shake well before each use. Store in the refrigerator for up to two weeks. Apply to skin with a cotton pad.

Aromatherapy Skin Spritz

Use this instant refresher to remove cleanser residue and excess perspiration and oil, especially during hot weather. Grapefruit and lemon oils have gentle astringent and bleaching properties, while apple cider vinegar balances the skin's pH.

> ½ cup carbonated mineral water
> ½ cup witch hazel
> 1 tablespoon apple cider vinegar
> 5 drops lavender essential oil
> 5 drops grapefruit essential oil
> 3 drops lemon essential oil

1. Place the water, witch hazel, and vinegar in a pump-spray bottle with a fine mist head. Add the lavender, grapefruit, and lemon oils.

2. To use, shake and lightly spritz over the face and neck, avoiding eyes. Store in the refrigerator for up to one month.

 # recipes for moisturizing

Daily Moisturizer

This moisturizer will leave your complexion moist and replenished and is perfect for normal or combination skin. Smooth on twice a day after toning. You can substitute virgin olive oil for the apricot kernel, jojoba, and wheat germ oils (available at any health food store), but the result won't be quite as light or nourishing.

> 2 tablespoons apricot kernel oil
> 1 teaspoon jojoba oil
> 1 teaspoon wheat germ oil
> 6 drops lavender essential oil
> 2 drops lemon essential oil (omit if using on sensitive skin)

Place all the ingredients in a sterilized glass jar with a tight-fitting lid and shake well. Store in a cool, dark place and use within two months.

Don't forget the sunscreen!

Many commercial moisturizers have built-in sunscreens, but homemade recipes don't. Remember to use sunscreen of at least 15 SPF or higher whenever you're outside in the sun.

galen's
cold cream

Recipe page 96

Galen's Cold Cream

The Greek physician-philosopher Galen supposedly first concocted this cold cream recipe in the second century AD. His ancient cream is just as effective today as it was two thousand years ago—and it's worth looking for the beeswax in your natural foods store just to try this soothing facial treat. Rosewater also is available at health food or gourmet stores. The cream doubles as a makeup remover and a moisturizer, and it's suitable for all skin types.

1 ounce beeswax
⅓ cup virgin olive oil
2 tablespoons water or rosewater
5 to 10 drops lavender essential oil

1. In a glass or stainless steel double boiler, melt the beeswax. In a glass or stainless steel saucepan, heat the oil slightly, then pour it into the melted wax. Beat until combined.

2. In the saucepan, heat the water or rosewater, then stir it, drop by drop, into the oil and wax mixture. Remove from the heat and stir until the mixture is cooled and thick. Blend in the lavender essential oil.

3. Spoon the mixture into a jar and store in a cool, dark place. It will last about three months.

Moisturizing Serum for Oily Skin

Even oily skin needs a light moisturizer to put a barrier between the skin and environmental pollutants. Olive oil is nourishing, the cinnamon reduces inflammation, and the essential oils are healing and antibacterial.

1 small cinnamon stick
½ cup virgin olive oil
5 drops tea tree essential oil
5 drops lavender essential oil

1. Lightly crush the cinnamon and place in a small container with a lid. Add the olive oil, cover, and steep for 10 days. Strain. Add the tea tree and lavender oils.

2. Pour the serum into a small, sterilized jar. To use, warm a few drops between your fingertips and lightly massage into clean, slightly damp skin. Store in a cool, dark place.

|||||||||||||||||||||||||||||||||||||||||||||||||||||||||||||||||||||||||||||||||||||||||||||||||||||||||||||||||||||||

Emergency moisturizer

If you're stuck somewhere without your toiletries, you can use jarred mayonnaise, olive oil, or even vegetable shortening as a stand-in for your daily moisturizer. Pat on gently and use sparingly to avoid feeling greasy.

Spa steams, scrubs, and masks

If you treat yourself to a facial at the day spa, part of the program will be these three treatments. Though you might miss the luxurious indulgence of the in-person experience, you can easily replicate many spa treatments at home for a fraction of their price.

Steaming opens the pores for a deep-down cleansing. Exfoliating scrubs remove dead skin cells and improve circulation to give your complexion a youthful glow. Facial masks moisturize and nourish skin—what's more, they give you a few minutes of relaxing down time (you can always pretend you're in the spa). Whip up these spa treats from inexpensive pantry staples.

Easy aloe exfoliant

Consider applying fresh aloe vera gel to skin before moisturizing. The gel contains acids that help remove dead skin cells to reveal a fresher, brighter complexion. To obtain the gel, cut off a leaf at the base and split it open with a knife. Scrape out the gel with a spoon.

recipes for scrubs and steams

Smooth Skin Rice Scrub

Japanese women swear by rice to keep their complexions crystal-clear and porcelain-smooth. This gentle exfoliant contains baking soda to slough off dead skin cells. The cinnamon and lemon zest combat inflammation and bacteria, making this a perfect pantry treatment for oily, pimple-prone skin.

> 2 tablespoons baking soda
> 2 tablespoons rice, ground in a clean coffee grinder or food processor
> 1 teaspoon finely grated lemon peel
> ½ teaspoon ground cinnamon

1. Combine the ingredients in a clean, dry wide-mouthed jar.

2. To use, gently massage the scrub into dampened skin, then rinse off.

Lemon Rosemary Steam

Lemon tones skin and is mildly antibacterial, and rosemary stimulates circulation.

> 1 lemon, sliced
> 1 tablespoon dried rosemary
> 5 drops lavender essential oil (optional)

1. Fill a bowl with boiling water. Add the lemon, rosemary, and lavender oil.

2. Drape a towel over your head and shoulders to create a tent and lean over the bowl, keeping your face about 10 inches above the water. Steam your face for 10 minutes. Splash with water, then pat dry.

Softening Oatmeal-Tea Scrub

Finely ground oats and almonds are gentle exfoliants. This scrub is perfect for dry skin, because it moisturizes and safely sloughs dead skin cells that can dull your complexion.

½ cup rolled oats
½ cup almonds
3 tablespoons green tea leaves (from loose or bagged green tea)
Virgin olive oil

1. Pulse the oats and almonds in a food processor till coarsely chopped. Add tea and pulse until the mixture reaches a fine, sandy consistency.

2. Store the mixture in a sterilized airtight jar.

3. To use, mix 1 to 2 tablespoons of scrub with enough olive oil to make a paste.

4. Let it thicken for 1 to 2 minutes, then gently massage it into damp skin with your fingertips; rinse off.

Honey-Almond Scrub

This simple scrub is nice to use on elbows, feet, legs, and other rough patches.

1 tablespoon honey, more as needed
2 tablespoons ground almonds
5 drops lavender essential oil (optional)

1. Warm the honey in a cup by sitting the cup in hot water for a few minutes.

2. Pulse the almonds in a food processor till fine. Put in a small bowl and stir in enough warmed honey to make a spreadable paste. Stir in the essential oil, if using.

3. To apply, first rinse your skin with tepid water. Then gently massage in the scrub, paying attention to any flaky skin. Keep any leftover mixture in the refrigerator, covered with plastic wrap. Rewarm before use.

Chamomile-Mint Tea Steam

Chamomile calms skin irritation and mint refreshes skin. You can use many culinary herbs or tea bags in facial steams. All have slightly different effects. For example: Sage, thyme, oregano, and citrus tea blends suit oily, blemished skin. Fennel seeds are great for dry or mature skin (crush or grind before using). Spicy tea blends are wonderful for boosting circulation.

2 chamomile tea bags
2 mint tea bags
1 pint boiling water

1. Place the tea bags in a heatproof bowl and cover with boiling water.

2. Drape a towel over your head and shoulders to create a tent and lean over the steaming bowl, keeping your face about 10 inches above the water. Close your eyes and steam your face for 10 to 15 minutes.

3. When you're finished, splash your face and neck with cool water, then pat dry.

Special care for extra-dry skin

Extremely dry skin can be the gateway to more serious skin problems, including ringworm and athlete's foot. That's because dry skin develops tiny cracks that allow fungi, bacteria, or other germs easy access to do their dirty work. The feet are especially vulnerable.

Smooth on some Mediterranean gold. Every evening, glide a few drops of olive oil over your face, elbows, knees, and the backs of your arms. The oil contains mono-unsaturated fat, which refreshes and hydrates skin without leaving a greasy residue.

Soothe with skin shortening. Any of these oily products will trap skin's own moisture: petroleum jelly, mineral oil, peanut oil, vegetable oil, or even vegetable shortening. Apply anywhere skin is particularly dry; just use sparingly to avoid feeling greasy.

Spritz dryness away. Rose, lavender, or bergamot essential oils are great for hydrating the skin. To create an herbal spritzer, mix a few drops of any or all these essential oils with water in a 4-ounce spray bottle and spritz on your face whenever your skin needs a little boost.

When to call THE DOCTOR

Most of the time, simple home remedies and consistent attention will take care of all but the most serious cases of dry skin. If you moisturize consistently and see no improvement after a week or two of treatment, seek advice from your doctor or a dermatologist.

5 soothing tub soaks

Simple pantry toss-ins can provide immediate relief for skin that's so dry it feels parched and itchy. When you leave the bath, slather your skin with one of the moisturizers in this chapter. Doing so while your skin is still damp locks in its natural oils. Note: Adding oil to the bath makes it slippery, so be extra careful when getting in or out of the tub.

• **Half a pound of sea salt and 1 pound baking soda.** Soak until the water is cool to soothe itching.

• **Two cups Epsom salts.** Toss the salt in the tub, and save some extra in a plastic container. Then, while you're soaking, rub handfuls of Epsom salts on knees, elbows, and feet to soften and soothe rough patches.

• **One cup uncooked oatmeal tied into an old stocking or muslin bag.** Oatmeal contains unique antioxidants that soothe skin, plus they leave a protective coating on your skin that seals in moisture.

• **Equal parts of apple cider vinegar, wheat germ, and sesame or olive oil.** Apple cider vinegar is both antibacterial and alkalinizing (meaning it helps maintain the proper acid balance), while sesame oil and wheat germ add moisture.

• **One cup powdered milk with 1 tablespoon grapeseed oil.** The lactic acid in the milk will exfoliate your skin, and the grapeseed oil will give your skin a powerful dose of antioxidants. Olive oil's a fine substitute.

recipes for dry skin

Moisturizing Aloe Toner

Many toners are just too drying for skin that's severely parched, but this lovely formula is absolutely perfect. Aloe vera moisturizes, vinegar soothes itchy skin, and fragrant lavender lessens redness. Orange blossom water (used in baking and cocktails) can be found in most supermarkets.

>   4 tablespoons aloe vera gel
>   2 400 IU vitamin E capsules
>   4 tablespoons orange blossom water
>   2 teaspoons apple cider vinegar
>   10 drops lavender essential oil

1. Scrape the aloe gel from the largest stalks of a fresh aloe plant (or buy 100 percent pure aloe gel at the health or natural food store). Put in a small, clean jar with a tight-fitting lid.

2. Pierce the vitamin E capsules with a clean needle and squeeze contents into the jar.

3. Add the rest of the ingredients, cap the jar tightly, and shake well. Use cotton pads to apply to skin after cleansing; don't rinse off. Store in the refrigerator.

Peppermint-Lavender Hand Quencher

Hands take a special beating from the elements and are quick to show signs of aging. Protect them with this soothing, rich lotion.

>   4 peppermint tea bags
>   1¼ cups boiling water
>   1⅛ cups olive oil (or use a blend of almond, apricot, or grapeseed oils)
>   1 ounce beeswax, finely chopped or grated
>   10 drops lavender essential oil
>   2 400 IU vitamin E capsules

1. Place the tea bags in a cup, and add the boiling water. Cover and steep for 15 to 20 minutes. Remove the tea bags.

2. In the top of a double boiler over simmering water, warm the olive oil. Add the beeswax and stir until melted.

3. Remove from heat and slowly add 1 cup of the peppermint tea, beating continuously until well combined. Stir in the lavender essential oil and squeeze in the contents from the vitamin E capsules (pierced with a needle).

4. Pour into a sterilized jar with a tight-fitting lid, and store in a cool, dark place.

Special care for extra-oily skin

Which do you want first: the good news or the bad? The good news is, people with oily skin are apt to develop fewer wrinkles as they age. The bad news is, they're also apt to be more blemish-prone. The great news? Oily skin can be tamed with simple, inexpensive, easy kitchen potions.

Take oil to beat oil. Adding oil to your diet to combat oily skin may not seem like sound advice, but trust us, it is—if it's the right kind of oil. Flaxseed oil is high in essential fatty acids, which can help improve many skin conditions, including oily skin. You'll find this highly perishable oil in the refrigerated case at health-food stores. Buy cold-pressed oil sold in opaque containers, and store it in your refrigerator. Alternately, grind up a tablespoon or two of flaxseeds in a clean coffee grinder and add to cereal, yogurt, salads, or other foods every day. You'll get the healthy omega-3s and a nice fiber boost.

Wipe with a witchy oil reducer. After you've washed your face, soak a cotton pad in distilled witch hazel and sweep it over your face. Use it twice a day for two to three weeks. After the third week, apply it once a day. Witch hazel contains tannins, which have an astringent effect, making the pores tighten so they release less oil.

Massage oil away. This oaty rub helps absorb oil and sloughs off dead skin cells that clog pores. Using a clean coffee grinder, buzz up 2 teaspoons of dry oatmeal (not instant or flavored varieties), then moisten the powder with enough witch hazel to form a paste. Using your fingertips, massage this paste gently into your skin, then rinse it away with warm water.

When to call THE DOCTOR

A shiny complexion can be a cosmetic challenge, but it's certainly not a medical emergency. If you have severe acne breakouts, however, consider seeing your dermatologist for advice.

oil-reduction recipes

Manly Astringent

This aromatic blend does double duty as an aftershave or stimulating astringent. It clears oil from the skin and helps fight blemishes.

> 1 bottle bay leaves, best quality
> 2 teaspoons whole cloves
> 1 teaspoon ground allspice
> 2 teaspoons ground ginger
> Dark rum

1. Put bay leaves into a clean, wide-mouth, 16-ounce jar.

2. Add the cloves, allspice, and ginger.

3. Add enough dark rum to cover the spices and bay leaves by a couple of inches.

4. Cover tightly, and put the bottle in the pantry for four weeks. Shake it every few days.

5. Strain and put the astringent in a clean bottle.

Sage-Chamomile Toner

Chamomile and sage are loaded with anti-inflammatory and skin-soothing properties. Sage is also a mild astringent. Adding vodka to the blend helps dry oily skin and preserves the toner.

> 16 ounces water
> 4 chamomile tea bags
> 4 tablespoons dried sage
> 8 ounces vodka

1. Bring the water to a boil and add the chamomile tea bags and sage. Remove from heat. Cover and steep for 4 hours. Strain.

2. Fill a 16-ounce glass jar halfway with the tea.

3. Add the vodka to the jar until full. Cap and shake well. To use, soak cotton pads in the toner and sweep over your face after cleansing once a day.

healthy nails

Well-groomed fingernails make a great first impression. But brittle, flaking nails or cracked, dry cuticles do not. As for toenail fungus, well, it can make you want to stash your sexy sandals in the closet. If you tend to hide your nails from sight, you'll be happy to discover these simple remedies. They all come straight from your kitchen cabinet and can make your nails so healthy and attractive that you'll want to show them off for all to see.

kitchen cabinet cures

Slather hands and cuticles. Frequent applications of moisturizer prevent scraggy looking cuticles and brittle nails. Keep hand lotion handy in several key places: beside the kitchen sink, near the tub or shower, in your purse or car, next to your favorite chair, in your desk drawer, and on your nightstand. Hiding lotion in plain sight will help you remember to slather it on several times a day.

Enrich nails from within. If your nails are brittle or flaking, try getting more essential omega-3 fatty acids in your diet. These are found in foods such as canned fatty fish, nuts, freshly ground flaxseeds, and flaxseed oil. Just a few servings per week of canned salmon, sardines, or mackerel can put you on the path to healthier nails. If you don't eat much fish, take 1 tablespoon flaxseed oil a day (use it in place of other oil in salad dressing), or sprinkle 2 tablespoons freshly ground flaxseeds on your cereal or other food every day.

Pantry HEALERS

Avocado oil

Canned fatty fish

Epsom salts

Flaxseed oil

Flaxseeds

Jojoba oil

Lavender essential oil

Moisturizer

Olive oil

Petroleum jelly

Tea tree oil

Thyme

Unless you suspect you have an underlying nutritional deficiency, nail problems are generally cosmetic problems, not health issues. As for nail fungus, it's tenacious and can take months or even years to clear up on its own. If the two-step soak and tea tree treatment doesn't clear up the problem after at least three months of diligent, regular use, consult your doctor to discuss options.

Do this before bedtime. For dry or brittle nails, rub petroleum jelly or olive oil into your nails to hold moisture around and under your nails. Then, slip a pair of thin cotton gloves on your hands before you to sleep.

Sooth ingrown toenails. If you don't clip your nails straight across, or if your shoes don't fit properly, you can wind up with a painful ingrown toenail. Here's a soothing treatment: Fill a 5-gallon bucket with about 2 gallons of hot water. Add a handful of Epsom salts and stir until the salt dissolves. Soak your problem foot for 15 to 20 minutes each day. Hot water softens the skin around the ingrown nail while the Epsom salts will combat infection and reduce swelling.

Treat toenail fungus with tea tree oil. Applying 100 percent tea tree oil for a minimum of three months has been shown to kill nail fungus equally as well as a prescription antifungal cream. In the study, 60 percent of both groups completely or partially eradicated their symptoms. Once or twice a day—every day—apply a drop or two of tea tree oil to the discolored nail. Be careful not to apply tea tree to the skin because undiluted tea tree oil may be irritating. Make sure to use 100 percent pure tea tree essential oil; products that only contain a little oil won't work.

Nail no-no's

Quick-drying nail polishes: They may save time, but at the expense of your nails. Most of these formulas contain more formaldehyde and alcohol than regular polishes, both of which are drying and make nails prone to splitting. To fast-dry nails naturally, do this: Fill your bathroom sink part way with ice cubes, then fill with cold water. After each coat of nail polish, dip your wet nails into the cold water for a minute or two. Miraculously, they'll be dry when you take them out.

Artificial nails: They can seem like a godsend to women who have problems with weak, soft, brittle nails, and for women who bite or pick at their nails. Trouble is, fake nails can breed fungus. What's more, when artificial nails are glued on top of your real ones, the gap in between creates a breeding ground in which you can develop a painful bacterial infection. So forgo the fakes, no matter how much you long for elegant nails.

Rich Aromatherapy Cuticle Oil

The essential oils in this rich, softening blend help to counter cracked and ragged cuticles. Tea tree oil is a proven fungus fighter, while lavender is anti-inflammatory and healing. You can find avocado and jojoba oil in health food stores, or you can substitute olive oil for either or both.

> 1 tablespoon jojoba oil
> 1 tablespoon avocado oil
> 10 drops tea tree essential oil
> 10 drops lavender essential oil

1. Pour the jojoba and avocado oils into a small, dark-colored glass bottle, which will help preserve the oil.

2. Add the tea tree and lavender essential oils, screw on cap, and shake to combine.

3. Before using the cuticle oil, shake the bottle well, then massage a few drops into your nails and cuticles daily to soften your cuticles and prevent them from splitting.

Double-Powered Nail Fungus Treatment

Thyme and tea tree oil annihilate fungal infections; lavender is soothing and healing. Use this soak several times a week, then follow with the aromatherapy oil regimen in the previous recipe. The key to this treatment is regularity and patience: You have to use this double-barrel treatment regularly for at least three months in order to send fungus packing.

> 2 teaspoons dried thyme
> 10 drops tea tree essential oil
> 10 drop lavender essential oil

Steep the thyme, covered, in 1 cup of boiling water for 15 minutes before straining. Allow to cool and then swirl in the tea tree and lavender essential oils. Soak affected nails in the liquid for 15 minutes twice a day.

healthy teeth & mouth

Pantry HEALERS

Aloe

Apple cider vinegar

Baking soda

Cinnamon

Cinnamon gum

Clove essential oil

Myrrh tincture

Peppermint
  essential oil

Peppermint tea

Salt

Tea (green & black)

Tea tree oil

Witch hazel

Xylitol gum & mints

When your teeth and gums are in tip-top shape, it's not just your appearance that benefits. Heart disease, diabetes, pneumonia, and even chronic lung disease are all linked to unhealthy gums. Researchers suspect that as bacteria from your gums travel throughout your bloodstream, they create low-level inflammation that can trigger or promote a variety of chronic diseases. Happily, effective and economical natural remedies for a sparkling smile and a healthy, sweet-smelling mouth are as close as your kitchen pantry.

kitchen cabinet cures

Stock xylitol gum and mints. This natural sugar alcohol (found in berries, vegetables, mushrooms, and birch trees) may look and taste just like sugar, but there's where the resemblance ends. Xylitol contains 40 percent fewer calories than sugar, and quite unlike sugar, it prevents cavities and plaque formation by inhibiting the growth of decay-promoting bacteria. A report published in the *Journal of the American Dental Association* said that chewing xylitol gum for five minutes after eating, three to five times a day, inhibits plaque accumulation and prevents cavities. And just recently, a team of Japanese dentists discovered that when pregnant women began chewing xylitol gum in their sixth month of pregnancy and continued using the gum for a year, their babies were much less likely to develop cavity-causing bacteria compared to pregnant women who didn't chew the gum. Look for gums or mints labeled "all xylitol" or those containing xylitol as the only sweetener.

Be a tea drinker. Flavonoids and other tea ingredients seem to prevent harmful bacteria from sticking to teeth and also block production of a type of sugar that contributes to cavities. Tea also contains high amounts of fluoride. Alternate between green and black tea and enjoy a few cups a day.

Gargle with apple cider vinegar in the morning. The vinegar helps remove stains, whiten teeth, and kill bacteria in your mouth and gums. Brush as usual after you gargle.

Brush your teeth with baking soda once a week. This will help remove stains and whiten your teeth. Use it just as you would toothpaste. You can also use salt as an alternative toothpaste. If your gums start to feel raw, switch to brushing with salt every other day.

Chew cinnamon gum once a day. Researchers at the University of Illinois at Chicago have found that cinnamon-flavored chewing gum reduces bacteria in the mouth that cause bad breath. The reason? The gum contains cinnamic aldehyde, an essential oil that inhibits the growth of bacteria responsible for cavities and periodontal infections. Actually, any kind of sugar-free gum chewed after meals will help remove food particles and wash away bacteria because it generates extra saliva.

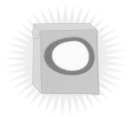

Some chewing gums actually help prevent cavities and plaque build-up.

 recipes for a healthier mouth

Cinnamon Tooth Powder

This easy-to-make recipe polishes and whitens teeth and leaves your mouth feeling super-clean. Cinnamon has antibacterial properties, while clove is both antiseptic and healing.

- 2 tablespoons baking soda
- 1 teaspoon fine sea salt
- ½ teaspoon powdered cinnamon
- 5 drops clove essential oil
- 3 drops peppermint essential oil

1. Sift the baking soda, salt, and cinnamon together into a bowl to remove lumps. Add the clove and peppermint oils, then sift again. Store the powder in an airtight container.

2. To use, dampen your toothbrush, dip it in the powder, and brush as you would with toothpaste.

Minty Mouthwash

Cooling peppermint sweetens bad breath and makes your mouth feel clean. Tea tree essential oil fights gum disease, and aloe vera soothes oral tissue.

> 2 peppermint tea bags
> ¾ cup boiling water
> 1 tablespoon fresh aloe gel
> 5 drops tea tree essential oil
> 3 drops peppermint essential oil

1. Place the tea bags in a small glass bowl and cover with the boiling water. Cover the bowl and steep for 30 minutes. Squeeze and remove the tea bags.

2. Add the aloe gel and tea tree and peppermint oils. Mix well. Store in a dark glass container.

3. Shake well, then swish 1 to 2 tablespoons around your mouth, and spit it out. Do not swallow. Store in a cool place and use within one week.

Mouthwash for Bleeding Gums

See your dentist if your gums bleed whenever you brush your teeth. Once you've ruled out any dental problems, try this soothing, healing mouthwash. It contains tannin-rich black tea and witch hazel, which have a toning effect on gums. Green tea is an antioxidant. Myrrh has antiseptic and astringent properties, and herbalists praise its powers for healing oral problems.

> 2 black tea bags
> 2 green tea bags
> ¾ cup boiling water
> 1 tablespoon witch hazel
> 5 drops myrrh tincture

1. Place the black and green tea bags in a glass bowl and cover with the boiling water. Cover the bowl and steep for 30 minutes. Strain.

2. Add the witch hazel and myrrh and mix well. Store in a dark glass bottle.

3. To use, shake well and swish 1 to 2 tablespoons around the mouth and spit it out. Do not swallow. Store in a cool place and use within one week.

mouthwash for bleeding gums

Recipe page 108

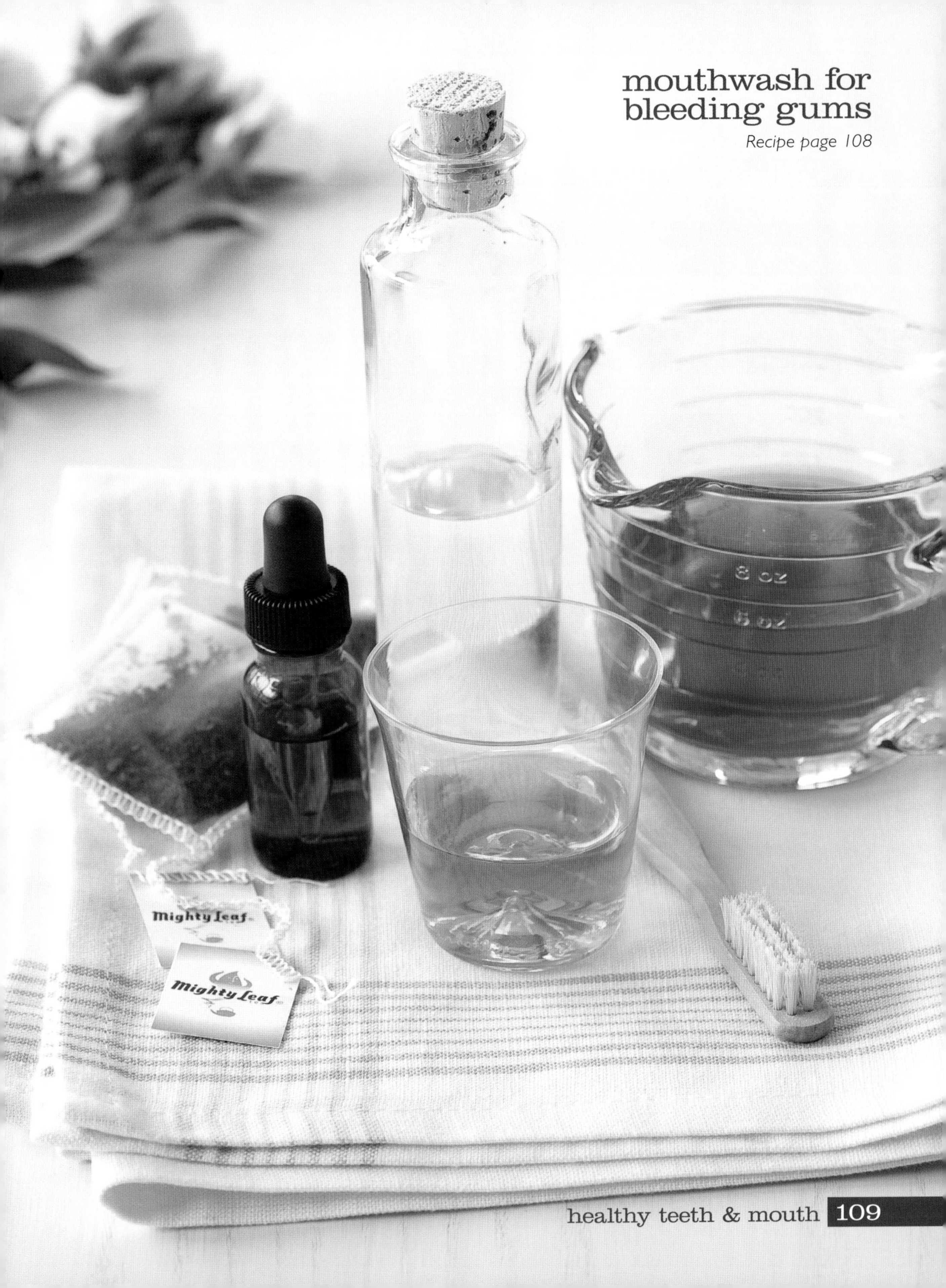

super-charged immunity

Your immune system is a complex network of cells, tissues, and organs. When operating at peak efficiency, these elements work together in harmony, like a well-conducted orchestra, to ward off attacks by bacteria, viruses, and fungi whose mission is to enter and infect your body. These days, it's more important than ever to keep your immune system in tip-top shape so that you can more effectively repel illnesses from the simple to the serious. In this chapter, you'll discover essential strategies for building and maintaining a powerful immune system. And we'll arm you with tools you can use to ramp up your immunity. Guess where you'll find those tools? By now, you know the answer: They're all in your kitchen cabinet.

first things first

These four key strategies are the places to start to turbo-charge your immunity:

Lay off the sweets. And the fatty foods, unhealthy trans fats, and junk-food carbs. All of these dampen a healthy immune system.

Eat farm foods, not factory foods. Unprocessed fruits, vegetables, dairy products, and even lean meats are packed with the nutrients you need for a powerful immune system. Packaged and processed foods not only get stripped of many of those nutrients, but add in chemicals that do you no good.

Pantry HEALERS

Brazil nuts

Canned fatty fish (salmon, sardines)

Dried mushrooms

Farm foods (unprocessed fruits and vegetables, lean meats, dairy products)

Fiber-rich foods

Flaxseeds

Garlic

Green tea

Pumpkin seeds

Raisins

Walnuts

Be active. Exercise is one of the best things you can do to power up immunity. In addition to a brisk 20- to 30-minute walk most days of the week, perform some muscle-building activities at least three times a week. Researchers are learning that muscle mass may help defend against disease-causing microbes—and even help speed recovery from infection and wounds.

Sleep deeply. Right up there with exercise is adequate sleep. Immunity experts say that getting to sleep by 9 or 10 p.m. and resting through the night seems to support immune defense and repair.

kitchen cabinet cures

Scan the shelves for fiber. Think beans, whole-wheat pasta, barley, dried split peas, lentils, nuts, seeds, dried fruits, and whole-grain bread containing 4 grams or more of fiber per serving. Fiber helps lower blood sugar levels and provides immune-enhancing vitamins and minerals.

|||||||||||||||||||||||||||||||||||||||||||||||||||||||||||||||||||||||||||||||||||||||||||||||||||||||||||||

4 reasons to rethink your drink

That innocent-looking can of soda pop—no matter what it's sweetened with—may be taking a toll on your immunity. Here's why:

1. People who drink sodas instead of healthy beverages (think low-fat milk and pure fruit juice) are less likely to get adequate vitamin A, calcium, and magnesium. What's more, soda contains phosphoric acid that depletes calcium and magnesium. These two nutrients help keep your immunity operating at peak efficiency.

2. Sodas containing high-fructose corn syrup also contain high levels of free radicals linked to tissue damage, the development of diabetes, and diabetic complications.

3. Plastic soda (and water) bottles contain a toxic chemical called bisphenol A (BPA) that can leach from bottles into soda…into you.

Emerging evidence links BPA to a myriad of maladies, including immune system depression. Public health experts recommend that we protect children from exposure to products containing BPA—especially those they consume or use every day.

4. Diet soda actually *contributes* to weight gain. A study of 1,550 people concluded that people who drink diet soda have a 41 percent increased risk of being overweight or obese—for every can or bottle they drink per day! Turns out, any sweet taste signals body cells to store fat and carbohydrates, which makes you hungrier. Sweet tastes also promote insulin release, which blocks your body's ability to burn fat. The hard truth: No published study has ever proven that drinking diet soda will help you lose weight.

Drink more tea than coffee. Harvard University researchers found that the immune activity of tea drinkers is significantly higher than that of coffee drinkers. They suspect that an amino acid in brewed tea called L-theanine may be involved in tea's immune-enhancing benefits. What's more, green tea is loaded with antioxidants that help damaged cells repair themselves.

Pump some seeds. Yummy pumpkin seeds are rich in zinc, a mineral that's key to a healthy immune system. Studies show that people who are zinc deficient (which is common as we age) have a harder time fending off garden-variety infections. A half cup of pumpkin seeds contains about 6 milligrams of zinc, which is about 40 percent of the recommended daily amount. Calorie alert: If you chow down on delicious, nutritious pumpkin seeds, consider cutting calories elsewhere because ½ cup of pumpkin seeds contains 374 calories.

Samba with selenium. Brazil nuts are packed with the immunity-enhancing antioxidant mineral selenium. Adequate selenium levels enable white blood cells to kill off microbes and tumor cells. Some researchers theorize that because selenium protects cells from free radical damage, a deficiency of the stuff could allow harmless viruses to mutate into more aggressive strains. Once your immune system has been compromised, these more dangerous viruses can then reproduce out of control. They suspect

Vitamin D alert

Are you getting too little of this vital immune-enhancer?

A new groundbreaking study found that nearly 60 percent of the study's participants had too little vitamin D in their blood—and nearly one-quarter of them had serious deficiencies. The study, conducted at the Children's Hospital Los Angeles of the University of Southern California, revealed that low levels of vitamin D put people at risk for a whole spectrum of diseases, including cancer, osteo-porosis, diabetes, and autoimmune disorders. What astonished the research team was that the volunteers were healthy, young women living in Southern California, who could logically be expected to benefit from good diets, exercise, and plenty of exposure to sunshine, which triggers the body to produce vitamin D.

Many experts have said that vitamin D's current recommended daily allowance, now set at 400 IU a day, is much too low, and are calling for it to be raised substantially.

that may be why selenium-deficient HIV patients are far more likely to develop AIDS and die faster. Getting enough selenium rejuvenates immune cells and empowers them to fight germs. Because Brazil nuts contain 75 to 100 micrograms of selenium each, just a couple of nuts a day gives you all the selenium you need. You'll also find selenium in canned salmon (between 34 and 40 micrograms in a 3-ounce portion), raisins, and walnuts.

Glorify the garlic. Rich in antioxidants, especially selenium, garlic can increase production of natural killer cells. Toss chopped or crushed garlic into foods at the very end of cooking, because high temperatures destroy garlic's medicinal action. Better still, use garlic raw whenever possible. For the most potent effect, chop, crush, or cut the cloves 10 to 15 minutes before using and toss directly into salad dressing, sandwich fillings, and other foods.

Opt for omega-3s. Omega-3 fatty acids can strengthen immune function. Omega-3 fatty acids, abundant in cold-water fish, like canned salmon and sardines, as well as in flaxseeds, help reduce acute inflammation, which occurs as part of the immune response to attack or injury. What's more, omega-3s activate parts of the immune system that rein in attack cells to stop them when their job is done.

Get friendly with fungi. Dried mushrooms, including shiitake, maitake, and morels, are packed to the gills with substances that enhance your immunity. Among these are vitamins D, C, K, and the B-complex vitamins riboflavin, niacin, and pantothenic acid. Dried mushrooms are also a rich source of potassium and phosphorous. They're a snap to reconstitute in water, and they add real gourmet flavor to sauces, stews, and casseroles. They last practically forever on the pantry shelf and are usually less expensive than fresh gourmet mushrooms.

Dried mushrooms are packed with nutrients that help prevent disease.

extra energy

When you were young, having plenty of energy was something you took for granted. But somewhere along the road to your middle years, you probably noticed that your engine stopped revving at high speed and started coasting along instead. Though you may never regain the party-all-night-play-all-day energy of your youth (and really, would you want to even if you could?), you can certainly repower your energy engine. And it won't take fancy supplements or complicated meal plans. Just open the door to your kitchen cabinet, and follow these simple tips.

kitchen cabinet cures

Nurse a coffee throughout the day. If you supersize your coffee to jump start your day, you may be driving yourself deeper and deeper into a low-energy rut. Compelling research from Brigham and Women's Hospital, Harvard Medical School, and other institutions finds that frequent low doses of caffeine—the amount in a quarter-cup of coffee—were more effective than a few larger doses of caffeine when it comes to keeping people alert.

Combine protein with good carbs. Snacks that include an ounce or two of protein with some complex carbohydrates give you a quick energy boost—without an energy crash a few hours later. Give these tasty pantry combos a try:

• Small pop-top can of salmon or tuna with whole grain crackers

Pantry HEALERS

All-bran cereal

Baked beans

Canned patés

Canned spinach

Coffee

Dried apricots

Kidney beans

Lemon or lime

Lemon essential oil

Peanut butter

Peppermint
essential oil

Peppermint or
spearmint gum

Pine essential oil

Rosemary
essential oil

Seltzer water

Whole-wheat bread

- Small box of raisins or dried cranberries with a handful of nuts
- Handful of trail mix (nuts and dried fruit varieties)
- Slice of multi-whole-grain toast and peanut butter

Have a slice with your seltzer. A refreshing glass or two of icy seltzer water with a slice of lime or lemon is a double-powered energy booster. First, since fatigue often signals dehydration, a couple of glasses of H_2O can restore your energy pronto. What's more, the citrusy scent of lemon or lime makes you feel awake and refreshed. Plus, the drink's iciness gives you a sensory wake-up call.

Do some iron-ing. If you're constantly dragging—but getting plenty of sleep—you might have iron-deficiency anemia, a common cause of fatigue. Iron is essential for producing hemoglobin, which carries oxygen to your body's cells, where it is used to produce energy. Risk factors include having heavy periods, being a vegetarian (iron that comes from meat is better absorbed than iron from vegetable sources) or having an ulcer or other problem that causes internal bleeding. Shoot for 18 milligrams a day if you're a nonvegetarian woman who has menstrual periods; nonvegetarian men and post-menopausal women need 8 milligrams a day. Canned patés that contain liver are super-rich iron sources. Kidney beans, baked beans,

Fragrant energy fixes

Aromatherapy is a natural healing art that uses fragrant essential oils distilled from plants. Some essential oils can give you an energy boost because their complex essences positively affect "feel-good" brain chemicals.

Clinical aromatherapists say that formulas like these, below, can give you an instant energy zing. You can pick up essential oils in a health or natural food store for a few dollars. Buy products labeled "100 percent pure essential oil" rather than synthetic perfume blends.

Concentration blast. As an herb, rosemary is a wonderful, savory seasoning. But in essential oil form, it enhances blood flow in the brain, so theoretically, a few whiffs could help you focus and be more attentive. The easiest way to use it: Just dribble a few drops of rosemary essential oil on a tissue and breathe in the scent as often as necessary.

Energy blast. To a water-filled spray bottle add 3 drops peppermint oil, 3 drops pine oil, and 3 drops lemon oil. Twist on the spray top, shake gently, and mist into the air around you any time you need instant energy.

Alertness blast. Add these essential oils to a spray bottle: 5 drops lemon, 3 drops peppermint, 5 drops rosemary. This is a great formula to rev yourself out of that afternoon slump.

whole-wheat bread, canned spinach, and dried apricots are also good choices. To boost your body's ability to absorb the iron in these vegetarian sources, eat them with a good source of vitamin C, such as canned tomatoes or mandarin oranges or a glass of orange juice.

Chew peppermint or spearmint gum. You'll get a little burst of energy from the invigorating flavor and scent, not to mention the physical act of chewing (it's hard to chew if you're asleep).

Eat a bowl of all-bran cereal. It contains 792 milligrams of phosphorous, an important mineral that the body needs to metabolize carbohydrates, fat, and protein so they can be used as energy.

Go high-fiber for breakfast. One study found that people who started their mornings with a high-fiber meal were more alert throughout the morning, probably because these meals take longer to digest than, say, a bowl of cornflakes or a doughnut, so blood sugar levels remain steadier. It also helps to include some protein with breakfast—and every other meal. Good breakfast options from the pantry include: whole-grain toast with a tablespoon of peanut butter and a handful of dried fruit; a bowl of high-fiber cereal (aim for at least 5 grams of fiber a serving) with milk; or a bowl of oatmeal sprinkled with 2 tablespoons of ground flaxseeds and ½ teaspoon of cinnamon.

good moods

Plenty of little things can give you a case of the blues, and some are simply beyond your control. What *is* within your control? Making some smart moves to improve your physical and mental state when the road gets bumpy. Even though you can't open your kitchen cabinet door and have a good mood jump out at you, a few items on those shelves can gently help you feel more upbeat.

kitchen cabinet cures

Eat some happy fish. The reasons for eating omega-3 rich fish keep piling up—especially when it comes to improving your state of mind. Researchers now know that omega-3s can improve mood problems by influencing the brain's "happy-making" neurotransmitters and by lessening inflammation that can damage brain cells. A new study published in the *American Journal of Clinical Nutrition* reported that when middle-aged women with symptoms of mild psychological distress took 1.5 grams of omega-3s (about the amount in a 3-ounce can of salmon) daily for eight weeks, their symptoms improved significantly.

If you like sardines, you can get even more mood-boosting omega-3s: A 3-ounce can of sardines packed in sardine oil contains 3.3 grams. Unfortunately, you can't expect one can of fish to blast you into a sunnier state of mind. Plan on eating a serving of canned fish, especially sardines and herring, several times a week. If you're not a fish eater, take a daily fish oil supplement instead.

Pantry HEALERS

Canned fish (salmon, sardines, herring, tuna)

Cashews

Chickpeas

Dried crimini mushrooms

Extra-dark chocolate

Flaxseeds

Fortified whole-grain cereals

Lentils

Vitamin D3

Zinc-fortified cereals

Boost your B$_6$. If you don't get enough vitamin B$_6$, your mood might not be all that it could be. In fact, this nutrient's deficiency symptoms include fatigue and malaise. As many as 50 percent of women don't get enough; some 15 percent get less than 25 percent of their B$_6$ needs. Getting even 1 milligram less of this vital nutrient can short-circuit your nervous system. What's more, vitamin B$_6$ deficiencies are linked to depression. Women under 50 need 1.2 milligrams a day; women over 50 need 1.5 milligrams. Men under 50 need 1.3 milligrams; over 50, 1.7 milligrams. Good pantry sources include yellowfin tuna (also known as "light"), salmon, dried crimini mushrooms, and flaxseeds.

Have a hearty breakfast cereal. Folic acid is called folate when it occurs naturally in food; folic acid is the synthetic form of this B vitamin found in supplements and added to fortified foods. And nearly 40 percent of people diagnosed with depression have folic acid deficiencies. When they start eating foods rich in folic acid, guess what? They begin to feel happier. Adults need 400 micrograms a day (women contemplating pregnancy and pregnant women need 600 micrograms). Some wholegrain breakfast cereals are fortified with a daily supply in one serving; read labels carefully to be sure. Other great sources of folate sitting in your pantry include lentils (358 micrograms in 1 cup of cooked lentils) and chickpeas (282 micrograms in 1 cup of cooked chickpeas).

Soak up the sunshine vitamin. Feel like you get more than your share of the blues? Maybe you're not getting enough blue—sky, that is. During the winter, in northern parts of the world where sunshine becomes limited, many people experience seasonal affective disorder, or SAD. Here's why: Your body uses sunlight to manufacture

Scent the air with happiness

Professional aromatherapists use essential oils of rose, lavender, lemon, and ylang-ylang to make folks feel happier. One (or more) of these may work for you, too. To find out, visit your local health or natural food store and sniff the essential oil tester bottles to see which scents appeal to you. To use your selected oil, you can pick up an inexpensive diffuser, which will be sold near the essential oils, or simply add several drops of the oil to a 4-ounce spray bottle of water. Then, spritz the air with a mood-lifting aroma to your heart's content.

vitamin D, which is actually a hormone, not a vitamin. Turns out, low vitamin D levels are common to depressed people; happy people have higher D levels. If you can get outside in the winter on sunny days, do so. If you can't, your best bet might be to take a vitamin D supplement. Experts now recommend that the current daily requirement of 400 IU be raised to 1,000 IU or even more. It's hard to get that much from food, so taking a daily supplement might help you lift your dark cloud. Choose vitamin D_3 supplements; this form of D is the one your body absorbs best.

Toss cashews on those bran flakes. Italian researchers discovered that blood levels of zinc are consistently lower in people with depression. A serving of a fortified breakfast cereals gives you 25 percent of your daily requirement. Toss in an ounce of tasty, crunchy cashews, and you'll get an extra-big zinc boost.

Low levels of both vitamin D and zinc have been linked to depression.

Savor a chocolate mood-lifter. Go ahead—reach for a few pieces of extra-dark chocolate the next time you feel a little blue. This delicacy interacts with the brain's chemical messengers responsible for regulating mood. French scientists recently learned more about its mood-lifting effects: When they gave rats some chocolate extract, the rats passed depression tests with flying colors. (Wonder how scientists figure out whether or not rats are depressed? It's simple. They put the rodents into a cylinder filled with water. Happy rats try to escape. Unhappy rats don't. All are rescued.)

Pantry HEALERS

Almonds

Broccoli

Canned fish (salmon, sardines, herring, tuna)

Cashews

Coffee

Dried fruit

Leafy greens

Rosemary essential oil

Sage

improved memory

Do you remember the title of the last book you read? Do you scratch your head and wonder whether you've taken your pills this morning? Are names sometimes just beyond your brain's reach? While forgetfulness isn't necessarily a sign that something's wrong, it can be frustrating and sometimes a little scary (especially when you've left that stove burner on…again). Memory boosters and simple do-it-yourself home remedies can help sharpen your memory now and keep it honed for years to come.

kitchen cabinet cures

Make memories with almonds. A recently completed study, conducted by researchers at the Massachusetts Institute of Technology and Tel Aviv University, has revealed just how critical magnesium is for enhancing memory and preventing its impairment. In the study, two groups of elderly rats were given identical diets, but one group was given a magnesium supplement. After testing both groups, the researchers learned the supplement improved the rats' short- and long-term memory and even enhanced their learning ability. The researchers figured out that the number of synapses (nerve endings in the brain that carry memories as electrical impulses) actually increased in the brains of the rats fed the magnesium. But don't race out to the drugstore to pick up bottles of this mineral just yet, warn the researchers. The magnesium supplements currently available don't work the same way as the one the researchers used. The researchers' advice to folks who need a memory boost? Get your magnesium the old-fashioned way, by eating pantry foods like almonds, cashews, and dried fruit. (Leafy greens and broccoli are also super sources.)

Count on coffee. If you drink caffeinated beverages, you'll get a short-term boost in your ability to concentrate. And long-term benefits could be yours as well, especially if you're an older adult. At the Faculty of Medicine in Lisbon, Portugal, researchers concluded that elderly people who drank three or four cups of coffee a day were less likely to experience memory loss than people who drank a cup a day or less. In a French study, women over 80 who drank three cups or more per day were 70 percent less likely to have memory decline than those who drank one cup or less.

Catch a whiff. Buy a little bottle of 100 percent pure rosemary essential oil at the health or natural food store. Tests of brain waves show that inhaling rosemary's aroma increases the brain's production of beta waves, which indicate heightened awareness. Another study showed that inhaling rosemary oil enhanced the memories of test-taking students. To get the memory-boosting benefits, just dab a few drops of the oil on your hair, wrists, clothing, or a handy hankie—anywhere you can get a whiff. Or put some of the oil in a diffuser, and let it fill the air.

Add sage to your cooking. A couple of small studies suggest that the anti-inflammatory effects of sage may boost memory for several hours after eating an extract of the herb. Though those supplements aren't commercially available, you might be able to replicate the results by adding savory sage liberally to various dishes. For example, roast a chicken or turkey with sage-seasoned stuffing; make a tea with 1 teaspoon of the dried herb; use sage in salad dressings and rice dishes; or sprinkle it liberally over pork, poultry, or fish before cooking.

Chow down on tuna or salmon salad. Or enjoy sardines on toast. The same reasons that make canned cold-water fish like salmon, sardines, tuna, and herring so good for your heart also make them good for your brain. The omega-3 oils in fish help "thin" the blood and prevent clogged arteries, and that can keep your brain healthy and, presumably, will help keep your memory sharp.

It's hardly a widespread or accepted form of healing, but there are many people who steadfastly believe that crystals and gems contain a vibrational energy that can help people heal. In fact, gemstone therapy has been around for thousands of years. Proponents note that each stone has its own talent. According to them, amethyst and amber calcite are the gems associated with improved memory. Their message: Carry or wear them everywhere you go, and it will help your mind function more clearly.

stable blood sugar

Pantry HEALERS

Buckwheat flour

Cinnamon

Coffee

Fenugreek

Flaxseeds

High-fiber breads

Soba noodles

Walnuts

Wine

Do you know what your fasting blood sugar level is? If you don't, you should—especially if you're overweight or have high blood pressure or if diabetes runs in your family. That's because diabetes, the disease that's reaching epidemic proportions in countries all over the world, is marked by elevated blood sugar levels. What's also on the rise? The number of people who have the silent conditions that predict they will someday get diabetes. Researchers now know that diabetes puts you at seriously increased risk for a host of health problems. Among them: heart disease, kidney failure, blindness, infertility, and even cancer. Even if diabetes isn't a concern for you, maintaining blood sugar stability should be. Here's why: Blood sugar levels that spike and dip excessively can trigger mood and energy issues. Help is close at hand if you keep your pantry stocked with weapons to help you win the blood sugar battle.

kitchen cabinet cures

Have a (lunchtime) coffee or two. Recent studies clearly connect coffee drinking with a lower risk for developing diabetes. In one of them, researchers followed the diets of nearly 70,000 nondiabetic French women for about 11 years. During that time, 1,415 of them developed diabetes. Turns out, the women who drank coffee at lunchtime had a significantly lower risk of developing diabetes—and it didn't matter whether they drank regular or decaf.

These studies build on what researchers already know from at least nine previous studies involving almost 200,000 people in the United States, Europe, and Japan: Coffee drinkers have a substantially lower risk of developing type 2 diabetes.

Do the cinnamon sprinkle. A few years ago, researchers from the U.S. Department of Agriculture studied cinnamon's effects on volunteers with type 2 diabetes. Those who took either 1, 3, or 6 grams of cinnamon (about ½, 1, or 2 teaspoons) or a placebo for 40 days saw their blood glucose levels drop 18 to 29 percent, depending on the amount they took.

More recently, 109 people with poorly controlled diabetes either received standard care, or took ½ teaspoon of cinnamon a day for 90 days (plus standard care). Those who took the cinnamon substantially lowered the critical blood sugar marker, HbA1C. When diabetics lower their HbA1C number to the extent the people in this study did, they lower their risks for developing heart disease by 16 percent, diabetic retinopathy (an eye disease that can cause blindness) by 20 percent, and kidney disease by as much as 33 percent.

Experts suggest that just ½ teaspoon of cinnamon a day can help lower your blood sugar and drop your risks for dangerous diabetic complications. This could be one of the easiest of all home remedies: Just sprinkle this delicious spice into hot and cold cereal, yogurt, coffee, or tea once a day.

Get friendly with fenugreek. If you have prediabetes or type 2 diabetes, meet this little brownish-yellow spice seed. It has a subtle, almost smoky flavor, and it's mostly used in Indian cuisine to flavor curries. Traditional Indian healers use it medicinally for a slew of health problems, including diabetes, and now researchers are discovering that those healers were apparently on the right track. Three different studies have determined that fenugreek lowers glucose levels in type 2 diabetics, increases glycemic control, and decreases insulin resistance. And in a new study, people who took 4 teaspoons of powdered fenugreek every day for eight weeks lowered their fasting blood sugar by 25 percent. They also slashed their triglyceride and LDL (bad) cholesterol numbers, too—by 30 percent each.

To reap fenugreek's blood sugar-lowering benefits, plan to use it daily. You can powder the seeds in a clean coffee grinder and mix with hot water for a tea, or you can mix

The diabetes epidemic

How widespread has the disease become? Over the past two decades, the number of people worldwide diagnosed with diabetes has gone from 30 million to 246 million. By comparison, in 2008, 33.4 million people worldwide were living with HIV, the virus that causes AIDS. While the diabetes epidemic has been well documented in the United States, it is home to less than 10 percent of the cases worldwide. Seven of the 10 countries with the highest number of diabetics are in the developing world, with China and India leading the way. The World Health Organization conservatively estimates that by 2030, 366 million people worldwide will have diabetes.

Pantry no-nos

There's more to stable blood sugar than adding certain foods and spices to your diet. Even more important is what you choose not to eat. In general, simple carbohydrates are the foods that most spark blood-sugar surges (and the blood sugar plunges that follow). The reason: Their chemical structure is so simple that they are digested into blood sugar almost instantly. For stable blood sugar—and to help avoid many conditions linked to wild blood-sugar swings—stay away from the following foods, which interestingly tend toward the color white:

- Refined sugar
- High-fructose corn syrup
- White bread
- Pancakes
- White-flour cakes and cookies
- White rice
- White potatoes
- Plain spaghetti
- Corn flakes

the powder into breads, muffins, and cooked foods. Aim for 4 teaspoons of powdered fenugreek a day. Do not use fenugreek during pregnancy because it can stimulate uterine contractions.

Stock soba noodles. This tasty Japanese pasta is made from buckwheat flour, which is milled from a fruit seed, so it's not a true grain. In a Canadian study on rats with type 1 diabetes, consuming regular amounts of buckwheat lowered their blood glucose levels by 12 to 19 percent. The study's authors concluded that buckwheat is "a safe, easy, and inexpensive way to lower glucose levels and reduce diabetic complications, including heart, nerve, and kidney problems." In another study, when researchers followed almost 36,000 women in Iowa for six years, they discovered that women who ate three servings of whole grains a day, including buckwheat, had a 21 percent lower risk of diabetes than women who ate just one serving a week. Buckwheat is also a good source of fiber and important minerals. Use buckwheat flour in recipes for pancakes, muffins, and breads.

Choose fiber-rich bread. Search for whole-grain breads that contain at least 3 grams of fiber and 3 grams of protein per slice (more is better). High-fiber whole-grain bread slows the absorption of glucose and decreases insulin spikes. According to the journal *Diabetes Care*, eating whole grains regularly reduces your risk for developing type 2 diabetes.

Enjoy a glass of wine with your dinner. One study found that women who had a drink of wine a day cut their risk of diabetes in half compared to teetotalers. Not a wine lover? The study found the same effects for beer. But cork the wine bottle once dinner is over. An Australian study found that drinking a glass of wine immediately after eating can result in a sudden drop in the insulin in your blood, meaning the glucose from your meal hangs around longer, eventually damaging arteries.

Make some walnut burgers. You'd be surprised how delectable—and easy—it is to use walnuts in recipes for burgers, meatballs, and other tasty treats. And they add a yummy crunch when toasted and tossed into salads. The latest research confirms that eating walnuts is a brilliant strategy for people with type 2 diabetes. In new study conducted at Yale University School of Medicine, researchers put 24 people with type 2 diabetes on diets containing a half cup a day of walnuts or on walnut-free diets. After eight weeks, the walnut eaters had significantly improved heart health markers. Separately, Australian researchers recently put 50 overweight type 2 diabetics on one of two diet plans—one group ate a daily quarter-cup serving of walnuts; the other group went walnut-free. After a year, the walnut eaters had significantly greater reductions in their fasting insulin levels.

Since a half cup of walnuts a day contains 327 calories, you'll want to cut an equivalent amount of calories elsewhere in your diet. You can find simple, tasty main-dish walnut recipes online. Not so incidentally, walnuts are an excellent source of omega-3 fatty acids, are proven to lower cholesterol, and even help prevent and control high blood pressure.

Go wild with freshly ground flaxseeds. Its toasty, nutty flavor enhances almost everything you sprinkle it on. Not only does it contain a healthy dose of fiber, it also contains omega-3 fats that help maintain flexible cell membranes. This is critical for people with diabetes, because flexible cell membranes respond to insulin and absorb glucose better. As a result, studies find that flaxseeds may help lower elevated blood sugar. Sprinkle freshly ground flaxseeds over your salad, yogurt, and cereal, for starters. You can also mix it into meatloaf or stir it into pancake and muffin batter.

Switch to buckwheat pancakes and noodles for flavor and your health.

healthy weight

Obesity absolutely devastates your health. It's linked not only to an increased risk of the problems you'd expect—heart disease and diabetes, as well as joint pain—but also to numerous others you may not consider, such as cancer, hearing loss, Alzheimer's disease, and gastrointestinal problems. For some people, keeping extra weight off seems almost impossible—but it's not. Just don't make the mistake of relying on short-term "dieting," which is surprisingly ineffective. Employ these wise kitchen moves, and you're likely to find that achieving your weight-loss goals will become a little bit easier.

kitchen cabinet cures

Portion nuts in snack-sized bags. Sure, you know that nuts are a healthy snack—we've certainly recommended eating these crunchy taste treats often enough throughout this book. Here's yet another reason to make them a snacking habit: A study from the City of Hope National Medical Center found that overweight people who ate a moderate-fat diet containing almonds lost more weight than a control group that didn't eat nuts. Really, any nut will do.

But if you're unaware of how many nuts you're eating, you could end up gaining weight instead of losing it. The appropriate serving size for nuts is 1 ounce, or about 200 calories, depending on the nut. To keep yourself from mindlessly nibbling more than you need, do this: When you buy nuts, open the container and put handful-sized

Pantry HEALERS

Anchovies

Canned fish

Canned soups and
vegetables

Capers

Cereals

Hot sauces

Lentils

Nonfat powdered
milk

Nuts

Oatmeal

Seltzer

Soba buckwheat
noodles

Tea (green or black)

Whole grains
(instant barley,
quinoa, tabbouleh)

Whole-wheat pasta

portions into ziplock snack or sandwich bags. And by handful, we mean the amount of nuts you can hold in the palm of your hand with your fingers closed. Then, limit yourself to a serving or two a day.

Buy the smaller size. It's a fact that the larger the portion in front of you, the more you'll eat. When researchers sent 79 parents home with a movie and either 1- or 2-pound bags of M&Ms along with either a medium or jumbo tub of popcorn for each family member, they ate more M&Ms from the 2-pound bag than from the 1-pound bag and about half a tub of popcorn, regardless of the tub size. Though we're certainly not promoting M&Ms as a weight-loss food (we sincerely wish we could), we do recommend ordering the small bag of popcorn when you're at the movies and buying single-serving–sized snack food packs instead of jumbo sizes. The extra money you might save buying larger sizes isn't worth derailing your weight-control efforts.

Stock these three cans. Canned beans, corn, and tomatoes stretch higher calorie dishes and also combine to make yummy, low-cal meals. Try these great ideas:

• Add a can each of corn, garbanzo beans, and plum tomatoes to your pasta salad recipe. You'll boost the salad's texture and flavor, and as a bonus, you'll be able to eat more salad for just a few more calories. As a double bonus, you'll get healthy amounts of fiber and important nutrients.

"Fast food" from your pantry

Eating out—particularly fast food—is a major cause of weight gain. One study found that people who consumed fast food more than twice a week gained 10 pounds more over a 15-year period than those who ate fast food less than once a week. What's more, fast foods are often loaded with way too much sodium and fat—especially the super unhealthy trans fats. To reduce the incentive to eat out, keep the pantry stocked with these "convenience" foods:

• Canned beans

• Canned fish (no sauce)

• Canned vegetables (no sauce—except for veggies canned in tomato sauce)

• Canned tomato products—pureed, chopped, or whole

• Whole-wheat pasta

• Packaged healthy whole grains, such as tabbouleh, quinoa, and instant barley

• Soba buckwheat noodles

• Dried lentils

• Canned soups (toss in a can of beans for a hearty, healthy main dish in minutes)

• Toss a can of light tuna with a can of white beans. Add a drizzle of olive oil, a squeeze or two of lemon, and a sprinkle of oregano.

• Mix a can of kidney or black beans with a can of corn, and add some canned salsa and a few shots of hot sauce for a tasty lunch.

• Simmer a can of Italian plum tomatoes with a little garlic for a superfast pasta sauce. Serve over 1 cup of whole-wheat pasta.

Pull a caper in your kitchen. You can add oodles of flavor to many foods—for next to no calories—by keeping capers and anchovies in your pantry. Since richly flavored foods are more satisfying than bland foods, you can eat less without feeling deprived. Capers are the tiny pickled buds that give a great zing to bean, tuna, and salmon salads. Rinse before using. And even if you think you don't like anchovies, try adding a few, well-minced, to chicken or tuna salads and tomato sauces. For a delicious low-cal pasta, simmer a large can of Italian plum tomatoes with a can of light tuna, minced garlic, a pinch of dried red pepper flakes, and a few minced anchovies for a few

Make 3 smart switches

See how many calories you can save by switching from high-fat, high-calorie indulgences to lower-fat, lower-calorie options. Just by making these three little dietary tweaks, you could lose 25 pounds in a year.

Skip the sugary drinks. If you drink non-diet soda, you can cut 160 calories (per 16 ounces) out of your day just by switching to a sugar-free quaff. What's more, a very recent study links sugar-sweetened soda, sport drinks, and fruit drinks (not 100 percent fruit juice) to excessive weight gain, diabetes, and heart disease. The best beverage choices: green or black tea (hot or iced) or seltzer flavored with a squeeze of lemon or lime, or, of course, just plain water, with or without lemon or lime. Try to live by

a simple rule: Don't get any calories from your everyday beverages.

Start with soup. Studies show that people who start a meal with soup—especially broth-based soup—end up eating fewer calories by the end of the day without feeling hungrier. Avoid high-calorie cream-based soups and watch the sodium content. Bean soups are especially filling.

Read the labels. Avoid any prepared food that lists sugar, fructose, or corn syrup among the first four ingredients on the label. You should be able to find a lower-sugar version of the same type of food. Also, seek out sugar-free pantry items such as ketchup, mayonnaise, and salad dressing.

minutes. Serve over whole-wheat pasta. Omega-3 alert: Anchovies are a rich source of this heart-healthy fat.

Use nonfat powdered milk in coffee. You get the nutritional benefits of skim milk, which is high in calcium and low in calories. And powdered milk doesn't dilute coffee the way liquid milk does. And it's far lower in calories and fat than half-and-half.

Eat cereal for breakfast five days a week. Studies find that people who eat cereal for breakfast every day are much less likely to be obese and have diabetes than those who don't. They also take in more vitamins, fiber, and calcium—and less fat—than people who eat other breakfast foods. Of course, that doesn't mean reaching for the ultrasweet kid choices (which is as unhealthy for them as it is for you, by the way). Instead, serve a high-fiber, low-sugar cereal like Kashi GoLean, Total, or Grape-Nuts. To sweeten, add berries (fresh or dried) or sliced banana. And check the package to see what is considered a single portion size. For many dry cereals, a healthy serving is just 1 cup—but many adults pour out at least twice that amount.

Have oatmeal on the weekends. You may not have time on weekday mornings to cook a bowl of oatmeal, so weekends are ideal for enjoying this satisfying, nutrition-rich breakfast. An especially toothsome, stick-to-the-ribs choice is steel-cut Irish oats. Oats are packed with unique compounds, like beta-glucan, which helps lower cholesterol and stabilizes blood sugar, and potent antioxidants called avenanthramides, which reduce heart attack risk. Oats also pack a healthy 4 grams of fiber and just 150 calories per 1-cup serving. Best of all, a bowl of oatmeal keeps you feeling fuller longer, so you're better able to resist food cravings between breakfast and lunch.

Spice it up! Use hot sauce, salsa, cayenne, and Cajun seasonings instead of relying on butter and creamy or sugary sauces. Besides providing lots of flavor with no fat and few calories, many of these spicy seasonings turn up your digestive fires, causing your body to temporarily burn more calories. What's more, capsaicin, the ingredient that puts the fire in hot peppers, can put the chill on your appetite. For a surprising taste treat, sprinkle a little cayenne pepper over air-popped popcorn.

A simple way to eat less

It's a fact that when you serve food on large-sized plates, you tend to load more food on the plate, making it easier to overeat. So switch your dinner-sized plates for smaller lunch-sized plates, and you'll automatically eat less. Need more help controlling portion sizes? Remember the basic rule of portion mix: one-quarter of your plate should hold a lean protein; one-quarter should hold a carbohydrate portion, preferably whole grain; the remaining half should be filled with vegetables.

easing what ails you

Proven kitchen-cabinet remedies for 74 of the most common health concerns

It wasn't that long ago that huge multi-purpose drugstores didn't exist. Doctors weren't a phone call away, and hospitals and clinics were few and far between. Back in our grandparents' or great-grandparents' day, everyone needed to have at least a smattering of homegrown healing ability to protect their family's health.

And what they learned was how to heal with whatever staples they had on hand. As it turns out, they knew what they were doing. Research confirms that many basic kitchen staples have legitimate, powerful healing properties.

In the pages that follow, we provide over 1,000 research-supported pantry cures. Some you'll probably recognize, like using honey to soothe a sore throat. But many others will surprise you—for example, that you can also use Tabasco to help your throat!

Just as importantly, we put these cures in proper perspective. Sometimes, they're all you need to remedy a problem. Other times, they should be used in conjunction with more conventional, doctor-prescribed cures. In all cases, we'll put you on the path toward fast and effective healing.

acne

Even though you're probably long past worrying about your prom-night complexion, acne at any age makes you want to live in a world without mirrors. The umbrella term for the condition in which pores become blocked and often infected, acne causes whiteheads, blackheads, and inflamed skin. Dozens of acne medications are available over the counter and by prescription, but many of them are harsh and can have serious side effects. Fortunately, simple remedies you find in the pantry can often eliminate mild acne—for you and your teenager.

first things first

Keeping your skin clean sounds like pretty obvious advice. But many of us really don't know the very best ways to do that. Here they are:

• Wash body parts where you sprout acne twice a day. Use a mild cleanser, and don't scrub or use exfoliants or facial masks, all of which can make acne worse.

• Keep your hair off your face. When oil from your hair meets oil from your forehead, breakouts may follow. Shampoo every day or two, depending on how oily your hair is, and keep combs, brushes, and anything you use on your hair scrupulously clean.

• Keep your fingers off your face and away from acne. Your hands spread oil, germs, and dirt to everything they touch, even if you can't see dirt on them. Plus scratching, pinching, or rubbing acne can lead to the blemishes getting infected.

Pantry HEALERS

Acidic fruit juices

Aloe

Aspirin

Chamomile

Echinacea

Epsom salts

Fish or
  fish oil capsules

Flaxseed

Green tea

Honey

Iodine

Peppermint

Walnuts

Witch hazel

- Don't wear a sweatband or tight clothing when you exercise. That can increase your skin's production of oil and lead to both acne and "bacne," those pimples that appear on your shoulders and back.

- If you have severe acne, avoid makeup and lotions. With mild acne, you can use water-based (as opposed to oil-based) makeup. Look for the words "noncomedogenic" or "nonacnegenic" on the label. Wash makeup off your face with soap and water before you go to bed.

kitchen cabinet cures

Dab on tea tree oil. A 5 percent solution of this essential oil from an Australian tree works just as well as the top drugstore acne remedy, benzoyl peroxide, in eradicating pimples, according to Australian researchers. Though tea tree oil doesn't work as quickly as the drugstore cure, it's gentler on your skin. But don't mop it all over your face. It's strong and can dry out your skin, triggering your body to overproduce oil, which can make acne worse. Just dilute a few drops of pure tea tree oil with 20 to 40 drops of witch hazel and apply to skin once or twice a day with a cotton swab. And stay out of the sun—tea tree oil can make you more sensitive to UV rays.

Go clear with green tea. A University of Miami study found that even a mild dose of green tea's antimicrobial and antioxidant compounds erases almost two-thirds of pimples from people with mild to moderate acne when used twice daily for six weeks. But save your money—you don't need to buy the cream. When you whip up a cup of green tea for sipping, whip up a second, let it cool and use it as a face wash, or lay the wet tea bag right on your face like a compress.

Dab on the honey. Honey kills bacteria, which explains why this old folk remedy may improve acne. A particular kind, Manuka honey from New Zealand, is being studied for its antibiotic properties, which are powerful enough to kill methicillin-resistant *Staphylococcus aureus* (MRSA). You don't need to import honey from the other side of the world, though. Just apply a teaspoon of plain honey to affected areas. Some home remedy experts recommend mixing ½ cup of honey into a cup of plain oatmeal, then

When to Call THE DOCTOR

If your blemishes don't respond to natural remedies or over-the-counter medications, you may need some extra help. Contact your doctor if your face becomes seriously inflamed with painful, fluid-filled lumps and a reddish or purplish cast. This could be cystic acne, which can be scarring.

the natural DOCTOR'S

- Switch to organic milk. Because it's hormone-free, it may help decrease acne outbreaks.

- Eat foods rich in antioxidants. Choose a rainbow of brightly colored fruits and vegetables—the more vividly colored, the better.

- Despite the legend, dark chocolate (60 to 70 percent cacao) doesn't promote acne. But, like other sugary and fatty foods, milk chocolate may worsen acne.

Echinacea, the popular herb for colds and immunity, can also help heal acne.

applying the paste to your skin. Leave on for 30 minutes, then rinse. Impurities on the skin adhere to oatmeal and are sloughed away. The oats reduce inflammation and leave a protective barrier on the skin, keeping it moisturized.

Say aloe. This herb, which may be growing on your windowsill right now, fights infection and promotes healing. What's more, applying the gel at least twice a day may reduce scarring. To use, just cut a leaf from the plant, scrape the gel off with a spoon, and apply to affected areas. Or pick up a bottle of 100 percent pure aloe gel at the health food store. Make sure it contains no additional ingredients.

Use your cold remedy herb. That's right, the echinacea you keep in the cupboard to ward off colds and flu may also help you clear up your complexion. It's actually a traditional herbalist's remedy that has been shown in some animal studies to help speed wound healing, which may be why it works for blemishes. What's more, it has bacteria-killing compounds, lessens inflammation, and even eases wound pain. Just place a few drops of tincture onto a soft pad or cotton ball and dab it right on pimples or soak a soft cloth with brewed echinacea tea and use as a daily wash.

Feel minty fresh. Mint is refreshment for your face: It may help remove some of the oil that clogs your pores and turns into unsightly blemishes. To make this herbal remedy, add the contents of two peppermint tea bags (or if available, 2 tablespoons of finely chopped fresh mint) to 2 tablespoons of plain unsweetened yogurt and 2 tablespoons of plain oatmeal (just whir some oats—not flavored

To pop or not?

Squeezing pimples or blackheads can increase inflammation, lead to infection, and cause skin damage, which can leave you with scarring and pitting. But if you can't stand the ugly whitehead for one minute longer, use the dermatologist-approved way for making it disappear. You'll need a needle, some rubbing alcohol, a cotton swab, and some hydrogen peroxide. Here's how to do it.

Clean the area. Take a needle and swab it with alcohol to sterilize it. Gently prick the

pimple. Use the swab to drain it. Clean it up with hydrogen peroxide, which is an antiseptic.

To remove a blackhead, you can find a tool called a blackhead extractor in the drugstore. Soften the area for 10 minutes with a hot-water compress (not so hot that you'll burn yourself). Then wash your hands well (keep scrubbing with soap and water until you finish reciting the alphabet) before using the extractor to reduce infection risk.

or instant—in your blender or food processor until finely powdered). Mix all the ingredients together and leave them on your face for 10 minutes, then wash off with plain water and dry.

Mash an aspirin. Aspirin contains salicylic acid, an old frontline remedy for acne. Aspirin helps reduce inflammation and dries up pimples. Mash an aspirin with a little water to form a paste and dab it on a blemish, or use a solution made from four adult aspirin dissolved in 2 tablespoons of water. (Make sure to use uncoated aspirin tablets.) You can also take an aspirin orally to help get the red out, but always check with your doctor before you start taking the drug regularly.

Consult the witch. Witch hazel, that is. Pour a little witch hazel onto a cotton ball to clean your face morning and night. Witch hazel is a natural astringent that helps to dry and shrink pimples.

Hit it with healthy acids. Any acidic fruit juice (lemon, lime, grapefruit) or vinegar can help flush pores. Dab onto acne with a cotton ball or swab.

Make a blackhead eradicator. To get rid of those tiny dark skin spots that look like specks of pepper, add 1 teaspoon of Epsom salts and 3 drops of iodine to ½ cup of water and bring to a boil. Let cool. Dip in a clean cotton pad and use it to clean your pores.

Fight oil with fat. But not just any fat—use the omega-3 fatty acids found in fish. One study found that people taking a multi-nutrient capsule containing fish oil had significantly less acne than they did before they started the remedy. Omega-3s are anti-inflammatory, and acne is all about inflammation. Fatty fish such as canned salmon, sardines, albacore tuna, and mackerel, and other foods such as flaxseed and walnuts are high in these healthy oils. Your acne RX: Two to three fish meals a week, or sprinkle a spoonful of freshly ground flaxseed on cereal or salads, and pop walnuts as a snack.

Relax and soothe with chamomile. The same tea you drink to reduce stress can lessen acne inflammation. Whir the contents of a chamomile tea bag in a blender or spice or coffee grinder, mix with just enough water to make a paste, and apply to inflamed skin. Or, brew up a strong

Weird & wacky

Early American settlers had some pretty strange notions when it came to eradicating acne. One involved the application of urine to the outbreaks. Another called for using the water that collected in old tree stumps to bathe pimpled skin. Needless to say, neither has been studied, and neither is worth trying.

chamomile tea with two tea bags to 1 cup boiled water. Cover and let steep for 15 minutes. Apply the cooled tea to your face with a cotton ball after cleansing.

recipes for healing

Pimple-Relieving Compress

This gentle treatment will help send a pimple on its way.

> 4 teaspoons hot water
> 2 drops tea tree essential oil

1. Put the hot water in a bowl. Swirl the tea tree essential oil through the water, then soak a cotton ball or gauze pad in the solution.

2. Gently squeeze out excess liquid and apply the cotton ball or pad directly to the area of the pimple. Cover with plastic wrap and secure with a bandage or tape. Leave in place for at least an hour. Repeat twice a day.

Clarifying Herbal Hot Pack

This soothing treatment will open pores and kill bacteria.

> 4 green tea bags
> I tablespoon dried thyme
> I tablespoon dried oregano
> I quart water

1. Put tea bags, thyme, oregano, and water in a pot and bring to a boil.

2. Cover and steep for at least 60 minutes.

3. Reheat after an hour until it's almost too hot to touch, then saturate a clean cotton face towel until soaked through.

4. Carefully wring out the towel, and gently place on your face. Sit back and relax for 10 to 20 minutes. For best results, soak towel in the hot tea again whenever it cools off.

age spots

Sometimes called liver spots, these unsightly brown splotches that appear on hands, shoulders, and face as you age should more accurately be called "sun spots." That's because they're actually the result of too much sun exposure. They're harmless and painless—except for the embarrassment you feel when you look at them. Bleaching ointments can make them less noticeable and certain medical procedures—laser therapy or cryotherapy—can make them disappear. But you can fade them naturally, too, using nature's chemical peels you've got stashed in the pantry.

first things first

You can prevent age spots—or keep the ones you have from getting worse—with these careful sun strategies:

• Avoid sustained sun on bare skin between 10 a.m. and 4 p.m. in the summer and 10 a.m. and 2 p.m. in the winter.

• Slather on the sunscreen 30 minutes before you go outside and reapply as needed. Use a minimum sun protection factor (SPF) of 15, though many dermatologists now say SPF 30 may be better. Look for products containing zinc oxide, ecamsule, avobenzone, and oxybenzone, all of which contribute to superior skin protection.

• Choose outdoor clothing designed to absorb the sun's ultraviolet rays or treat your clothing with Rit's SunGuard, a product that treats fabric with a compound that blocks 96 percent of UV light.

Pantry HEALERS

Aloe
Apple cider vinegar
Buttermilk
Castor oil
Chickpeas
Lemon juice
Oatmeal
Onion
Yogurt

When to Call
THE DOCTOR

If a skin spot changes color, starts growing, tingles, or itches, it might not be an age spot but melanoma, a form of skin cancer. Call your dermatologist immediately for a skin check.

kitchen cabinet cures

Squeeze on some lemon. The juice from a fresh lemon is like a mild acid peel—it can erase the upper layer of skin (just like acid treatments you'd get from a dermatologist) and reduce the look of some age spots. It also acts as a weak bleach. Put some on a cotton ball and rub the skin twice a day.

Try buttermilk. There's science behind this old folk remedy. Milk contains lactic acid, and when dabbed on age spots or other sun-damaged areas of skin, it may help enough to slough off the top layers of skin.

Dot on the aloe vera. Just break off a leaf and dab the gel right on your age spots.

Try onion juice. A popular folk remedy is to apply a mix of apple cider vinegar and onion juice to the spot. Finely chop or blend an onion and use a strainer or cheesecloth to squeeze out the juice. Mix equal parts vinegar to onion juice, and apply for 30 minutes, once a day.

Try chickpeas. Mash about one-third cup of chickpeas (garbanzo beans) and add a little water. Smear the paste onto the spots and leave it until it dries. Repeat each day and the spot should start to fade, say many folk healers.

Try castor oil. Apply it on the spots once or twice a day, rubbing the oil into the skin. The spots should disappear within a month.

recipe for healing

Anti-Age Spot Mask

This beauty treatment could help lighten age spots—and it serves double duty as a purifying skin mask.

> 2 tablespoons plain yogurt
> 2 teaspoons old-fashioned oatmeal
> 1 teaspoon lemon juice
> 1 teaspoon sea salt

1. Blend all ingredients together thoroughly to form a paste.
2. Massage into age spots on your hands (it might be too drying for facial age spots).
3. Leave in place for 20 minutes or so, then rinse with water. Use weekly.

anti-age spot mask

Recipe page 138

allergies

If you step outside and are immediately sneezing, sniffling, and rubbing your eyes, you're not allergic to the great outdoors—you're allergic to the pollen, dust, or mold floating in the air. All manner of harmless things, from your pet cat to peanuts, can make you react as if they were dangerous toxins. There's no cure for allergies, but you can reduce and treat your symptoms naturally with remedies you make yourself from stuff you already have in the house. Happy breathing!

first things first

There are lots of tricks for avoiding allergens. Here are several popular ones for the most common allergy triggers, including dust, mold, and pollen:

• Keep indoor humidity levels below 35 percent to prevent growth of mold and mites.

• Stay in the air-conditioning during pollen season.

• If you can, hire someone to mow the lawn.

• Breathe through your nose, not your mouth, to help filter out pollen.

• Immediately shower and wash your hair after coming inside.

• After spending time outdoors, immediately wash your clothes to prevent bringing pollen inside.

• Create an asthma-safe and allergy-free garden, using female plants (no pollen), pollen-free grass, and plants without strong perfume.

Pantry HEALERS

Apples

Black, green, and
   white tea

Chili peppers

Fish

Garlic

Greens

Honey

Horseradish

Lemon tea

Olives

Onions

Nuts

Red wine

Salt

Thyme

Wheat germ

- In spring and early summer, avoid exercising in the evening when you're more likely to breathe in pollen and pollutants.
- In late summer and fall, don't exercise in the morning when pollen counts are highest.
- Use a vacuum with a high-efficiency particulate air (HEPA) filter.
- If you have pets, don't let them in your bedroom, and wash them once a week.
- Choose washable throw rugs instead of wall-to-wall carpeting.
- Run a dehumidifier in your basement to remove moisture and prevent mold.
- Get a plastic, dust-proof cover for your mattress to thwart dust mites.
- Wash bed linens once a week in hot water or dry in a hot dryer to kill mites.
- Don't put plants in your bedroom.
- Use exhaust fans in the kitchen and bathroom to remove excess moisture and odors from the air.
- Get rid of unnecessary stuffed animals, drapes, carpeting, and pillows. All harbor dust and allergens.

kitchen cabinet cures

Have tea in bed. A nice hot cup of steaming lemon tea with honey in the morning will wake up your nasal cilia, the itty-bitty hairs in your nose that whisk pollen and dust out of your nasal passages. If you have allergies, those cilia are liable to be sluggish. A cup of tea will rouse the cilia to keep pollen and air particles at bay so you're not sneezing and coughing first thing in the morning. Add a little sage, fennel, or anise from your spice rack to help stimulate your nasal cilia even more.

In fact, have tea any old time. Black, green, and white teas are rich in flavonoids, plant chemicals that protect against inflammation.

Cue into quercetin. This plant chemical is also a flavonoid, a plant compound that's been found to protect us against everything from heart disease and cancer to

When to Call
THE DOCTOR

If you've never had allergies before or if home remedies, over-the-counter antihistamines, or prescription medications aren't working, or if you're wheezing, it's time to make an appointment.

It may be time to call for emergency help if you have trouble breathing, experience swelling of your lips or throat, feel dizzy or light-headed, or have gastrointestinal symptoms. In severe form, those are the symptoms of anaphylactic shock, more common with food allergies than respiratory allergies.

the natural
DOCTOR'S $\mathcal{R}x$

Painful as it may be to your allergic child, get rid of her stuffed animals, and consider finding nonallergenic replacements. Also consider eliminating drapes, carpeting, decorative pillows, or other decorative accessories that attract dust and allergens.

Weird & wacky

Actually, this remedy for hay fever may not be as wacky as it sounds—it's endorsed by many reputable healers, and it's a popular treatment in England. Honey that's produced locally—say, within 25 miles of your home—may contain pollen from the plants that trigger your allergies. If you eat a spoonful or so of this honey daily during the winter, it's just possible that it could act similarly to allergy shots and blunt your allergic reaction. We think it's a sweet remedy that can't hurt and just might help. (Note: Never give honey to babies under a year old.)

cataracts, allergies, and asthma. In test tubes, it prevents immune cells from releasing histamine. You can take a supplement, but quercetin comes in some attractive food packages, including tea, red wine, apples, garlic, and onions.

Go Mediterranean. A study of children living in Crete, Greece, found far fewer allergies and less asthma among those who ate the healthy Greek diet—fish, loads of vegetables and fruit, olive oil, and nuts. Among the most protective foods in their diets were nuts. Of course, make sure your child doesn't have an allergy to nuts before adding these to her diet.

Sprinkle on the wheat germ. In one study, men and women with allergy symptoms who took 800 IU of vitamin E every day (in addition to taking their regular allergy meds) discovered they didn't need as much medication as similar sufferers who took a placebo, particularly for stuffiness. Vitamin E is a potent antioxidant that appears to calm the part of the immune system involved in allergies. You can certainly reach for the vitamin E in your kitchen vitamin drawer, but studies suggest being cautious about taking more than 400 IU, the amount found in the average multivitamin. Get the rest from food. Wheat germ is one of the best sources. Mix it into cereal, oatmeal, salads, meatloaf, or casseroles. To increase your vitamin E intake further, snack on almonds, hazelnuts, peanuts, and pistachios. Peanut butter also supplies vitamin E, as do fortified cereals.

Unstuff with horseradish. You know it makes your eyes water and your nose run, but there's also scientific evidence that this spicy root may act as a natural decongestant. Spread some jarred horseradish on whole-wheat crackers—it tastes better than you think!

Find some folate. This B vitamin is abundant in fortified whole-grain products, as well as in canned, dark green veggies like canned spinach, collard or mustard greens, and canned peas. A study of the diets of more than 8,000 American adults and children found that those who had the least folate in their diets were the most likely to have high levels of antibodies to pollen, dust mites, and animal dander, and to have wheezing problems, a symptom of asthma.

Chow down on chili. The capsaicin in the chili pepper may calm the inner lining of the nasal passages (called the mucosa), making them less sensitive to irritants and less likely to become inflamed and secrete the protective fluids that stuff you up. And if you've ever eaten a hot pepper, you know it will help clear your nasal passages pronto.

Make a saline solution. Mixing ¼ teaspoon salt and ¼ teaspoon baking soda in 8 ounces of warm water. Place the saline solution in the neti pot, and, tipping your head to one side, pour the solution into one nostril. It will run into the other nostril and down the back of your throat. Drain by spitting out the remnants and blowing your nose.

This simple treatment will remove irritants and even some inflammatory cells from your nose. Use it at least once a day, and make sure to give yourself a rinse when you come in from the outdoors to wash pollens away.

Make a hay fever inhaler. Old-time herbalists believed that inhaling certain brews could ease allergy symptoms. They had a point: The herb in this brew contains thymol. Research shows that thymol reduces bronchial tract swelling and has anti-inflammatory and some antibacterial action. To make it, put ½ ounce dried thyme in a 1-pint canning jar and cover with boiling water. Close the jar tightly. Let steep and cool for 30 minutes. Remove the lid. Breathe in the vapors deeply several times. Keep the jar with you and inhale as needed during the day.

Eating hot peppers can help battle allergies by making nasal passages less sensitive.

If you're allergic to what you eat

The most common food allergies are to the proteins in cow's milk, eggs, peanuts, wheat, soy, fish, shellfish, and tree nuts (like walnuts or almonds). If you break out in hives, have respiratory symptoms, or are likely to go into anaphylactic shock after eating the offending food, you need to be vigilant:

• Always ask about ingredients when you are eating away from home, such as in a restaurant or at someone else's house.

• Read food labels and know what you're looking for. Soy can be soy or it can be "natural flavorings." When in doubt, avoid the product until you contact the manufacturer.

• Always carry antihistamines or injectable epinephrine with you in case you eat something by accident. You should also wear an ID bracelet that describes your allergy.

anal itching

The itch you dare not scratch (at least in public) is usually more annoying, not to mention embarrassing, than it is a symptom of something serious. It generally yields to some tender loving basic care and home remedies you can concoct from pantry staples.

Pantry HEALERS

Baking powder

Chamomile

Echinacea

Oats

Tea

Witch hazel

first things first

Many cases of anal itching can be blamed on "cling-ons," fecal material left over from a bowel movement. Constipation, diarrhea, and hemorrhoids can increase your risk. Here's how to tend to the down under:

• Make sure your personal hygiene is above reproach by bathing regularly and washing your anal area with soap and water. Dry well.

• After a bowel movement, wipe gently with toilet paper. If there is any indication of fecal material on your skin, use a soft wet cloth or a flushable wipe to remove any remains. Dry thoroughly.

• Avoid bath oils, salts, and anything containing perfume or dyes that might irritate sensitive skin.

• Finally, avoid tight clothes, especially in hot weather. Clothing that presses your buttocks together, combined with sweat, can cause irritation and itching. Roomy, breathable cotton undies will help, especially if you sit all day, sit on a plastic seat, or ride a bike.

kitchen cabinet cures

Try chamomile. Add two chamomile tea bags to 8 ounces of boiling water. Steep for 5 minutes. Soak a cotton pad in the mixture and apply. (Don't use this remedy if you have ragweed allergies.)

Clean with witch hazel. This astringent will not only clean the anal area but will cool it down and reduce swelling, another itch trigger. Soak a cotton pad in witch hazel and apply it to the affected area. Get even more cool relief by storing the witch hazel in the refrigerator.

Take a baking powder soak. Add a quarter cup of baking soda to warm bath water and soak in the soothing mixture for 15 minutes. Give your clothes a baking soda treatment too. It's a mild detergent.

Roll some oats. Oatmeal is a traditional treatment for irritated skin; it eases inflammation and is soothing. Place 2 cups of rolled oats in a piece of cut-off panty hose, seal it tightly, and place it in your bath water. Gently roll the oatmeal bundle over the itchy area.

Take the tea bag treatment. The same tea you drink can provide cool relief to swollen, irritated tissue. Brew a bag and allow it to cool, then hold it against your itchy parts.

Watch those spicy foods. Anything that can burn you up on the way in can irritate you on the way out. Spicy foods, coffee and other caffeinated drinks, alcohol, and acidic foods such as citrus fruits and tomatoes are common itch-makers.

Check your toilet paper and laundry. You may be sensitive to a chemical, such as a dye or perfume, in your toilet paper or laundry detergent or softener. Even creams and ointments meant to be used in the anal area can irritate you. Switch to perfume- and dye-free products.

Make this soothing compress. Echinacea isn't just for preventing colds. It has wound-healing ability and can deaden pain. Blend 1 teaspoon of echinacea tincture into 1 cup of cool water. Dip a clean handkerchief into it, and apply to the anal area for 5 minutes. Store any leftover mix in the refrigerator and use again.

When to Call THE DOCTOR

If you notice blood or other discharge or feel a lump in the rectal area, it could be the symptom of something that requires medical treatment. If your child complains of an itchy butt, it's time to see the doctor. Kids can pick up pinworms and other parasitic travelers. A tell-tale symptom: nighttime itching. These ickies are contagious, so if you also itch down below, tell the doc.

When there's pain with the itch

That's a common symptom of anal fissures, tears in the lining of the anal canal often caused by hard stool. Drink lots of water to soften stool, use over-the-counter stool softeners, and call your doctor if there's excessive bleeding or your problem doesn't resolve in four weeks.

anxiety

Pantry
HEALERS

Canned chicken

Chamomile

Flaxseeds

Fortified cereal

Honey

Lavender oil

Rosemary

Tuna or salmon
  (canned)

Vitamin G12

Walnuts

A little anxiety is a good thing. It's the appropriate response to stress: It's what makes you look both ways before you cross a busy street, rehearse your words over and over before a speech, and recheck the math on your tax return three times over. But you can overdo anxiety, worrying yourself into a frenzy over every little thing or nothing at all until it becomes a habit. Instead of preparing you for dealing with a major stressor, overblown or chronic stress can virtually paralyze you with both physical and emotional symptoms. Fortunately, you can find some simple and natural ways to ease your mind without ever leaving your kitchen.

first things first

If you're suddenly feeling anxious, follow this sequence of actions to restore your calm:

• Take stock of the situation and consider the source. Rationally considering what's going on often helps to soothe the raw emotions.

• If possible, remove yourself from the situation.

• Then do some deep breathing. Focus on breathing in slowly and deeply, then breathing out. Regulating your breath will usually bring your anxiety under control. To slow and deepen your breathing, sit down, put one hand over your abdomen, and slowly inhale so that your belly expands under your hand but your shoulders do not rise. Hold your breath for 4 or 5 seconds, then very slowly exhale. Repeat until you feel calmer.

kitchen cabinet cures

Have a bowl of cereal. A deficiency in B_{12} vitamin can cause anxiety. If you're a vegan—meaning you don't eat any animal-based foods—you may miss out on B_{12} because it's found mostly in meat, dairy products, and eggs. The vitamin is also available in fortified foods such as breakfast cereals, which supply a quarter of this vitamin's recommend daily value of 6 micrograms.

But you could be lacking B_{12} even if you're not a vegan. One Tufts University study of 3,000 men and women found that up to 39 percent of people have low B_{12} levels, while about 9 percent are deficient. Tufts researchers speculated that the problem is because many people have trouble absorbing this nutrient. The B_{12} in cereal may be better absorbed than other foods, because the vitamin is sprayed on, like a supplement. (Make sure you slurp up all the milk, which is where the vitamins in breakfast cereal often end up.)

Cut out the caffeine. It could be java that's making you jumpy. It's not unusual to feel anxious after drinking too much coffee or other caffeinated quaffs. In fact, "caffeine-induced anxiety disorder" is an official medical diagnosis. Caffeine is a psychostimulant, meaning it stimulates your central nervous system and then stays in your bloodstream and tissues for as long as six hours. Most people can consume as much as 300 milligrams of caffeine before they begin to have issues (that's about three 8-ounce cups of coffee or five cups of hot or iced tea). If you're drinking more than that, cut back by a cup a day and see if your anxiety abates.

Switch to chamomile tea. Sweet-tasting chamomile is the classic remedy for frayed nerves. The herb contains the chemicals apigenin and luteolin, which promote relaxation. In one study, patients about to undergo a cardiac catheterization were given chamomile tea to see what effect it had on their cardiovascular systems. While it had no measurable effect, 10 of the 12 patients fell asleep throughout this anxiety-producing procedure! One caveat: People with severe allergies to ragweed, asters, and chrysanthemums may have an allergic reaction to chamomile. For maximum calming action, use two chamomile tea bags to 1 cup of water and steep, covered, for 10 minutes. Drink three cups a day when you're going through nerve-racking times.

When to Call THE DOCTOR

Having anxiety before taking a test, while making a speech, or waiting for the results of a medical test is perfectly normal. But you may have an anxiety disorder if you dread everyday situations; feel intense fear; worry excessively; experience physical symptoms such as chest pain, heart palpitations, shortness of breath, dizziness, or stomach problems; or have frightening and persistent memories. Treatment may include talk therapy, particularly cognitive behavior therapy, and anti-anxiety and antidepressant medications.

Tuna contains several nutrients that can actually help your body relax.

the natural
DOCTOR'S
Sunshine is a terrific anxiety-beater. Try to get out in the sun for 15 minutes a day, and during that time, don't use sunscreen. This will naturally increase your vitamin D levels, which can decrease depression and anxiety.

Open a can of calm. Canned chicken and tuna are high in the essential amino acid lysine, one of the building blocks of the brain's chemical messengers called neurotransmitters. In one 2004 study, men who were experiencing high levels of anxiety started to feel much better once their diets were fortified with lysine. The amino acid is highest in meat, fish, and beans, among other sources. One 4.5-ounce serving of canned chicken a day may be all it takes to calm you down—it contains about the amount of lysine that reduced anxiety and tamped down stress hormones in a group of healthy volunteers in a 2007 Japanese study.

Switch from sugar to honey. A 2009 New Zealand study found that rats fed high-antioxidant honey exhibited less anxiety in a complex maze than animals that were given an equivalent amount of sucrose. This may also work in the stressful maze of your life.

Have the tuna melt. Or salmon salad. Or a handful of walnuts. There's some evidence that omega-3 fatty acids, the kind abundant in canned fatty fish, walnuts, and flaxseeds, may ease anxiety symptoms by lowering levels of stress chemicals such as adrenaline and cortisol in the body. An Israeli study found that students given fish oil supplements had less test anxiety as measured by their eating and sleeping habits, cortisol levels, and mental states.

Lavender up. A few drops of pure lavender essential oil on your pillow, in your bath, or on a hanky can whisk your cares away. You can even rub it right on your skin—it's one of the few essential oils that can be applied directly. One study found that people who received a massage with lavender oil were more upbeat and had less anxiety than people who had a lavender-free massage. Another found lavender massages can even lower systolic pressure, the top blood pressure number that's associated with stress. You can also add 5 drops to a cup of boiling water and inhale for a quick calm-me-down.

Try some rosemary. If you're taking a test, you might want to tuck a little sprig of rosemary in your pocket or roll some dried rosemary in a tissue: A group of nurses taking an important test said it not only calmed their nerves, they thought it helped them "dredge up" the answers!

arthritis

Almost everyone gets a "touch" of arthritis as they age. Usually it's osteoarthritis, a joint disease caused by the wear and tear of a life filled with tennis games, toting kids, and even that great fitness program you've stuck to all these years. Rheumatoid arthritis, on the other hand, is a painful, joint-disfiguring condition that occurs when your immune system mistakes normal tissue for something foreign and attacks it. It can occur at any age. Drugs—some powerful—will help, but some easy, soothing home remedies also carry the promise of a pain-free life.

first things first

There's more to treating arthritis than just alleviating pain when it occurs. Doctors increasingly are recommending that people with arthritis go on an anti-inflammatory diet. That means nixing foods that trigger inflammation. On the no-no list are the usual suspects: fast foods, junk foods, fried foods, and processed foods. Instead, adopt a healthy Mediterranean-style diet with plenty of fresh fruits and veggies, fish, olive oil, garlic, onions, and herbs. A Swedish study of patients with rheumatoid arthritis found that those who switched to the Mediterranean eating plan had less inflammation and regained some physical function as a result.

To start improving your diet right away, look to your pantry for nuts, dried fruits, canned fruits (in juice, not sugary syrups), canned fish, and whole grains such as barley, oats, tabbouleh, couscous, and brown rice.

Pantry HEALERS

Capsaicin

Cayenne

Chamomile

Cloves

Eucalyptus essential oil

Ginger tea

Green tea

Lavender

Rice

Rosemary

Thyme

Turmeric

Vanilla essential oil

When to Call
THE DOCTOR

Since you can't be sure what kind of arthritis you have or whether your symptoms suggest another condition entirely, see your doctor if joint stiffness, swelling, redness, or pain persists more than a few days—especially if it becomes red, hot, swollen, and very painful. You could have gout (in which uric acid crystals collect in the joint, causing inflammation). You're at risk for gout if you're overweight, if your diet is loaded with red meat, or if you're a heavy beer or spirits drinker. Sometimes, infections are responsible for joint pain.

If you've already been diagnosed with arthritis, call your doctor if you notice a different type of swelling in your joints.

kitchen cabinet cures

Fill your socks with rice. No, not while you have them on! Fill a cotton sock (there's a microwave involved, so you don't want a synthetic fiber that will melt) with any kind of uncooked rice you have in your cabinet and seal it. Put it in the microwave on high for 2 to 3 minutes. Remove carefully—it will be hot. When it cools down slightly but is still nice and warm, place it on a sore, stiff joint for pain relief. It should stay warm for about half an hour. You'll love how the rice shapes to your body and provides soothing heat. If you have some lavender or other fragrant herb on hand, toss it in for a little relaxing aromatherapy, too. Reuse as often as you wish.

Sip some ginger tea. Numerous studies have found that ginger mimics nonsteroidal anti-inflammatories (NSAIDS), the front-line drugs for arthritis. It seems to work by curbing pain-causing chemicals that are part of the body's inflammatory response—and does it without the side effects of medication. Use powdered, raw, or lightly cooked fresh ginger liberally on food. Make tea by slicing three or four quarter-sized pieces of ginger into a couple of cups of boiling water. Simmer, covered, for 15 minutes and enjoy two or three times a day. You can also pick up ginger tea bags at the supermarket or health food store.

Make some spice rack rubs. Add a little cayenne, rosemary, or thyme to ½ cup of olive or vegetable oil and use it as a soothing rub. All these herbs have pain-soothing properties.

Give joints the cold-hot treatment. You'll need two containers: Fill one with cold water and a tray of ice cubes, the other with hot water at a temperature you can tolerate to touch. Always start with cold, and immerse the hurting joint for a minute, then switch to the hot water and immerse for 30 seconds. After this, switch from cold to hot for about 15 minutes, immersing the affected joint in each for 30 seconds each time. Finish with cold water for a minute.

Wash the dishes. If your hands ache, this simple kitchen task is just what the doctor ordered. First, you're dipping your hands in hot water, which can help relax muscles and joints and relieve stiffness. Second, you're exercising your hands, which helps keep your hands and fingers mobile.

Turn on the kitchen radio. Study after study has found that listening to your favorite music can ease the ache, in part by distracting you and in part by raising levels of hormones that reduce your pain sensitivity. In one Cleveland Clinic Foundation study of people with back, neck, or joint pain, one group was given a play list of relaxing tunes, a second group chose their own sound track, and a third didn't get a musical prescription. The two music groups had lower rates of arthritis pain, depression, and disability than the non-music group, which experienced a 2 percent rise in pain. The study also indicated that the kind of music you listen to doesn't matter. Classical, country, or hip-hop—you just have to like it. The people who chose their own pain-relief tunes experienced a greater reduction in pain, depression, and disability than those who listened to generic relaxing music.

Sniff some pretty spices. Studies have found that pleasant aromas like lavender can alter the perception of pain. Japanese researchers think they know why: They found that lavender reduces levels of the stress hormone cortisol, which can make you feel relaxed and less likely to be aware of pain. But lavender isn't the only pleasant aroma that works. In one study, Korean researchers found that people with arthritis had less pain and were less depressed when exposed to the aromas of a variety of kitchen spices, including marjoram, rosemary, and peppermint. Make a pain-soothing blend to inhale by adding a teaspoon or so of one of these dried herbs to a quarter-cup of vegetable oil. Take a whiff frequently.

Make your own capsaicin cream. This old home remedy is now an over-the-counter treatment for arthritis and back pain. A substance extracted from spicy cayenne pepper, capsaicin reduces levels of a compound called substance P, which transmits pain signals to the brain. You can whip up some kitchen cabinet relief by mixing a few dashes of ground cayenne with 2 to 3 teaspoons of olive oil. Apply it with gauze to unbroken skin at the painful joints several times a day. The first few doses will cause a mild burning sensation, but you'll become desensitized after a week or so. Just keep it away from the mouth, eyes, and other mucous membranes, and avoid direct contact with the pepper's seeds—cayenne is highly irritating. Mild skin irritation is a common side effect of this treatment.

Pain-relieving perfume

There's no more convenient place to stash your favorite pain-relieving scent than on your skin. You can easily whip up a skin oil that will be there—right on your arm or wrist—when you really need it.

Take 15 drops of an essential oil known to relieve pain—lavender, chamomile, eucalyptus, or vanilla—and mix it with about 2 tablespoons of a neutral oil like almond, jojoba, coconut, or avocado. Dab on your skin. You can also use it as massage oil.

Don't use the same scented oil every day. You'll soon get used to the scent and will no longer respond to its pain-relieving ability.

Weird & wacky

An old cure for "rheumatism" was to kill a rattlesnake before it had a chance to strike (always a good idea), skin it, dry it, and then put the remains in a jug of corn whiskey. Then, drink the whiskey. No surprise: There's no science to support this (and it's a little too dangerous to recommend). But there have been studies at Israel's Shulov Institute for Science looking at the possibility that snake venom, with toxins removed, could become a potential remedy for arthritis. Venom contains certain peptides—a molecule containing amino acids—that can turn off pain signals, which is handy for a reptile that needs to immobilize its prey. Of course, there's a fine line between momentary paralysis and death, so we don't want you trying this one at home.

Apply a chamomile tea poultice. Along with calming your nerves, chamomile tea is an anti-inflammatory that may help ease arthritis pain. Brew a strong infusion using four chamomile tea bags in a cup or so of hot water. Steep, covered, for 20 minutes, then squeeze and remove tea bags. Soak a clean cloth in the liquid and apply. One caveat: If you're allergic to ragweed, asters, or chrysanthemums, you may be allergic to chamomile.

Go green. Sip four cups of green tea a day. In a recent study conducted at Case Western Reserve University, researchers gave mice the equivalent of four cups of green tea a day. Then they gave the mice a substance that would normally produce rheumatoid arthritis. The tea-drinking mice were far less likely to develop arthritis than the mice that drank water. Other research found that tea's polyphenols—antioxidant properties—were also anti-inflammatory and improved arthritis-related immune responses.

Stir in some turmeric. Researchers have discovered that turmeric—the yellow spice found in curries and ballpark mustard—contains a powerful compound called curcumin, which inhibits enzymes and proteins that promote inflammation. Several studies have found that turmeric specifically reduces pain and swelling in people with arthritis. In one study of people with knee osteoarthritis, those who ate just 2 grams a day (less than a teaspoon) had pain relief and increased mobility equal to those who took 800 milligrams of ibuprofen, an over-the-counter nonsteroidal anti-inflammatory. Sprinkle about ½ teaspoon on rice or in vegetables daily. Or keep some packets of ballpark mustard in your pocket—they're the perfect dose.

Clove up! Cloves contain an anti-inflammatory chemical called eugenol that interferes with a bodily process that's linked to the kind of immune response that triggers arthritis. In one animal study, eugenol prevented the release of COX-2, a protein that spurs inflammation. That's the same protein that COX-2 inhibitor drugs like celecoxib (Celebrex) target. In another, clove compounds inhibited the inflammation process involved in conditions like arthritis, asthma, and allergies, to name a few. Cloves also contain antioxidants, important in slowing the cartilage and bone damage caused by arthritis. Cloves are used liberally in Indian cuisine and spice up everything from stew to meat loaf and even quick breads. Aim for ½ to 1 teaspoon a day.

Stick to low-allergenic foods. There's some evidence that food allergies may play a part in autoimmune illnesses like rheumatoid arthritis. At the University of Oslo in Norway, researchers found that people with the autoimmune disease had higher levels of antibodies to cow's milk, eggs, codfish, and pork than people who didn't have the disease. In one study, people with rheumatoid arthritis who followed a diet that eliminated common allergens like grains (especially gluten-containing wheat products), nuts, milk, and eggs for 10 to 18 days had significant symptomatic improvement. When they started eating these foods again, they felt worse. Other studies have found that corn, wheat, oranges, oats, rye, eggs, beef, and coffee may also be problem foods. Interestingly, many of these foods help produce arachidonic acid, a body chemical that's linked to inflammation.

 recipes for healing

Gingery Poultice

Applying crushed ginger to a painful joint can deplete the body's stores of substance P, a brain chemical that carries pain messages to your central nervous system. One study of 56 people found that ginger eased symptoms in 55 percent of people with osteoarthritis and 74 percent of those with rheumatoid arthritis.

> 3-inch piece of fresh ginger
> Olive oil

1. Peel and finely mince the ginger.
2. Mix it with just enough olive oil to form a paste.
3. Apply to the painful joint. Depending on where the pain is, you may need to wrap the ginger in place with a gauze or ace bandage. Leave in place for 10 to 15 minutes. Don't wrap too tightly. For extra relief, gently warm the ginger before applying.

Minty Pain Relief Oil

Hard to believe that the most ubiquitous flavor in the world—it's in your toothpaste!—can also kill pain. In one study, peppermint oil rubbed on the forehead and temples of chronic headache sufferers eased their pain. Mint is also a traditional ingredient of salves and oils for soothing aching muscles.

> 2 cups, more or less, fresh mint leaves
> Olive oil
> 1 tablespoon vodka or rubbing alcohol
> Few drops tincture of benzoin

1. Loosely fill a small clean jar with fresh mint leaves.
2. Cover with olive oil to fill the jar.
3. Add the vodka or rubbing alcohol. Allow it to sit on a sunny window and steep for at least 2 weeks. Then strain it and transfer it to a clean jar or bottle. Add the tincture of benzoin (available at drugstores and health food stores) to preserve the oil. Store it in a cool dark place. Rub onto aching joints as needed.

Spicy Massage Oil

This rub is packed with herbs that relieve pain and inflammation. Use it twice a day, every day, for a week or until pain abates.

> 1 tablespoon dried rosemary leaves
> 3 teaspoons celery seeds
> 1 teaspoon crushed cayenne or other red pepper
> 8 ounces olive, almond, or jojoba oil

1. Whir the rosemary, celery seeds, and red pepper until pulverized in a clean coffee or spice grinder.
2. Spoon into a glass jar with a tight-fitting lid and add the oil.
3. Shake vigorously, then cover and leave for 10 days, shaking periodically.
4. Strain through a paper coffee filter into a sterilized glass bottle and keep in a cool, dark place for up to 6 months, longer if you refrigerate it.
5. To use: Rub 1 to 2 drops onto the skin to test for any adverse reaction. If there is no reaction, gently massage a little of the oil onto the aching joint twice a day.

asthma

This inflammatory respiratory condition is more than just an allergy in hyperdrive. Asthma can narrow your airways and make breathing difficult. It's a chronic lung disease, and it can be life-threatening. Asthma should be treated by a doctor, and your asthma medications should always be at hand. But there are some pantry-ready remedies that can help reduce your symptoms and be effective during minor emergencies.

first things first

When an asthma attack occurs, take it seriously and follow these first steps:

• Use your emergency inhaler at the first sign of an attack.

• If you don't have your medications with you, take a chill pill. When your airways are acting up, panicking will only make matters worse. Begin taking slow, measured, deep breaths and focus on the breath going into your nose to a count of four and then coming out of your mouth to a count of four.

• Next step, grab a cup of coffee, a glass of cola, or another highly caffeinated beverage to help open your airways. Caffeine is chemically similar to the asthma drug theophylline. It is effective both as a remedy and a preventive measure. In an Italian survey of 72,284 people, those with asthma who drank one cup of coffee per day had 5 percent fewer asthma attacks than those who drank none; drinking two cups a day cut the rate by 23 percent, while three cups cut

Pantry HEALERS

Antacids

Apples

Coffee

Fatty fish (herring, salmon, mackerel, tuna)

Greens

Mandarin oranges

Nuts

Olive oil

Spinach

Tomatoes

Vegetables

If the emergency inhaler that your doctor has prescribed doesn't bring relief within 15 minutes, call your doctor, ask someone else to call your doctor for you, or call 911 or your local emergency number.

Severe asthma attacks can be fatal. Always carry your inhalers and medications with you. Never hesitate to seek emergency help if your attack seems particularly severe.

it by 28 percent. The researchers suspect that the caffeine in coffee acts as a bronchodilator, expanding airways that become constricted when you have asthma.

kitchen cabinet cures

Go fishing—and take your vitamins. An Australian study found that kids who ate fatty fish like herring, salmon, mackerel, and tuna were 75 percent less likely to be asthmatic. Why would fish protect against asthma? The omega-3 fatty acids found in fish reduce inflammation, which is at the root of most airway problems. Another study found that when asthmatic kids took omega-3 supplements, along with vitamin C and zinc, their lung function improved and they had better control over their asthma.

Get magnesium. One study found that adults with roughly 500 milligrams of magnesium in their diets had better airflow and more control of their asthma than those who consumed less. Foods high in magnesium: nuts, particularly almonds, cashews, and peanuts.

Crunch a Granny Smith. A number of studies that have looked at the diets of children and adults with asthma have found that an apple a day keeps the wheezing away. No apples in your pantry? Apple juice helps, too.

Veg out big-time. Eating lots of fresh vegetables helped protect residents of three townships in China from asthma, according to one study. But people who consumed fewer vegetables had more wheezing and lung problems. The key: Produce contains myriad antioxidants that can protect airways against stress and damage, the kind that lead to increased asthma incidence and more difficult symptoms. Good news: Canned veggies are also loaded with antioxidants. So mine your pantry (or the supermarket shelves) for fresh or canned spinach, carrots, collard greens, mustard greens, and other yummy veggies, all ready to serve up in a flash.

Take an antacid. Particularly before bedtime. Studies have found that inhaling even tiny amounts of stomach fluids that have backed up into the esophagus may trigger asthma symptoms. And surprisingly large numbers of people have the problem of backed-up stomach acids—it's called gastroesophageal reflux disease, or GERD. For many people, GERD can be more pronounced when you're lying down, so among the lifestyle changes to consider: Don't eat up to three hours before going to bed, and elevate the head of your bed four to six inches. Avoid caffeine, alcohol, and chocolate after dinner, while you're at it. These can relax the muscles of your esophageal sphincter, which can allow stomach contents to back up. Instead of three big squares a day, eat more frequent smaller meals. Eating heavily at one sitting is also a GERD risk factor.

Check your other drugs. In some people, popping a nonsteroidal anti-inflammatory like aspirin or ibuprofen for a headache can bring on another problem—an asthma attack. Another drug culprit: beta-blockers, often prescribed to treat heart disease, hypertension, migraine headache, and glaucoma. If you've noticed the connection, talk to your doc about alternatives.

Use more olive oil. In a study of children on the island of Crete, researchers found that those who had high consumption of margarine were more likely to have allergies and to wheeze, a symptom of asthma. One likely reason: Margarine is high in omega-6 fatty acids, which can trigger inflammation. Kissing cousins to margarine are cooking oils high in omega-6s, such as corn, safflower, and sunflower oils. To avoid omega-6s, use olive oil as a dip for bread and for your everyday cooking.

Be cautious about allergy provokers in your pantry. Just as respiratory allergies can trigger asthma symptoms, so can food allergies. Among the leading culprits are nuts and soy (which is ubiquitous in processed foods).

Pour on tomato sauce. Add salsa to your omelet, toss canned tomatoes in your chili and casseroles, and add tomato paste or sauce to meat loaf and vegetable dishes. Several studies have found that eating tomatoes is linked to fewer asthma symptoms. In one study, researchers found that people who ate tomatoes three times a week experienced less wheezing and fewer asthma-like symptoms.

Toss mandarin orange segments in your spinach salad. Increasing your intake of vitamins C and A may help reduce your risk of asthma. A recent review of studies

Your nose knows

Inhale through your nose, not your mouth. That's a fundamental part of Buteyko breathing, a breathing retraining method that was developed in the 1960s and is starting to catch on again. Several small studies have found the program of nasal breathing, breath-holding, and relaxation reduces asthma symptoms and the use of emergency medications. While Buteyko breathing requires some study and practice, you can start breathing through your nose right away. Nasal breathing helps protect the airways in part by preventing dryness and warming and cleaning the air that's inhaled into the lungs. It also helps maintain normal levels of carbon dioxide and nitric oxide in the lungs, both of which help prevent tightening of the airways.

Studies show that eating tomatoes is linked to fewer asthma symptoms.

related to asthma and diet found that people who had low levels of both these vitamins were more inclined to have the lung disease. How they may work: Vitamin A helps maintain the integrity of the cells that line the airways. Vitamin C is a potent antioxidant that can help prevent damage to the immune system—including the mucosa, a first line of defense. It may also help regenerate other antioxidants, such as vitamin E, which can be damaged in the fight against oxidative stress. Vitamin A is also abundant in fortified foods such as cereal and canned veggies like spinach, collard or mustard greens, sweet potato, pumpkin, and carrot.

Place "vacancy" signs outside the roach motel. Every bit of these nasty critters is allergenic, from their saliva and feces to their eggs. Studies have shown that if you're allergic to them, it can make asthma symptoms worse. So, give them the heave-ho by placing roach traps all around the kitchen—under the sink, behind the refrigerator or stove—flush with the wall. Also scatter them in other rooms where roaches like to congregate, like bathrooms and basement. If you get a lot of little visitors, you may need to bring out the boric acid and sprinkle behind appliances and under the stove, as well as placing it in cracks in walls or floors, which you should seal with caulk. Don't do this if you have pets or small children though.

Prevent mice infestations. Soak a rag or paper towel with peppermint oil and wipe it along baseboards. This common, nontoxic home remedy is recommended by some professional pest control experts for repelling rodents. Apparently, they're not fans of the mint fragrance.

Preventing asthma from day one

You may protect your baby from developing asthma if you eat a diet rich in vitamin E, according to several scientific studies. It's been estimated that E-deficiency during pregnancy may explain up to a third of childhood asthma cases. Scientists hypothesize that the antioxidant powers of vitamin E protect the immune system and early development of the airways. Wheat germ and wheat germ oil are excellent sources, but you can also get it in nuts, peanut butter, mango, and fortified cereals. Another gift you can give your baby: Eat yogurt during your last month of pregnancy and while you're breast-feeding. The probiotic Lactobacillus GG seems to decrease asthma in children whose mothers followed this dietary tip.

recipes for healing

Toxic cleaning products can trigger an asthma attack. Be gentler on your system and your home by using just two simple pantry staples to make your own surprisingly effective cleaners.

Baking soda

Porcelain. Place a little baking soda on a wet rag and use to scrub porcelain tubs and sinks and the toilet bowl.

Ovens (not self-cleaning ovens). Mix a cup of baking soda with enough water to make a paste. Apply to oven surfaces and allow to stand for 15 minutes. Scrub off with a scouring pad.

White vinegar

Windows. Fill a spray bottle with ¼ cup white vinegar and enough water to reach the top. Spray windows and wipe clean with crumpled newspaper.

Floors. Mix ½ cup of white vinegar in a pail of warm water. Don't worry about the salad smell—it evaporates as the floor dries.

Clogged drains. Pour ½ cup of baking soda down the drain, followed by ½ cup of vinegar. It will fizz. Let it sit for a few minutes, then pour down a teakettle full of boiling water.

Copper. Mix equal parts vinegar and salt (about 1 tablespoon to start), rub on surfaces, and rinse completely with water.

athlete's foot

Pantry HEALERS

Aloe

Baking soda

Cloves

Mustard powder

Onion juice

Oregano

Tea tree oil

Thyme

Vinegar

Yogurt

That itching, burning sensation in your sneakers means that a fungus called tinea pedis is taking up residence between your toes. (Yes, go ahead and say, "Ewww!") Athlete's foot also causes blisters, scaling, oozing, and crusting and, if left untreated, can spread to your heels, palms, and between your fingers. Fortunately, nature has provided a plethora of antifungals and soothing remedies that you probably already store right in your kitchen.

first things first

A few basics can help protect feet from the infernal itch. These are tops on our list if your feet are prone to athlete's foot:

• Regularly wash your feet with soap and water or use a basin of water with about an ounce of vinegar added. Pay special attention to the space between your toes where tinea fungus love to settle.

• What's good for a baby's bottom is good for your tootsies, too. After washing and drying feet well, sprinkle on some talcum, cornstarch, or antifungal powder.

• Be selective about footwear. You may love the latest celebrity-endorsed sports shoe, but if it's all leather, it could turn into a steamy condo for fungus.

• When your feet sweat, you want socks that will wick the moisture away, and cotton socks—well, they just stay wet. Wear sports socks specially designed to keep your feet dry.

- If your feet sweat a lot, change your socks a couple of times a day and alternate pairs of shoes to allow them time to dry out. You may need to do this more frequently with shoes and socks you use during exercise.

- Never go barefoot in public places! Wear sandals or water shoes, especially in gym showers or at the pool.

- But go barefoot at home. Going shoeless around the house will allow your feet to dry and "breathe," which will discourage fungal growth.

kitchen cabinet cures

Let baking soda quench the burning itch. Add enough water to 1 tablespoon of baking powder to make a paste. Rub it on the parts of your foot that itch. It will provide quick relief. Let the paste sit for 5 to 10 minutes, then rinse thoroughly and dry your feet completely. Dust your piggies with talc or cornstarch afterward.

Try powdered mustard. Put a tablespoon or so of mustard powder from your spice rack into a warm footbath and give your feet a good, long soak. Mustard has antifungal properties.

Dunk those dogs in yogurt. The live acidophilus bacteria in yogurt send in friendly microorganisms to vanquish the unfriendly fungus that's causing the burning, itching, and flaking between your toes. Dab a little plain yogurt on the affected areas, let it dry, then rinse off and dry thoroughly.

Give your feet and your socks the vinegar treatment. Soak a cotton ball in vinegar and dab affected areas several times a day. Likewise, kill fungus in your socks by soaking them in vinegar for a half an hour.

Fight odor with odor. An old home remedy that seems to have some merit is using fresh onion juice to treat athlete's foot. One reason it may work: Onions have antimicrobial properties, meaning they're the natural enemy of bacteria and fungi. To use, whir a roughly chopped onion in a food processor with enough water to make a paste. Place your feet in a basin and slather on the smelly slurry. Let it sit for 30 minutes or so before rinsing off and thoroughly drying your feet.

When to Call THE DOCTOR

If you have diabetes and a case of athlete's foot, make an appointment. The disease can cause circulation problems and nerve damage that makes any wound or infection more serious.

Call your physician if you notice your feet are warm to the touch, swollen, or have red streaks, all symptomatic of infection. Ditto if a fever or pus or other discharge accompanies the condition. Finally, consult your doctor if you've tried lots of remedies and the condition doesn't go away. Stronger antifungal medication may be your only solution.

Check your pet

If you've tried it all, and you *still* have athlete's foot, consider your pet. In one study of 211 dogs, researchers found 89 fungal strains on them that can infect humans. In fact, 11 dog owners who had athlete's foot or jock itch (infection of the groin area by the same group of fungi that cause athlete's foot) were infected with a fungus strain also carried by their pets. If you think your pet might be causing your fungal troubles, ask your veterinarian to check your canine or kitty.

Try tea tree oil. If you don't have tea tree oil in your medicine cabinet, you should. It's an essential home remedy item for scores of problems. This potent antiseptic has been used for all kinds of skin conditions for more than a century. One study found that tea tree oil was as effective as an over-the-counter remedy for athlete's foot for relieving burning, itching, inflammation, and scaling. Add a few drops to a tablespoon of witch hazel and apply to the affected area with a cotton swab three times a day. It can cause dermatitis (skin inflammation) in some people, so use sparingly the first time and don't use further if a rash develops.

Give your feet some thyme. Mix up a cup of strong thyme tea (2 tablespoons of dried thyme to 8 ounces of boiling water, covered and steeped for 10 minutes). Strain it, and when it cools, soak a cotton cloth in the tea and wipe your feet, particularly the reddened areas and between your toes. Dry thoroughly with a clean cloth. Thyme has antifungal properties. You can also try the same brew substituting cloves or oregano, two other powerhouse antifungal agents in your spice rack. (For a one-two punch at the visiting fungi, dab tea tree oil diluted in a little witch hazel on afterward.)

recipe for healing

Aloe Ointment

Aloe-based remedies bought at the drugstore are expensive, but are made from the same gel you get for free from the aloe plant on your windowsill.

> 1 aloe stalk
> ½ teaspoon tea tree oil
> 10 drops lavender oil

1. Slit the aloe stalk and use a teaspoon to scoop off all the gel.

2. Blend in the tea tree and lavender oils.

3. Rub the salve into the affected areas. The aloe helps heal raw, cracked skin, and the two oils fight fungi. Use as often as necessary.

back pain

If you've never had back pain, you belong to a very small club. As many as 8 out of 10 people have had an aching back at some time in their lives. Often, the pain is just the result of an injury—a fall on the ice, lifting a too-heavy load, twisting in a way the body was not designed to twist. A little ice, a little heat, and a few days of painkillers and the problem is over. But for too many of us, back pain is an ongoing dilemma. There are many natural ways to ease the hurt when it happens and keep it from happening in the first place. Here are many of a kitchen-cabinet nature.

first things first

Home remedies have their place in dealing with back pain, but when it really hurts, start with these steps:

• Apply a heating pad for 20 to 30 minutes at a time. Or use the hot rice-sock remedy detailed in the Arthritis section.

• Use an over-the-counter pain medication, such as acet-aminophen, ibuprofen, naproxen, or ketoprofen.

• To take pressure and weight off your back, lie on your back with pillows under your knees and your hips and knees bent. You can also rest your feet on a chair from that position.

• Don't rest longer than one or two days. Bed rest can weaken your muscles even further. Try to walk around as much as possible.

Pantry HEALERS

Canned fish

Cherries

Dark chocolate

Flaxseed

Fruits and vegetables

Nuts

Olive oil

Tea

Vanilla

Vitamin D

Walnuts

THE DOCTOR

If you try traditional methods, plus one or more kitchen cabinet cures, and still have pain after two to three weeks, check in with your doc. Do so as well if you have any numbness or pain that travels down your leg or if pain is so intense you can't move. Likewise, give the doc a call if an injury triggered the pain or if you have other symptoms such as fever, nausea, vomiting, abdominal distress, weakness, or sweating.

• To reduce any curve in your spine, sleep on your side with your knees bent. You can also put a pillow between your knees. If you're a back sleeper, make sure you have a pillow under your knees and your lower back.

• Avoid sleeping on your stomach unless you have a pillow under your hips.

kitchen cabinet cures

Get your daily D. One of the little-known contributors to back pain is lack of vitamin D, the "sunshine" vitamin. In one study, more than 80 percent of people between the ages of 15 and 52 who had chronic low back pain were deficient in this vitamin, which is necessary for maintaining normal levels of calcium in the blood. When they supplemented their diets with vitamin D, their back pain improved. And in the small number of people with normal vitamin D levels, 69 percent also experienced less pain when they took extra vitamin D.

The best way to get vitamin D is to spend 15 minutes a day three times a week in the sun, although for people in

Eat away back pain

Certain foods can quench the inflammation that contributes to all kinds of pain. Your back pain diet should include:

• Olive oil

• Canned salmon, sardines packed in water or olive oil, mackerel, albacore tuna, flaxseed, walnuts

• Cherries. One study showed that drinking 12 ounces of tart cherry juice twice a day for eight days, reduced muscle pain and strain. Canned tart cherries, packed in their own juice, would also be helpful.

• Vegetable protein (such as soy)

• Vegetables and fruits of every hue—canned or frozen are fine, as long as they're not packed with heavy syrup or salt

• Nuts

• Tea

• Dark chocolate in moderation (1 ounce a day)

Then, there are the foods NOT to eat. These foods can increase inflammation inside the body, fanning the pain:

• Vegetable oils such as corn, safflower, sunflower, cottonseed, and mixed vegetable oils

• Margarine and vegetable shortening

• Processed foods

• Products containing high-fructose corn syrup

• Saturated fats, including meat, butter, and full-fat dairy products

• Foods made with trans fats

northern climes the sun may not be strong enough to activate the vitamin D raw material that's stored in the skin. And getting that much sun can be nearly impossible during winter months. Some nutrition experts suggest taking 1,000 IU of vitamin D_3 every day.

Hit the vanilla. Dab a few drops of vanilla onto a handkerchief and sniff it to make the pain go away. It will help relieve your stress, which can exacerbate pain of any kind. A study done at the Columbia University Medical Center found that people who smelled vanilla while doing stress tests had more stable heart rates and lower blood pressure—markers of relaxation—than those who took the same tests without any exposure to scent. If you're tense, studies have found, you can be more pain-sensitive.

Listen to the kitchen radio. A study done at the Cleveland Clinic Foundation found that people with back and other kinds of aches who listened to music they enjoyed for an hour a day experienced a 25 percent decrease in their pain. Researchers aren't sure if it's relaxation or distraction that does the trick, but if you're in pain, music can be, well, music to your ears.

the natural
DOCTOR'S Rx

The first thing to do when you have a bad back, once the pain resolves, is to strengthen your abdominal muscles. Stronger muscles in your body's midsection will take lots of pressure off your spine and hips. Take up a program of "core" and abdominal strengthening exercises, such as crunches.

Weird
& wacky

We just love this old North Carolinian folk remedy for a bad back: Lie down (presumably outside) and when you hear the call of a whip-poor-will, roll over three times. This remedy may have been inspired by one that hails from Sussex, England. There, folkloric advice calls for the back pain sufferer to roll on the ground at the sound of spring's first cuckoo. We suspect the rolling had something to do with stretching out sore back muscles—and birdsong is one of the best soul lifters around.

recipes for healing

Classic Mustard Plaster

You may remember this one from your childhood. It worked well when you had chest congestion, and it works equally well on back pain.

> 2 or more tablespoons white or brown mustard seeds, ground in coffee grinder (or 2 tablespoons powdered mustard, such as Coleman's)
> 3 tablespoons flour
> 1 egg white
> 1–4 tablespoons warm water

1. Stir the mustard and flour together in a small bowl.
2. Blend in the egg white and add enough water to form a thick paste.
3. Spread the mustard plaster on a cloth or paper towel.
4. Have someone place the cloth or towel on your back, mustard side on the skin, and leave on for about 20 minutes. Mustard seeds act like a counter-irritant to help reduce pain, much like over-the-counter capsaicin creams.

Camphor Oil Rub for Back Pain

You don't have to shell out dough for an over-the-counter cream for back pain. Instead, try this effective, easy-to-make rub.

> 1 tablespoon finely minced fresh ginger (or 1 tablespoon powdered ginger)
> 1 tablespoon dried rosemary
> ¼ cup olive oil
> 5 drops peppermint oil (optional)
> 2 drops camphor or wintergreen essential oil (optional)

1. Whir the ginger and rosemary in a clean coffee grinder till very fine and blended.
2. Mix the olive oil and the peppermint and camphor oils together in a small bowl.
3. Blend in the rosemary-ginger mixture.
4. Have someone rub the fragrant mixture into the painful area of your back and cover with a piece of flannel or an old T-shirt. Then put a heating pad over the cloth for 15–20 minutes and rest while the rubs soak in. You can double the recipe for larger areas. Wash it off during a soak in the tub, if you like.

belching

In some countries, belching after a meal is interpreted as "My compliments to the chef!" In many others, it's interpreted more as "My disrespects to the chef!" Of course, most belches are neither—they are just sudden, uncontrolled releases of gas, without any intended meaning at all. Belching is almost always caused by swallowing too much air when you eat or drink (aerophagia). That means it's easy to turn down the volume. Mother Nature has remedies—and you can find them in your kitchen pantry.

first things first

To prevent everyday belching, try these measures:

• Eat and drink slowly. Most everyday belches are caused by swallowing too much air while you're eating—because you eat too fast, gulp your food, or sip through a straw.

• Use anti-gas products like Beano more frequently. They contain an enzyme that helps digest the substances that most often cause gas. Most people think to use it just with beans, but there are many other "gassy" foods, including apples, bananas, lentils, cruciferous vegetables such as broccoli and Brussels sprouts, and onions.

• Avoid chewing gum, sucking on hard candy, and drinking "sparkling" or carbonated beverages (the carbon dioxide they contain produces gas in the warm climate of your stomach).

• Take a walk. A little stroll after you eat can help move food through the digestive system.

Pantry HEALERS

Chamomile

Fennel

Fenugreek seeds

Ginger

Papaya (dried)

Peppermint

Pineapple juice

Yellow
  mustard seeds

• Gastroesophageal reflux disease

• Gastritis or stomach inflammation, which may be caused by infection from the bacterium *Helicobacter pylori*

• A hiatal hernia

• A problem called gastroparesis, which prevents the stomach from emptying. It can be a symptom of diabetes, thyroid disorders, or pancreatitis

• Intolerances to certain foods including dairy products, fructose (fruit sugar), and sorbitol (a carbohydrate-based sweetener)

kitchen cabinet cures

Sip peppermint tea. Steep one or two peppermint leaf tea bags in hot water for 10 to 15 minutes. Keep a cover on the tea to prevent the medicinal oil from evaporating. Drink a cup before each meal. Peppermint calms your stomach muscles and helps food—especially belch-worthy fatty stuff—move along a little faster. But don't use it if you have gastric reflux or heartburn—peppermint relaxes the sphincter muscles that keep stomach contents from backing up into the esophagus.

Head gas off at the pass. If you're a post-meal burper, try this 30 minutes before lunch and dinner. Add ½ teaspoon of whole yellow mustard seeds to a half cup of water. Drink it down without chewing the seeds and see what a difference a little mustard can make.

Serve pineapple juice. Pineapple contains bromelain, a digestive enzyme. It can help prevent gas and bloating after a meal. Dried papaya slices may also curb belching.

Chew some fenugreek seeds. This ancient Indian digestive helper (and curry powder ingredient) is now being studied for its ability to control blood sugar by slowing down sugar absorption from foods. It also helps move food through the gastric tract. Fenugreek seeds have a pleasingly exotic, smoky taste.

Brew some chamomile. It doesn't prevent belching per se, but it does calm you down. And that's useful, because stress and anxiety can cause you to swallow large amounts of air, due to more irregular and excited breathing patterns. Chamomile also calms gastrointestinal spasms.

Try fennel. This relative of dill has a pleasant licorice taste and is an antispasmodic, meaning it relaxes the smooth muscles of your digestive tract. You can eat fennel seeds raw or boil 1 teaspoon in a cup of water for 10 minutes, covered. Then strain and drink warm or cool.

Go the ginger route. Promote better digestion with some ginger tea, either with a tea bag or by steeping 1 teaspoon of dried ginger (or 1 tablespoon chopped fresh ginger) in a cup of boiling water for 10 to 15 minutes. Cover while steeping to preserve the essential oils. Sip slowly after meals to relieve gas.

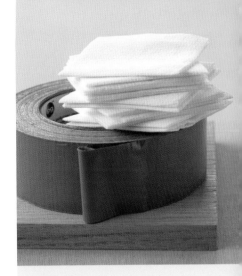

blisters

Perhaps you took a long walk in new shoes. Or you double dug a flower bed without wearing gloves. Or you played 18 holes of golf rather than your usual nine. And what do you have to show for it? Blisters, literally a symptom of something that's rubbed you the wrong way. Not to worry: They're easily mended and easily prevented with home remedies. Start with the basics.

first things first

To keep blisters at bay, follow these simple suggestions:

• Wear shoes that fit properly. You should have a thumb's width of space between your longest toe and the tip of the shoe.

• Wear socks designed to wick moisture away from the feet. Usually, those are made of synthetic fibers. And skip tube socks—they rarely fit well. You want a well-fitted sock with a heel and no visible seams that could rub your foot. Change socks frequently when you're especially active.

• When doing any repetitive task with handheld tools or sports gear—be it raking leaves, swinging a golf club, or digging a hole—wear gloves made for the task. They protect your skin and improve your grip.

• Apply antiperspirant to your feet. Yes, the same kind you use under your arms will reduce sweat on your feet, too. Some studies have found that reducing moisture also reduces blister formation.

Pantry HEALERS

Alcohol

Aloe

Baking soda

Chamomile

Duct tape

Seek medical care if your blister is more than 2 inches across or if it appears to be infected. Symptoms of infection: redness that extends beyond the borders of the blister, yellow crusting, oozing pus, prolonged pain, or a fever. If your blister isn't caused by friction, it could be poison ivy, poison oak, chicken pox, eczema, shingles, or another condition. If you're not sure, call the doctor. It's also a good idea to make the call if you have diabetes and have a blister on your foot. Diabetes can cause poor circulation, which slows healing, and may cause nerve damage so you can't feel pain.

If a blister appears, your first steps should be these:

• Apply an antiseptic. As soon as a blister rears itself, give it a wipe with hydrogen peroxide if it's intact. Use an antibiotic ointment if it's ruptured.

• Trim the flap. Using small scissors that you've wiped with alcohol, cut the flap of loose skin from a ruptured blister to avoid a sudden tear which can cause bleeding (and open up a wound to bacterial infection).

• Keep it covered. Even if it's intact, you will still want to keep a blister covered with something like moleskin or other bandage to protect yourself from irritation and potential infection—not to mention so that you can wear your shoes without making matters worse.

kitchen cabinet cures

Soak in fortified chamomile tea. Use three tea bags to a pint of boiled water, and brew, covered for 10 minutes. Stir in a teaspoon of baking soda for a soothing and antiseptic soak. If the blister is on a place you can't soak, dip a cotton gauze pad in the tea and apply.

Use duct tape. It was good enough for McGyver, and runners use the sticky stuff all the time. Clean your feet and apply alcohol to the blister. Place a small layer of gauze over it, then lay a piece of good-quality duct tape (with a fabric core) over the area. Make sure it lays smoothly with no wrinkles. Duct tape is also good for preventing blisters. Just make sure your foot is fully extended when you put on the tape.

Leaf it. That aloe vera plant on the windowsill will come in handy here. Snap off a leaf and gently rub the healing gel on the blister.

Find your sewing kit. If a blister is large or in an inconvenient spot where you might rupture it anyway, it might be better to drain it. However, be aware that an open blister is more prone to infection. To pop it, wipe a sewing needle (and the blister) with alcohol, then prick the blister in one or two places and gently press out the fluid. Apply an antibiotic ointment and a bandage immediately.

body odor

When the answer to the question, "What's that terrible smell?" is "Yikes! It's me!" it's time to take some action. Though a dousing of perfume might replace one smell with a more pleasant one, it's probably better to attack the problem at a more fundamental level. And you can do it with ease, naturally.

first things first

These may seem painfully obvious, but just in case, here's a basic checklist to perform before you try more involved remedies:

• Wash daily. Use an antibacterial soap to stifle the bugs that make you smell in the first place.

• Dry thoroughly, especially your feet. Bacteria love damp spaces, such as the gaps between your toes, so give various parts of your body a blast from your hair dryer for about 30 seconds after bathing to make sure you are really dry.

• Use antiperspirant if you tend to sweat. These products block pores that produce sweat under the arms.

• But if you rarely sweat, use deodorant. It makes your skin acidic, which discourages bacterial growth. It usually contains perfume to mask odor. And yes, you can use it on other parts of your body that generate odor.

• Wear natural fibers. Cotton, wool, and silk allow your skin to breathe. If you exercise (and/or sweat) a lot, choose clothing designed to wick moisture away from the body.

Pantry HEALERS

Baking soda
Chamomile
Hydrogen peroxide
Lavender
Lemon
Parsley
Peppermint
Rosemary
Sage
Rubbing alcohol
Vinegar
Witch hazel

When to Call THE DOCTOR

Nearly all cases of body odor are harmless and the causes obvious. But in rare cases, body odors are an indication of a more serious condition. Call your doctor if:

• You suddenly develop a strong, unusual body odor. This is characteristic of kidney failure or a condition called diabetic ketoacidosis, in which you have too little insulin in your body to use glucose for energy.

• You smell like fish. You may have an uncommon genetic condition called trimethylaminuria, or fish odor syndrome, in which your body can't break down a nitrogen-containing compound in some foods.

• You smell like maple syrup. This is a symptom of—and we're not making this up—maple syrup urine disease, a genetic metabolic disorder in which your body can't metabolize certain amino acids. It's managed with a special diet, but if not diagnosed in time, can cause brain damage.

• You have unusual body odor and a rash. A bacterial infection called erythrasma is associated with a strong odor and brownish-red, scaly patches under the arms, in the groin area, or between the toes. It's treated with a topical antibiotic.

kitchen cabinet cures

Tone down the garlic and onions. Though we often recommend these two for their power to prevent infections, take them off the pantry shopping list if you have body-odor issues. They're not only the cause of bad breath, but in some folks, their scent can literally ooze out of their pores. Cumin is another body odor culprit. You don't have to eliminate them from your diet—they're good for you. But if you're going to be in close quarters, take a temporary pass.

Drink some chamomile tea. Body odor is often caused when perspiration—which is odorless—meets bacteria on the skin. Exercise is the healthy reason for sweat. Stress, on the other hand, can cause your sweat glands to get busy as well. When you're feeling nervous, overwhelmed, and anxious, brew a cup of this chamomile tea, which will calm you down immediately. And no one will ever see—or smell—you sweat.

Have a baking soda bath. It removes odors in your fridge and works on you, too. Baking soda is also mildly antiseptic. Alternatively, use it as a dusting powder like you would use talcum.

Swab on sage. This herb, which you probably associate with poultry seasoning, has antibacterial and antiperspiration properties. Add a teaspoon or two of dried sage to a cup of boiling water, allow it to cool, and apply with a cloth to sweat-prone areas, avoiding the face and genitals. You can also drink a cup or two a day to cool you off, though pregnant women should abstain.

Slice a lemon. Like over-the-counter deodorants, acidic fruits can change the pH of your skin, making it a hostile environment for the bacteria that cause odor. Slice a lemon in half and rub under your armpits and on the soles of your feet.

Have a witch hazel splash. Apply this astringent (drying), deodorizing liquid directly to your skin or apply with a cotton pad.

Hit on the germs. Use rubbing alcohol, vinegar, or hydrogen peroxide on underarms to discourage bacteria.

Make your own herbal bath solution. All you need is a piece of cheesecloth or a stocking, which you can fill with fragrant herbs of your choice, including lavender, sage, parsley, peppermint, or rosemary. Tie securely and toss into the tub. You can also rub the pouch over the areas where odor is problematic.

Pass on the hot stuff. Some foods, like chili peppers, can cause you to break out in a sweat. If smelly sweat is a problem for you, stay away from any food that increases it.

Chew on some parsley. This kitchen herb is 70 percent chlorophyll, which is known to clean up bad odors. It's also antibacterial. Nibble on a few sprigs after you've indulged in something especially odiferous.

Weird & wacky

We wouldn't do this ourselves, but an old, traditional body-odor treatment was to add 2 or 3 cups of tomato juice to bathwater and soak in the solution for 15 minutes. The effectiveness of this harmless treatment has never been verified—but since it's also used for bathing dogs who've gotten "skunked," there must be something to it.

recipe for healing

Herbal Bath Deodorant

This lovely and fragrant bath will not only freshen you, but also will kill the bacteria that cause odor.

> 1 tablespoon dried rosemary
> 1 tablespoon dried sage
> 1 tablespoon dried peppermint
> 1 tablespoon dried lavender, if available

1. Whir the rosemary, sage, peppermint, and lavender in a clean coffee grinder.

2. Place them in a doubled piece of cheesecloth. Gather up the corners of the cheesecloth and tie securely.

3. Toss the bundle into a hot bath to scent the water. Rub the herbal pouch all over the skin, paying particular attention to areas where odor is a problem.

boils

Pantry HEALERS

Black tea

Chamomile

Epsom salts

Lavender

Oregano

Tea tree oil

Thyme

Turmeric

It looks like a pimple on steroids, but a boil is a different kind of skin infection—usually caused by a specific bacteria called *Staphylococcus aureus*. They can be as small as a pea and as large as a golf ball and are most common on the face, neck, armpit, shoulders, and bottom, generally "boiling" up from a hair follicle or oil gland. They can be quite painful. But with a few home remedies, they can also be treated effectively.

first things first

When a boil boils up, start your home treatment simply:

• Dip a soft cloth into warm water and press against the boil for 20 minutes at least three or four times a day to encourage it to drain. Unless it drains, it can't heal. The heat also increases the amount of blood around the boil, sending more infection-fighting white blood cells to the site to fight it.

• Wash your hands frequently. Because boils are usually caused by a staph germ, you don't want to spread the infection to other parts of your body or other people in your life. Wash hands thoroughly with hot water and soap after touching the boil.

• Don't squeeze or pierce the boil. This can spread the infection.

• Take over-the-counter painkillers. Unlike most skin eruptions, boils can really hurt until they rupture, but a low dose of ibuprofen or acetaminophen can ease the pain.

kitchen cabinet cures

Add some natural antiseptics. Go plain water one better. Prepare a cup of thyme tea (1 teaspoon of dried thyme to 1 cup of boiling water) and use as a compress, particularly after the boil has ruptured. Thyme contains a natural antiseptic called thymol. Or try chamomile tea; it's anti-inflammatory and can ease redness and pain. Lavender and oregano also have antibacterial properties.

Try black tea. A plain warm tea bag can act as a compress, too—it contains tannins, which also have antibacterial properties.

Treat with tea tree oil. Studies have found that this oil from an Australian tree is highly effective against staph infections, even those that are antibiotic-resistant. Just dab a little on the boil several times a day.

Make a turmeric paste. An old Ayurvedic remedy from India involves making a paste of 4 to 5 tablespoons of the spice with water and applying it to the boil. Studies have found that turmeric is effective against staph and other common bacteria.

Soak with Epsom salts. Much as the salt you eat draws fluids into your bloodstream, a soaking solution of Epsom salts can draw fluid out of the skin, shrinking the underlying tissues and reducing inflammation. That's why Epsom salts are such a popular folk remedy for skin troubles, ranging from insect bites to poison ivy to boils.

When to Call THE DOCTOR

If a boil lasts longer than two weeks, feels warm, has red streaks stretching out from it, or is on the spine or the middle of the face, you may have a more serious infection that requires medical help. Likewise, if a boil is unusually deep or large, or there's more than one in the same area, you might need to have it lanced by a doctor.

Weird & wacky

This old English remedy, gets our vote for strangest of them all. Apply a poultice to the boil. When you remove the poultice, place it in a corpse-containing coffin. Theory was, the boils would leave you and pass on to the dead person, where they could do no harm.

recipe for healing

Germ-Killing Poultice

¼ cup hot water
5 drops tea tree essential oil
5 drops lavender essential oil

1. Put the hot water in a bowl. Swirl the essential oils through the water, then soak a gauze pad in the solution.

2. Gently squeeze out excess fluid and apply it directly to the boil. Cover with plastic wrap and secure with a bandage or tape. Leave in place for at least an hour. Repeat twice a day.

breast tenderness

Pantry HEALERS

Castor oil

Decaf coffee

Flaxseed

Magnesium-rich foods (bran cereals, almonds, brown rice, spinach)

Oatmeal

Vitamin E

You're shifting in bed, turn over onto your stomach, and ouch! Your breasts feel like they've been punched. Most breast pain is harmless and cyclic—it accompanies your period, fueled by hormones. Some women may also have lumpy breasts along with the tenderness, a condition called fibrocystic breast disease. You may find instant relief right in your kitchen.

first things first

Before you open your pantry door for a cure, open your closet door and consider your bras. Poor fit can cause your breasts to sag, droop, or be pinched. That lack of support can cause breast tenderness (and back pain). And when your breasts are tender from premenstrual syndrome, a supportive bra can minimize movement and ease pain.

To measure yourself for a bra, run a tape measure just under your breasts around your back and rib cage. It should rest flat on your skin, neither tight nor sagging. Take that number and add five to it. If you get an odd number, round it down rather than up. Over time bras tend to sag anyway, and there are hooks on the back that will allow you to adjust the tightness.

Determine your cup size by measuring across the fullest part of your breasts while wearing a non-padded bra. Subtract the chest measurement. If the difference is an inch, you're an A; 2 inches, you're a B; and so on. Always try on a bra before buying—and shop during the time in your menstrual cycle when your breasts aren't swollen.

kitchen cabinet cures

Switch to decaf. Cyclic breast pain is a hormonal issue. It may be exacerbated by foods containing methylxanthine, including coffee, tea, and cola (and some strange bedfellows like bananas, mushrooms, cheese, wine, beer, pickles, and chocolate). Caffeinated coffee is probably the biggest culprit, so stick with decaf.

Have oatmeal for breakfast. A recent survey of more than 3,000 midlife women found that those who ate lots of fiber (bountiful in vegetables, whole grains, beans, and fruit) had less breast tenderness than those who ate less roughage. Most women should consume 20 to 25 grams of fiber a day. A bowl of oatmeal or high-fiber cereal for breakfast is the perfect kitchen cabinet cure.

Sprinkle on the flaxseed. In one study, women who took 2 tablespoons of crushed flaxseed every day for three months had less breast pain with their periods. Flaxseeds are high in omega-3 fatty acids, the healthy fats found in fatty fish, which your body needs to form anti-inflammatory hormones that can help relieve pain. They also contain lignans, estrogen-like compounds that may contribute to their ability to ease breast pain. Beans, including soybeans, nuts, and seeds, all contain lignans and may also work. As a bonus, studies show, flaxseeds may help prevent breast cancer. To use, just buzz a couple of tablespoons of whole flaxseeds in a clean coffee grinder and sprinkle on cereal, yogurt, salads, or other foods. You'll love the rich, nutty flavor.

Pop some E. A number of studies have found that women with breast pain and tenderness get relief at doses of vitamin E ranging from 150 to 800 IU. It doesn't work for everyone, but it's worth a try. It's hard to get that much vitamin E in food, but you get the highest amounts in fortified foods such as breakfast cereal, as well as in wheat germ and wheat germ oil, seeds, nuts, and leafy green vegetables like greens and spinach.

Massage your girls. Some practitioners recommend giving yourself a lymphatic breast massage. Here's how: Using oil or soap, massage breasts from the breast bone outward to the armpits. This improves circulation and

When to Call THE DOCTOR

If you have breast pain and you're nursing a baby, you may have mastitis, an infection that is typically treated with antibiotics. Mastitis is usually accompanied by swelling, fever, or a feeling of warmth, pain, or burning.

Also call your doctor if you notice dimpled or wrinkled skin on your breast, which may resemble an orange peel. And certainly call if you find a lump or thickening of any kind. Other symptoms that warrant a doctor's quick attention include:

• Bruising on your breast though you didn't have an injury

• Unusual discharge or bleeding from your nipples

• A nipple that suddenly turns inward

• Symptoms that interfere with your sleep or daily life

In Russia, an old folk remedy for breast tenderness is to wrap cabbage leaves on your breasts, wear warm linens, and go to sleep. We can't fathom how this might have worked, but cabbage leaf poultices pop up time and time again in folk remedies from all over the world.

helps lymph fluid flow, which may relieve swelling and pain.

Make a castor oil pack. Alternative medicine practitioners often use cloth soaked in castor oil to relieve inflammation and increase circulation. Place the cloth on your breasts and cover with a piece of plastic (cut from a plastic supermarket bag or plastic food wrap) and then cover with a hot water bottle to heat the oil. There's no scientific evidence that it works, but it sounds soothing.

Cut out salt. If your breasts swell and hurt with your period, trying cutting out salty foods and hide the salt shaker two weeks before you menstruate. Sodium causes body tissues to retain fluid.

Eat magnesium-rich foods. Studies have found that taking 200 to 400 milligrams of magnesium daily two weeks before a period can reduce breast soreness. If you'd like to do that with food, have 100 percent bran cereal with a cup of milk for breakfast every morning (that's about 100 mg), a handful of almonds as a snack (78 mg for 23 almonds), and brown rice and a side of spinach with dinner (about 86 mg per cup for the rice, 156 mg for a cup of cooked spinach) every day.

bruises

You smacked into something—or something smacked into you—and you'll soon have an ugly purple splotch to mark the spot. If you race to the kitchen cabinet for some help, you just might be able to prevent the Technicolor display, or at least shorten the time it takes your bruise to fade from black. The key to bruise control is to take action quickly.

first things first

Kitchen cabinet cures really *are* effective for bruises. But always start with this approach: Press a cold, wet compress made of paper towels, napkins, handkerchiefs, or even tissues onto the bruise right away. Or wrap ice in a towel and firmly apply to the bruise (a bag of frozen veggies works in a pinch). This helps stop the bleeding under the skin and can lessen swelling.

kitchen cabinet cures

Add arnica to your kitchen cabinet. *Arnica montana* is an alpine flower with a long history of healing bruises and other wounds. Though you probably don't stock the stuff (or even know what it is), you should—especially if you have an active family. It's harmless, inexpensive, and when it works, it works really well. Buy arnica in homeopathic pill form at pharmacies and health-food stores. It comes in little vials that contain tiny sugar pills infused with minute doses of the herb. In 2006, plastic surgeons from a practice in Connecticut studied its effects on

Pantry HEALERS

Arnica

Arrowroot

Castor oil

Lavender oil

Oregano

Sugar

Vinegar

Witch hazel

Weird & wacky

We admit that this ancient Chinese treatment is probably more fun to read about than to use. And we can't vouch for its effectiveness. But it's harmless and may be worth a try—at the very least, it will amuse a bruised child and take his mind off his boo-boo. You need two things: a U.S. silver coin (dimes, quarters, and half dollars minted before 1964 are mostly silver) and a peeled, freshly hard-boiled egg. Slip the coin vertically all the way into the egg until its top edge is even with the top of the egg. Place the warm (not hot) egg on the bruise and leave it there for 30 minutes. This is said to immediately erase the discoloration.

29 people who'd just undergone face-lifts. They concluded that those who took arnica had smaller bruises than those who didn't. Key to success: Take it immediately after you've banged into something; the longer you wait, the less effective arnica is. Others swear by arnica cream. Spread it quickly on a bruise, as long as there aren't any cuts or scrapes on the site.

Lift the bruise with sweetness. This only works if you're close to the sugar bowl when you get bruised. Wet your fingers, dip them in sugar, and give the entire bruise a brisk, firm massage with your sugary fingers. This may help seal the capillaries that are bleeding under the skin and could prevent the bruise from forming.

Got some arrowroot? Many cooks keep this powder in the spice rack to thicken sauces. If you have some handy, take a tablespoon or two, depending on how large the bruised area is, add just enough water to make a paste, and slather it on the spot. When it dries, you may find that the bruise has disappeared.

Try vinegar. This remedy is as old as the hills, and like many folk remedies, no scientific studies exist to explain exactly how the sour liquid helps heal bruises. Simply mix equal parts of apple cider vinegar and warm water, soak a paper towel or cloth in the solution, and press it gently on the bruise. It's possible that the vinegar and warm water compress increases blood flow near the skin's surface. That could help dissipate the blood that has pooled in the area. Witch hazel will also do the trick.

Erase that black eye with castor oil. A shiner is embarrassing to explain, so short of making like a pirate and wearing an eye patch (which is even more embarrassing) try this: Gently massage castor oil on the discolored

Busting the pineapple myth

Think that eating lots of pineapple can help fade a bruise? Think again. It's true that bromelain, a natural substance found in pineapples, helps fade bruises because it has anticlotting and anti-inflammatory effects. Trouble is, you only find bromelain in pineapple stems, not in the yummy fruit. If you're planning surgery and want to minimize bruising, talk to your doctor about taking bromelain supplements.

fragrant oil compress

Recipe page 182

skin. Be sure to keep the oil out of your eye. This is a tried and true folk remedy that's said to ease the pain, bring down the swelling, and lessen the unsightly color.

Rub in this simple massage oil. Mix 5 drops of lavender essential oil with 1 teaspoon vegetable oil, and massage into the bruise. The pressure of the massage will help the pooled blood reabsorb, and the scent of lavender will relax and calm you. Perfect for soothing your jangled nerves after a minor accident.

recipes for healing

Pizza Spice Poultice

This simple tea poultice can reduce the swelling and the pain of a bruise.

> 1 heaping tablespoon dried oregano
> 1 cup boiled water

1. Steep the oregano in the hot water for 10 minutes. Strain. Reserve the oregano and the liquid.

2. Wrap the damp oregano in a piece of cheesecloth roughly the size of the bruise to make a poultice.

3. Place the poultice on the bruise and leave it on for about 15 minutes. When the cheesecloth dries, re-wet it with the oregano water, and reapply.

Fragrant Oil Compress

This simple formula can ease an achy bruise, and it's a cinch to make. You can use all, one, or none of the essential oils, depending on what you have handy.

> ¼ cup water
> ¼ cup witch hazel or apple cider vinegar
> 5 drops lavender essential oil
> 5 drops rosemary essential oil
> 5 drops peppermint essential oil

1. In a bowl, mix together the water, witch hazel (or vinegar), and the essential oils. Soak a cloth in the liquid, wring it out until nearly dry, and then place over the injured area.

2. Cover with plastic wrap so the skin absorbs the essential oils, and cover the whole thing with a towel. Apply the compress for 30 minutes, and repeat up to three times daily.

bursitis & tendinitis

Bursitis and tendinitis are usually caused by excessive, repeated motion. Bursitis is an inflammation of the fluid-filled sacs (bursa) that cushion joints; tendinitis is an inflammation of tendons or ligaments. Both painful problems can affect fun-seekers and worker bees alike, from weekend warriors who overdo it on the tennis courts to folks who shovel out after snowstorms. To quickly ease the aches of either "itis," march into your pantry and reach for some potent anti-inflammatory ingredients. You might be surprised to learn that some household standbys are as effective as over-the-counter painkillers.

Pantry HEALERS

Curry powder
Ginger
Ice pack
Tart cherry juice
Tiger Balm
Turmeric

first things first

Here's what to do when a joint starts to hurt after a prolonged period of repeated motion:

• Stop what you're doing. Pain is a signal that you need to take a break from whatever triggered it.

• Next, wrap an elastic bandage around the affected joint—firmly enough to contain it but not tight enough to restrict blood flow. Think girdle, not tourniquet.

• Elevate the joint above the level of your heart. Both the bandage and the elevation will help restrict blood flow to the area, which lessens inflammation. If your elbow hurts, keep it on a high armrest, or sit in a low chair with your elbow propped up on the table. If you're treating your knee, lie on your back with the knee propped up on pillows.

• Beyond that, doctors usually recommend an anti-inflammatory painkiller, such as ibuprofen.

The following pantry cures can also help a whole lot.

kitchen cabinet cures

Treat it to the cold shoulder. Ice your sore joint to ease pain and inflammation. Wrap up an ice pack in a towel and apply it for 10 to 20 minutes every four hours. Or freeze a paper cup full of ice, tear off the top edge, and rub the ice where it hurts. Repeat three or four times a day, allowing two to five minutes for each treatment.

Then run hot and cold. After about three days of giving joints the cold treatment—or until the joint is no longer warm to the touch—start alternating cold with heat. Heat increases blood flow to the injury, helping it to heal faster. Use a microwavable heat pack or an electric heating pad. Or, for form-fitting warmth, place 2 to 3 cups of rice in a large sock, tie off the sock, and microwave for 60 to 90 seconds. The rice will mold nicely to a knee, elbow, or ankle.

Take a vitamin-mineral-omega-3 cocktail. Together, these essential nutrients, many of which may be sitting in your medicine chest or kitchen vitamin drawer, reduce inflammation and help injured connective tissue and muscles heal. Take this combo daily for at least two weeks.

Vitamin A	15,000 IU	daily
Vitamin C	500 mg	twice a day
Vitamin E	400 mg	daily
Calcium	1,500 mg	daily
Magnesium	750 mg	daily
Fish oil	1,500 mg	daily

Try a cherry cocktail. Tart cherry juice is a traditional arthritis remedy that some natural healing experts also recommend for bursitis and tendinitis. It's a sensible notion, since cherries are rich in inflammation-relieving antioxidants. But aside from a few studies on mice, there's no science to back it up. Try drinking two 8-ounce glasses per day until the pain goes away. Just make sure the juice you buy contains no added sugar or other ingredients, and consider the calories if you're watching your weight.

Drink some ginger. Ginger contains lots of powerful compounds that relieve pain and ease inflammation. Enjoy a cup of strong ginger tea three times a day when you're recuperating from bursitis or tendinitis. Make the tea with pure gingerroot tea bags, and use two per cup of boiled water. Steep, covered, for 10 minutes before drinking. No ginger tea bags? Slice three or four quarter-size pieces of fresh gingerroot and simmer in a cup or so of water for 10 to 15 minutes. Or add 1 teaspoon of powdered ginger to a cup of boiled water, cover, and steep for 10 minutes. Strain before drinking.

Or apply some ginger. You can also harness ginger's pain-relieving powers by making a ginger compress to help ease the hurt from the outside in. Chop 2 tablespoons of fresh ginger, drop it in 3 cups of boiled water, and let it steep for 20 minutes. Soak a folded piece of cloth in the warm tea and wring it out. Making sure it's not too hot to touch, place the cloth over your sore joint for five minutes. Repeat three or four times a day. If you notice any irritation, discontinue using.

Try Tiger Balm. This menthol-laced salve is a pantry staple in many traditional Chinese households for pain relief. Rub some on the sore spot once or twice a day. But test a small patch of skin first. This is hot stuff, and some sensitive people develop a rash or redness if they use it often.

Next time at an Asian market, pick up Tiger Balm. It's a wonderfully useful topical pain reliever.

Become a curry enthusiast. Turmeric, the Indian spice that's a key ingredient in curry and ballpark mustard, contains several potent antioxidant and anti-inflammatory compounds. The most researched and best known of these is curcumin. This pigment, which gives turmeric its brilliant yellow color, inhibits the synthesis of prostaglandins, hormone-like compounds in the body involved in pain signal transmission. Turmeric researchers suggest adding a teaspoon or so of the spice—it has a warm, tangy, citrusy flavor—to foods like scrambled eggs, rice, stews, meat loaf, and other hearty dishes. Since you need to use turmeric regularly to reap its benefits, you could also try curcumin supplements, which you can pick up at health food stores. Take 350 milligrams of the standardized extract twice a day for best results.

calluses & corns

You don't have to run out (make that walk over, since your corns and calluses render your feet too painful to run) to the podiatrist every time you have painful corns or calluses. Chances are, you'll find simple solutions much closer to home—right inside your kitchen cabinet.

Pantry HEALERS

Aspirin

Castor oil

Lemon peel

Vinegar

Vitamins E and A

White onion

first things first

Essentially, a callus is thick layering of dead skin caused by constant rubbing or usage. Calluses form to protect you from further injury, and because they are the outermost layer of skin, usually are painless and safe. A corn is a callus that has formed a hard core in its center. By nature of its size and hardness, corns can press on a nerve or bone, making them painful and sensitive.

To attack calluses—not corns—always start with these two fundamentals:

• First soak your feet in warm water with a handful of Epsom salts for about 10 minutes to soften the dead skin.

• Then use a pumice stone or callus file to gently rub off the top layers of the callus. Don't grind the whole callus away in one sitting—you could go too deep and make matters worse. Instead, sand it down a little after a soak or while you're in the shower. If the callus is thick or hard, the sanding project might take a few weeks.

Never use this technique on corns, because it will make them even more painful.

kitchen cabinet cures

Try a medicine cabinet cure. Take five or six crushed uncoated aspirin tablets and add just enough equal parts of apple cider vinegar and water to make a paste. Rub the paste onto the corn or callus, then place an adhesive bandage over it to hold it in place. Wait at least 10 minutes before removing the bandage. The callused skin should easily come loose when rubbed with a pumice stone. Aspirin and corn pads contain similar forms of salicylic acid, which helps skin cells shed when you apply it topically.

Employ some vinegar and oil. Add a cup of apple cider vinegar to a basin of hot soapy water. Soak your feet for at least 15 minutes, or longer if you can. This will help soften calluses, which you can then file down gently with a pumice stone. To remove corns, dab on some castor oil after you soak. It may take 10 days or so of the double treatment, but the corns should peel right off.

Squirt on some vitamin E or A. In the evening, pierce a vitamin E or A capsule with a clean needle and rub the oil into the corn. Allow it to penetrate for a few minutes, then wear a white cotton sock to bed. Repeat this for a week or so till the corn disappears.

Peel some lemon. Use a potato peeler to slice off an inch-long band of lemon peel, about as wide as your toe. Wrap it over the corn, pith side down, and secure with a bandage or a piece of bandage tape. Cover with a white cotton sock and wear to bed. Repeat as often as necessary until the corn is gone.

Get in step with dancers' relief. It's said that ballet dancers use this corn remedy. Put a slice of white onion in a small glass container. Pour white vinegar over it and leave it in a warm place all day. At night, put the onion on the corn and cover with a bandage or bandage tape. The corn may be soft enough to remove in the morning, though stubborn corns may need repeat treatments.

When to call THE DOCTOR

If you have diabetes or poor circulation, consult a doctor instead of treating corns or calluses yourself. In rare cases, being too aggressive in treating a corn—such as using scissors to remove it—can cause an infection for which you'll need a doctor's help to cure.

Weird & wacky

Here's an odd-sounding folk cure that home remedy experts swear by. Soak a half slice of stale bread in apple cider vinegar. Use adhesive tape to secure it to the affected part of your foot. Wrap with plastic wrap and cover with a cotton sock. In the morning, your corn or callus may be history!

Ditch the ill-fitting shoes

Almost all corns have the same cause: shoes that rub you the wrong way. If your sexiest shoes hurt your toes, see if a good shoemaker can ease the fit over the affected spot. If he can't, you must lose the shoes to escape your corn problem.

canker sores

Pantry HEALERS

Aloe

Baking soda

Hydrogen peroxide

Licorice tea

Milk of magnesia

Sage

Tea

Tea tree oil

You've probably never called these mouth irritations by their real name, which is aphthous ulcers. But you've certainly had at least one or two of them in your lifetime. Stress, abrasions, and allergies are just a few causes for the sores, which, though annoying, are rarely cause for alarm. These kitchen cabinet cures should be able to shave at least a few days off their normal healing time, which is usually about a week.

first things first

Whether you have just one or a few canker sores, you'll want to apply some common-sense solutions in addition to the remedies below:

• Forego spicy or very acidic foods.

• Pass on crunchy or chewy foods.

• Rinse your mouth with salt water a few times a day.

• After brushing, rinse your mouth with an antibacterial mouthwash.

kitchen cabinet cures

Try aloe. Instead of buying an over-the-counter preparation in the drugstore to coat that painful canker sore, make your instant, natural cure. All you need is a cotton swab and an aloe vera leaf. Dry the sore area with a cotton swab, then slice into the leaf and scrape off a bit of gel with a clean spoon. Dab directly on the sore. Repeat as often as necessary.

Reach for baking soda. Rinse your mouth with a solution of 1 teaspoon baking soda in ½ cup of warm water. The baking soda helps kill the bacteria, which will ease the pain.

Use milk of magnesia. Sip a small amount and use it as a mouth rinse, making sure to rinse the canker sore itself. You can also dab milk of magnesia directly on the canker sore with a cotton swab three or four times a day.

Or, add this to the milk of magnesia. A variation on the milk of magnesia remedy above is to mix a teaspoon of it with a teaspoon of Benedryl liquid allergy medicine. Swish this blend around in your mouth.

Do the tea bag trick. Apply a damp tea bag to the sore for 5 minutes. Tea is alkaline, so it neutralizes acids. It also contains compounds that may help relieve pain.

Make like a sage. The culinary herb sage kills bacteria and viruses and contains compounds that reduce inflammation. Steep 2 teaspoons dried sage in a cup of boiling water, covered. Let cool, and use as a mouth rinse two or three times a day, making sure to swish the tea in the area of the mouth with the canker sore.

Climb the tea tree. Using a cotton swab, dab a single drop of tea tree oil, an antiseptic, directly on the sore.

When to Call THE DOCTOR

If you get more than your fair share of canker sores, let your doctor know so that he or she can rule out any medical problems. And make an appointment if your canker sores are so painful that you can't drink—you could become dehydrated, which is dangerous.

the natural DOCTOR'S Rx

Tasty licorice tea, which you can find in tea bags at health food stores, is an excellent way to treat and eliminate canker sores. Use one tea bag per cup of boiled water and steep, covered for 10 minutes, then drink.

recipe for healing

Disinfecting Mouth Rinse

Hydrogen peroxide is a strong disinfectant. That's a plus, since a canker sore is an open wound that's vulnerable to infection, which increases the pain. And since baking soda is alkaline, it provides extra relief by neutralizing acids.

> ¼ cup hydrogen peroxide
> ¼ cup water
> 1 teaspoon baking soda
> 1 teaspoon salt

1. Blend the peroxide and water in a glass.

2. Add the baking soda and salt and stir to dissolve thoroughly.

3. To use, swish the solution around in your mouth and spit it out.

carpal tunnel syndrome

Pantry HEALERS

Bromelain supplements

Canned fish (salmon, sardines, herring, mackerel)

Capsaicin cream

Caviar

Cayenne pepper

Flaxseed

Many people believe that carpal tunnel syndrome (CTS) is a condition of modern times, a result of countless hours spent typing on a computer keyboard. While research shows this isn't true, what's certain is that some old-fashioned kitchen remedies can help ease this increasingly common and painful wrist and hand problem.

first things first

Let's debunk the "computers are the primary cause of CTS" issue. A Mayo Clinic study found that people who use computers all day weren't at increased risk for developing this painful wrist or hand problem. More recently, a Danish study also concluded that there isn't enough evidence to blame computer work for CTS.

So who is at risk? According to a 2009 study, the likeliest victims of CTS are people who work in the meat or fish processing industries, foresters who work with chain saws, or workers on assembly lines producing electronic products. So while some office workers who spend lots of time on computers do get the condition, so do many other people who work far away from computers.

While home remedies and kitchen cabinet cures like the ones below can assist in fast and effective healing, you should also use these common-sense tactics:

• As with any inflammation-caused pain, heat and cold are your allies in relief. Apply an ice pack wrapped in a thin towel for 10 minutes to ease inflammation. You can repeat every hour. Once you are past the inflammation stage, use heat to relax muscles. A warm bath before bed is a good approach.

- Stop doing the things that caused the damage to your wrists! If the repetitive task is job related, that might be hard. But at minimum, arrange at least a few days to let healing occur.

- If you have to keep doing the task after healing, alter your technique. Can you change how you grip the tool? The way you position your hands? Having more than one approach to a task can help prevent CTS.

- To ease the pain, stabilize the wrist with a splint. Wear as often as possible, but especially at night when you're apt to sleep in positions that can aggravate the inflammation (like with your hand under your pillow).

kitchen cabinet cures

Go salmon fishing. There are no studies as to whether eating fatty fish, such as canned salmon, sardines, herring, or mackerel can ease carpal tunnel syndrome. But since eating fatty fish is proven to have strong anti-inflammatory effects, it's a safe and healthy move to have two or three servings a week.

Scarf up some caviar. No, not the expensive stuff that will set you back a month's pay. Scientists recently discovered that salmon and lumpfish caviars are the food world's number one dietary source of inflammation-fighting omega-3 fatty acids. You can find these tasty, inexpensive fish roes on many supermarket shelves in the gourmet or canned fish aisle.

When to Call
THE DOCTOR

It's a good idea to make a doctor's appointment when you first experience three or more consecutive days of wrist pain. Seeking help early can prevent permanent damage to the median nerve. You'll also want to rule out other painful conditions, such as arthritis, whose symptoms mimic carpal tunnel. If it is CTS, your doctor may suggest you wear a special splint and rest your wrist for a week or so. In advanced cases, you may require surgery.

Could it be an infection?

Recently, Australian hand surgeons wrote up a case report titled "An uncommon cause for a common complaint." Turns out that in rare cases, carpal tunnel syndrome can be caused by an infection. Known as infectious tenosynovitis, it comes in two forms. The gonococcal type is a sexually transmitted disease that commonly affects teenagers and young adults. The nongonococcal variety can occur following a puncture wound, cut, bite, or even a bout of dry, cracked skin. Sometimes, the wound can't even be found. So if your symptoms persist even after treatment and your doctor still can't pinpoint a cause, ask her to test you for this infection.

Add flaxseed to your cereal. Freshly ground flaxseed is extremely rich in plant-based omega-3 fatty acids, which reduce inflammation. Enjoy a couple of tablespoons every day in your yogurt, oatmeal, salad, or cereal—they add a nice nuttiness. Give it a couple of weeks to have an effect.

Use a spicy rub. The same kinds of remedies that ease arthritis pain may also ease CTS pain. One good choice is red pepper, which has a reputation as an arthritis remedy. Also known as cayenne, this spice contains a substance called capsaicin, which reduces the levels of the chemical compound substance P, which transmits pain signals to the brain. Mix a few dashes of ground cayenne pepper with 2 to 3 teaspoons olive oil. Apply with gauze to your wrist several times a day. Allow a week or more of continued use for the desensitization to take place. The first few doses will cause a mild, but usually tolerable burning sensation. Don't apply this remedy to inflamed or broken skin.

Find relief in the bathroom pantry. That pain-relieving capsaicin cream you bought the last time someone suffered a muscle ache or arthritis pain makes a great carpal tunnel treatment. Be sure to give it a few days to work.

Use bromelain. This protein-digesting enzyme derived from pineapple combats inflammation in the carpal tunnel from inside your body. Take 500 milligrams in supplement form when your stomach is empty (otherwise, it'll consume itself dissolving the food you've just eaten). It's easy to find in the vitamin aisle at the drugstore or in health food stores.

chapped lips

On anyone's list of health woes, chapped lips ranks way down at the bottom. But that doesn't mean they aren't annoying, irritating, and uncomfortable. Happily, many things can cure the problem, including some you can make at home from stuff that's right inside your pantry.

first things first

Prevention is easy when it comes to chapped lips: Just keep lip moisturizer in your purse or pocket. As soon as the weather gets cold and dry, treat your lips several times a day with a store-bought lip moisturizer or one of our recommended balms.

kitchen cabinet cures

Smooth on some honey. Plain honey is a great moisturizer. Apply some morning and night and just try not to lick it all off. Don't use honey on children under the age of one, because it may contain dangerous spores that infants' immune systems can't handle.

Squeeze out some vitamin E. Puncture a vitamin E capsule and apply the oil to your lips for some very healthy and effective relief.

Use shortening. When nothing better is at hand, olive oil or vegetable shortening, such as Crisco, will help to soften and moisturize chapped lips quite nicely. Just smooth directly on your lips.

Pantry HEALERS

Beeswax

Honey

Lavender
  essential oil

Olive oil

Tea tree essential oil

Vegetable
  shortening

Vitamin E capsules

Wintergreen
  essential oil

recipes for healing

Cocoa Lip Balm

Although this concoction smells tasty, it's not meant to be eaten. If you plan to give it to a child, label it accordingly and explain how to use it.

½ cup extra-virgin olive oil
1 tablespoon grated beeswax
½ teaspoon unsweetened cocoa powder
1 capsule vitamin E

1. In a microwave or the top of a double boiler, melt the oil and beeswax together. Do not boil. If the mixture starts to boil, remove from the heat and allow it to cool. Once the beeswax and oil are blended, stir in the cocoa powder. Pierce the vitamin E capsule with a needle, squeeze out half the contents, and stir it in. Pour the resulting mixture into clean containers with tops.

2. Let the lip balm sit for 48 hours at room temperature, or until it arrives at the proper consistency for spreading. You can carry a small container of lip balm around with you during the day, but you may find it keeps better in the refrigerator overnight.

Healing Lip Balm

If your lips are cracked and painful, this extra-soothing balm will help heal them before you know it.

4 tablespoons olive oil
1 tablespoon grated beeswax
1 teaspoon honey
1 capsule vitamin E
10 drops lavender essential oil
10 drops tea tree essential oil
10 drops wintergreen essential oil

1. In the top of a double boiler, warm the oil, beeswax, and honey over low heat until the wax melts. Remove from heat. Pierce the vitamin E capsule with a needle and squeeze its contents into the mixture.

2. Stir in the essential oils. Store in a cool, dark place and use by dipping a finger into the balm and smoothing it on your lips.

When to Call THE DOCTOR

Chapped lips usually clear up as soon as you moisturize them diligently. However, if you have chronically chapped lips, or if your lips regularly crack or bleed, see your doctor to rule out any medical conditions.

chicken pox

Chicken pox lasts only a week or two, but it can be a miserable time for little kids, especially when they're covered head to toe (and everyplace in between) with the spotty, itchy pox. And it can be an exhausting couple of weeks for moms and dads, too—this is one of those childhood illnesses that calls for round-the-clock loving care. Even though the preventive vaccine may result in fewer children coming down with chicken pox, there will always be kids (and even some adults) who'll benefit from using these gentle kitchen pantry remedies in addition to the standard cures.

first things first

In addition to your arsenal of cures, take these actions the minute you know your child has chicken pox:

• If it's winter, turn down the heat to the lowest comfortable temperature. In summer, use air conditioning. Not available? Then put fans in your child's room. Heat brings more blood to the skin, which exacerbates the itch.

• Trim his or her fingernails as far back as you can, and keep them short. The goal is to make it as hard as possible to scratch open blisters. This helps prevent infection—and scarring.

• Offer your child a cool, wet washcloth to press against her skin when she feels like scratching. She'll be able to satisfy her urge to scratch but won't do any damage.

Pantry HEALERS

Bran flakes

Calamine lotion

Milk of magnesia

Oatmeal

Orange pekoe tea

Petroleum jelly

Salt

Tea tree essential oil

Shun the blistering sun

If your child has recently been exposed to someone with chicken pox, keep her out of the sun. A dose of sunshine may make the blisters worse when they finally erupt. After the chicken pox is over, your child's skin will remain sensitive to the sun for as long as a year. You don't have to barricade her in the house, but do apply sunscreen every day.

• For extra insurance against scratching, have your child wear cotton gloves to bed and clean, extra-soft, long-sleeve cotton pj's with long pants. Cotton is gentler to the skin than synthetic fabrics.

• Let your child get plenty of rest, and serve plenty of clear liquids and soft, bland foods, especially if there are sores in the mouth.

• Never give your child aspirin when she has chicken pox—or any other viral illness, for that matter. Doing so could cause Reye's syndrome, a complication that is potentially fatal.

kitchen cabinet cures

Go for an oatmeal swim. A nice cool (not cold) bath laced with a cup or so of baking soda or oatmeal will make your child feel much more comfortable. You can buzz a couple of handfuls of plain oatmeal in a food processor or blender and toss right in the tub. Or you can stuff finely ground oatmeal into a clean piece of panty hose and put that in the bathwater. Your child can use the oatmeal sock to rub gently on the pox.

Offer sips of orange pekoe tea. Home remedy advocates swear that drinking warm orange pekoe tea can speed the eruption of chicken pox sores—and the faster they emerge, the faster they'll dry up and heal. Sweeten with honey to make the tea more palatable. Don't use this for children under the age of one.

Dab on some milk of magnesia. Its soothing, drying action can work some magic on itchy pox.

Find the calamine lotion. Then swab onto the blisters. This pink lotion is made in large part of zinc oxide, which helps soothe and dry up the blisters.

Tap the tea tree. Blend a few drops of tea tree essential oil with 1 tablespoon of olive oil, and use a cotton swab to apply the oil to sores two or three times a day. Tea tree oil is a powerful natural antiseptic.

Prevent the crack-up. After sores have crusted over, coat them with some petroleum jelly to prevent them from cracking and bleeding. When you do this, however, make sure you don't transmit the virus to the stuff in the jar.

Instead of using your finger, apply the petroleum jelly with a cotton swab. Use a fresh swab every time.

Mind the mouth. If your child has chicken pox in his mouth (yes, it can happen), have him gargle with salt water. Serve soothing, bland foods like soups, gelatin, and bananas—items that won't hurt the blisters. Ice pops can also be soothing.

When to Call THE DOCTOR

Chicken pox is usually more of an annoyance than a danger; most cases clear up in 10 to 14 days without problems. Only in rare cases do serious complications emerge. Still, call your pediatrician once you suspect your child has chicken pox. The doctor can prescribe medications, if necessary, to lessen the severity of the disease. Seek immediate attention if your child has a high fever accompanied by severe headache, has a fever that lasts more than a few days, feels severe pain in his limbs, repeatedly vomits, develops a cough, or has a large area of warmth or redness surrounding one or more blisters—this is a sign of infection.

 recipe for healing

Anti-itch Poultice

This poultice provides soothing relief for an itchy child. What's more, it contains that invisible ingredient—a mom or dad's loving touch—that makes it more powerful than any over-the-counter treatment you could ever buy.

> Water to cover
> 1 cup bran (pulverize plain bran flakes in the blender or food processor)

1. Boil the water and remove from heat.

2. Steep the bran in the water until it is room temperature. Strain, reserving the liquid.

3. Place the bran in a piece of cheesecloth and tie it securely so it's completely contained in the cloth.

4. Apply the bran bundle on the sores and let sit for 10 seconds, moving it from place to place until all the pox have been treated. Then rewet the bundle with the reserved bran water and repeat the application. Use the bran treatment every couple of hours for maximum relief.

cold sores

Canker sores might have many causes, but cold sores have just one: a particular type of herpes virus. And that's not the only difference between these mouth maladies. Canker sores mostly occur inside the mouth; cold sores usually appear on or around the lips. But in both cases, healing comes naturally and relatively quickly. And kitchen cabinet cures can help speed up and improve the process.

Pantry HEALERS

Aloe

Aspirin

B$_{12}$ supplements

Black tea

Cornstarch

Lavender
  essential oil

Lemon balm
  essential oil

Lysine supplements

Olive oil

Red wine

Tea tree essential oil

first things first

Sometimes, you can prevent a cold sore from emerging—or reduce its severity—if you react quickly to the first sensations of one forming. Here's what to do:

• Apply a drop or two of lemon balm essential oil to the area as soon as you feel the tingle of a cold sore forming. Recent studies have proven that lemon balm essential oil effectively kills the herpes virus.

• Then hold an ice cube on top of the area for 10 minutes. Repeat the whole procedure several times a day.

kitchen cabinet cures

Dry up a little red wine. If you have an opened bottle of red wine handy, put a little bit in a saucer and let it sit until the liquid evaporates. Slather the sore with the solidified dregs and it will ease the pain on contact. Theory is that resveratrol, red wine's potent antioxidant, can relieve the inflammation. Despite the fact that experts say there's probably not enough resveratrol in wine dregs to make much of a difference, some folk healers swear by this trick.

Make a cornstarch paste. An old home remedy calls for making a cornmeal poultice for a cold sore. Here's an easier adaptation: Make a paste of a little cornstarch and water and dab it on the sore a few times a day. It will soothe and cool the inflammation.

Take lysine supplements. Along with lemon balm essential oil, this amino acid emerges as a hands-down best healer for cold sores. Take 3,000 milligrams daily until the sore goes away. Research shows it thwarts the replication of the virus.

Try a tea bag poultice. At the first twinge of a cold sore, apply a damp, cooled black tea bag to the area where you expect the outbreak to occur. Keep it on for 10 minutes. Repeat three or four times a day to reduce the duration and severity of an outbreak. It's been said that Earl Grey tea bags seem to be the most effective.

Beef up your B$_{12}$. Studies have shown that people who tend to get cold sores also tend to have low levels of vitamin B$_{12}$. Taking a daily B$_{12}$ supplement might lessen your chances for developing the sores.

Dab on some aloe. Cut off a little piece of your aloe plant, scrape off a bit of the gel, and swab the cold sore three or four times a day until the sore goes away.

Apply some tea tree oil. Apply tea tree essential oil directly on the cold sore three or four times a day.

Have an aspirin. It will offer you some pain relief. Research also shows that 125 milligrams of aspirin a day can cut the time a herpes infection remains active by 50 percent.

When to Call THE DOCTOR

If you have frequent bouts of cold sores, it could indicate a weakened immune system or that you're under undue stress that could be affecting your health in other ways. Check with your doctor to rule out medical causes, and ask her advice about ways to reduce your stress.

Weird & wacky

We found this one in a book about old home remedies: "To heal a cold sore quickly, put earwax on it." Naturally, we don't recommend the earwax treatment, though we do wonder what prompted its inventor to try it.

recipe for healing

Lemon Balm Cold Sore Treatment Oil

This recipe combines ingredients known to help heal cold sores. It also feels good on the sore.

5 drops lemon balm essential oil
2 drops lavender essential oil
10 drops olive oil

Blend the essential oils with the olive oil and dab on the sore three or four times a day.

colds & flu

Scientists studying the 99 known strains of rhinoviruses made a headline-worthy breakthrough in 2009. By decoding the viruses' genome, they discovered weaknesses they believe can finally lead to a cure for the common cold. The bad news is that cure is still a long way off. In the meantime, you can rely on trusted home remedies as your first line of defense against sniffling, sneezing, sore throat, coughing, and aches. These cures come right from your kitchen cabinet and help get you back on your feet fast.

first things first

There are certain hard-and-fast rules we should all follow when a cold or flu comes along. Among them:

• Stay home in a warm (but not overheated) room.

• Increase the moisture in the air with a humidifier if it makes you feel better (it won't speed your healing, though).

• Drink plenty of fluids.

• Get lots of rest.

• To keep the virus from spreading, cover your mouth when you sneeze or cough, and wash your hands frequently with soap and water.

• Do your friends, coworkers, and the public at large a favor by staying home until the symptoms pass.

kitchen cabinet cures

Eat garlic. There's no question that garlic boosts your immunity and fights viruses; researchers keep working to find just how effective it is. Though its effectiveness at easing colds is a matter of debate, herbalists often advise eating raw cloves at the onset of cold or flu symptoms (if you cook or dry garlic, it loses its antibiotic properties). To make it more palatable, chop up a clove of garlic and mix with a spoonful of honey, yogurt, or applesauce before eating. Chopping or crushing raw garlic activates its medicinal compounds.

Swallow a mustard-honey remedy. Mix ¼ teaspoon mustard powder with 2 tablespoons honey and swallow. This sweet-savory blend will help loosen chest congestion. Never give honey to babies under one year of age.

Try this wonderful tea. Put 5 slices of fresh gingerroot in a small saucepan and add 2 cups of water. Bring to boil, then simmer for 20 minutes. Drink the tea warm. The ginger is loaded with anti-inflammatory, germ-killing compounds. Make it even more delicious by adding some honey and orange juice. You'll get a shot of vitamin C from the OJ and a burst of soothing antiseptic power from the honey.

Breathe in these spices. Aromatic, germ-killing herbs and humidity can do wonders for a stuffed-up head. This treatment takes only minutes to put together, and the

When to Call THE DOCTOR

If you're sidelined with a miserable cold, especially if it's accompanied by a fever and aching, call your doctor's office even if you think it's "just a cold." You'll learn about any flu hitting the community, and your doctor's office will suggest the best course of action. Generally, they'll want to see you in person if a fever lasts for more than three days or if your temperature is over 102°F. Never give aspirin to a child with a virus; this increases the risk of Reye's syndrome, a rare but life-threatening disease.

Is sweating healing?

You'd certainly think so, since so many home remedies, like mustard plasters and steaming cups of ginger tea, make you perspire. These remedies have their place: Mustard plasters can help break up chest congestion, and ginger tea lowers fevers and kills cold viruses.

But you can't get rid of a cold by simply sweating it out—unless you're working up that sweat by exercising. Turns out, hopping on a treadmill or getting some other form of aerobic exercise gives you a little relief. It opens up sinuses and allows them to drain. And according to doctors at the Mayo Clinic, exercising gives you a shot of a natural cold-fighting drug, adrenalin. Chemically related to all the drugs used to treat cold symptoms, adrenalin levels go up when you exercise. What's more, when researchers asked people with colds to work out on treadmills, they learned that their colds didn't limit their ability to exercise.

results are priceless. Put 1 tablespoon each of dried thyme, sage, and peppermint into a medium bowl and add boiling water. Lean over the bowl with a towel draped over your head, close your eyes, and inhale for 10 minutes. For safety, keep your face at least 10 inches above the water. Repeat two or three times a day as needed.

Use saline spray for clogged sinuses. Breathe easier quickly by thoroughly mixing ¼ teaspoon table salt into 1 cup of boiled water. Let cool until it's a comfortably warm temperature. To get the solution into your nose, use an ear bulb syringe (like the kind used to clean out a baby's nose), a neti pot (an Indian sinus-cleaning tool available in health food stores), or a water pick(also know as an oral irrigator) on the lowest setting (you'll need a special adapter for this). Flush your nasal passages two or three times a day.

Find some zinc lozenges. Zinc gluconate lozenges are among the top remedies for colds and flu. In one study, people who sucked on a lozenge containing about

Soup's on!

We're hard-pressed to think of a country that doesn't have its own version of Mom's chicken soup. From Mexico to China and ports of call in between, mothers serve up bowls of the fragrant liquid whenever their loved ones come down with cold and flu miseries. In some circles, it's known as "Jewish penicillin," and in fact, studies show that hot chicken soup seems to be more effective at clearing nasal passages than other hot liquids are. Somehow, chicken soup inhibits the movement of white blood cells, which contributes to inflammation of the lining of the respiratory tract. And, of course, it offers plenty of nutrition and fluids—and if you're lucky, a dumpling or noodles and some soft vegetables.

For greater healing power, add chopped garlic to your chicken soup. But be sure to toss it in just before you serve it, because heat destroys garlic's medicinal compounds. Also consider spiking your chicken soup with a dash of red pepper sauce, red pepper flakes, or wasabi, the condiment (usually made from horseradish) that's eaten with sushi. All of these red-hot add-ins can increase the broth's decongestant power. In fact, adding any of them to any food can help you breathe more freely.

Other hot beverages also have a place in your cold-healing arsenal. Hot lemonade, like any hot drink, decreases congestion (although the effect is short-lived), and it also provides a healthy dose of vitamin C, which may help fight off colds and lessen their severity. Tea with honey also helps break up congestion and soothes a sore throat. Herb teas made with sage and thyme have germ-killing properties and can decrease inflammation.

13 milligrams of zinc every two hours while awake, shook off their symptoms three to four days sooner than people who didn't. Just don't take them continuously for more than a week.

While you're at it, grab some elderberry. At the first sign of the flu, take an elderberry syrup called Sambucol. Elderberry has been used in Europe for centuries to fight viruses. One lab study showed that Sambucol killed 10 flu strains, and in a human study, it reduced flu recovery time to three or four days. More recently, in a test tube study conducted at a Florida research lab, elderberry extract killed the H1N1 virus. Another option: elderberry flower tea. Make it by putting 10 elderberry tea bags in a quart canning jar filled with just-boiled water. Cover and steep for 20 minutes. Sweeten with honey to taste. Drink one cup every four hours, reheating the tea when necessary. Elderberry flower products are sold in health food stores.

Attack with pepper spray. This is a classic case of fighting fire with fire—and it works like a charm to ease sore throat pain. In a clean 8-ounce spray bottle, combine

Elderberry is emerging as one of the world's top flu remedies.

Cold or flu: an update

Both colds and flu are caused by viruses. There are many more cold viruses than strains of the flu, but they are relatively minor infections. Cold viruses primarily inflame the mucous membranes that line your nose and throat. The all-too-familiar symptoms include a runny nose, sneezing, watery eyes, and sometimes a sore throat, aches, and coughing. Most colds clear up within a week or so.

Influenza is a more serious illness. It usually brings with it fever, chills, muscle aches, and sometimes back pain, in addition to cold symptoms. The flu typically comes on suddenly and can lead to secondary infections, such as bronchitis and pneumonia, which require much more serious medical treatment. For that reason, the flu can pose a serious health threat, especially to the elderly.

Flu viruses are notorious shape shifters. The most recent flu incarnation, the H1N1, is sweeping its way around the world. This strain has proven to be dangerous to otherwise healthy young people, as well as to pregnant women and people with chronic conditions like asthma and diabetes. If you've been exposed to the flu or suspect you may be coming down with it, see your doctor right away. He or she can prescribe drugs called Tamiflu or Relenza, which can stop the flu virus from spreading through your body. Taking one of these drugs can lessen flu symptoms and shorten their duration. They may also be able to prevent the flu once you've been exposed.

1 tablespoon of cayenne pepper with just enough water to almost fill the bottle. Shake well and use as a spray to numb the back of your throat. You can also use the mix as a gargle. Just don't get it near your eyes.

Lap up some lemon. The traditional sore-throat gargle—a squeeze of lemon juice in a glass of hot water—works because it creates an acidic environment that's hostile to bacteria and viruses.

Stir up some honey and lemon tea. There's something about this simple throat-soothing tea that makes you feel nurtured when you're fighting a cold. And it's remarkably effective. The honey soothes and coats your throat and is a natural antiseptic. The lemon acts as an astringent, shrinking swollen throat tissue.

Bare-cupboard throat fix. Even if your pantry is empty, you've got these two ingredients on hand—and they work remarkably well. Just fill an 8-ounce glass with warm water, mix in 1 teaspoon salt, and gargle away. The salt really does soothe the pain.

Cut short a cold with your...blow-dryer. As crazy as it sounds, inhaling heated air may help kill a virus working its way up your nose. In one study conducted at Harvard Hospital in England, people who breathed heated air had half the cold symptoms of people who inhaled air at room temperature. Set your hair dryer on warm (not hot), hold it at least 18 inches from your face, and breathe in the air through your nose for as long as you can—at least 2 or 3 minutes, and preferably 20 minutes.

Weird & wacky

Consider using the wet sock cure. This oddly soggy strategy really does help ease a fever and clear congestion by drawing blood to the feet, which helps increase circulation throughout your body. The best method is to warm your feet in hot water, soak a thin pair of cotton socks in cold water, wring them out, and put them on just before going to bed. Put a pair of dry wool socks over the wet ones. The wet socks should be warm and dry in the morning, and you should feel much better.

recipes for healing

Minty Chest Rub

This homemade chest rub can relax you and calm your cough.

> 12 drops eucalyptus essential oil
> 4 drops peppermint essential oil
> 2 tablespoons olive oil or vegetable oil

1. In a small dish, mix the eucalyptus and peppermint essential oils with the olive oil.

2. Rub the mixture onto your chest and cover with a damp, warm towel (try warming the damp towel in the microwave). Leave on until the warmth fades.

Simple Mustard Powder Plaster

This mustard plaster produces heat without being hot to the touch. Mixing water with the powdered seed forms a volatile oil which irritates (and can burn) the skin, increasing blood flow. When using a mustard plaster, do not let the skin become too red. To soothe any burning, wash the area with cold water. Protect the skin beforehand by applying petroleum jelly to the area. To make a milder plaster, use less mustard powder or replace the water with milk or an egg. Do not leave on longer than 10 to 15 minutes.

> 1 tablespoon mustard powder
> 2 tablespoons all-purpose flour

1. In a bowl, mix the mustard powder with the flour. Add enough water to make a paste.

2. Spread the paste over half of a dish towel. Fold the towel in half, covering the paste, and apply to the chest. Don't apply the mustard paste directly onto the skin. Check the chest skin often and remove the mustard plaster if there are signs of irritation.

Nighttime Breathing Relief

Getting a good night's sleep is probably the best thing you can do for a cold. This recipe allows you to breathe so you can sleep through the night. The key oil in this formula is eucalyptus; you can triple the amount you use if you omit the other two oils.

> 2–4 drops peppermint essential oil
> 2–4 drops eucalyptus essential oil
> 2–4 drops wintergreen essential oil

1. In a small bowl, mix the oils together. Dip a cotton ball into the mixture and put it near the vent of a steam humidifier.

2. Place the humidifier and the cotton ball near your bed when you have a cold.

Extra-Strength Mustard Plaster

This recipe makes a slightly thicker, stronger mustard plaster. Do not leave on longer than 30 minutes.

> 2 tablespoons or more olive oil
> 1/3 cup yellow mustard seeds
> 2 tablespoons grated beeswax

1. Put 2 tablespoons olive oil and the mustard seeds into a blender and blend. Continue adding olive oil until you have a thick liquid.

2. Pour the mixture into the top of a double boiler over low heat; add the beeswax and heat, stirring, until the wax melts. Spread a dish towel on a flat surface. Once the mustard-wax mixture is warm and can be spread, apply it to the towel and let it cool to room temperature.

3. Place the towel salve-side-down on the chest and cover with a T-shirt or old flannel, then apply external heat on top with a heating pad or hot-water bottle. You should start to feel warmth seeping into your chest in about 10 to 15 minutes. Leave it on another 15 minutes. You can store the plaster in the fridge for several days; when needed, remove and let it warm to room temperature before using.

Flaxseed Toddy

This old farmers' remedy is said to be a good cold cure. At the very least, it's hot, tasty, and soothing.

> 2 ounces flaxseeds
> 2 ounces sugar
> 1 cup honey
> Juice of 3 lemons

1. Boil the flaxseeds in 1 quart of water for 5 to 10 minutes. Strain out the flaxseeds.

2. Add the sugar, honey, and lemon to the hot water and blend.

3. Drink 1/2 cup before meals and a cup at bedtime. Refrigerate the remaining toddy, but heat before using.

Herbal Inhalant

Make this soothing breathing reliever and tote it along to help ease congestion.

> 1/4 to 1/2 teaspoon rock salt
> 2–4 drops peppermint essential oil
> 2–4 drops eucalyptus essential oil
> 2–4 drops wintergreen essential oil

1. Put the rock salt in the bottom of a small glass bottle or jar with a tight-fitting lid. Add the oils.

2. Carry with you and sniff as needed to open clogged nasal passages.

Decongestant Salve

This rub can give that expensive stuff from the pharmacy a run for its money.

   ½ cup olive oil
   1 tablespoon peppermint essential oil
   1 tablespoon eucalyptus essential oil
   1 tablespoon wintergreen essential oil
   ½ ounce grated beeswax
   4 drops tincture of benzoin (available at drugstores)

1. In the top of a double boiler over low heat, heat the olive oil and the essential oils. Add the beeswax and tincture of benzoin and stir until the beeswax is melted and the oils are well mixed.

2. Pour the mixture into a clean, wide-mouthed jar with a tight-fitting lid and allow to cool. Put under your nose or rub on your chest as a decongestant. You can keep this mixture, covered, in a cool, dark place for up to two weeks. Wash your hands after applying so you don't accidentally get any salve in your eyes.

Sore Throat Gargle

This old-fashioned gargle will soothe a sore throat, and the sweetness may tempt kids to gargle a little longer.

   2 heaping tablespoons brown sugar
   ½ teaspoon salt
   ¼ teaspoon baking soda
   2 cups warm water

1. In a jar with a tight-fitting lid, combine the brown sugar, salt, baking soda, and warm water. Shake well before each use.

2. Gargle with up to ½ cup four times a day as needed. Make a fresh batch each day.

Fever-Relief Spray

Spraying pulse points with a cool, soothing solution might help lower a fever. At the very least, spritzing on this refreshing blend will soothe you and make you feel more comfortable. The pulse points are the places on the body where you can easily feel your heart rate when you touch them with your fingers—typically inside your wrists, just under each side of the jaw, and the back of the knees.

   ¼ cup rubbing alcohol or vodka
   ¼ cup witch hazel
   3 drops peppermint essential oil
   2 drops lavender essential oil

1. In a clean spray bottle, combine the rubbing alcohol, witch hazel, and peppermint and lavender oils. Shake to mix and then chill in the refrigerator.

2. Spray onto pulse points to reduce fever, avoiding your eyes and mouth.

conjunctivitis

Pantry HEALERS

Black tea

Boric acid

Eyebright tea

Fennel seeds

Flaxseeds

Honey

Vitamins A and C

Zinc

More commonly known as pinkeye, this red, itchy, crusty eye condition stems from inflammation of the membrane that covers the white part of the eye and lines the inner eyelids. It can be caused by viruses or, less commonly, bacteria, or by seasonal allergies. Conjunctivitis is so contagious that if your child comes down with it, you're liable to get a call from the school nurse asking you to bring her home until the infection clears up. Having infectious conjunctivitis in one eye practically guarantees it will spread to the other eye.

first things first

Follow these steps immediately if you or a loved one might have conjunctivitis:

• Take out your contact lenses, if you wear them, and clean them thoroughly. If you can, wear glasses until your eye(s) heal thoroughly. If your child has pinkeye and wears contacts, have her do the same. Removing contact lenses speeds healing and prevents reinfection.

• Toss any eye makeup products you've been using (they may be infected), and don't wear eye makeup again until the pinkeye disappears.

• Wash your hands several times a day.

• Don't share towels, eyedrops, tissues, eye makeup, washcloths, or pillowcases with family members who have pinkeye.

• Launder sheets, pillowcases, and towels of infected family members in hot water separately from those of the rest of the family.

kitchen cabinet cures

Use a honey soother. Put 3 tablespoons honey in 2 cups boiling water, stir to dissolve, and let it cool. Dip a makeup remover pad into the mixture and use it to wash the crust and pus from your eyes, using a different pad for each eye. Repeat several times a day. Studies show that applying raw honey to the eyes reduces the swelling, pus, and redness. Make sure you use raw honey; pasteurization destroys honey's antibiotic properties. You can find raw honey at health food stores.

Soothe with a wet tea bag. Place a warm, wet black tea bag over your infected eye for 5 minutes, followed by a cool, wet tea bag for 2 minutes. The tannins in the tea bags help reduce the swelling. Repeat several times a day with a fresh tea bag.

Try some boric acid. Boil 1 teaspoon of boric acid in 1 cup of water, cool, and apply with a sterile eye cup or gauze pad.

Boil up some fennel seeds. Fennel seeds help fight infection. Boil 1 teaspoon of seeds in 1 cup boiling water for 5 minutes, strain, cool, and apply with a gauze pad over closed eyes for 10 minutes.

Make a flax poultice. This soothing treatment will help soothe itchy, painful eyes. Bruise 1 ounce (about a small handful) of flaxseeds with a rolling pin or the bottom of a flat pot or frying pan. Steep them in 4 ounces water for 15 minutes. Wrap in gauze or cheesecloth and apply to closed eyes for 10 minutes or so.

Don't forget to take your vitamins. Take 10,000 IU vitamin A and 50 milligrams zinc once a day, and 500 milligrams vitamin C twice a day to strengthen your immune system and help speed the healing process. Note: These are adult doses. Ask your pediatrician about appropriate dosages for children.

When to Call THE DOCTOR

If the infection doesn't clear up after a few days, or the condition worsens, see your doctor. She may want to prescribe antibiotic drops.

the natural DOCTOR'S Rx

Health food stores carry eyebright tea, which is especially good for soothing conjunctivitis. Dip the tea bag into hot water for a minute or two to wet it, then let it cool before applying to the eye.

Weird & wacky

In some Italian neighborhoods, where coffee making (and drinking) is elevated to a high art, you might find a mother using cold brewed espresso as a pinkeye treatment. Odd? Absolutely—but it just might work. Here's why: Coffee's acidity is similar to boric acid, and caffeine works to constrict blood vessels so it could reduce puffiness.

constipation

Feeling "all backed up" is uncomfortable in so many ways. There's the bloated feeling, the unproductive straining, and the insecurity of knowing that you might suddenly need to let go at a most inopportune time. Constipation can have a slew of causes, including a fiber-poor diet, not drinking enough fluids, stress, laxative dependence, lack of exercise, and certain prescription drugs or health conditions. As luck would have it, constipation also has a slew of solutions, many of which can be found right in your kitchen pantry.

first things first

Here are the basic approaches to start with when things just don't seem to be moving the right way:

• The best way to become "regular" again is simply to eat more fiber—20 to 35 grams a day. Fiber absorbs water and makes your stool softer and larger, which speeds it through your system.

• To cope with all that fiber, you'll need more fluids too. Drink more water than usual.

• And don't forget about exercise, which can also help keep things moving.

• When you feel the urge, head to the bathroom. If you "put it off till later," you're asking for a case of constipation.

• On the other hand, don't try to force a bowel movement. You may give yourself hemorrhoids or anal fissures. These not only hurt, they aggravate constipation.

kitchen cabinet cures

Fix up a flax drink. Boil a couple of cups of water with 2 tablespoons flaxseeds. Strain and cool, then add a teaspoon of apple cider vinegar and drink. The fiber and liquid combo can help move things along.

Open some sesames. An Amish remedy for constipation—and one espoused by Chinese folk healers—is sesame seeds. Their oily composition helps moisturize the intestines, which can help if dry stools are a problem. Spin ½ ounce of the tasty seeds in a clean coffee grinder and sprinkle on food like a seasoning.

Syrup trick for infants. If your baby is constipated, add 1 teaspoon of corn syrup to 4 ounces of water or formula. It can work as a stool softener and make stools easier to pass.

Pop some psyllium. The seeds of a plantain relative, psyllium, is the laxative most recommended by modern herbalists and doctors. It can also be an effective treatment for irritable bowel syndrome and hemorrhoids. Though it's probably not something you'll find in your kitchen cabinet, you may want to run out to the health food store to pick some up. Relief is very likely to follow. Add 2 teaspoons of the seeds to a little water and let them swell slightly. Take in the morning and at night with 1 or 2 glasses of fluid. Although rare, allergic reactions or intestinal obstruction may occur.

When to Call THE DOCTOR

Chronic constipation can signal serious conditions, colorectal cancer and bowel obstruction among them. Tell your doctor if the problem lasts two weeks or more despite using the remedies in this chapter. Call your doctor immediately if you see blood in your stool or if constipation is accompanied by fever, severe abdominal pain, cramps, or unexplained weight loss. Also, if you've recently started a new medication that seems to cause constipation, advise your doctor. Possible drug culprits include antihistamines, diuretics, blood-pressure drugs, sedatives, calcium supplements, certain antidepressants, and antacids that contain calcium or aluminum.

Lay off the laxatives

Stimulant laxatives can be addictive, and using them regularly can lead to loss of important nutrients and permanent loss of bowel control. Even worse, their abuse has been linked to colon cancer. If you're dieting, you might be taking these unwittingly, because stimulant laxatives can be hidden in over-the-counter weight loss teas and supplements. Avoid diet aids that contain senna leaf (*Cassia senna*), cascara sagrada bark (*Rhamnus purshiana*), or castor oil.

Not all laxatives are dangerous, however. The bulk-producing laxatives, such as Metamucil, contain psyllium seed husks. This natural substance absorbs liquid in the intestines, swells up, and naturally triggers the urge to move the bowels. Other safe choices are the emollient laxatives, or stool softeners. They allow water or fat to penetrate the stool, or they help lay down a smooth coating that lets stools pass easier. Examples include Colace, mineral oil, and glycerin suppositories.

Get-up-and-go

There's a reason a daily walk is called a constitutional. When you move your body, you also help move food through your bowel more quickly. Aim for a 15-minute daily walk at the very least. The more you move, the more you "move."

Drink coffee to loosen up. If you're a java drinker, you may have already discovered that the caffeine in coffee has a bowel-loosening effect. It induces a bowel movement by stimulating the colon. Just don't drink too much of it—caffeine is a diuretic and will eliminate fluid from your body.

Or try other hot drinks. If you don't like coffee, try any other hot beverage first thing in the morning. Herbal or decaffeinated tea or a cup of hot water with a little lemon juice or honey may stimulate the colon as well. (Lemon juice is a natural laxative.)

Grab some prunes. The number one classic kitchen remedy for getting bowels back on track is fiber-rich prunes. (Three prunes contain 3 grams of fiber.) What's more, a prune compound called dihydroxyphenyl isatin helps trigger the intestinal contractions that make you want to go. An old grandmother's remedy for

Kitchen cabinet fiber foods

If you're wondering how to get more fiber in your diet for better regularity, look to these kitchen pantry staples, all excellent sources of fiber.

Food	Portion size	Fiber Grams
Bran cereal	½ cup	10–14
Red kidney beans	½ cup	8.2
Shredded Wheat'N Bran cereal	1¼ cups	7.9
Lentils, boiled	1½ cups	7.8
Black beans	½ cup	7.5
Figs, dried	3	6.9
Navy beans	½ cup	6.7
Whole-wheat spaghetti, cooked	1 cup	6.3
Pinto beans	½ cup	5.5
Oatmeal, cooked	1 cup	5.0
Green split-pea soup	1 cup	5.0
Almonds	1 ounce	3.3
Prunes, canned	5	3.3
Pearl barley	½ cup	3.0
Dates	5	3.0
Prunes, dried	5	3.0

constipation: Soak a handful of prunes in boiled water overnight. First thing in the morning, drink the water, then eat the soaked prunes. Another great dried fruit choice is figs, which will get your move on and may not cause as much bloating as prunes can.

Reach for raisins. Raisins are also high in fiber and contain tartaric acid, which has a laxative effect. In one study in which people ate 4½ ounces (one small box) of raisins a day, doctors determined that it took half the time for digested food to make it through the digestive tract.

Stir up some honey and lemon. Try having a cup of hot water mixed with a tablespoon of lemon or lime juice and a tablespoon of honey. The juice stimulates the release of bile, and that can kick-start intestinal contractions.

Get out the salts. Since its discovery in a mineral spring in the village of Epsom, England, in 1695, Epsom salts have been a popular constipation remedy. They work because they draw water into the intestines, and that's what enables bowel flow. To use, stir 2 or 3 teaspoons into a glass of warm water and drink in the morning. Don't use this remedy for more than seven days—it can cause dehydration and laxative dependence.

coughs

You're coughing so hard that the floor is shaking. Your chest hurts, you're keeping yourself and your family awake at night, and you're utterly miserable. Though it feels absolutely awful, a bad cough is actually a good thing. It's part of your body's sophisticated defense system and helps rid the respiratory tract of phlegm. Coughs can be caused by a cold, influenza, bronchitis, or pneumonia. Dust or smoke can trigger a dry cough—as can a case of nerves. In all cases, there are plenty of options for quick, soothing relief.

first things first

When you have a cough, there are basic steps to follow, in addition to trying the following remedies:

• Of course, cover your mouth when you cough. And then wash your hands frequently (consider keeping a bottle of hand sanitizer next to you until you get better).

• Drink plenty of liquids, especially hot tea. Coughing can be dehydrating; hot tea not only replenishes your fluid levels, but relieves your throat.

• Let yourself cough, particularly if it's productive (meaning it is bringing up phlegm). That means not taking cough suppressants.

• If your cough is productive, speed up the healing process by inhaling lots of steam, either from a vaporizer, shower, or steam treatment. It'll help break up and expel the congestion.

Pantry HEALERS

Almonds

Black pepper

Eucalyptus
  essential oil

Flaxseeds

Honey

Lemon

Milk

Onions

Peppermint

Sage

Salt

Thyme

kitchen cabinet cures

Pick some thyme. Thyme is an officially approved German treatment for coughs, upper respiratory infections, bronchitis, and whooping cough, with good reason. Those tiny leaves are packed with cough-relieving compounds. For starters, thyme flavonoids relax tracheal and ileal muscles, which are involved in coughing. The flavonoids also reduce inflammation. To make a tea, mix 2 teaspoons crushed leaves in 1 cup boiling water, cover, then steep for 10 minutes and strain.

Fight back with flax, honey, and lemon. Boiling flaxseeds in water gives you a thick, gooey gel that soothes the throat and the bronchial tract. Honey and lemon act as mild antibiotics and make this syrup super-soothing. To make it, boil 2 to 3 tablespoons of flaxseeds in 1 cup of water until the water becomes thick. Strain, then add 3 tablespoons each of honey and lemon juice. Take 1 tablespoon as needed.

Brew black pepper tea. This remedy is rooted in two very different traditions: New England folk medicine and traditional Chinese medicine. The rationale behind it is that black pepper stimulates circulation and mucus flow; honey is a natural cough reliever and mild antibiotic. To make the tea, place 1 teaspoon of freshly ground black pepper and 2 tablespoons of honey in a cup. Fill with boiling water and let steep, covered, for 15 minutes. Strain and sip as needed. This remedy works best on coughs that produce mucus and isn't suitable for dry coughs.

Another sour approach. This isn't for the feint of heart, but it is a commonly used folk cure: Quarter a fresh lemon, sprinkle it with lots of black pepper and salt, and suck on it for quick relief.

Try some warm milk. Another popular folk cure for a cough is to drink a cup of hot milk sweetened with honey.

Consider almonds. Some ancient traditions believe almonds help relieve bronchial problems, including coughs. They recommend blending a few teaspoons of finely ground almonds with a cup of orange juice and sipping it for relief.

When to Call THE DOCTOR

If you have difficulty breathing or swallowing, have thick greenish-yellow or bloody phlegm, a fever, stiff neck, or wheezing, see your doctor. Call 911 if you can't catch your breath or if your face swells and you have hives. Finally, check in with your doctor if an otherwise uncomplicated cough lasts longer than two weeks.

the natural DOCTOR'S Rx

Believe it or not, rinsing your nasal passages with a mild saline solution can ease your cough. That's because coughs are often caused or worsened by postnasal drip. Spritzing the inside of your nose helps wash out mucus that would otherwise drip, drip, drip down your throat. Here's how: Make a saline solution with ¼ teaspoon salt and ¼ teaspoon baking soda in 8 ounces of warm water. Place the saline solution in a neti pot (a little container made exactly for this purpose and found at health food stores). Or you can also use a small plastic bottle with a nasal tip, or even a water pick (also known as an oral irrigator) fitted with a special nasal tip.

super onion cough syrup
Recipe page 217

recipes for healing

Lemony Cough Syrup

This tasty formula works brilliantly to ease coughs. Both honey and lemon are antibacterial, and the honey is soothing. What's more, it's scientifically proven to work. Researchers at Pennsylvania State University studied 105 coughing kids who received buckwheat honey, a honey-flavored preparation containing dextromethorphan (the ingredient in many cough syrups), or no treatment at all. Parents reported that kids who got honey saw the greatest reduction in coughing severity and frequency. Never give honey to children under the age of one. It's not safe for them.

> 1 lemon
> 1 pint raw honey

1. In a small saucepan, cover the whole lemon in water and simmer for 5 minutes.
2. In a separate saucepan, warm the honey, but don't let it boil. A slow cooker works perfectly.
3. Remove the lemon from the pan and wait until it's cool enough to handle, then slice it and add it to the honey. Let the honey and lemon cook on warm heat for an hour—do not allow to boil.
4. Cool, then strain into a sterilized jar and refrigerate. Have a teaspoon of the syrup whenever you need cough relief.

Super Onion Cough Syrup

After honey, lemon, and whiskey, onion is the ingredient most commonly included in cough remedies. Turns out, there are two good reasons why. First, onions relieve inflammation that can reduce irritation. And they contain a substance called protocatechuic acid that attacks viruses, like the one that may be causing your cough.

> 5 or 6 onions
> ½ cup honey
> Juice of 1 lemon

1. Chop the onions and place them in the top of a double boiler.
2. Add the honey and lemon and cook over very low heat for 3 or 4 hours.
3. Strain and take a tablespoon or two as needed.

Steam Cough Relief

This herbal steam treatment is a triple threat against coughs. First, the steam opens up breathing passages and thins mucus, making it easier to expel. Thyme reduces spasms in muscles that control coughing, and eucalyptus kills many of the bacteria that cause bacterial respiratory infections, plus it reduces bronchial inflammation.

> 4 cups water
> 3 tablespoons dried thyme
> 5 drops eucalyptus essential oil

1. In a saucepan over medium heat, heat the water until nearly boiling (but don't boil). Pour into a heat-safe bowl and add the thyme and eucalyptus oil.

2. Hold your head about 8 inches above the water, drape a towel over your head and the bowl to make a tent, and breathe in deeply until the water cools. Keep your eyes closed throughout.

Herbal Steam Treatment for Congestion

Aromatic herbs and humidity can do wonders easing coughs and chest congestion. This treatment takes only minutes to put together, and it's heavenly to use.

> I tablespoon dried thyme, chopped
> I tablespoon dried sage, chopped
> I tablespoon dried peppermint, chopped
> Boiling water

1. Put the thyme, sage, and peppermint in a medium bowl and add boiling water.

2. Let steep for a minute.

3. Lean over the bowl with a towel draped over your head and the bowl and inhale for 10 minutes. Keep your face 8 to 10 inches above the steaming water. Repeat two or three times a day as needed.

cuts & scrapes

Oops! The knife slips, the glass shatters, the bike skids, there's an icy patch on the sidewalk, and next thing you know, you're bleeding from a minor cut or scrape. Kids, in particular, get scraped and cut on a seemingly regular basis and run to Mom or Pop for reassurance and treatment. Most minor injuries can be easily treated with simple, soothing, kitchen remedies—plus a big hug and a kiss, no matter if the "kid" is 7 or 70.

first things first

The first two steps are almost always the same when you get a cut or scrape:

• Stop the bleeding. Most minor cuts and scrapes will stop bleeding on their own. If you're treating one that doesn't, apply pressure with a clean cloth for a few minutes.

• Then clean the wound. Rinse with water, but don't use soap; it can irritate the wound. Remove any debris with tweezers you've sterilized in boiling water.

From there, treat the wound using remedies like those below, and cover it with a bandage to prevent infection.

kitchen cabinet cures

Go Krazy on it. Krazy Glue contains the same ingredients as "liquid bandage," and just a drop on a cut will seal it closed for quicker healing.

Pantry HEALERS

Beeswax

Black tea

Chamomile
essential oil

Echinacea

Honey

Krazy Glue

Olive oil

Tea tree essential oil

Vitamin E capsules

If the cut is deep or very long and bleeds heavily, you need stitches right away. Go straight to the emergency room, your doctor, or a walk-in clinic. If a cut or scrape reddens, fills with pus, or has red streaks, it's probably infected and will require a doctor's attention. And see the doctor if you've cut yourself with something that's dirty or rusty, especially if you're uncertain when you had your last tetanus shot.

Spread on the honey. The high sugar content of honey pulls moisture from wounds and denies bacteria the moisture they need to survive. It also locks out harmful external contaminants. As far back as the 1970s, surgeons reported that women who had gynecological surgery had shorter hospital stays and showed no signs of infection when incisions were coated with honey. Studies in India show that burns dressed with honey heal more quickly and with less pain and scarring than burns slathered with silver sulfadiazine, a conventional burn treatment. What's more, a recent scientific review found that six out of seven studies showed honey to be an effective treatment for healing wounds and eradicating infections. Medicinal honey is available at health food stores, but you can use regular honey on small cuts and scrapes.

Press on with tea. Black tea contains tannins, which act as astringents that can stop bleeding. Gently press a cool, damp tea bag on a cut or scrape, which will feel soothing and can stop any swelling.

Dab on some echinacea. If you have a bottle of echinacea tincture lying around, dab some right on the cut. It might sting for a couple of seconds, but the herb (and the alcohol it's prepared with) will kill any germs. Echinacea also helps relieve pain and reduces inflammation.

 recipe for healing

Herbal Healing Ointment

You can have this ointment on hand to treat everyday cuts and scrapes as they arise. It's easy to make and just as effective as store-bought antiseptic creams.

   1–1½ ounces grated beeswax
   1 cup olive oil
   2 capsules vitamin E, 400 IU
   30 drops tea tree essential oil
   20 drops lavender essential oil (optional)
   10 drops chamomile essential oil (optional)

1. In the top of a double boiler over low heat, melt the beeswax. Stir in the olive oil. Remove from the heat. Pierce each vitamin E capsule with a needle and squeeze the contents into the mixture. Then stir in the tea tree, lavender, and chamomile oils.

2. Pour into a small sterilized jar with a tight-fitting lid and store in a cool, dark place. Use as needed on wounds. It should last a year.

dandruff

Although you'd think dandruff is a hair problem, because its telltale white specks are usually spotted on the hair or the shoulders, dandruff is actually a skin condition. It has many causes: a dry or oily scalp, sunburn, an allergic reaction, a deficient diet, residue from harsh hair products—even stress. The most common cause, however, is seborrheic dermatitis, an itchy, scaly rash that can affect the scalp, face, and chest. To lessen the flaking and itching, concoct a kitchen cabinet cure or two.

first things first

Sometimes, the solution to dandruff is simpler than you think. Be sure you are doing the following before moving on to more serious remedies:

• Use a dandruff shampoo that matches your hair. Dandruff shampoos are available for all types of hair, be it thin, thick, dry, or oily. Match up carefully.

• Don't go more than two days without shampooing.

• Don't just lather your hair when shampooing; thoroughly massage your entire scalp.

• Be sure to rinse out all the shampoo. Sometimes, dandruff isn't dandruff, but just dried soap residue!

kitchen cabinet cures

Treat your scalp to ginger. Finely mince or grate a 3-inch piece of ginger. Place in a saucepan along with four

Pantry HEALERS

Aloe

Apple cider vinegar

Chamomile tea

Ginger

Olive oil

Rosemary

Thyme

chamomile tea bags and a quart of water. Simmer, covered for 15 to 20 minutes. Let the tea cool, then strain. After shampooing, massage ½ to 1 cup (depending on how long your hair is) into your scalp for a few minutes. Don't rinse. You can refrigerate any leftover tea for your next shampoo.

Prune your aloe plant. This old folk remedy could do the trick. Cut a thick stalk or two off your aloe plant, and squeeze out as much gel as you can. Apply the gel to your scalp and massage in. You can do this right before bed, and cover your hair with a bandanna. Or, just massage it in and leave it in for an hour or two. Then, hop in the shower and foam the aloe with water, massaging for a few minutes before rinsing. Don't use shampoo.

Grab the vinegar. An apple cider vinegar rinse is perhaps the most popular dandruff remedy of all time. Theory is that the acid in the vinegar helps restore the scalp's chemical balance and quash any bacteria that may be contributing to the flakes. To use, simply soak a cotton ball with vinegar and apply all over the scalp. Or, just pour a cup or so over your hair and massage your scalp for a few minutes. Allow to dry. No vinegar in the house? Juice a few lemons instead.

Make an herbal oil. Ginger and rosemary are often chosen as antidandruff weapons—possibly because both calm irritation. This remedy works especially well if your scalp is dry and itchy. Combine ¼ cup olive oil with 1 tablespoon each of minced ginger and dried rosemary. Warm over low heat for a few minutes. Massage into your scalp and leave in for 15 to 30 minutes. Wash with a gentle shampoo and rinse well.

Squeeze-bottle cures

Many of the home remedies for dandruff involve making teas, rinses, or other liquid treatments that should be used frequently. How do you manage this without having to constantly make new batches? Easy: Start by making one large batch. Then put enough for the coming week into a plastic kitchen squeeze bottle, and put the bottle in the shower. They're perfect for dousing your scalp without excess waste. Any leftovers should be packaged tightly and put in the freezer for later usage. Be sure to label carefully to make sure no one tries to cook with it!

Rinse with rosemary. Rosemary helps control the over-production of seborrhea, the scalp oil that contributes to dandruff. Make an antidandruff brew by adding 2 table-spoons of dried rosemary to 1 cup boiled water. Cover and steep for 20 minutes, then strain and cool. Use as a final rinse after shampooing and conditioning, and massage it well into the scalp. For best results, don't rinse out. Rosemary can darken hair, so avoid this if you're a blonde and want to stay that way.

Give it some thyme. This fragrant herb combats bacteria that could contribute to your dandruff problem. Simmer 3 heaping tablespoons of dried thyme in a couple of cups of water in a covered pot for 15 to 20 minutes. Strain and cool. Apply to hair after shampooing; don't rinse out.

 recipe for healing

Dried Herb Dandruff Treatment

This fragrant infusion combines rosemary's oil-reducing power with thyme's bacteria-clobbering capability. It smells heavenly and, as a bonus, will make your hair nice and shiny.

2 teaspoons dried rosemary
2 teaspoons dried thyme
$2/3$ cup boiling water
$2/3$ cup cider vinegar

1. Place the rosemary and thyme in a heatproof glass or ceramic bowl. Pour in the boiling water. Cover and steep for 15 to 20 minutes.

2. Strain the liquid into a clean, 10-ounce bottle with a tight-fitting lid. Add the vinegar and shake. Store in a cool, dark place.

3. After shampooing, rinse hair thoroughly and then massage a small amount of the herbal treatment into the scalp. Between shampoos, massage a small amount into the scalp before going to bed.

depression

The blues can strike anyone, any time, out of nowhere. But if you've become a glass-is-half empty person most of the time and have lost your ability to get a kick out of life, you might have more than just a case of the blues. Clinical depression is a real condition that requires real treatment. Maybe you've experienced a traumatic event—a death in the family, a divorce, or a job loss. New mothers sometimes cope with postpartum depression. Or maybe, for no reason you can put your finger on, you just feel perpetually sad and empty. Happily, whether you are just a little down or under a doctor's care for depression, you may be able to lift your mood a bit just by opening your pantry door.

first things first

Everyone—*everyone*—has periods in their lives when their moods darken. But that is not the same as having clinical depression. If you've started to feel a little down, don't ignore the situation. Ask yourself a few basic questions:

• Am I feeling perpetually hopeless?

• Is my mood interfering with my normal activities?

• Do I cry often or have thoughts of suicide?

• Am I abusing alcohol or drugs?

• Have I gained or lost weight without intending to?

If the answer to all these questions is "no," then there's a good chance you can turn gray skies to blue again merely by following some of the uplifting remedies ahead.

kitchen cabinet cures

Take your vitamins and minerals. If you're down and you can't figure out why, you just might have a vitamin or mineral deficiency. One recent study linked depression to low levels of vitamin D among women during the winter. When the women took vitamin D supplements, their moods improved. In another recently announced Chinese study, researchers uncovered a link between depression and low levels of B_{12} and folate in adults over the age of 55. Finally, in a third new study, women with PMS-related depression who took calcium supplements were able to lose their blues. What's more, nutrition experts note that vitamin B_6, magnesium, and calcium have mood-lifting capabilities.

Become a fishetarian. In countries where fish consumption is high, such as Japan, Taiwan, and Finland, rates of depression tend to be low. But in areas where fish consumption is low, like North America and Europe, depression rates are much higher—as much as 10 times higher. Women who rarely eat fish have more than twice the risk of developing depression compared to those who dine on "fin food" often. To treat depression, you'll need between 1 and 3 grams of omega-3s a day to lift your mood, an amount you'll have to get from taking fish oil supplements. However, eating more canned fish, such as sardines, salmon, herring, and mackerel, could potentially help protect you from developing depression in the first place. Start by eating at least two fish meals a week.

Flip for flax. Flaxseed is rich in omega-3s. Bump up your daily take by adding a couple of tablespoons of freshly ground flaxseed to cereal, yogurt, or salads every day.

Cook up a bowl of oatmeal. Around the turn of the 20th century, a school of physicians known as the Eclectics treated "nervous exhaustion" with oats. And they were probably onto something. First, oats are a nutritional powerhouse, containing more than half the recommended daily amount of essential fatty acids, folic acid, and zinc, among other essential minerals. What's more, oatmeal contains plenty of fiber, which can help prevent blood sugar spikes that affect mood. For this treatment to be effective, have a bowl of whole-grain oatmeal for breakfast three or more

When to Call THE DOCTOR

If you answer "yes" to any of the questions in the "First things first" section, or if your sadness lasts more than two weeks, seek treatment promptly. Effective solutions can include talk therapy, medication, or a combination of both. If you're feeling suicidal, call 911 or, if you live in the United States, the National Suicide Prevention Lifeline at 1-800-273-TALK (8255) for the immediate help you need.

times a week. Avoid instant or other varieties that are loaded with sugar or artificial ingredients.

Make your cereal whole grain. Just ¾ cup of whole-grain cereal contains about 800 micrograms of folate, a B vitamin. Many people who are depressed are deficient in folate. Studies find that men who get 234 micrograms of folate for every 1,000 calories they eat are half as likely to become depressed as men who get 119 micro-grams. Other great pantry sources of folate include lentils (358 micrograms in 1 cup of cooked lentils) and chickpeas (282 micrograms in a cup).

Try a mood-lifting tea. Herbalists call lemon balm the "gladdening herb" and say it lifts the spirits. If you don't already have lemon balm tea bags on hand, pick some up at the health or natural food store. Brew up a cup using one tea bag to a cup of boiled water. Cover and steep for 10 minutes. Enjoy up to three cups a day, sweetened to taste with honey.

A plain vanilla remedy

Certain aromas can lift your mood by influencing the production of endorphins—the brain's "feel-good" chemicals. Among them are vanilla and lavender. In fact, vanilla helps reduce anxiety, which is often associated with depression. According to a study done at Memorial Sloan-Kettering Cancer Center, patients undergoing MRIs who breathed vanilla-scented air reported 63 percent less anxiety than those who breathed unscented air.

Use this fragrant strategy by adding a drop or two of vanilla extract to the pot before the coffee brews to fill your kitchen with the pleasing scent, or simply light some vanilla-scented candles around your home or add vanilla essential oil to your bathwater.

In another study, conducted on college students, inhaling the aroma of lavender essential oil improved depression symptoms and also eased insomnia symptoms. You can dab lavender oil on your wrists and temples or diffuse it in the air with an inexpensive device you can pick up at the health food store.

diarrhea

There's nothing subtle about diarrhea. A bout of loose bowels can overtake you suddenly, out of the blue. The siege can resolve quickly or linger for days and will certainly disrupt your life as long as it lasts—chances are, you'll be going nowhere until it abates. Common causes include food poisoning, a change in eating habits, or traveling to countries where foreign water and foods disagree with you. Viral, bacterial or even parasitic infections could also be to blame, as can stress. Happily, most cases are minor and pass quickly, and several handy items from your kitchen cabinet can contribute to a speedier recovery.

first things first

Here's the immediate response you should have to the arrival of diarrhea:

• Resist that urge to run to the drugstore for an over-the-counter anti-diarrhea medicine. Diarrhea is your body's defense mechanism against noxious substances, so let yourself purge before you put a stop to the process.

• While you're under siege, keep eating to a minimum, and drink plenty of fluids. Best are electrolyte drinks like Gatorade, which can restore fluids and help prevent dehydration.

kitchen cabinet cures

Sip clear broth or juice. Apple juice and clear broth will help replace salts and minerals lost to diarrhea. But

Pantry HEALERS

Apple cider vinegar
Apple juice
Applesauce
Baking soda
Blackberry leaf tea
Black tea
Broth (clear)
Buttermilk
Caraway seeds
Chamomile tea
Honey
Lemon
Lime
Oranges
Raspberry leaf tea
Rooibos tea
Salt
Sugar
Vinegar
White rice

When to Call THE DOCTOR

Call your doctor if your diarrhea lasts more than 24 hours. And if you have any of these symptoms, call your doctor right away or seek emergency care:

• Pain, fever, or the presence of blood or mucous in the stool

• Persistent diarrhea or an inability to diagnose the diarrhea's cause

• A sense of becoming dehydrated (symptoms of this include constant thirst, dark-colored urine, dry mouth, fatigue, weakness, or chills)

the natural DOCTOR'S Rx

Friendly bacteria—often called probiotics and which include well-known types like acidophilus—are great for helping resolve diarrhea. You can find probiotics in yogurt that contains "live active cultures," or you can buy them in supplement form at drugstores and health food stores. Read yogurt labels to be sure the ones you choose contain high numbers of several strains of these good bugs, and stick with plain or vanilla nonfat yogurt while you're ill.

As to food, stick to the tried-and-true BRAT diet while your bowels are under siege: bananas, plain rice, applesauce, dry toast, and tea.

avoid citrus, pineapple, tomato, and other juices that you can't see through because the acid in them can irritate already inflamed intestines. Start with small sips and work your way up to drinking a cup every half hour.

Sip orange peel tea. A traditional diarrhea remedy and general digestive aid, orange peels stimulate digestion. You need organic oranges for this brew; nonorganic orange skins may contain dyes and pesticides. Peel an orange and chop the peel finely. Place in a pot and cover with a pint of boiling water. Cover the pot tightly and steep till cool. Strain, sweeten with honey, and drink.

Calm yourself with chamomile. This tea, known for its gentle relaxation powers, can also calm bouts of diarrhea. It attacks the problem on two fronts, via compounds that ease intestinal spasms and combat inflammation. To brew, use two chamomile tea bags per cup of boiled water. Let steep, covered, for 15 minutes. Drink a cup three times a day while you're under the weather.

Sip some vinegar water. If a bacterial infection is at the root of your diarrhea, apple cider vinegar could help contain the problem, thanks to its antibiotic properties. What's more, some folk remedy experts contend that apple cider vinegar contains pectin, which can help soothe intestinal spasms.

Offer caraway tea. To calm the intestinal spasms and discomfort that accompanies diarrhea, try sipping caraway tea. Brew it by adding a teaspoon of caraway seeds to a cup of boiling water, cover, and let steep for 15 minutes. Strain through a fine sieve before serving.

Or try these other teas. Tannins in black tea have an astringent action on the mucous membranes in the intestines. This helps the body absorb fluids and calms intestinal inflammation. In particular, blackberry and raspberry leaf teas are praised by herbalists for their ability to ease diarrhea. Be sure to choose teas made from real leaves (some berry teas are mainly flavoring). Choose decaffeinated black teas; caffeine is dehydrating. (There is no caffeine in herbal teas.) Red teas, such as rooibos, can calm spasms in the colon.

Bind yourself up with rice. Plain white rice is known for its "binding effect" on bowels. Eat small portions of white rice, butter-free, until diarrhea is under control.

Honey to the rescue. Many cultures swear by honey as a cure for diarrhea. Mix 4 tablespoons of honey into a cup of hot water. Let cool and drink. It's very sweet, but effective.

Try some applesauce. Applesauce contains pectin, which helps to firm soft bowel movements. Consider applesauce spread on a slice of toast. But avoid apple juice—it contains little pectin and could make the situation worse.

Consider this ancient approach. Many cultures swear by buttermilk as a diarrhea remedy. An Ayurvedic healing approach is to mix ½ teaspoon of dry ginger into a cup of buttermilk and drink that three to four times a day.

Weird & wacky

Though we absolutely don't recommend this treatment for treating an infant's diarrhea, we do find it fascinating and would love to know what inspired its creation. We offer it up strictly in the interest of history: Cut the lining from a chicken gizzard and let it dry. Then put it in boiling water to make a tea. Give 1 teaspoonful to your baby every half hour.

recipes for healing

DIY Electrolyte Drink

This simple formula helps maintain your body's equilibrium.

> 1 cup apple juice
> 2 cups water
> 1 teaspoon salt
> Juice from a lemon or a lime

1. In a pitcher, combine apple juice, water, salt, and the lemon or lime juice. Store in the refrigerator.

2. Drink throughout the day to maintain hydration and proper balance of electrolytes.

Pantry Rehydrator

Sip this solution all day long to make sure you're replenishing fluids flushed by diarrhea. Drink up to 3 quarts a day.

> ½ teaspoon salt
> ½ teaspoon baking soda
> 4 tablespoons sugar
> 1 liter of water

Mix all ingredients in a pitcher until dissolved and drink as needed.

earache

Pantry HEALERS

Pantry healers

Apple cider vinegar

Garlic

Olive oil

Peppermint
  essential oil

Salt

Sesame oil

Vodka

Xylitol gum

Ears are prone to problems that make them hurt. Blame it on their delicate architecture. Inside your ear, the moist, dark, narrow canals that loop-di-loop like a snail's shell are ideal harbors for bacteria. While young children are most prone to earaches, they're not the only ones who suffer from their pain; ear infections can strike at any age. Plus water enthusiasts of any age can contract swimmer's ear (otitis externa), the ear canal infection caused when bacteria invade the skin that lines the canal. Fortunately, there are easy ways to deal with most earaches, and they all start with ingredients found in your pantry.

first things first

• Don't race to the doctor the minute an earache strikes. These days, most docs recommend taking a 72-hour "wait-and-see" approach—both for grownups and kids (as long as your baby is otherwise healthy and her symptoms are mild). Since most cases of otitis media (the official name for inner ear infections) clear up on their own, waiting it out can prevent the overuse of antibiotics.

• Apply a warm, moist cloth over the ear to help relieve pain.

• Take a mild over-the-counter pain reliever to reduce the pain. If it's a child with the earache, ask his or her doctor first before giving pain medicine.

kitchen cabinet cures

Shake up the Italian salt trick. Heat a cup or so of coarse salt in a pan till hot. Put the heated salt in a thick cotton sock (using a funnel makes this easier) and tie the end. Test against your inner wrist to make sure it's not too hot, then hold the sock against your child's hurting ear. At the very least, the warmth will ease discomfort. And it's also possible that the salt will draw fluid from the infection, which theoretically could relieve middle ear pressure.

Put vinegar to work. Mix 2 tablespoons apple cider vinegar with 2 tablespoons warm water and put it in a dropper bottle. Instill four drops in the painful ear four times a day.

Harness the healing power of vodka. Try putting three drops of room-temperature vodka in a painful ear to relieve pain and help kill bacteria.

Surprise! An ingredient in sugar-free gum helps prevent ear infections.

Make a salty gargle. Gargling with warm salt water when ear pain begins can help some children. The liquid's heat increases the flow of blood to the eustachian tubes, which link the ears and throat.

Xylitol gum to the rescue. The sweetener xylitol, which comes from birch trees and is also found in strawberries and plums, cuts down the growth of bacteria that cause middle-ear infections. In one study, children who chewed two pieces of the gum five times a day for two months had 40 percent fewer ear infections. Trident chewing gum is one of several brands that contain xylitol.

Open sesame (oil). If you cook Asian cuisine, you probably have a bottle of sesame oil in your pantry. Turns out it is a popular folk remedy for earaches. Add half a clove of

||||||||||||||||||||||||||||||||||||||||||||||||||||||||||||||||||||||||||||||||||||||||||||||||||||||||||||||||

Remove wax safely

To remove earwax, put 10 drops of hydrogen peroxide in each ear and let it stay there for three minutes. Then tilt the head so the liquid runs out—and the wax with it. Never, ever try to excavate wax with cotton swabs, paper clips, hair pins, or similar tools. Granny's advice is still best: Never stick anything smaller than your elbow in your ear.

Weird & wacky

These cures should be labeled "weird, wacky, and disgusting." The first, mentioned in several compilations of old home remedies, calls for putting drops of urine in the affected ear. It's even been written that Elvis Presley's mother relied on this creepy remedy whenever The King had a childhood earache.

Another gross-sounding trick was to stuff the painful ear with a moist wad of chewing tobacco—or even to blow tobacco smoke into the ear. Thanks, but we'll pass on all of these. There's no known science to support any of them.

garlic to a teaspoon of sesame oil and heat until warm. Lie on your side and put four drops into the painful ear. Leave it in for 10 minutes, then drain.

Or try olive oil. Many folk healers say that olive oil is an effective earache remedy. As with sesame oil, heat until warm, then put about four drops into your ear. Let sit for 10 minutes, then drain.

Use peppermint. A similar remedy from days gone by is peppermint essential oil. Thoroughly blend one drop of peppermint oil with 20 drops of olive oil and put four drops of the mix in the infected ear. Drain after 10 minutes. Other old-timers say to apply the peppermint oil around the outside of your ear. Just make sure pure peppermint oil never enters your ear.

When to Call THE DOCTOR

Ear pain isn't usually an emergency. If it's a baby with the earache, see the doctor if the pain seems extreme or the child has a fever over 100°F. As for you, call the doctor if the pain doesn't go away after two days. Tell the doctor about any fluid discharge from the ear, dizziness, or painful sensations when you chew. Sudden, intense pain, followed by some relief, could indicate a ruptured eardrum. Other common signs of ruptured eardrum are discharge (sometimes with blood), muffled hearing, a ringing in the ears, and a feeling of dizziness or vertigo. If you or your child has these symptoms, see your doctor before trying any of the remedies in this chapter.

Garlic: the bacteria slayer

If you have garlic in the pantry, you might never need to give your child that pink prescription medicine ever again. Here's why: Garlic is Mother Nature's antibiotic. It contains compounds that kill bacteria and relieve inflammation. Some experts speculate that garlic combats bacteria differently than antibiotics. Since garlic doesn't rely on mimicking and interrupting the bacteria's defense mechanisms (like antibiotics do), bacteria don't fight against it. Thus, they don't mutate and become resistant to the cure.

Herbalists and doctors schooled in natural medicine say that using garlic oil in the ear eases ear pain because it migrates past the eardrum to alleviate the infection.

Here are five ways to harness garlic's power to clear up ear infections, including how to make garlic oil.

1. If your children get ear infections frequently, peel and finely chop garlic cloves from two or three bulbs. Place in a clean glass jar. Cover completely with olive oil and steep in the refrigerator for a week. At the end of the week, strain out the garlic and pour some oil into a little dropper bottle. To use, warm it slightly by standing the dropper bottle in a bowl of hot water. Add three or four drops to the affected ear and gently cover the opening with a cotton ball. Store the leftover oil in the refrigerator in a labeled and dated jar.

2. If you need garlic oil immediately, use a garlic crusher or mince the garlic as fine as you can and let it steep, covered in olive oil, for at least 15 minutes. Strain it and keep leftover oil in the refrigerator. Warm it slightly before dropping it into the affected ear with an ear dropper. Lightly cover the ear opening with a cotton ball.

3. Eat one or two raw cloves every day while you or your child is fighting the infection. One approach: Chop the fresh garlic, mix it with olive oil, and spread it on toast.

4. Mix chopped garlic with some warm honey and eat it right off the spoon. Never give honey to babies under 1 year old.

5. Squeeze a clove of garlic and put a few drops of the juice in the ear. Repeat three times a day.

eczema

This maddeningly persistent, baffling, unsightly skin condition might make you long to be a skin-shedding snake. Compounding your frustration is the fact that doctors are often at a loss to determine eczema's cause or effective treatment. During acute flare-ups, skin erupts in small, itchy, fluid-filled blisters. Over time, scratching makes the skin look thick and scaly. Home treatments focus on keeping skin moisturized, which helps prevent the itch—and triggers the healing.

first things first

Before trying home remedies, be sure to take these tried-and-true steps:

• During winter months, use a humidifier in your bedroom to help keep your skin moist. Make sure to clean the machine frequently so you don't end up breathing in mold and fungi, which thrive in dirty humidifiers.

• To minimize sweating in the summer, which can aggravate eczema, run the air conditioner.

• Rely on your dishwasher as much as possible to avoid contact with detergents and water. When you do wash dishes, wear a pair of cotton-lined rubber gloves or wear rubber gloves over a pair of thin cotton gloves. Avoid skin contact with latex, since it can cause allergic reactions—and make eczema worse—in some people.

• Slash or eliminate your use of laundry chemicals. Instead, use toxin-free products whenever possible—

Pantry HEALERS

Aloe

Canned fish (herring, mackerel, salmon, sardines, tuna)

Flaxseeds

Honey

Lavender essential oil

Nuts

Olive oil

Turmeric

Vegetable shortening

or those that are fragrance-free and dye-free. Avoid bleach, fabric softeners, and dryer sheets.

• Give your clothes an extra rinse in the washing machine to remove all traces of detergent.

• Consider whether something you've touched has caused a breakout, and steer clear of these substances in the future. Contact dermatitis can be caused by nickel used in earrings and other jewelry, as well as latex, cosmetics, perfumes, and cleaning agents.

kitchen cabinet cures

Change up your fats. If you have eczema, examine the fats you consume. Omega-6 fatty acids (found in safflower, sunflower, and corn oils) can worsen inflammation. On the other hand, omega-3 fatty acids (found in olive oil, flax-seeds, nuts, and fatty fish) enhance the body's production of anti-inflammatory compounds and can help ease eczema and other inflammatory skin conditions. Good first move: Grind fresh whole flaxseeds in a clean coffee grinder and sprinkle a couple of tablespoons on breakfast cereal, smoothies, salads, or yogurt every single day.

Love the shortening. Having a heavy hand with moisturizers is essential to healing eczema. One super-easy route: Immediately after your shower or bath, baste your outbreaks (and outbreak-prone skin) with a rich, neutral moisturizer. Believe it or not, an excellent choice is vegetable shortening, such as Crisco. Apply to wet skin to seal in as much moisture as possible.

Heal outbreaks with aloe. Aloe gel, straight from the plant, is rich in anti-inflammatory and healing compounds. Split open a stalk, scrape out the gel with a spoon, and slather it on eczema outbreaks several times a day. If you don't have a plant on your windowsill (and if you have eczema, growing your own makes a lot of sense), you can buy aloe gel at most drugstores and health food stores. Read the label to be sure products contain 100 percent pure aloe gel with no added ingredients.

Combat redness with yellow. The bright yellow spice turmeric, which gives ballpark mustard its vivid hue, has well-studied antioxidant, anti-inflammatory, and immune-stimulating properties, thanks to a compound called

When to Call THE DOCTOR

If your eczema covers a large area or keeps recurring despite your self-care treatments, contact your doctor. And you'll need a doctor's attention as soon as possible if an itchy patch of skin begins to show signs of infection. These include crusting sores, pus, red streaks on the skin, excessive pain, swelling, or fever.

||||||||||||||||||||||||||||||||||||

Is it an allergy?

Many experts feel that food allergies play a big role in eczema, particularly in children under the age of two. In kids, the problems most often come from eggs, dairy, peanuts, soy, wheat, and tree nuts. In adults, the troublesome foods are usually dairy, wheat, eggs, yeast, and citrus products. Keeping a food and symptom diary can help you link offending foods to flare-ups. You could also try eliminating all these foods from your diet for about a month. Then reintroduce the suspect foods one at a time for three days to see if the skin reacts. In children, this food elimination diet has been known to produce a visible change in a short time. Dramatic change is rarer in adults, but still, it can't hurt and it might help.

the natural
DOCTOR'S

There's a connection
between a healthy gut and
healthy skin. Probiotics are
known to maintain a healthy
balance within your digestive
organs. Find these healthy
bacteria in yogurt, kefir (a
delicious yogurt-like drink),
and other cultured foods, as
well as in supplements available at pharmacies and health
food stores. Probiotics in
your diet have been shown
to improve eczema.

curcumin. It has a warm, citrusy flavor that mixes well with eggs, rice, and most casserole dishes. It's also a principal ingredient in curry powder. To enlist turmeric's help for fighting eczema, add ½ to 1 teaspoon to stews, rices, soups, or other dishes every single day—it won't help if you don't take it regularly. If you can't manage that, consider taking curcumin supplements, which are available at health food stores. Look for extracts standardized to contain 95 percent curcumin and take 350 milligrams twice a day.

Hook some pantry fish. Canned salmon, sardines, herring, and mackerel are loaded with omega-3 fats that help your body regenerate skin, prevent inflammation, and stave off inflammatory problems like eczema. Studies on relieving the symptoms and causes of eczema have focused more on fish oil supplements than on fish itself, but the evidence has convinced plenty of dermatologists to empha-size the importance of fish in the diet. Specifically, dine on canned fish two or three times a week. Enjoy a sandwich of canned salmon, stuff a tomato with tuna salad, or sauté some onions, add a tin of sardines, and enjoy over a bowl of whole-wheat pasta.

recipe for healing

Honey-Lavender Salve

Honey is frequently mentioned as an eczema healer. This recipe makes the most of it. The honey draws in moisture, which eases the skin irritation produced by eczema and dermatitis.

    I ounce grated beeswax
    I cup olive oil
    ¹/₃ cup honey
    I capsule vitamin E, 400 IU
    60 drops lavender essential oil

1. In the top of a double boiler over low heat, melt the beeswax, stirring occasionally. Stir in the olive oil. Remove from the heat and let cool slightly, then add honey. Pierce the vitamin E capsule and squeeze in the contents. Add up to 60 drops of lavender oil.

2. Pour mixture into a clean jar with a tight-fitting lid, and use as needed to keep skin smooth and hydrated.

eye irritation

The world can be a dusty, gritty place, and when one of those specks lands on your eyeball, the discomfort is nothing to blink at. Happily, tears come to the rescue, cleaning the surface of your eyes, nourishing their cells, and countering the desiccating effects of dry air. Without them, your eyes become irritated and red. But as we age, we produce fewer tears, which is one reason older people tend to have more eye irritation. Allergies also irritate eyes, making them red and itchy. So can exposure to dry air and cigarette smoke. For simple solutions, look no further than your kitchen cabinet.

first things first

There are many measures you can take to prevent eye irritations. Here are some to try:

• Consciously blink when you're concentrating. Your "blink rate" drops from a normal 17 to 22 blinks per minute to as few as 4 when you're maintaining intense visual focus. In one study, people playing computer games blinked just once every two to three minutes. When your eyes remain wide open, their tear coating evaporates. So cue yourself to blink whenever you turn a page in your book or check your rear-view mirror while driving (which should be several times each minute). If you're working at a computer, try the 20-20 rule: Give your eyes a 20-second rest every 20 minutes. Look out a window or at something across the room and be sure to blink.

Pantry HEALERS

Black tea

Canned fish (herring, mackerel, salmon, sardines, tuna)

Chamomile tea

Flaxseed oil

Flaxseeds

Nuts

Pumpkin seeds

If you get a speck on your pupil or a foreign body embedded in your eye, call your doctor. He may want you to come to the office or head to the emergency room. Also call the doctor if you remove a particle from your eye but still feel something there, if your eye is red, or if you have trouble seeing. You may have scratched your cornea. Treatment with drops is often required to avoid infection and control pain. If the scratch was inflicted by a dirty object, have it checked promptly.

|||||||||||||||||||||||||||||||||||||||||||||

Skip it!

Avoid eye drops that clear the "red" out of your eyes. These constrict your blood vessels but don't provide the moisture your eyes really need. They can wind up making your eyes drier—and you can become dependent on them. Instead, use artificial tears or plain saline solutions.

• Lower your computer monitor. Shifting your eyes upward to read the top lines on your screen could double your odds for dry eyes. The reason: Looking up exposes more of the surface of your eyes to the air. (This is one reason computer use dries out eyes more than reading a book does—when you read, you tend to look down, which partially closes your eyes.) Raise your chair or lower your monitor so you can see the top third of the screen while looking straight ahead.

• Eat better fats. When researchers from Brigham and Women's Hospital in Boston checked the diets and eye health of nearly 32,500 women, they found that those who ate the healthiest fats had the lowest risk of dry eyes. In fact, those who ate tuna or tuna salad sandwiches at least five or six times a week were 68 percent less likely to have dry eyes than those who had less than one weekly serving of tuna. Choose "light" tuna if you go this route; it's far lower in mercury than albacore. Better still, make that a salmon salad—salmon is much richer in omega-3s than tuna and contains low levels of mercury. Other good pantry food sources include flaxseed, flaxseed oil, pumpkin seeds, and nuts.

kitchen cabinet cures

Find some flaxseed. Teardrops contain fat and mucus, in addition to water. To have a healthy tear film, you need to eat plenty of omega-3 fatty acids. One outstanding way is to add a tablespoon or two of freshly ground flaxseeds to cereal, yogurt, salads, or other foods. Its nutty flavor complements meatloaf, breads, cookies, and muffins. Omega-3 fatty acids are also plentiful in nuts and canned fish.

Brew up chamomile tea. Make chamomile tea, using two tea bags, and steep, covered, for 15 minutes. Remove tea bags and cool to lukewarm. Soak two cotton balls with the tea and place them on your eyes for 10 minutes.

Soothe with tea bags. Soak two black tea tea bags in warm water for 10 minutes. Press out excess liquid and place on your eyes for 10 minutes.

fatigue

People complain of feeling drained and exhausted so often that doctors say fatigue is the leading reason for doctor's office visits. Often, simple measures can combat the problem. Sometimes the remedies may seem counterintuitive: Exercise, for example, is one of the best ways to beat fatigue. Sleeping too much, on the other hand, may not be helpful at all. But these quick kitchen pick-me-ups can be just what the doctor ordered.

first things first

Often, fatigue problems are nothing more than a symptom of bad sleeping habits. So start there. Are you getting seven to eight hours of sleep every night? If not, take these measures to remedy the situation:

• Establish a regular bed and wake time, and stick to it—even on the weekend.

• Likewise, establish a consistent "wind-down" bedtime routine, and give yourself enough time to complete it.

• As part of that wind-down period, turn off the television and the computer. But feel free to play relaxing music.

• Avoid nicotine, alcohol and caffeine close to bedtime. Any of these will disrupt your sleep.

• Increase your daytime activity level, including getting exercise. In addition to so many other health benefits, it helps to make you legitimately tired at night.

• Create a sleep-conducive environment that is dark, quiet, and comfortable.

Pantry HEALERS

Apple cider vinegar

Bitters

Blackstrap molasses

Cranberry juice

Iron-rich foods

Lime juice

Peppermint essential oil

Rosemary essential oil

Tea

If your fatigue persists, even after you've taken steps to treat it, let your doctor know. When fatigue accompanies a sudden onset of abdominal pain, shortness of breath, or severe headache, seek immediate medical attention or call 911. Extreme exhaustion, alone or along with other symptoms, can signal a heart attack, especially for women. Other chronic symptoms that require a doctor's attention are muscle aches, nausea, depression, fever, or difficulty seeing.

kitchen cabinet cures

Drink something bitter. A traditional herbalists' cure for fatigue—which is still prescribed today by doctors in Germany—is to drink a tonic made of bitter herbs. The thinking was that because these herbs improve digestion, they might also enhance nourishment. Thus, if fatigue was due to nutritional deficits, a bitter tonic could turn things around. Whether or not that's true is debatable, but this modern take on an old-fashioned tonic is a real eye-opener—and there's a good chance you've got a bottle stashed along with your cocktail-making supplies. Shake several dashes of Angostura bitters into a tall glass of club soda or tonic water on ice. If nothing else, the sprightly taste will refresh and enliven you.

Spritz yourself awake. The scent of peppermint is known for its invigorating properties. Add 30 drops peppermint essential oil to water or witch hazel in a 4-ounce spray mister. Use freely to mist the air around you when you need some reawakening.

Or try this fragrant refresher. For a quick pick-me-up, put two drops of peppermint or rosemary essential oil on a tissue or handkerchief, hold it to your nose, and breathe deeply. If you have more time, try adding two drops of peppermint oil to cool bathwater along with four drops of rosemary oil for an invigorating soak.

Try tea and see. If you need a caffeinated pick-me-up, choose tea over coffee. One study found that drinking tea all day improved alertness and performance just as well as coffee and was less likely to disrupt sleep.

Have a cocktail. No, not a martini. Alcohol will only make you more fatigued. As a quick pick-me-up, try drinking a small glass of chilled cranberry juice with a splash of fresh lime juice.

Beat workout exhaustion. Exercise and sometimes extreme stress cause lactic acid to build up in the body, causing fatigue. Interestingly, the amino acids contained in apple cider vinegar act as an antidote. What's more, apple cider vinegar contains potassium and enzymes that may relieve that tired feeling. Next time you're feeling beat, add a tablespoon or two of apple cider vinegar to a glass of chilled vegetable drink or to a glass of water.

Drink something sweet. An old remedy for fatigue is molasses, probably on the theory that it contains iron, which could counter anemia. Try stirring 1 tablespoon blackstrap molasses into 1 cup of hot water next time fatigue catches up with you.

There's an iron mine in your pantry

Iron deficiency is the most common cause of anemia, leading to a low volume of red blood cells in your body. Symptoms include weakness, pallor, fatigue, and brittle nails. If you suspect anemia, check with your doctor. Most cases are caused by blood loss (for example, from a bleeding ulcer or heavy menstrual flow).

The solution to anemia is right there in your pantry, where many iron-rich foods are stocked.

Aim for: The recommended amount of iron is 8 milligrams per day for men and menopausal women and 18 milligrams for menstruating women.

Helpful hint: Our bodies absorb iron much better from meat than from plant foods. If you get most of your iron from vegetarian sources like beans and peas, eat them with foods like citrus fruits that are high in vitamin C, which aids iron absorption.

Food	Standard Amount	Iron (mg)	Calories
Clams, canned, drained	3 oz.	23.8	126
Fortified ready-to-eat cereals (various)	about 1 oz.	1.8–21.1	54–127
Fortified instant cooked cereals (various)	1 packet	4.9–8.1	Varies
Pumpkin and squash seed kernels, roasted	1 oz.	4.2	148
White beans, canned	½ cup	3.9	153
Blackstrap molasses	1 tablespoon	3.5	47
Lentils, cooked	½ cup	3.3	115
Kidney beans, cooked	½ cup	2.6	112
Sardines, canned in oil, drained	3 oz.	2.5	177
Chickpeas, cooked	½ cup	2.4	134
Prune juice	¾ cup	2.3	136
Shrimp, canned	3 oz.	2.3	102
Cowpeas, cooked	½ cup	2.2	100
Lima beans, cooked	½ cup	2.2	108
Soybeans, green, cooked	½ cup	2.2	127
Navy beans, cooked	½ cup	2.1	127
Refried beans	½ cup	2.1	118

fever

You're miserable when you have a fever. You're likely to feel boiling hot one minute, shivery cold the next. You're weak as a kitten and feel just plain awful all over. Bacterial or viral infections, such as tonsillitis or the flu, are usually the cause. Though they make you feel miserable, a fever is actually part of your body's sophisticated immune system. You can make yourself feel better with these easy pantry fixes.

first things first

When you have a fever, the last thing you want to do is push through it by maintaining your usual schedule. Instead, follow this tried and true advice:

• Get into bed or onto your couch, and cover yourself up.

• Have hot tea and plenty of liquids at the ready.

• Settle in for a day or two of pure rest and relaxation.

kitchen cabinet cures

Bathe away a fever. To help bring down a high fever, take lukewarm or cool sponge baths once an hour or more frequently if necessary. Or just soak washcloths in cool water and apply them to your wrists, forehead, and neck. If you like, suck on ice chips spritzed with a little lemon juice to moisturize your mouth. Finally, drink water and other liquids liberally to prevent dehydration. Lukewarm

Pantry HEALERS

Cayenne

Chamomile tea

Cinnamon

Coriander

Cream of tartar

Ginger

Lavender
  essential oil

Lemon

Mustard powder

Peppermint
  essential oil

Rosemary

Rubbing alcohol

Thyme

Witch hazel

sponge baths cool the body slowly, and drinking liquids prevents dehydration.

Fight fire with spices. According to Ayurvedic healers who practice traditional Indian medicine, cinnamon, coriander, cayenne, and ginger promote sweating and can help break a fever. Use as much of the spicy stuff as you can comfortably stand. Add coriander, ginger, and cayenne freely to chicken broth to sip while you're recuperating. Sprinkle toast liberally with cinnamon or add it to tea.

Try a German fever cure. This is a popular concoction for lowering a fever, especially among folks of German descent. Add the juice of 1 lemon and 1 teaspoon cream of tartar to 16 ounces of hot water. Sweeten to taste with honey and sip slowly.

Work up a sweat with ginger tea. This fever remedy hails from all over the world—healers throughout North America, China, India, and the Middle East swear by it. Ginger contains anti-inflammatory compounds, some of which have mild aspirin-like effects. What's more, herbalists classify ginger as a diaphoretic, which means it makes you sweat, and sweating is a sure path to fever reduction. To make an effective fever tea, thinly slice a 2- to 3-inch-long piece of ginger and put it in a pot with a quart of water. Bring to a boil, then simmer over very low heat for 30 minutes, covered. Cool for another 30 minutes. Strain and drink a cup three times a day, sweetened with honey. No fresh ginger? Raid your spice rack for ginger powder. Add a teaspoon to a cup of boiled water, cover, and steep for 10 minutes. Strain before drinking. As with any remedy, check with your doctor before using if you're pregnant.

When to Call THE DOCTOR

If a fever lasts longer than three days, rises above 103°F, or is accompanied by a severe headache with stiff neck, a productive cough, abdominal pain, or painful urination, see a doctor. Also consult a doctor for fever in babies under six months old or in the elderly. Note that the body's temperature varies by as much as 2°F during the day, being lowest in the morning. Rectal temperature is usually about 1°F higher than other temperature measurements.

Caution: aspirin and children

Never give aspirin to a child with a fever, as it may increase the risk of a serious neurological illness called Reye's syndrome. Acetaminophen will bring the fever down safely. If a child has a temperature of 104°F or above, give acetaminophen and a sponge bath of lukewarm water. Continue sponge bathing until the temperature drops below 102°F. In adults as well as children, high fevers pose the risk of dehydration, so be sure to drink plenty of liquids.

Go soak your feet. A spicy foot bath can help ease fever by drawing blood to the feet. This eases the pressure on the blood vessels in your head and increases circulation. To a basin full of hot water, add a teaspoon of mustard powder. Stir well and soak your feet for 15 minutes or so. Wrap the rest of yourself up in a cuddly blanket.

 recipes for healing

Fragrant Fever Spritzer

Spraying pulse points with a cool, soothing solution feels great when you're hot and feverish. The pulse points are the places on the body where you can easily feel your heart rate when you touch them with your fingers—typically inside your wrists, just under each side of the jaw, and the back of the knees.

> ¼ cup rubbing alcohol
> ¼ cup witch hazel
> 3 drops peppermint essential oil
> 2 drops lavender essential oil

1. In a clean spray bottle, combine the rubbing alcohol, witch hazel, peppermint oil, and lavender oil. Shake to mix and then chill in the refrigerator.

2. Spray onto pulse points to reduce fever, avoiding eyes and mouth.

Coriander-Cinnamon Fever Chiller

This pungent tea contains spices with strong anti-fever properties.

> ½ teaspoon powdered coriander
> ½ teaspoon cinnamon
> ¼ teaspoon of powdered ginger

1. Add spices to cup of boiling water. Let it steep, covered, for 10 minutes, then drink.

Herb Tea Footbath

These herbs have a combination of powers that can help bring down a fever.

> 1 tablespoon dried peppermint
> 2 chamomile tea bags
> 1 tablespoon dried thyme
> 1 tablespoon dried rosemary

1. Bring the peppermint, chamomile tea bags, thyme, and rosemary to a boil in 2 quarts of water, then cover and simmer for 20 minutes. Allow the brew to cool till it is comfortably hot, then strain into a foot basin.

2. Wrap up in a blanket and immerse your feet in the tea for 15 to 20 minutes, during which time you should start sweating.

flatulence

You go to great lengths to avoid it. Teen comedies trumpet it. From Aristophanes to Chaucer to Mark Twain, great writers have satirized it. Since the dawn of human existence, for reasons that are unclear to folks of delicate sensibilities, public flatulence makes people laugh. Until it happens to you. At that point, it's just one great social faux pas you wish you could erase. Most healthy people pass gas several times a day, but excessive intestinal gas can point to a digestive disorder. It's an easy problem to remedy with these simple home remedies.

first things first

We all know that certain foods, like beans, are almost certain to fill up your gas tank. If that's a problem for you, try taking Beano, an over-the-counter supplement that counters the bean-gas effect.

kitchen cabinet cures

Spoon up some soda. To remedy a gassy digestive system, mix 1 teaspoon baking soda in a small glass of water, spritz in some lemon juice, and sip slowly.

Chew up a spoonful of seeds. Fennel seeds have a specific action that releases trapped intestinal gas. Simply chew up—thoroughly—a teaspoon or so of fennel seeds after a meal.

Pantry HEALERS

Baking soda
Brandy
Cayenne
Chamomile tea
Crystallized ginger
Cumin
Epazote
Fennel seeds
Marjoram
Peppermint tea
Turmeric

When to Call
THE DOCTOR

Rarely does flatulence signal a medical problem. If you're frequently plagued, try changing your diet to avoid gas-producing foods, such as beans and lentils and dairy products containing lactose. If your problem is associated with vomiting, diarrhea, constipation, heartburn, or unexplained weight loss, see your doctor for a checkup. He or she may want to examine you for other indications of the condition known as irritable bowel syndrome or other ailments. Also, severe flatulence that doesn't go away can sometimes be a symptom of gallbladder problems, an inflammatory condition in the intestines, or colon cancer.

Brew some mint tea. Peppermint tea is such a gentle and time-honored treatment for flatulence that hospitals often give it to new mothers following Caesarean section births. Simply steep a peppermint tea bag in just-boiled water, covered, for 10 minutes, and sip slowly after eating.

Seek spicy antidotes. For some gas-producing foods, there's a corresponding anti-gas spice. Take beans, for example. Adding a teaspoon or so of ground cumin not only perks up their flavor, but it will counteract their propensity to produce flatulence. Other anti-gas pairings include chopping crystallized ginger into ice cream (it complements most flavors) or sprinkling cayenne onto cheeses. The leafy Mexican herb epazote has a long-held reputation for "de-gassing" foods. Add some to your chili or stew.

Try turmeric for relief. Ayurvedic healers swear by turmeric as a quick source of gas relief. Boil a teaspoon of turmeric in a cup of water. Strain and drink immediately.

Tap into the liquor pantry. Many home remedy experts say that a little brandy after a meal will help with digestion and reduce gassiness. Either take a teaspoon straight, or add 2 teaspoons to a cup of water and drink.

recipe for healing

Anti-gas Tea

Herbalists call these herbs "carminative," which means they help dispel gas, aid digestion, and ease intestinal spasms. This makes enough tea to take in a thermos and sip all day long.

> 4 chamomile tea bags
> 4 peppermint tea bags
> 1 teaspoon crushed fennel seeds
> 1 teaspoon dried marjoram

Steep tea bags, fennel seeds, and marjoram in 1 quart boiling water, covered, for 10 minutes. Strain. Chill and drink it cold or keep it hot in a thermos.

foot odor

There's nothing more embarrassing than standing in the security line at an airport, taking off your shoes, and having the guards mist the area around you with air freshener. That should tip you off to the fact that you have a foot odor problem to clear up, pronto. Though smelly feet are most often the bane of teenage boys whose hygiene is somewhat under par, it can also affect folks who spend a lot of time on their feet and whose footwear doesn't wick away perspiration. A few odor-eating pantry remedies can quickly make feet fit for public exposure again.

first things first

Follow these basics of foot hygiene, and never worry about foot odor again:

• Wash your feet regularly in warm soapy water, using a deodorant soap.

• Expose your feet to air frequently; this will encourage evaporation of sweat.

• Air shoes after wearing to discourage mold growth.

• Change shoes every other day to allow moisture buildup to dry completely.

• Wear cotton socks, which absorb moisture better than synthetic ones.

• Dust the inside of shoes with baking soda.

Pantry HEALERS

Antibiotic ointment

Apple cider vinegar

Baking soda

Black tea

Cornmeal

Cornstarch

Epsom salts

Gingerroot

Lavender essential oil

Lemon essential oil

Oatmeal

Peppermint

Peppermint essential oil

Rosemary

Sage

Sugar

Tea tree essential oil

Witch hazel

Yogurt

Zinc-rich foods

||||||||||||||||||||||||||||||||||||||

Did you know?

Your feet have more sweat glands than any other part of your body.

kitchen cabinet cures

Dust on some starch. Cornstarch absorbs sweat. Once or twice daily, sprinkle it liberally onto your feet before putting on your socks. Do not use if your feet have sores or open wounds.

Try a black tea footbath. Boil two tea bags in a pint of water for 15 minutes. Remove the bags and dilute the tea with two quarts of water. Let the mixture cool if necessary, then soak your feet for 15 to 30 minutes. Repeat daily. The tannic acid in strong black tea kills bacteria and closes pores to help your feet sweat less.

Fragrant foot rub. Lavender oil not only smells good, it helps kill bacteria. Rub a few drops onto your feet and massage it in before you go to bed at night. Cover your feet with socks.

Salt your dogs. Mix 2 cups of Epsom salts into 1 to 2 gallons of warm water in a bucket or basin. Soak your feet for 15 minutes twice a day. The Epsom salts act as an astringent to reduce sweating and may kill bacteria.

Zing it with zinc. Some experts suggest that adding zinc to your diet can help eliminate foot odor. Top pantry food sources of this mineral include beans, oatmeal, fortified breakfast cereal, almonds, and cashews.

Neutralize odor with vinegar. Soak feet in a solution of about a third of a cup of apple cider vinegar to a foot basin full of warm or cool water. The acid in the vinegar will neutralize the odor.

Try antibiotic ointment. Sweat, on its own, doesn't smell. It's when it interacts with bacteria that it begins to stink, just as it is for armpit odor. So how do you kill bacteria? Some home-remedy gurus suggest that before you go to bed, rub your feet and nails with a thin coating of antibiotic ointment like Neosporin, put on some socks, then go to sleep. In the morning, the bacteria will be gone, and with it, your foot-odor problems.

Refreshing Minty Scrub

Peppermint cools and deodorizes the skin, and sugar buffs away dead skin cells. Your feet will smell wonderful after you use this fragrant scrub.

> 1 tablespoon coarse-ground oatmeal
> 1 tablespoon cornmeal
> 1 tablespoon sugar
> 2 teaspoons dried peppermint
> 1 tablespoon natural yogurt
> Juice of 1 lemon
> 5 drops peppermint essential oil

1. Combine oatmeal, cornmeal, sugar, and peppermint in a bowl.

2. Add yogurt, lemon juice, and oil. Mix to form a gritty paste.

3. To use, sit on the edge of the bathtub and massage the mixture into your feet, paying particular attention to heels and soles.

Refreshing Deodorant Foot Spray

For some quick help for your feet, this simple, pleasant spray delivers instant freshness.

> 4 ounces boiling water
> 2 tablespoons dried sage
> 4 tablespoons witch hazel
> 10 drops lavender essential oil

1. Pour boiling water over the sage. Cover and steep for 15 minutes. Strain and cool.

2. Add witch hazel and lavender oil.

3. Pour into a 4-ounce spray bottle. Refrigerate. Shake well before use. Spritz on feet after bathing or anytime you need a pick-me-up. Use within 10 days.

super deodorant foot soak

Recipe page 251

Super Deodorant Foot Soak

The herbs and essential oils in this aromatic blend help to reduce sweatiness, fight odor, and leave feet fresh and clean. Rosemary and ginger stimulate circulation, and sage discourages perspiration.

- 1 tablespoon dried rosemary
- 1 tablespoon dried sage
- 1 tablespoon fresh gingerroot, finely grated, or 1 teaspoon dried powered ginger
- 4 cups water, plus extra as needed
- 1 tablespoon baking soda
- 1 tablespoon Epsom salts
- 10 drops tea tree essential oil
- Small ice cubes or crushed ice

1. Place rosemary, sage, and ginger in a large saucepan with water. Bring to a boil. Remove from heat, cover, and steep for 10 minutes. Strain.

2. Add baking soda, Epsom salts, and tea tree oil. Mix well. Pour into a foot spa or shallow basin big enough for both feet. Top with extra water and add ice.

3. Soak feet for 15 minutes; pat dry. Follow with a dusting of fragrant foot powder, below.

Fragrant Foot Powder

Cornstarch makes feet feel silky, and the essential oils eliminate odor-causing bacteria.

- ½ cup baking soda
- ½ cup cornstarch
- 15 drops lemon essential oil
- 15 drops lavender essential oil
- 10 drops tea tree essential oil

1. Sift baking soda and cornstarch to remove lumps. Add the lemon, lavender, and tea tree oils and sift again.

2. Store powder in an airtight, lidded container in a cool, dark place.

3. To use, dip a powder puff into the mixture and apply after bathing, or decant the mixture into a small shaker.

Pantry HEALERS

Apple cider vinegar

Cayenne

Cinnamon

Olive oil

Peppermint tea

Thyme

foot problems

So many things can make your dogs ache that it's hard to know where to begin. Shoes that don't fit properly or that force your feet into impossible angles are a good place to start. Running, jogging, or performing other athletics in shoes that don't offer proper support also make the list. Beyond foot pain are these discomforts: feet that feel perpetually chilly and ingrown toenails. You'll find answers to all these minor woes right behind your pantry door.

first things first

In most cases, healthy feet are directly related to right-sized shoes:

• Have your feet measured properly at a good shoe store. Measure width as well as length. You might be surprised to learn that you've been scrunching your feet into the wrong-sized shoes for years.

• Find out from your doctor whether you have flat feet or fallen arches. Or merely show your worn shoes to a good shoe salesperson; they can often tell from the wear pattern whether you have either. Some podiatrists and chiropractors now use a special gizmo that you step on, and it instantly assesses any problems.

• If you learn that your feet need more support, consider getting special shoe inserts (called orthotics) from your podiatrist or medical supply store.

kitchen cabinet cures

Give tootsies a vigorous rub. To stimulate circulation and relieve pain, massage your feet (better yet, get your loving partner to do it for you) in equal quantities of olive oil and apple cider vinegar.

Try some hydrotherapy. You'll love this one because it makes your feet feel like new. Fill one basin with cold water and another with water as hot as you can comfortably stand. Sit in a comfortable chair, and place your feet in the cold water. After 5 minutes, switch to the hot water. Repeat. This "hydromassage" alternately dilates and constricts blood vessels in your feet, boosting circulation.

Soak in thyme tea. In a just-released study, researchers discovered that thyme contains the same kind of COX-II inhibitors as nonsteroidal anti-inflammatory drugs, such as ibuprofen. Make a strong tea with 2 tablespoons of dried thyme in a quart of boiling water. Cover the pot and simmer for 20 minutes. Let it cool until it's hot enough for you to comfortably stand the temperature. Then soak your feet in the tea for 15 to 20 minutes.

Minty foot energizer. After hours of standing all day, especially during the summer, refresh your aching feet with this tea: Add three or four peppermint tea bags to a quart or two of just-boiled water, let steep for 15 minutes, and cool the tea. Pour it in a foot basin or a foot spa, add some ice cubes, and soak for 15 minutes or so.

Spice up cold feet. If you're going to be outdoors on a frigid winter day, try this warmer-upper. Sprinkle a little ground red pepper (cayenne) into your socks. The stimulating heat will keep tootsies warm. Tote a clean pair of socks with you in case you find the cayenne irritating.

Have a glass of cinnamon. Chinese healers say that drinking a little cinnamon water will stimulate circulation and keep feet (and hands) warm. Just mix a half-teaspoon into a glass of hot water. Let it steep for a few minutes and drink three times a day. Bonus: Cinnamon also helps lower blood sugar and cholesterol.

When to Call THE DOCTOR

Don't worry if your feet hurt occasionally. But be sure to visit a podiatrist if walking first thing in the morning is difficult or if the painful area is swollen or discolored. You may have a broken bone, an inflamed tendon, or a pinched nerve. And see the doctor if you regularly have pain after walking long distances or working out on treadmills or elliptical machines—this could indicate flat feet or other structural problems. A painful, burning sensation in the feet might mean you have diabetes or thyroid disease. If you have diabetes, see your doctor at once if a cut, sore, bruise, or blister on your foot doesn't start to heal after one day.

gout

If you think Henry the Eighth when you think "gout," you're not alone. This condition has a reputation for striking the rich and well-fed. Among its well-known sufferers: Benjamin Franklin, King George IV, Benedict Arnold, and Dick Cheney. But the truth is, gout is an equal opportunity affliction that can strike anyone. This often-hereditary form of inflammatory arthritis causes uric acid—which is naturally secreted by the kidneys—to deposit in and near the joints. The result is swelling, redness, and severe pain. You're more apt to contract it by eating rich meaty foods, drinking beer, and being overweight, which is why it historically was associated with the upper crust. Typically, a gout attack lasts just a few days and affects only one joint (famously, the big toe), which can become exquisitely painful. A healthy diet can help head it off, and simple home treatments can ease the pain.

first things first

A few years ago, researchers in the United States analyzed the Third National Health and Nutrition Survey (a database containing detailed health information on some 15,000 people) to see whether long-held treatment recommendations for gout needed updating. What they discovered may surprise you—and your doctor.

• Eat less rich meat and seafood. This basic advice for gout sufferers turns out to be correct: People who eat a lot of meat and seafood are at a higher risk for gout.

• Put dairy back on the menu. Dairy products, as it turns out, *aren't* a gout no-no, as doctors once thought. Researchers learned that people whose diets include dairy products actually have a lower risk for having gout, and foods like milk, yogurt, and cheese may help prevent attacks. Choose low-fat products to limit calories and unhealthy fats.

• Don't say no to vegetables. Doctors used to advise gout patients to limit eating purine-rich veggies like spinach. But the researchers found no correlation between gout and vegetable intake. They theorize that vegetables have bountiful beneficial compounds that may offset any purine/gout connection.

• Not all booze is bad. Based on their studies, the researchers suggest that standard advice about nixing all alcoholic beverages be fine-tuned a bit. Lay off the beer, absolutely. Its high purine content is definitely linked to gout risk. Hard liquor raises gout risk, too, but to a slightly lesser degree than beer. But moderate wine consumption seems to have little effect on gout risk.

• Enjoy your morning coffee. At one time, doctors told gout patients to limit coffee drinking, on the theory that its diuretic effects could lead to attacks (becoming dehydrated can trigger gout). To the contrary, the researchers learned that drinking four or more cups a day significantly lowers urate levels (a major gout risk factor). Drinking decaf was also helpful. But tea had no effect on lowering urate levels.

• Say no to sweet sodas. Researchers connected the dots between the sharp rise in gout cases over the last 50 years and this: In the 1960s, soft drink makers began using high-fructose corn syrup instead of sugar. Scientists who study fructose metabolism say that it affects urate levels. Examining their database, the researchers were able to prove that people, particularly men, who drink fructose-sweetened sodas or eat other high-fructose treats have higher levels of gout than people who consume fewer sweet drinks or foods. Diet sodas are OK; people who drink them don't have a higher gout risk.

• Choose healthy cooking oils. Put olive and canola oils on your shopping list, and use them instead of butter, margarine, corn oil, and soy oil. These omega-3 rich oils may lower uric acid levels. In a South African study, after

When to Call THE DOCTOR

If you develop a tender, swollen joint, see your doctor, even if you've had similar attacks in the past. Gout can mimic other conditions, such as joint infections and even spider bites, so your doctor will want to confirm the diagnosis. During the exam, your doctor may draw liquid from the affected joint and examine it to confirm the presence of uric acid crystals.

patients with gout replaced saturated fats with unsaturated ones, their blood levels of uric acid dropped 17.5 percent after 16 weeks.

A new study shows that thyme can help battle inflammation.

kitchen cabinet cures

Chop down a cherry tree. Eating tasty cherries is proven to lower uric acid and prevent gout attacks, and drinking an 8-ounce glass of cherry juice helps, too. You can buy delicious dried, sugar-free cherries to keep handy in the pantry, as well as jars of juice made without sugar, at health and natural food stores.

Become a flax fan. Another rich and important source of omega-3 acids is nutty-tasting flaxseeds. Buy them whole at a health food store and grind up a couple of tablespoons or so in a clean coffee grinder. Sprinkle on cereal, yogurt, or oatmeal, or tuck them into meat loafs, breads, muffins, and other baked goodies.

Take thyme for gout pain. In a very recent Japanese study, researchers discovered that thyme contains compounds that inhibit the production of prostaglandins. These play a key role in the inflammation process connected to painful conditions such as arthritis and gout. Make thyme one of your go-to seasonings and use it liberally, especially during gout attacks. You can also brew it into tea. Use 1 teaspoon dried thyme to 1 cup boiling water. Cover and brew for 10 minutes, then strain. Sweeten to taste with a little honey.

Visit the cranberry bog. Cranberry has a long-held reputation for easing and preventing gout. No studies prove the connection, but theoretically, cranberry's ability to acidify could affect uric acid production. Avoid cranberry juices that contain high-fructose corn syrup. Instead, buy pure cranberry juice at health or natural food stores. Add a couple of splashes of the tart stuff to club soda. Sweeten with a touch of honey, if you like.

Try celery seed tea. Known for its ability to relieve pain and inflammation, celery seed is an herbalist-recommended gout treatment. Make celery seed tea by brewing 1 teaspoon of the tiny seeds in a cup of boiling water, and steep for 10 minutes, covered. Strain and drink.

gum problems

Spend a few minutes each day being compulsive about your oral hygiene, and you'll stand a good chance of warding off gum problems, including gingivitis and periodontal disease. Deal with plaque by visiting your dentist at least twice a year, and invest extra time in brushing (use a soft-bristled brush and pay special attention to your gum line) and flossing your teeth. You can also keep your gums nice and healthy with some easy pantry treatments.

first things first

Mouth-cleaning gear keeps getting fancier and more high-tech, but the fundamentals haven't changed:

• Brush your teeth and gums every morning and evening, and even better, after every meal.

• Use floss or interdental brushes between the teeth at least once a day.

• Use an antibacterial mouthwash containing tea tree or myrrh.

• Avoid smoking.

• Don't chew on toothpicks or other hard objects.

• See your dentist for cleanings at least twice a year. Most gingivitis will resolve quickly and easily if the plaque is removed from around the necks of the teeth.

Pantry HEALERS

Aloe

Antibacterial mouthwash

Black tea

Chamomile tea

Echinacea

Green tea

Hydrogen peroxide

Myrrh essential oil

Orange pekoe tea

Salt

Sesame seeds

Sunflower seeds

Thyme

Witch hazel

If symptoms such as bleeding, tenderness, or pain persist for more than a week, see a doctor or dentist. Gum disease that does not clear up quickly with home care may indicate a more serious underlying condition.

kitchen cabinet cures

Massage gums with aloe. Aloe helps damaged tissue heal and soothes irritation, which makes it a perfect treatment for sore gums. Scrape a few spoonfuls of aloe gel from a cut stalk into a saucer. Dip a soft-bristled toothbrush into the aloe and gently massage the gums by stroking the brush over them in a back and forth motion. Dip the brush in the aloe every time you move to a new spot. Work your way bit by bit until you've covered the entire surface of your gums. This helps stimulate blood circulation and heals the tissue.

Swish some salt. To sooth gum pain and reduce swelling, swish your mouth for 30 seconds or so with salt water (1 teaspoon salt mixed into a glass of warm water). Or mix hydrogen peroxide 50:50 with warm water and swish through your mouth for 30 seconds or so.

Gnaw on sesame seeds. Both sesame seeds and sunflower seeds contain minerals that contribute to healthy teeth and gums. Chew a spoonful slowly every day to help strengthen gum tissue.

Use a cold herb to treat gums. That bottle of echinacea you use to head off colds comes in mighty handy as a treatment for sore gums. It promotes healing, and it acts as a local anesthetic to relieve pain. You can apply liquid echinacea directly to sore gums with a cotton swab, or you

Treat your teeth, protect your heart

Here's a health flash you don't want to miss: People with chronic bacterial infections of the gums are nearly twice as likely to have fatal heart attacks as those with healthy gums. That's right. Brushing and flossing your teeth don't just brighten your smile—they can also save your life.

In a University of Minnesota study of more than 700 men and women with no history of heart disease, researchers found a direct link between missing teeth (an indicator of serious dental disease) and plaque buildup in the arteries. Other studies have linked periodontal (gum) disease with increased resting heart rate, abnormal electrocardiograms, and poor blood sugar control—all symptoms of or contributors to heart disease.

University of Michigan researchers who studied 320 U.S. veterans went so far as to conclude that dental disease was a larger risk factor for heart disease than being overweight, having high cholesterol, not exercising, or smoking. So run, don't walk, to the phone, and make that dental appointment right now.

can add a teaspoon of echinacea tincture to a half cup of warm water and swish vigorously through your gums for at least a minute. Repeat daily.

Make an herbal mouthwash. Add 1 teaspoon dried thyme to a cup of just-boiled water. Thyme contains compounds that relieve pain and kill bacteria. Steep, covered, for 15 minutes before straining. Cool and use as a mouthwash two or three times a day.

Press on some orange pekoe. Tea contains astringent tannic acid that shrinks swollen tissues and helps staunch bleeding. If bleeding and inflammation persist, fold the bag in half and bite down on it.

Calm gums with chamomile. Studies have shown that using chamomile tea as a mouthwash reduces gum pain and helps heal gingivitis. Just pour a cup of hot water over two chamomile tea bags, cover, steep for 10 minutes, and cool to room temperature. Remove the tea bags, take a mouthful of tea and swish it around vigorously for several minutes before spitting out. Repeat until you've used the entire cup. Do this daily for best results. You can also press the wet tea bags for a minute or two against any areas that are particularly irritated.

 recipe for healing

Super Healing Mouth Rinse
Black tea and witch hazel are rich in tannins, which improve tissue tone. Green tea is an antioxidant and lessens inflammation, and myrrh is a time-honored treatment for gum problems.

- 2 black tea bags
- 2 green tea bags
- ¾ cup boiling water
- 1 tablespoon witch hazel
- 5 drops myrrh essential oil (optional)

1. Place black and green teas in a bowl and cover with boiling water. Cover bowl and steep for 30 minutes. Strain.

2. Add the witch hazel and myrrh oil. Mix well. Store in a dark glass bottle.

3. To use, shake well and swish 1 to 2 tablespoons around the mouth. Do not swallow. Store in a cool place. Use within one week.

hangover

Pantry HEALERS

Baking soda

B-complex vitamins

Bouillon

Coffee

Consommé

Ginger

Honey

Lime

Salt

Sauerkraut

Sports beverage

As human miseries go, hangovers are pretty inconsequential. They can't kill you, they don't last that long, and they're 100 percent preventable. Still, they can make the hardiest of people curl up in a ball and whine like a baby. What causes the miserable malaise? No, that's not a trick question. You probably don't know that too much alcohol overwhelms the capacity of the enzyme known as alcohol dehydrogenase (ADH), which metabolizes alcohol through the liver. That's what makes your head pound, your stomach rebel, and your body feel practically lifeless. Temperance or abstinence is the only way of preventing a hangover, but some pantry cures can make the day after a little more livable.

first things first

Prevention, prevention, prevention! Do these simple things, and never have to use hangover cures again:

• Chow down before you drink. Having food in your stomach—especially starchy and fatty foods—will slow the body's absorption of alcohol.

• Stick to clear spirits, such as vodka and gin (the higher the quality, the better). Darker liquors contain higher amounts of toxic substances called congeners. These contribute to hangovers.

• While you're drinking, aim to sip one glass of water between every alcoholic drink. This will slow your intake and help prevent dehydration.

• Take a 50-milligram B-complex vitamin before you start drinking and another one while you're drinking. Doing so may help lessen a hangover.

kitchen cabinet cures

Brew up ginger tea. Ginger settles your stomach on the morning after and eases nausea. Sweeten it with lots of honey—it will help your body burn off any alcohol still left in your system.

Drink something sauer. A popular, standard folk cure for hangovers is to drink a glass or two of sauerkraut juice. We're honestly not sure why—perhaps the friendly bacteria it contains help balance the damage done by the alcohol.

Pour some consommé on the rocks. Consommé or bouillon replaces salt and potassium and will help your body rehydrate. Drinking it chilled will refresh you a bit.

Wake up to coffee. Caffeine, a central nervous system stimulant and vasoconstrictor, may temporarily ease your aching head and may give you enough get-up-and-go to head out the door the morning after. But never, ever make coffee your "one-for-the-road" nightcap, and then think you're sober enough to get behind the wheel. You're not. Call a cab or rely on your (sober) designated driver instead.

Rehydrate like a player. Before you go to bed, have two 8-ounce glasses of a sports beverage like Gatorade. It will help prevent dehydration and could head off a headache.

When to Call
THE DOCTOR

Call 911 if you're with someone who's drinking heavily and becomes dazed, confused, vomits persistently, or becomes unconscious. These are symptoms of alcohol poisoning. And if you're having hangovers regularly, you need to assess whether or not you have a drinking problem. You can do so easily and anonymously at www.alcoholscreening.org, a program sponsored by Boston University.

Weird
& wacky

If you feel so miserable that you'd try anything, try this. Take a piece of cut lemon and wipe the juicy side under each armpit. Proponents swear it works, though there is no science to explain it.

recipe for healing

Hangover Brew

This is no cure, but it might get your morning off to a less rocky beginning. It will rehydrate you and lessen acidity.

> 2 teaspoons fresh lime juice
> 1 teaspoon honey
> ½ teaspoon baking soda
> Pinch of salt
> 8 ounces cool water

Stir the lime juice, honey, baking soda, and salt into the water and drink.

headache

So many things can make your head ache. Deadlines. Arguments. Irksome bosses. Traffic jams. Even good things can give you a pain in the head—on the Mayo Clinic Web site, "ice cream headaches" has its own category (many of us know it as "brain freeze"). Generally speaking, headaches are your body's response to physical or emotional stress. That stress can make the muscles in your head and neck contract to create tension headaches. Or it can make blood vessels constrict and later expand to produce migraines or vascular headaches. And if your sinuses are congested or infected, pounding headaches often result. Despite the discomfort, most headaches are temporary and respond quite nicely to do-it-yourself pantry treatments.

first things first

Sometimes the obvious solutions *are* the best solutions. When a simple, run-of-the-mill headache starts coming on, do these two things:

• Immediately take an over-the-counter pain reliever, such as acetaminophen, aspirin, ibuprofen, or naproxen, as directed on the bottle.

• Distance yourself from whatever triggered the headache, be it a stressful situation, bright sunlight, or loud music. If you can, get to a quiet, calm room with dim light and relax for 15 minutes.

kitchen cabinet cures

Soothe on fragrant oil. To relieve headache pain, dab a drop or two of thyme or rosemary essential oil on each temple and on your forehead. Rub gently into the skin, then sit quietly for several minutes. In a 2010 study, researchers discovered that thyme and rosemary oils contain carvacrol, a substance that acts as a COX-II inhibitor, much like non-steroidal anti-inflammatory drugs, such as ibuprofen, do.

Enjoy some ginger tea. Ginger may work against migraines by inhibiting prostaglandin synthesis. What's more, ginger helps quell the nausea that often accompanies migraines. Make a tea by gently simmering three quarter-sized slices of gingerroot in 2 cups of water, covered, for 30 minutes.

Pain-easing sweet tea. Taking a break in your busy schedule can relieve some of the tension that causes many headaches. Chamomile tea has compounds that help ease pain and relax you. Brew up a cup using one chamomile tea bag to a cup of just-boiled water. Allow to steep, covered, for 10 minutes. Sweeten with honey, if desired. Take a few minutes to sip the hot tea slowly while sitting in a quiet spot.

Have an herbal footbath. Some natural healers believe footbaths are powerful remedies for headaches. The hot water draws blood to your feet, easing the pressure on the blood vessels in your head. By adding a few drops of peppermint and/or lavender essential oils, the aroma provides soothing relief.

Mine some magnesium. Headache researchers say that migraine sufferers should keep this essential mineral in their medicine chests. Turns out, migraineurs (the term docs use to describe folks who get these head-splitters) have low levels of magnesium in their brains during attacks and may also have a general magnesium deficiency. In fact, two placebo-controlled clinical studies have shown that taking magnesium supplements can prevent the headaches. Experts recommend taking 400 milligrams a day of chelated magnesium, magnesium oxide, or slow-release magnesium, all of which are available over the counter at your local drugstore. Note: Magnesium may cause diarrhea in some people.

When to Call THE DOCTOR

Most headaches are easily dealt with on your own and are of no medical concern. But if your headache is accompanied by any of these symptoms, see a doctor immediately. It could be a symptom of a much more serious condition.

- Sudden awakenings from sleep
- Blurry vision
- Confusion or slurred speech, especially after a blow to the head
- Difficulty moving any one part of your body
- Fever and a stiff neck
- Nausea
- Pain in or around your eyes
- Pain that is sudden and more severe than your typical headache

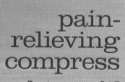

pain-
relieving
compress

Recipe page 265

Take vitamin B$_2$. In one study, taking 400 milligrams of this vitamin, known as riboflavin, daily for three months slashed migraines by 50 percent in 59 percent of the volunteers, as opposed to just 15 percent in volunteers who took a placebo.

Go herbal on migraines. An herb called butterbur has proved itself so effective for migraine relief that physicians who specialize in treating migraines often recommend it. At least three studies have been conducted on Petadolex, an over-the-counter butterbur extract, and in each study, the herb has significantly reduced migraine attacks when compared to a placebo. Recommended dosage is 75 milligrams twice a day for one month, then 50 milligrams twice a day.

 recipes for healing

Pain-Relieving Compress

These herbs all contain carvacrol, a compound that suppresses the COX-II enzyme—which means they have the same action as ibuprofen and other nonsteroidal anti-inflammatory drugs.

 1 tablespoon dried thyme
 1 tablespoon dried rosemary
 1 teaspoon cloves, crushed
 1 teaspoon fennel seeds, crushed

1. Add the thyme, rosemary, cloves, and fennel seeds to 3 cups of water in a pot. Bring to a boil, then simmer gently, covered, for 30 minutes. Let cool till it's comfortably warm.

2. Soak a cotton cloth in the brew and wring out excess liquid.

3. Place the compress on your forehead or the back of your neck to relax the tight muscles that are often the cause of a tension headache. You can also chill the brew and make a cold compress. This will constrict the blood vessels and reduce blood flow, which may relieve a vascular headache.

Headache Rub

The combination of fragrant aroma and gentle massage can quiet a painful headache.

 10 drops olive oil
 3 drops peppermint essential oil
 3 drops lavender essential oil

1. In a small bowl, mix the olive oil and the essential oils.

2. Dip your fingers into the oil and then massage the oil into the temples, along the hairline and the base of the skull, being careful not to get the oil in your eyes.

3. Wash your hands thoroughly after each application.

Pantry HEALERS

Apple cider vinegar

Baking soda

Bay

Bitters

Caraway

Cardamom

Chamomile tea

Cinnamon

Cumin

Dill

Fennel

Fennel seeds

Ginger

Honey

Horseradish

Lemon

Marjoram

Mint

Tarragon

heartburn

Given the number of over-the-counter treatments and prescription medicines dedicated to curing it—not to mention the endless television ads that promote them—you'd think heartburn must be humankind's greatest affliction. It just might be—according to one estimate, nearly half of all Americans experience heartburn at least once a month. Large meals and foods to which you're sensitive can lead to heartburn. Being pregnant, overweight, or a smoker raises your chances for having this digestive problem. So does a condition called hiatal hernia. However, in most cases, heartburn is a one-time affair dealt with simply enough using at-home cures.

first things first

To head off heartburn at the pass, work your way down this list of things that might be contributing to the problem:

• Heavy, large meals

• Acidic foods and beverages, including orange juice, coffee, and decaf

• Alcohol, chocolate, spearmint, and peppermint—these relax the lower esophageal sphincter

• Carbonated beverages

• Fatty foods, including full-fat milk

These actions can help you lessen or even eliminate heartburn:

• Lose weight

• Quit smoking

• Avoid lying down for two to three hours after eating

kitchen cabinet cures

Tried and true quick fix. Baking soda is alkaline, which means it neutralizes stomach acid. Mix ½ teaspoon baking soda and a few drops of lemon juice in ½ cup warm water. But don't forget to add the lemon juice! It dispels some of the gas baking soda creates in the stomach when it contacts stomach acid.

Find some fennel. Used throughout the world to treat heartburn, fennel seeds contain at least 16 compounds that sooth spasms. Buzz 3 teaspoons of the seeds in a coffee grinder and place in a heat-resistant bowl or saucepan. Add 3 cups of boiling water, cover and steep for 10 minutes, then strain. That makes 3 cups of tea; drink in 1-cup portions throughout the day, preferably on an empty stomach.

Calm the burn with chamomile. In Germany, where they take herbal medicine very seriously, chamomile is an officially approved heartburn treatment. It contains some 20 compounds that ease spasms, plus other compounds that have gentle sedative effects. Use one tea bag per cup of boiling water, cover and steep for 10 minutes. Remove the tea bag and drink. Shoot for having three cups a day on an empty stomach, and continue for two or three weeks. Then take a break for a week or two.

Mix the sour with the sweet. Honey and vinegar is an old Amish remedy for easing heartburn. Just mix a teaspoon of honey with a teaspoon of apple cider vinegar in a glass of warm water. Drink 30 minutes before you eat, and you just might avoid heartburn.

Toss in some herbs. Many herbs are known to ease your digestion. Among them are mint, dill, caraway, horseradish, bay, fennel, tarragon, marjoram, cumin, cinnamon, ginger, and cardamom. No matter what you're cooking up, chances are there's an herb that complements it. Use one or more liberally, especially when you're cooking something that you know might give you heartburn after eating.

Try a daily dash of bitters. Angostura bitters, a tincture of the gentian root, is an ingredient often used to make cocktails. Taking bitters has long been recommended by herbalists for chilling out heartburn. The bitters stimulate digestion. Try several dashes in water before eating to promote digestion and stop heartburn before it starts.

When to Call THE DOCTOR

Frequent heartburn attacks could signal that you have a viral infection. Or, they could be a sign of gastroesophageal reflux disease (GERD), which can cause or contribute to various other conditions. See your doctor if you get heartburn three or four times a week for weeks on end or if you wheeze or become hoarse, find it difficult to swallow, or lose weight rapidly. **Warning:** The symptoms of severe heartburn often mimic those of a heart attack. If symptoms arrive after a meal and are quelled by water or antacids, it's probably heartburn. But if you have a feeling of fullness, tightness, or dull pressure or pain in the center of the chest, shortness of breath, and/or light-headedness, call 911 immediately.

Weird & wacky

As interesting as these two old folk remedies may be to read about, we don't think they have much appeal as heartburn treatments:

• Mix a couple of tablespoons of olive oil with an egg white and drink it down.

• Take a pinch of coffee grounds, swirl them around in your mouth for a couple of minutes, then spit them out.

hemorrhoids

Pantry HEALERS

Aloe

Apple cider vinegar

Black tea

Chamomile tea

Epsom salts

Lavender
  essential oil

Witch hazel

Topping the list of infernally irritating problems is hemorrhoids. Making matters worse, it's an intimate condition that most folks find too embarrassing to discuss—even with their doctors. These swollen varicose veins that appear in or around the anus have a variety of causes. Constipation (common during pregnancy) and dry stools rank high on the list. Also to blame are prolonged sitting or standing. Straining to pass hard, dry stools is a culprit, as is catching up on your reading while sitting on the "throne." A fiber-poor diet is a major contributor to the problem. The good news is, many pantry remedies are remarkably effective and may help you avoid more invasive medical treatments.

first things first

You can ease or even prevent hemorrhoids by losing weight, increasing water and fiber intake, and enjoying dried figs, prunes, and dates, which all have laxative properties. Other easy tips include:

• Wear cotton undies.

• Use plain white fragrance-free toilet tissue.

• Don't scratch itchy hemorrhoids.

• Take a warm sitz bath for 10 to 15 minutes twice a day.

• Limit the amount of time you sit on the john (forgo reading while you sit).

• Don't strain to move bowels.

• Cleanse with flushable, moistened wipes after each bowel movement.

kitchen cabinet cures

Try witch power. Witch hazel is a natural anti-inflammatory that shrinks swollen veins and can bring immediate relief. Chill the bottle for 15 minutes in the refrigerator, then soak a wad of cotton in it and place the cotton ball on the hemorrhoid. At night, tuck a soaked cotton ball against the area and put on cotton undies. You'll find it helps relieve pain and itching so you can sleep.

Dab on some vinegar. Apple cider vinegar helps bring down the swelling and eases inflamed hemorrhoids. Apply to a cotton ball and wipe across the anal area. If it stings or burns, dilute the vinegar 50-50 with water.

Smear on some aloe. Soothing, healing aloe gel is an ideal hemorrhoid healer. Just slash open a stalk and dip a gauze pad into the gel, then apply.

Bag the pain. Place a warm, wet black tea bag directly on those painful swellings. You can do it while sitting on the toilet. The warmth is soothing, and you get added benefit from one of tea's main components, tannic acid. It helps reduce swelling, and its astringent action helps stop the bleeding. You can also use a wet chamomile tea bag, which will lessen the inflammation.

Take an Epsom soak. Sit in a tub of warm water in which you've dissolved a cup or so of Epsom salts. The warm water eases pain, and the salts constrict the hemorrhoid. Do not try this if hemorrhoids are bleeding.

When to Call THE DOCTOR

It's risky to self-diagnose hemorrhoids. You can't really see what's going on, and the hemorrhoid can be symptomatic of something more serious. That's why doctors prefer you make an appointment rather than assuming you can figure out the problem and solution on your own. Severe pain can be a sign of a thrombosed hemorrhoid, which occurs when a vein ruptures or a blood clot occurs in the hemorrhoid. If these are treated within 24 hours, the blood clot can be removed with a local anesthetic. Rectal bleeding may be a hemorrhoid symptom, or it can signal something more serious, such as colon cancer.

recipe for healing

DIY Hemorrhoid Pads

These soothing, cooling pads work just as well as store-bought—and smell heavenly.

> ¼ cup witch hazel
>
> 10 drops lavender essential oil
>
> 2 tablespoons aloe vera gel, scraped from inside a fresh aloe leaf

1. In a shallow, open-mouthed jar with a tight-fitting lid, combine the witch hazel, lavender oil, and aloe vera gel. Saturate cotton gauze pads in the liquid and refrigerate for at least an hour.

2. Use a pad on the affected area when it burns and after each bowel movement. Store in the refrigerator for several days.

hiccups

Pantry HEALERS

Chocolate (powdered drink mix)

Dill seeds

Honey

Hot sauce

Paper bag

Paper towel

Peanut butter

Sugar

Vinegar

Water

There's something silly about having hiccups. Invariably, they make anyone within earshot giggle at you. But they probably weren't such a laugh riot for poor Charles Osborne from Anthon, Iowa, who hiccuped continuously from 1922 to 1990—producing an estimated 430 million hiccups over 68 years! Fortunately, most attacks are far more fleeting. In a nutshell, a hiccup is just an involuntary contraction of the diaphragm. This makes you suddenly draw in a breath, which is checked by the abrupt closing of the glottis (the space between the vocal cords). The result is the characteristic hiccup sound. Hiccups are usually harmless. If there's no one around to scare the wits out of you, try some of these simple tricks to make them go away.

first things first

As soon as hiccups start, drink some water and take some deep breaths. Often, that's enough to stymie an attack. If they continue, try some of our proven home remedies.

kitchen cabinet cures

Swallow something sweet. A spoonful of sugar is popular because its graininess could slightly irritate the esophagus, causing the phrenic nerves to "reset" themselves, although there is no proof of this.

...Or something sour. Take a teaspoonful of vinegar. Its sour taste could stop a hiccup in its tracks.

Sip some hot sauce. This probably works because the heat and burn are distracting enough to turn your body's focus on the burn, instead of the hiccup process.

Brown bag 'em. Breathe slowly and deeply into a small paper bag. (Stop if you feel light-headed.) This increases the carbon dioxide level in the blood and makes the diaphragm contract more deeply to bring in more oxygen, which may stop the spasms.

Chew up some dill. Here's a simple, pleasant-tasting trick: Slowly chew a teaspoon of dill seeds. This traditional cure may work because swallowing the seeds stimulates the vagus nerve to make the hiccups stop.

Try the paper towel trick. Place a single layer of paper towel over the top of a glass, then drink through the towel. You'll have to "pull" harder with your diaphragm to suck up the water, and concentrated gulping counteracts spasmodic muscle movements.

Enjoy a little honey. Put 1 teaspoon of honey, stirred in warm water, on the back of your tongue, and swallow it. Like dill, honey could potentially tickle the vagus nerve to make the hiccups stop.

Have some PB. A classic hiccups remedy involves eating a big spoonful of peanut butter. In the process of chewing and getting it off your tongue and teeth, your swallowing and breathing patterns are interrupted. And hence, the hiccups will be history.

Yummy chocolate remedy. Eat some powdered chocolate drink mix (cocoa or Ovaltine) right off the spoon. Swallowing the spoonful isn't easy and should short-circuit the hiccups.

When to Call THE DOCTOR

Usually, hiccup attacks abate quickly. However, occasionally they can last for days, making it difficult to eat or sleep. If this occurs, see a doctor. In rare cases, a serious condition could be the cause.

Weird & wacky

We actually like this oddball remedy we discovered. It's just silly and distracting enough to make you forget to hiccup: Hold a penny between two toes and transfer it to two toes on your other foot. Don't let the penny touch the floor.

Try the love cure

It's not scientifically proven, but this hiccup remedy that hails from North Carolina is sweet indeed: While you're hiccuping, focus on the person you love best. This bit of folklore goes on to state that if your beloved loves you back, your hiccups will cease.

hives

Pantry HEALERS

Apple cider vinegar

Baking soda

Basil

Chamomile tea

Cornstarch

Cream of tarter

Milk of magnesia

Pepto-Bismol

White vinegar

Witch hazel

They seem to appear out of nowhere. They're red, they itch, and they're as annoying as an unwelcome guest. Typically, hives (also known as urticaria) are an allergic reaction to foods. Shellfish, fish, nuts, eggs, chocolate, and milk are frequent culprits. Medications can also trigger an attack of hives, as can pollen, animal dander, contact with certain plants, and insect bites. You can calm them down quite nicely with one of several pantry items.

first things first

One of the best ways to prevent hives is with your memory. If day-old shrimp caused a breakout of hives in the past, never eat day-old shrimp again. If you are highly allergic to cats, don't let cats rub against your arm. We rarely grow new allergies as we age; if you know what your body has responded badly to in the past, simply avoid it.

kitchen cabinet cures

Open a bottle of whup-witch. This may be the most soothing thing you can do for an outbreak of hives. Simply apply witch hazel liberally and frequently all over the affected area. This astringent helps shrink blood vessels, so they don't leak so much histamine, plus it has a cooling effect on irritated skin. You can magnify the effect by chilling the witch hazel in the refrigerator.

Open your medicine cabinet. Alternatives to witch hazel include milk of magnesia and Pepto-Bismol. Because they are alkaline, they help to relieve the itching. Use a cotton ball and dab either one on the hives.

Make a vinegar paste. Mix enough cornstarch with white vinegar to make a paste, and smear it all over the hives. This remedy eases itching and could counteract the irritants that caused the problem.

Wash with basil tea. Chinese healers rely on basil to ease itchy hives. They know that this herb is rich in the anti-allergy compound caffeic acid. To use, put 4 heaping tablespoons dried basil into a 1-quart canning jar, then fill it with boiling water. Cover tightly and cool to room temperature. Strain. Use the solution as a wash for hives and apply frequently. Refrigerate the leftover solution.

Take a baking soda soak. Baking soda is a classic time-honored remedy for itchy skin. Simply toss a handful or two into a warm or cool tub of water and soak for at least 15 minutes.

Try this pastry ingredient. The same cream of tartar that you use in pinches to stabilize meringues might also help relieve itchy hives. Just make a paste with a teaspoon of the stuff blended with a little water. Smooth on the hives and allow to dry.

Sooth with sour hive relief. Dab apple cider vinegar onto hives with a cotton ball or tissue to soothe the itching.

Use the inside-out chamomile treatment. Stress can make a hives-producing allergy attack worse. Chamomile's calming effects can make it better by soothing your jumpy nerves. But that's not all this apple-sweet herb can do for your hives. Chamomile contains anti-inflammatory compounds that can ease the swelling and the itching. Use 4 chamomile tea bags to 2 cups of boiling water, cover, and steep for 15 minutes. Then, drink 1 cup of the tea while you soak a clean cloth in the other cup and lay it on the affected area. Don't use chamomile if you are allergic to ragweed, aster, or chrysanthemums.

When to Call THE DOCTOR

Hives usually disappear on their own in a day or two and respond well to home remedies. See your doctor if they stick around for longer than a couple of days. Go to the emergency room if you feel light-headed, have trouble breathing, or feel that your throat is swelling. You could be having a life-threatening allergic reaction that requires immediate medical care.

indigestion

Pantry HEALERS

Anise seeds

Apple cider vinegar

Baking soda

Bitter beer

Candied ginger

Caraway seeds

Chamomile tea

Dill seeds

Fennel seeds

Honey

Lemon

Mint tea

The term "indigestion" means different things to different people, and the territory of troubles it covers is huge. Just to clear up any confusion, indigestion and heartburn are two different problems. Heartburn produces a painful or burning sensation in the center of your chest, due to acid spilling upward into your esophagus. Indigestion happens further south: It produces bloating, a feeling of uncomfortable fullness during or after a meal, or pain or burning concentrated in the upper abdomen. Smokers, pregnant women, and people who are overweight are especially susceptible. Luckily, indigestion symptoms are especially easy to tame by employing simple lifestyle tweaks and easy home remedies.

first things first

These simple suggestions can help make bouts of indigestion a thing of the past:

• Eat smaller, more frequent meals.

• Avoid your triggers. Spicy or fatty foods, carbonated drinks, and alcohol are frequent tummy troublers.

• Don't smoke.

• Maintain a healthy weight.

• Take your time when you dine.

• Be active—exercise improves digestion.

kitchen cabinet cures

Make a four-seed chew. Mix a batch of this seedy chew, which combats indigestion by helping your system expel excess gas. Take 1 teaspoon each of fennel, dill, anise, and caraway seeds and blend. Chew up a half-teaspoon or so, slowly, when you're having indigestion after you've eaten a big, spicy, or fatty meal. You might see this same mix in Indian restaurants, where it is often put in bowls for customers to sample as they leave.

Order up some mint or chamomile. A steaming cup of one of these teas will quickly dispel that dyspeptic feeling. Simply use one of either kind of tea bag to a cup of water. Cover and steep for 10 minutes before drinking. Many restaurants stock these two calming brews, so have it after dinner if you've eaten something rich that might not agree with you.

Sip this before eating. If you know you're going to indulge in foods that will make you sorry later, try this folk remedy first. Add 1 teaspoon of honey and 1 teaspoon apple cider vinegar to a glass of warm water and drink it 30 minutes before you dine.

Soda to the rescue. Stir a teaspoon of baking soda into a glass of water, add a few drops of lemon juice, and drink it. If your stomach is too acidic, this solution neutralizes stomach acid and helps relieve painful gas. In very rare cases, baking soda has been known to explode in the stomach and cause tearing, so squirt the lemon juice into the water first, to dispel some of the gas before it hits your stomach.

Nibble on candy. Candied ginger, that is. Ginger slices that have been dried and sugared are sold in supermarkets and health or natural food stores. They keep forever in the pantry and taste yummy. Two or three pieces can tame your tummy woes. This makes a great remedy for children's minor stomach aches.

Have half a bitter beer. Beers that have a bitter bite are rich in hops, an herb that helps stimulate digestion. But don't get carried away—more than a half glass of beer will depress your digestion.

When to Call THE DOCTOR

The vast majority of indigestion cases are simple, one-time affairs, easily cured with home remedies. But call 911 if you experience nausea along with sweating or an ache or pain in the chest; you may be having a heart attack. See your doctor if you have intense abdominal pain, especially if you also have black or bloody stools or if you're vomiting. And you need a checkup if indigestion lingers for more than a couple of weeks, despite your best attempts at self-care.

Weird & wacky

It's no surprise to us that a condition so ubiquitous would rack up scores and scores of crazy treatments. But these three tickled our funny bones:

• Bend over, turn over a rock, and walk forward without looking back.

• For a child's indigestion: Pass him backward around a table leg seven times.

• Execute a somersault.

insomnia

Pantry HEALERS

Chamomile tea

Lavender
  essential oil

Mandarin oranges

Milk

Pumpkin seeds

Sesame seeds

Sugar

Sunflower seeds

Tarragon

If you listen to the chatter around the office coffee machine every morning, you'd think that tossing and turning is our national pastime. So few people admit to getting a good night's sleep these days that everyone seems to have an opinion on the subject. The reasons we sleep so poorly are many: the stresses of 21st-century living, multitasking, financial and family concerns, health problems, bedrooms loaded with blinking, high-tech electronics…the list goes on and on. Take comfort from knowing that, as with any other health issue, admitting that you have a problem puts you on the path to solving it. These easily made home remedies will help improve your sleep.

first things first

One of the first pieces of advice you'd be likely to hear from a sleep medicine specialist is to "improve your sleep hygiene." Interpretation: Sleeping poorly can often be traced to having bad habits that can be easily fixed. Here, from the National Sleep Foundation, are some tips to help you have good hygiene of the sleep variety:

• Establish a regular bed and wake time.

• Avoid nicotine altogether and avoid caffeine close to bedtime.

• Avoid alcohol in the hours approaching sleep time.

• Exercise regularly (but complete your workout at least three hours before bedtime).

- Establish a consistent relaxing "wind-down" bedtime routine.

- Create a sleep-conducive environment that is dark, quiet, and comfortable.

- Discuss the appropriate way to take any sleep aid with a health care professional.

kitchen cabinet cures

Brew this herbal nightcap. Sip a strong cup of chamomile tea (made with two tea bags) before going to bed every night. When sleep comes more easily, cut back to using one tea bag (continued use of the stronger concentration can cause sleeplessness to return).

Make lavender oil your friend. In at least one study, inhaling lavender essential oil before bedtime helped people with insomnia sleep better. You can use the sweetly scented oil in several ways:

- Massage a few drops of lavender essential oil into your temples before going to bed.

- Sprinkle a few drops of oil onto your pillowcase each night (it won't stain).

- Use an aromatherapy diffuser to waft the scent throughout your bedroom.

- Take a relaxing hot bath before bedtime. Add lavender essential oil or lavender bath salts to the tub. Light some lavender candles and play relaxing music, then dry off and slip into bed.

Lavender essential oil is widely available at health and natural food stores. Make sure to buy 100 percent pure essential oil, rather than a cheaper perfumed oil product.

Weird & wacky

There's certainly no science for this nutty-sounding folk remedy, but who knows? Maybe onion vapors contain a sleep-inducing substance that researchers have yet to discover. We'd consider trying this one only as a last resort. Cut up a yellow onion and put it into a canning jar. Screw on the cover and put the jar on your nightstand. If you have trouble falling asleep, or wake up in the middle of the night, open the jar and take a few deep breaths. Then close the jar, lie back, and visualize calming images. With any luck, the next time you open your eyes it will be morning.

Go on, count those sheep

Believe it or not, there's something to the age-old ritual of counting sheep. Picturing the woolly livestock engages the right side of the brain, while counting them uses the left, effectively preventing you from concentrating on anything else: work problems, worries, or the fear of not falling asleep.

lavender at bedtime

See page 277

Nosh on some seeds. Pumpkin, sesame, and sunflower seeds all contain L-tryptophan, a substance the body uses to convert to the calming neurotransmitter serotonin. Try nibbling on a handful of seeds nightly 30 minutes before bedtime.

Sleep like royalty. If you're a terrible sleeper, you owe it to yourself to make an investment in the most comfortable bedding you can afford. Look for 100 percent cotton sheets with a thread count of 250 or higher for the most softness. If you've been sleeping on the same mattress for more than five years, consider getting a new one—and take your time picking one out. And change your pillows: Some people find that "memory foam" pillows can make sleeping more comfortable.

Try a fruity dessert. Canned mandarin oranges are mentioned in folk medicine as having sleep-inducing properties. There's no science to back this remedy, so it's on the list of otherwise healthy remedies that certainly can't hurt and might just help the situation. Choose brands canned in their natural juice rather than heavy sugar syrups.

Go from pancakes to pillows. Buckwheat pillows are stuffed with the well-cleaned hulls of a buckwheat stalk. Users swear by their comfort. In one study of customer satisfaction of 10 pillow types, buckwheat came in second. Originally from Japan, buckwheat pillows are becoming available worldwide as healthy, ultra-comfortable alternatives to foam or feather pillows.

Try tarragon. A traditional French home remedy for insomnia is to make a tea from dried tarragon. Put about 2 teaspoons of the herb into 2 cups of boiling water, cover, and let steep for about 30 minutes. Strain, then have a cup shortly before going to bed.

Make a milk cocktail. One of the best-known home remedies for insomnia is warm milk. But few know that having some carbs at the same time helps get the milk's tryptophan—the key amino acid for inducing sleep—to enter the brain. So folk healers say to heat the milk to just before boiling, then stir in a teaspoon of white or brown sugar. Consider adding a teaspoon of vanilla and a sprinkle of cinnamon on top, both for flavor and your health.

When to Call THE DOCTOR

If you've tried the remedies in this chapter and nothing helps you sleep, see your doctor for a checkup if insomnia persists. Many conditions and some medications have sleeplessness as a symptom. After ruling out physical problems, your doctor may refer you to a sleep clinic for treatment.

jock itch

This condition's name is misleading—you don't have to be the slightest bit athletic to acquire jock itch. In fact, the condition's signature—a red, itchy, chafed groin area—is often caused by the athlete's foot fungus, tinea pedis. Becoming itch-free is a matter of keeping your parts dry and relying on some homemade fungus fighters.

first things first

These simple suggestions can prevent your private itch:

• Wear sandals when you're walking around the pool deck or in the gym shower or steam room.

• Put a thick towel on the locker room floor when changing clothes.

• If family members have athlete's foot, you're at risk, too. Keep the tub extra-clean and be sure they use antifungal creams to clear up the problem.

• After a shower, dry yourself from head to toe. We mean that literally—start with your head and dry your feet last. That way, if there's fungus on your feet, you won't transfer the infection to your groin. If you have or suspect you have jock itch, consider using a hair dryer on the coolest setting to dry your privates instead of using the towel.

• When you get dressed or change your underwear, dust your groin with talc or baby powder. It will absorb moisture.

Pantry HEALERS

Apple cider vinegar

Antidandruff shampoo

Baby powder

Diaper rash cream

Talc

Tea tree essential oil

Thyme

• If you have athlete's foot, put your socks on first when you get dressed. You can transfer the fungus to your underwear if you pull your undies over your bare feet.

kitchen cabinet cures

Make it tea thyme. Thyme contains thymol, a compound with potent fungus-fighting abilities. What's more, thyme contains carvacrol, which researchers recently discovered has potent anti-inflammatory properties. To make the tea, stir 2 teaspoons dried thyme in 1 cup boiled water, cover, let it steep for 20 minutes, and strain. Once the tea cools, soak cotton balls in the tea and apply generously to the itchy area several times a day.

Enlist a potent fungus fighter. Tea tree oil is a germ-fighting and fungus-fighting antiseptic. Rub a thin layer of the oil onto your skin twice a day—but dilute it first: Mix 10 drops into 2 tablespoons olive oil or witch hazel.

Yes, get the vinegar out. Fungi can't thrive in acidic environments, so make your groin area acidic. A few times a day, dab on some apple cider vinegar with a clean cotton ball.

Shampoo the itch away. We're not aware of research to confirm this, but many people report that washing the groin with antidandruff shampoo helps eradicate jock itch because shampoos have antifungal properties.

Baby the area. Diaper rash creams containing zinc oxide often can do the trick on jock itch. Clean the area well, then put on a thin coating before getting dressed.

When to Call THE DOCTOR

If the itchy area has blisters or if the itch doesn't clear up after a few weeks of self-treatment, talk to your doctor. You might have something other than jock itch, such as an allergic reaction to some irritant in your clothing or the laundry detergent you use. In rare cases, jock itch is associated with serious illnesses such as diabetes or cancer.

Surprise culprit: Fido

Dogs and cats can harbor hard-to-see fungal infections on their skin, and you can pick one up when you pet or groom them. In one study of 211 dogs, researchers found 89 fungal strains that can also infect humans—and in fact, 11 dog owners who had athlete's foot or jock itch were infected with the same strain carried by their pets. Look for areas of skin where fur is missing or ask your veterinarian to check your canine or kitty.

laryngitis

Pantry HEALERS

Cayenne

Chicken broth

Gum

Honey

Hot pepper sauce

Lozenges

Myrrh tincture

Onions

Sage

Salt

You're croaking instead of speaking—that is, if you can make any noise at all. Chances are, you've either got a bad sore throat, which has swollen your vocal chords, or you've been overusing your voice (think politicians on election night). The result is laryngitis, an inflammation of the larynx (voice box), the part of the windpipe that houses your vocal cords. Normally, the vocal cords open and shut when you speak. When the vocal cords swell, they vibrate differently, which causes hoarseness. Smoking, allergies, sinus infections, dust, fumes, or even heartburn or bronchitis can cause a froggy voice. Key to home treatment is soothing the irritation, and that's easily done with ingredients you're likely to have on hand.

first things first

In addition to home remedies to soothe your vocal cords, do these for quick relief:

• Give your voice a rest and do your best not to talk until you're well on the way to healing.

• Don't whisper, either—it dries out your vocal chords.

• Whatever you do, don't smoke.

• Try not to "clear your voice."

• Don't drink alcohol.

• Use a humidifier or take herbal steams.

• Keep your throat moist by sucking on lozenges.

- Gargle several times a day with ½ teaspoon salt in a glass of warm water.

kitchen cabinet cures

Get some myrrh tincture. Unless the Wise Men visited you recently, you probably don't have this remedy in your medicine chest. But maybe you should: Herbalists consider myrrh the go-to treatment for healing oral problems. It kills pain and germs on contact and quickly combats inflammation. You can find myrrh tincture at health food stores—a little bottle lasts a long time. To treat laryngitis, add 30 drops to a glass of warm water and gargle six times a day. Don't use without diluting, and don't swallow it. Also, avoid if you're pregnant or nursing.

Have some sage-honey tea. Sage is said to help restore the voice, and honey is soothing and antiseptic. Use 1 teaspoon of dried sage to 1 cup of boiling water, cover and steep for 10 minutes, then strain. Sweeten with a couple of spoonfuls of honey and drink.

Spoon up a bowl of hot soup. Warm liquids, such as chicken broth, can help ease the discomfort. But spicy hot liquids help even more. Spike your soup with a sprinkle of cayenne or a few dashes of hot pepper sauce.

Sip some onion juice. Onions are a folk medicine staple. Like garlic, they're rich in compounds that quell inflammation and combat germs. An old home remedy for laryngitis is to drink a mixture of 2 teaspoons onion juice followed by a "chaser" of 1 teaspoon honey. Take those 3 teaspoonfuls every three hours. To get onion juice, press an onion half between two cutting boards and collect the juice that runs out. Of course, if you own a juicer, you don't have to use all that elbow grease.

Grab some gum before takeoff. When you travel by plane, chew gum or suck on lozenges. The cabin air is excessively dry, and your vocal cords suffer. If you keep your mouth closed and increase saliva production, you help prevent dehydration. And make it a point to down a glass of water each hour you're in flight.

When to Call THE DOCTOR

Usually laryngitis isn't serious, and you'll have your voice back in a few days. But if you're still hoarse after four or five days or if you're running a fever, let your doctor know. Persistent, unexplained hoarseness could signal something serious, especially if you're a smoker or tobacco chewer. See a doctor immediately or call 911 if your laryngitis is accompanied by pain so severe that you have trouble swallowing or if you're coughing up blood or wheezing.

Weird & wacky

For reasons we couldn't fathom, chestnut shells turn up in folklore as a laryngitis remedy. The directive is to chew the shells as if you were chewing gum. Frankly, we thought this treatment was just plain nutty until we came across a 2007 medical study—it suggested that the shells are actually loaded with antioxidants.

memory problems

Pantry HEALERS

Blueberry juice

Canned fish (salmon, sardines, herring, mackerel)

Cinnamon

Flaxseeds

Green tea

Prunes

Pumpkin seeds

Raisins

Sage tea

Sesame seeds

Shiitake mushrooms

Spinach

Sunflower seeds

Turmeric

Most middle-aged folks can lay claim to at least a few of these so-called "senior moments" in which our memory seems to fail us. As we age, our brains store information differently, making it harder for us to recall facts. But aging isn't always the problem. Simply trying to juggle too many important details can wreak havoc on your focus. Thyroid disorders can affect memory, as can medications, including those for high blood pressure, anxiety, and cancer. Believe it or not, you can often rescue a less-than-perfect memory with simple pantry cures.

first things first

Feeling forgetful lately? Take a close look at how much sleep you've been getting. Chronic sleep deprivation can shrink the hippocampus, the region of the brain responsible for accurate memory. In fact, studies have shown that just a few days of insufficient sleep time stresses the brain and could potentially mess up your memory. Other memory-slayers include smoking (even secondhand smoke can affect memory) as well as abusing alcohol and recreational drugs.

kitchen cabinet cures

Become a seed freak. Brain experts recommend nibbling on seeds to help protect your memory. That's because seeds—especially flax, sunflower, sesame, and pumpkin—are rich in magnesium, a mineral that helps protect brain cells from overstimulation, which is deadly to cells. What's more, seeds are laced with brain-healthy omega-3 fatty acids that help keep cell membranes flexible enough to function properly. Add a small handful of tasty sunflower or pumpkin seeds to your breakfast cereal, or snack on them at midday. Use sesame seeds liberally in cooking and baking—they add a subtle, nutty taste. And grind up tiny flaxseeds in a clean coffee grinder and stir into yogurt, cereal, or smoothies.

Eat with the fishes. When granny told you to eat your fish because it was brain food, she knew what she was talking about. Canned salmon, mackerel, herring, and sardines are loaded with omega-3 fatty acids. Another function of these healthy fats is that they help prevent inflammation in brain cells. Inflammation destroys cells, and when that happens in the brain it hastens cognitive decline. In a six-year study involving 4,000 Chicago residents age 65 and older, researchers found that the folks who ate the most fish were better able to preserve their memories than non-fish eaters.

Pal around with prunes. If the only time you reach for prunes is when you're a little, um, backed up, you're missing out on a marvelous opportunity to protect your memory. That's because prunes, and to a lesser extent, raisins, are superstars on the ORAC (oxygen radical absorbance capacity) chart. These tasty dried fruits are like the Terminator when it comes to neutralizing free radicals, which are unstable, cell-damaging molecules. When free radicals go on a rampage against brain cells, memory loss ensues. Have three or four prunes a day, or tuck a little box of raisins into your purse or briefcase.

Try the Popeye diet. Spinach is also way up there on the ORAC chart, and it's one of the few food sources of a-lipoic acid (ALA). This antioxidant seems to have a special affinity for protecting brain cells. In a study conducted on aging mice, researchers learned that ALA helped mice remember their way through a maze as well as mice that were much younger. Need more reasons to open a can of spinach (or enjoy it fresh or frozen) a few times a week? It's also a great source of the B vitamin folic acid, which helps neutralize a substance called homocysteine. High homocysteine levels can increase the risk for Alzheimer's disease in people over 60 by a whopping 150 percent.

When to Call THE DOCTOR

It's hard for people to assess memory problems on their own. So schedule an appointment with your doctor if you feel that your memory has slipped significantly over the last six months. And make an appointment right away (or have a loved one or a friend make one for you) if you have trouble remembering how to do things you've done many times before, can't remember how to get to a familiar place, or have trouble accomplishing activities that involve step-by-step instructions, such as following a recipe.

the natural DOCTOR'S Rx

Blueberry juice may boost your memory—aim for 16 ounces of 100 percent pure, unsweetened blueberry juice a day. And sage tea also has memory-enhancing properties. Brew a cup with 1 teaspoon of dried sage to 1 cup boiled water. Cover, steep for 10 minutes, and strain before drinking.

Weird & wacky

An old, traditional memory-booster calls for dipping garlic cloves in chocolate and eating one to three of them a day. In theory, we think this makes tons of sense—the garlic and the chocolate are loaded to the gills with the kind of antioxidants that protect brain cells. But seriously, in practice? No thanks—we'll have the chocolate-covered cherries instead, please.

Crave some curry. The bright yellow spice called turmeric, used in traditional Indian curries and other dishes, gets its neon glow from an antioxidant compound called curcumin. Turmeric drew the attention of researchers who study Alzheimer's disease when they noticed that people in India, where turmeric is used liberally in cooking, have relatively low rates of the disease. And now we know why: Curcumin deters the formation of brain deposits called amyloid plaques, which are the classic sign of Alzheimer's disease. Although turmeric is part of the curry spice blend, it doesn't taste spicy hot. Its exotic, slightly citrusy flavor complements rice (and turns it a beautiful bright yellow), soups, meat loafs, stews, casseroles, and baked goods. For maximum effect, try to get at least a teaspoonful or so every day.

Seek out shiitake. In research conducted recently at UCLA, scientists discovered that the combination of vitamin D and curcumin (the key ingredient in turmeric) could help stimulate the immune system to clear amyloid plaques found in the brains of people suffering from Alzheimer's disease. Turns out, one delectable source of vitamin D is shiitake mushrooms. Although you can find them fresh in markets, dried shiitake mushrooms have a richer, more concentrated flavor.

Sprinkle on some cinnamon. Helping preserve your memory is only one reason to use this tasty cookie spice as often as possible. It reduces inflammation and is a potent antioxidant. As an added bonus, it's been proven to lower cholesterol and blood sugar. To get those benefits, as well as a potential memory boost, freely sprinkle cinnamon on sliced fruit, toast, hot or cold breakfast cereal, lattes, and even soups and stews. Aim to get ¼ to ½ teaspoon every day.

Have a spot of tea. Researchers from the Netherlands confirmed in a very recent study that two green tea components, L-theanine and caffeine, can significantly boost levels of attention and alertness. This builds on what we already knew about tea's brain benefits. In another study published in the *American Journal of Clinical Nutrition*, researchers discovered that drinking just one cup of green tea a day made folks (55 and older) 38 percent less likely to experience a decline in their mental abilities. And drinking a second cup daily made them 54 percent less likely to show mental declines.

menopause

You may be one of those lucky women who sails right through menopause without ever experiencing hot flashes, mood swings, night sweats, or insomnia. But if you're not, and you wonder when you'll feel like your old self again, we've got the answer: Soon, very soon. That's because remedies already on standby in your pantry can quickly help you ease most mild menopause problems.

first things first

It sounds nutty, telling women dealing with sweat-drenching hot flashes to work up yet more sweat by exercising. But a really vigorous 20-minute daily session (via a fast-paced walk, gentle jog, or cardio machine) will do you a whole world of good. Besides helping you lose weight (pounds tend to creep on around menopause time), a short daily burst of high-powered activity will decrease hot flashes and night sweats, improve your mood and sleep, and help balance your hormone levels. What's more, weight-bearing exercises like walking, running, and resistance training help keep your bones nice and sturdy.

Other good, standard strategies for reducing discomfort include:

• Eat a diet rich in fruits and veggies.

• Cut your red meat intake.

• Use healthy fats, such as olive and canola oils.

• Put more beans, nuts, and low-fat dairy products on your menu.

Pantry HEALERS

Almonds

Beans

Canned fish (salmon, sardines, mackerel, tuna)

Canola oil

Flaxseeds

Nuts

Olive oil

Sage tea

Sunflower seeds

Wheat germ

Whole-grain cereals

See your doctor if you're experiencing irregular periods or unusual flow to make sure that the changes are related to menopause and not a signal of some other problem. If you have urinary discomfort, see a doctor to check for bladder infections, which occur more frequently among women who have vaginal dryness. Finally, schedule an appointment if you miss a period or develop bleeding between periods or if your symptoms interfere with daily activities.

kitchen cabinet cures

Try sage for the sweats. You may know sage best as the herb that gives sausages and turkey stuffing their delectable savor. What you may not know is that sage is the herb clinical herbalists frequently recommend for easing night sweats. In fact, studies on sage tea dating back to 1896 demonstrated its ability to suppress perspiration. Use sage tea as a short-term treatment only. Sage contains an essential oil called thujone, which is toxic. However, thujone is not water soluble, so sage tea contains limited amounts of the stuff. To use sage to treat night sweats, steep 1 teaspoon dried sage in 8 ounces boiled water, covered, for 15 minutes. Sip 4 ounces, three times a day. Because of the thujone toxicity issue, steer clear of taking sage essential oil or sage tincture.

Buzz up some flax. Flaxseed is a great dietary addition during menopause, because it offers a triple bonus of fiber, heart-healthy omega-3 fatty acids, and lignans, which are plant compounds that reduce the risk of breast cancer. The best way to use flaxseed is to grind 2 tablespoons a day in a clean coffee grinder and enjoy its nutty flavor sprinkled in cereal, yogurt, salads, and soups.

Entertain some E. Almonds, sunflower seeds, wheat germ, and olive oil are among the pantry foods that are rich in vitamin E. Though the research is limited, one study suggests vitamin E can lessen the frequency and severity of hot flashes. And a recent Tufts University study indicated that vitamin E helps prevent blood vessel blockage by keeping vessels dilated. This is important for menopausal women, whose risk of heart disease is two to three times higher than that of premenopausal women. Whole-grain cereals fortified with vitamin E are also excellent sources.

Eat something fishy. Canned salmon, mackerel, sardines, and tuna are loaded with omega-3 fatty acids that help reduce bone loss and lower risk of heart disease—two risk factors that directly target menopausal women. Having two or three servings of one of these tasty fish each week may lessen the severity of hot flashes and will absolutely have a healthy impact on your heart. What's more, a 4-ounce serving of canned tuna contains your daily requirement of vitamin B_6, which can help menopausal mood swings.

menstrual problems

Whether you have premenstrual syndrome or just the occasional menstrual cramps, you've probably heard all the PMS jokes, and you probably don't find them very funny. Of course, bad moods and tempers are just as likely to be triggered by the stresses of 21st century living as by menstrual discomfort. But if you find yourself staring a little too long at the knife rack during *that* time of the month, these home remedies should repair your jangled nerves and ease your cramps.

first things first

What you eat can make a big difference in how you feel before and during your period. Research has shown that eating foods rich in omega-3 fatty acids, calcium, and vitamin B_6 seems to ease mood-related PMS symptoms. And eating vitamin B_1-rich foods may ease cramps.

kitchen cabinet cures

Get sunnier with seeds. Sunflower seeds are chockfull of vitamin B_1 (thiamin). In one study, 556 young women with painful periods were given 100 milligrams of vitamin B_1 or a placebo for three months. After 60 days, 55 percent of the women taking the vitamin said their pain had disappeared. In the group who took the sugar pills, 99 percent said they didn't notice any difference in their symptoms. Though researchers couldn't explain how B_1 relieves cramps, they did note that vitamin B_1 deficiencies cause decreased pain tolerance, muscle cramping, and fatigue.

Pantry HEALERS

Canned fish (salmon, sardines, mackerel, tuna)

Celery

Chamomile tea

Cinnamon

Cloves

Collard greens

Epsom salts

Fennel seeds

Ginger

Ginger tea

Lavender essential oil

Nuts

Olive oil

Seeds

Shiitake mushrooms

Spinach

Wheat germ

Whole-grain cereals

the natural
DOCTOR'S R_x

If you're among the women who get that bloated feeling before or during your period, make celery sticks your go-to snack. They're a natural diuretic and are great at helping you beat the bloat.

Moodiness is a classic PMS symptom that responds nicely to doses of sunlight—whether from Mother Nature or from full-spectrum lightbulbs. Exercise is also a perfect way to dispel bad PMS moods.

A quarter-cup serving of tasty sunflower seeds supplies more than half your daily B_1 requirement.

Feast on canned fish. Fatty fish like canned sardines, salmon, tuna, and mackerel are high in omega-3 fatty acids, which may help ease menstrual cramps. What's more, a serving of yellowfin tuna (canned as "chunk light") provides almost 60 percent of your daily requirement for vitamin B_6, which seems to improve PMS symptoms for some women.

Brew a spicy tea. Ginger tea is a cross-cultural cramp reliever, known to folk healers as well as to practitioners in America, China, India, the Middle East, and beyond. Ginger contains compounds that work very much like nonsteroidal anti-inflammatory drugs, such as ibuprofen, to suppress prostaglandins. These are the hormone-like substances that are thought to trigger menstrual cramps. Ginger also contains four antispasmodic agents that relax muscles to ease cramps. To make an anti-cramp brew, just put ½ teaspoon of powdered ginger in a cup. Fill with boiling water, cover, and steep for 5 minutes. Strain before drinking. Have a hot cup two or three times a day.

Mine your cabinets for calcium. A diet rich in calcium and vitamin D (which helps the body absorb calcium) seems to ease PMS symptoms. No one is certain exactly why this combination works—it's possible that PMS actually stems from a calcium deficiency—but it does help some women. A large study of about 3,000 women found that those who got about 1,200 milligrams of calcium and 400 IU of vitamin D from food were about a third less likely to have PMS than those who got considerably less. A serving of spinach or collard greens provides almost one-fourth of your daily calcium requirement. And dried shiitake mushrooms are an excellent source of vitamin D.

Bag some chamomile. Chamomile tea has been easing menstrual cramps for hundreds of years. The apple-scented brew has antispasmodic properties to calm cramps, and its mild sedative effects calm jangled nerves. To make a tea, pour 1 cup boiling water over two tea bags, cover, steep for 10 minutes, and enjoy two or three cups a day. Make sure to have a cup before bedtime, too—it'll help you get a great night's sleep.

Seek out magnesium-rich treats. Baked goods made with whole-grain flour, buckwheat, or whole-grain cornmeal—all rich in magnesium—could help put a stop to the PMS blues. Although it's unclear how magnesium affects PMS, the nutrient is essential for dopamine production. This mood-boosting hormone also helps balance adrenal and kidney function, which in turn helps minimize fluid retention. And in a two-month British study, women who took just 200 milligrams of magnesium daily—about the equivalent of a quarter cup of almonds or two servings of spinach—had less weight gain, bloating, and breast tenderness during the second month of the study than women taking a placebo. Another study found that the ratio of magnesium to calcium was significantly lower in women with PMS than in women without it.

Get a little nutty. Nuts, seeds, wheat germ, and other foods high in vitamin E may help relieve symptoms of PMS. In a small three-month study of 46 women with PMS, those who took a daily 400 IU dose of vitamin E— admittedly the equivalent of far more nuts than you'd want to eat in one day—saw their mental and physical symptoms of PMS abate.

||||||||||||||||||||||||||||||||||||||||||||||||||||||||||||||||||||||||||||||||||||||||||||||||||||||||||||||||

Eat to beat period problems

A study of 33 healthy women found that reducing the amount of animal fat in their diets from the typical 40 percent to 20 percent made a huge difference in their PMS symptoms. Overall, their bloating, mood swings, and concentration problems lessened substantially.

Why does eating more vegetables and whole grains help women with PMS? It could be that doing so flattens the hormone rollercoaster by lowering levels of estrogen in the blood.

Another reason: Complex carbs boost levels of the feel-good neurotransmitter serotonin, the same one targeted by certain antidepressants. In a study at the Massachusetts Institute of Technology, researchers found that women who ate lots of complex carbs became less depressed, angry, and anxious and had more stable moods than women who ate fewer complex carbs.

That makes sense, because high-fiber carbs are digested more slowly than carbs that come from white sugar, flour, or rice, for example, so they help keep blood sugar levels stable. When blood sugar drops too low, fatigue and irritability ensue and magnify mood-related PMS symptoms. Complex carbs also help prevent the constipation that's common in women with menstrual cramps.

Many women admit to craving chocolate and ice cream before and during their periods. But instead of having a sugar fix, eating meals packed with whole grains, fruits, and vegetables may double-cross PMS symptoms, including the cramping that often accompanies heavy bleeding.

Find fiber in your pantry. Think of dietary fiber as a natural sponge that sops up excess estrogen. Lowering estrogen levels could mean fewer PMS symptoms. Increase your fiber intake by chowing down on whole-grain cereal or oatmeal for breakfast. Read labels and select those with the highest fiber content per serving. For an additional fiber fix, sprinkle a couple of spoonfuls of freshly ground flaxseed over your cereal (or add it to low-fat yogurt, which will also give you a symptom-reducing calcium boost).

Change your oil. Try substituting extra-virgin olive oil as often as you can for butter, margarine, and other less healthy fats. Butter is high in saturated fat, which may contribute to inflammation that exacerbates PMS symptoms. On the other hand, olive oil is rich in polyphenols, which are antioxidant substances that reduce inflammation.

Take a slow soak. Mix 30 drops of lavender essential oil with a cup of Epsom salts. Add to hot bath water and soak until the water cools. The Epsom salts will help with water retention and will ease muscular aches and pains. The fragrant oils will relax you and lift your spirits.

 recipe for healing

Herbal Cramp Pillow

This soothing little sack has its roots in traditional Chinese medicine. It contains spice rack herbs that are known to relieve pain.

> 2 tablespoons powdered ginger
> 2 tablespoons cloves
> 2 tablespoons ground cinnamon
> 2 tablespoons fennel seeds

1. Put the ginger, cloves, cinnamon, and fennel seeds into a bag made with several thicknesses of cheesecloth or a piece of cotton cloth. Tie securely with cotton string.

2. Put an inch or two of water in a small pot and bring to a boil.

3. Set the bag in a sieve or steamer a few inches above the boiling water and heat until the bag is comfortably hot.

4. Lie down on the couch, and place the herb bag on your lower abdomen. Relax and rest for 15 minutes or so. You can reuse the bag a few times; make a new one when the herbs lose their aroma.

herbal
cramp pillow
Recipe page 292

morning sickness

Pantry HEALERS

Almonds

Anise seeds

Chamomile tea

Dry cereal

Fennel seeds

Ginger (crystallized, fresh, powdered, syrup, tea)

Ginger ale

Honey

Lemon

Peppermint essential oil

Peppermint tea

Plain crackers

Water

You should be jumping for joy, but instead you're jumping for the bathroom every morning...or afternoon...or whenever. Despite its name, morning sickness can occur at any time of day, but it usually disappears after the first three months of pregnancy. There's still no definitive answer as to what causes the distress, but some doctors think rising levels of estrogen could cause it. Other potential triggers could be mild dehydration or the lower blood sugar that's characteristic of early pregnancy. Stress, traveling, certain foods, prenatal vitamins, and aromas can make matters worse, but soothing strategies from pantry ingredients can make matters better.

first things first

To prevent or ease nausea and vomiting, try these strategies:

• Eat dry cereal, plain crackers (such as saltines or oyster crackers), or dry toast before you get out of bed. These snacks soak up the saliva in your mouth and some of the acid in your stomach.

• Avoid greasy, fried, and spicy foods.

• Instead of three big meals, eat several small meals during the day.

• To quell nausea, sip ginger tea or nibble on candied ginger.

• Try wearing an acupressure bracelet, such as those used to prevent motion sickness.

• Have someone else prepare food if cooking odors provoke nausea.

kitchen cabinet cures

Go with ginger. Here's a case where many modern docs agree with traditional healers: Ginger is a safe and effective treatment for morning sickness. In one study, when pregnant women with morning sickness were given ginger or a sham treatment, 28 of 32 women in the ginger group said their symptoms improved, compared to 10 of 35 women in the placebo group.

The chemical compounds that give ginger its zesty taste—namely gingerol and shogaol—seem to reduce intestinal contractions, neutralize digestive acids, and curb the brain's "vomiting center." Doctors often recommend ginger to prevent nausea because it doesn't cause grogginess the way antinausea drugs can. It's even been used to lessen chemotherapy-induced nausea and postoperative nausea.

Here are four ginger remedies that ease morning sickness:

• Nibble on a couple of pieces of crystallized ginger before getting out of bed (store in a plastic bag on your night table).

• Drink ginger tea first thing in the morning.

• Have a spoonful of ginger syrup, which you can buy at many health food stores. Take a spoonful first thing, right off the spoon, or stir into a cup of hot water for tea.

• Sip (real) ginger ale. Several companies, including Reed's, make ginger ale with real ginger. Find it at health and natural food stores.

As with any medication or supplement you take during pregnancy, make sure to talk with your doctor about using ginger.

Hide some nuts in your bag. Bring a handful of almonds along when you leave the house in the morning. They help calm queasiness, plus they're packed with calcium, vitamin B_2, vitamin E, and other essential nutrients.

Sip a citrus soother. Make a warm, tummy-soothing drink by squeezing the juice of 1 lemon in a cup of water sweetened with 1 teaspoon of honey. Sip, as needed. Keep the drink warm in a thermos when traveling.

Drink a combo tea. The combination of chamomile and peppermint tea unleashes gentle but powerful antinausea compounds that can be especially helpful for combating morning sickness. On its own, each tea has a long tradition of easing nausea. Chamomile contains plant compounds that may lessen the gag reflex. Peppermint eases digestive

When to Call THE DOCTOR

Despite your misery, don't worry about morning sickness unless you can't keep down any food or fluids and you begin to lose weight. Let your doctor know if nausea or vomiting continues after four months and home remedies aren't working. Seek immediate attention if you vomit blood or a substance that looks like coffee grounds; if you lose more than two pounds; or if you have prolonged, severe vomiting that can cause dehydration and malnutrition.

Thinking of conceiving?

Studies show that women who are taking multivitamins when they conceive are less likely to experience severe morning sickness.

disturbances and helps curb vomiting. To make a tea, use one tea bag each of chamomile tea and peppermint tea to 1 cup boiled water. Cover, steep for 10 minutes, and drink. You can also prepare the tea the night before and chill overnight to sip first thing in the morning.

Employ a little aromatherapy. Put several drops of peppermint essential oil on a tissue, hold it close to your nose, and breathe in through your nose and out through your mouth until your nausea abates.

Zip some seeds. Anise and fennel seeds soothe upset stomachs and are easy to tote along with you. Mix a tablespoon of both (or just one) in a ziplock bag, and chew in ½ teaspoon pinches as the need arises.

Hurry up and hydrate. Simple as it sounds, women who drink a glass of plain old H_2O every hour have a lot less morning sickness. Get into the habit of downing a glass at night, too, whenever you get up to go to the bathroom.

recipe for healing

Ginger Tea for Morning Sickness

This simple brew will calm your stomach in the morning and reduce nausea without making you sleepy.

> 1 cup boiling water
> 1 teaspoon minced fresh ginger or ½ teaspoon powdered ginger

1. In a large cup, pour the boiling water over the ginger. Cover, steep 10 minutes, strain into a container, and refrigerate.

2. Sip in the morning when you wake. You can easily double or triple the recipe to make enough to sip throughout the day.

motion sickness

Maybe seagoing vessels upend your equilibrium, or perhaps you can't bear to take a bus or a train. Some folks can ride for hours in the front seat of a car, but put them in the rear and they quickly turn green as grass. No matter which kind of movement provokes you, you'll find that simple kitchen remedies can help put the brakes on your distress.

first things first

Following these suggestions may help keep motion sickness in check while you're traveling.

On a plane:

• Eat low-cal snacks and light meals 24 hours before departing.

• Choose a seat toward the front of the plane or by the wing.

• Direct the air vent above your seat toward your face.

In a car:

• Sit in the front seat.

• Keep your eyes on the horizon.

• Don't read or look at maps.

• Keep your head still by resting it against the seat back.

• Turn the air vents toward your face.

On a boat:

• Ask for a cabin on the upper deck or toward the front of the ship.

• When on deck, keep your eyes fixed on the horizon or land.

Pantry HEALERS

Cloves

Ginger (candied, fresh, powdered)

Honey

Lemon

Nutmeg

Peppermint (dried)

Vegetable oil

Usually, your bout of motion sickness will end shortly after you've exited the moving vehicle or boat. Call for emergency assistance on board if lethargy, confusion, headache, stiff neck, or severe abdominal pain accompanies your nausea or vomiting. Do the same if there is a danger of dehydration (especially if the patient is a child). Symptoms of dehydration include dry lips and mouth, sunken eyes, decreased urination, and rapid pulse. Call your doctor if vomiting lasts for more than several hours in a child or a day in an adult.

kitchen cabinet cures

Pack the ginger. Without question, the most effective motion sickness remedy is ginger. The herb has been tested on people sailing in rough seas, watching dizzying visual displays, and sitting in rotating chairs. In all cases, ginger lengthened the time it took people to become nauseous and lessened their tendency to vomit.

The chemical compounds that give ginger its zingy taste—mainly gingerol and shogaol—reduce intestinal contractions, neutralize digestive acids, and quell activity in the brain's "vomiting center." But ginger is better at preventing motion sickness than stopping it. If you're susceptible, take ginger *before* you start your journey.

To use ginger, mix a pinch of powdered ginger in water or eat ½ teaspoon chopped fresh ginger every 15 minutes for one hour before traveling; continue this if any signs of illness occur. You can also drink ginger tea or nibble pieces of candied ginger before your trip.

Chew on some cloves. Cloves contain compounds that help stop spasms, so they might also relieve that sudden lurching feeling. Try grinding a few cloves between your teeth before you get into a situation that might trigger motion sickness.

Have some warm "lemon-aid." Make a warm, tummy-soothing drink by squeezing the juice of 1 lemon in a cup of water sweetened with a teaspoon of honey. Sip, as needed. Keep the drink warm in a thermos when traveling.

recipe for healing

Spicy Tummy Rub

Many kids are prone to motion sickness, especially during car rides. This fragrant rub might help settle your child's tummy during your trip. Make it before you set out.

   1 teaspoon ground ginger
   ¼ teaspoon powdered nutmeg
   2 tablespoons dried peppermint
   ¼ cup vegetable oil

Blend the ginger, nutmeg, and peppermint in the oil, and let steep for an hour or so. Then strain. Massage the oil into your child's feet, temples, and wrists. If you're not driving, do it during car rides or on boat or plane rides.

muscle cramps

You're booted from dreamland by a sudden, severe pain in your calf muscle. Or, you're out for a run and suddenly your forward motion stops because your leg cramps up. Muscle cramps happen to just about everyone at one time or another and usually pass as quickly as they appear. Workouts can cause them, but so can remaining frozen in one position for too long. In most cases, employing a tried and true kitchen remedy can neatly end the pain.

first things first

These instant responses can help manage the problem without resorting to painkillers or other remedies:

• If you're jolted awake in the middle of the night by a leg cramp, immediately flex your foot toward your head. Then, pull your foot toward you with your hands, if need be, to give your calf muscle a good stretch. After your stretch, give your calf muscle a firm, brisk massage. If it still hurts, apply a bag of frozen veggies to the ache.

• Place an electric heating pad or a hot washcloth on the misbehaving muscle to relax the cramp and increase blood flow to the affected tissue. Set the pad on low, apply for 20 minutes, and then remove it for at least 20 minutes before reapplying.

• Take a long, warm shower, or soak in the bath. For added relief, pour in a half-cup Epsom salts. The magnesium in Epsom salts promotes muscle relaxation.

Pantry HEALERS

Apple cider vinegar
Honey
Rosemary
Tonic water
Water

Muscle cramps are usually temporary and don't cause any damage, even though they can feel excruciating. You'll need emergency help if you suddenly experience severe cramping that doesn't go away or if you experience night leg cramps and you've been exposed to a toxin, such as lead. Call your doctor if leg cramps interrupt your sleep so often that you have trouble functioning the next day or if you also experience muscle weakness or atrophy.

kitchen cabinet cures

Hydrate with H$_2$O. Since cramps are often caused by dehydration, drink plenty of water, especially before and during exercise or exertion. Here's the plan:

• Drink at least 2 cups of water before each workout.

• Stop and drink 4 to 8 ounces of water every 10 to 20 minutes during exercise sessions.

• If you perspire heavily, consider a sports drink, such as Gatorade, that replaces lost sodium and electrolytes.

• If nighttime leg cramps trouble you, drink a full glass of water before you head to bed.

Rosemary: drink and apply. This remedy works from the outside in and the inside out. Rosemary contains four anti-inflammatory substances, including rosmarinic acid, which works to ease pain much like aspirin does. What's more, rosmarinic acid is easily absorbed through the skin, and it's approved as a topical painkiller by German medical authorities. To use, put an ounce of dried rosemary into a 1-pint canning jar and fill with boiling water. Cover tightly and let stand for 30 minutes. Apply as a wash to the painful muscle two or three times a day. Every time you apply the wash, drink two shot-glass–sized doses.

Sip some vinegar water. This old folk remedy should please apple cider vinegar fans. Add 2 tablespoons apple cider vinegar and a little honey to a glass of water and drink to ease nighttime leg cramps. Of course, by the time you walk to the kitchen to put the drink together, your cramp is likely to be history—but maybe that's just the point.

Put night cramps to sleep. If cramps wake you in the wee hours, drink a glass of tonic water (make sure it contains quinine) before you go to bed. Research suggests that quinine can ease nocturnal leg cramps. But never take quinine tablets, which the FDA has banned due to serious side effects.

nausea & vomiting

There's no mistaking what your body's trying to do when you're vomiting—it's ridding itself of something noxious. Nausea, on the other hand, though more subtle, is also disturbing—especially when the "am I going to throw up or not?" feeling continues for hours, or longer. Causes for the unpleasant duo are many, but most commonly the culprit is a case of stomach flu, more properly called viral gastroenteritis. Morning sickness and medications (especially chemotherapy), overindulging in alcohol, motion sickness, migraines, food poisoning, and disorders of the stomach or intestines can also throw you into a state of distress. In most cases, though, you can help your system ease up with easy remedies you already have on hand at home.

first things first

As awful as it feels to throw up, a brief bout of vomiting usually serves a purpose. It rids the body of toxic substances, and once it's over, nausea and stomach pain should cease.

Repeated vomiting, on the other hand, can lead to dehydration. To prevent that from happening:

• Drink clear liquids as soon as you can keep them down. Mint tea can be soothing.

• Wait six hours or so after your last episode of vomiting before you start eating again. Then, eat lightly: Nibble on saltines, Jell-O, and toast. Next, try bland foods, such as

Pantry HEALERS

Apple cider vinegar

Apples

Bananas

Cayenne pepper

Cereal

Chamomile tea

Cinnamon

Ginger (powdered, fresh)

Fennel seeds

Jell-O

Peppermint essential oil

Peppermint tea

Rice

Salt

Saltines

Toast

Most nausea is easy to diagnose and a short-term issue. But if nausea and vomiting are accompanied by these symptoms, seek emergency attention. It might be indicative of a more serious health issue:

- Chest pain
- Severe abdominal cramping or pain
- Blurred vision
- Fainting
- Confusion
- Cold, clammy, pale skin
- High fever and stiff neck
- Fecal material or fecal odor in the vomit
- Severe headache
- Inability to keep food or liquid down for 12 hours (8 hours for a child)
- Vomit that contains blood, resembles coffee grounds, or is green

Make an appointment with your doctor if:

- You have diarrhea or a temperature of 100°F or above.
- Bouts of nausea and vomiting have lasted longer than a month.
- You've had unexplained weight loss.

cereal, rice, and non-citrus fruit. like bananas or apples. Avoid spicy or fatty foods.

- Give yourself a few days before you resume your normal diet.

kitchen cabinet cures

First, try ginger. Ginger is proven for its ability to relieve nausea and vomiting due to morning sickness, motion sickness, and even for the vomiting that accompanies chemotherapy treatment. In fact, a research paper published in the *Journal of Gynecological Oncology* listed ginger treatment for chemotherapy-related nausea among the top 10 major research advances in gynecological cancer in 2009.

To prevent nausea after chemotherapy: First, talk to your doctor and discuss taking ginger. With her OK, starting one week before your treatment, take ½ teaspoon powdered ginger a day.

For motion sickness: Take ½ teaspoon fresh ginger or a pinch of powdered ginger every 15 minutes for 1 hour before traveling and continue the dose if you feel sick during your trip.

For migraine-related nausea: Take ½ teaspoon powdered ginger at the first sign of a migraine.

Bathe if you can't drink. If you tried taking ginger but vomited anyway, try soaking your hands or feet in a ginger bath. You're likely to absorb enough of the herb through your skin to calm things down. Put a tablespoon of minced fresh or powdered ginger in a quart of hot water in a bowl or basin. Make sure it's not hot enough to burn you, then soak your hands or feet in the ginger bath until your nausea subsides. Alternately, wrap the ginger in a cheesecloth bag and float it in a bath tub of hot water and take a nice long soak.

Sip mint tea. This traditional remedy is one of the top nausea treatments all over the world. Herbal experts believe peppermint may reduce the gag reflex by anesthetizing the stomach lining. Use a peppermint tea bag in a cup of boiling water and cover it for 10 minutes, or make a stronger brew this way: Put 1 tablespoon dried peppermint or three or four tea bags in a 1-pint canning jar. Fill with boiling water. Let stand for 30 minutes, shaking the bottle a few times while it steeps. Then strain and sip as needed.

Have a cup of chamomile. This delicate herb contains potent anti-inflammatory and pain-relieving compounds that may ease the gag reflex. To treat nausea, put four or five chamomile tea bags (to equal about 2 tablespoons of dried chamomile flowers) in a pint jar and fill with boiling water. Steep for 30 minutes before drinking.

Crush some fennel seeds. Pleasant-tasting fennel seeds contain a compound called anethole, which has antiseptic and antispasmodic properties. Like mint and chamomile, it also contains anesthetic elements that may reduce the stomach's gag reflex. To use, buzz a tablespoon of fennel seeds in a clean coffee grinder. Put in a cup, fill with boiling water, cover and steep for 10 minutes. Strain before sipping.

Try a tummy rub. If your little one has an episode of vomiting or nausea, you can make him feel better by giving him a gentle belly rub. Mix a few drops of peppermint essential oil in a tablespoon or so of olive oil, and gently massage his belly in a clockwise direction.

Drink this for food poisoning. If you suspect food poisoning and have diarrhea in addition to nausea and vomiting, make a cup of cinnamon-ginger tea. Mix 1 teaspoon powdered cinnamon with ½ teaspoon grated fresh or powdered ginger. Add both spices to a cup of boiling water, cover, and steep for 15 minutes, then strain and sip. The cinnamon can help kill bacteria that might be causing the problem.

the natural DOCTOR'S Rx

After you've experienced a nasty bout of vomiting, your doctor will tell you to forgo dairy products until you've recovered. She's also likely to put you on the "BRAT" diet for a few days or so. That means limiting what you eat to bananas, plain rice, applesauce, and dry toast. This diet is also doctor-recommended for diarrhea.

Weird & wacky

We don't think this old folk remedy for nausea sounds very appetizing, but perhaps it worked for someone: Air-pop some popcorn and put it in a bowl. Cover with boiling water and let stand for 15 minutes. Eat a teaspoon of the soggy stuff every 15 minutes or so.

recipe for healing

Spicy Stomach Soother

This home remedy for vomiting turns up time and time again in collections of folkloric treatments. Experts suggest it might work by counter-irritating the stomach lining—think of it as fighting fire with fire.

> 1 teaspoon salt
> 1 teaspoon cayenne pepper
> ¾ cup apple cider vinegar

Mix the salt, cayenne pepper, and vinegar together in a cup or small bowl and take 1 tablespoon every 15 to 30 minutes as needed.

nosebleed

A sudden gush of blood coursing (or even trickling) down your face can really put a dent in your day, not to mention in your laundry budget. Nosebleeds can appear out of nowhere, as in when you scratch your nose and unwittingly nick a blood vessel with your nail. More often, a bloody nose results from an accidental whack while you're having fun on a sports field or court. Whatever the cause, don't panic. If you keep your wits about you, you can usually stop a nosebleed in a matter of minutes.

first things first

Some nosebleeds occur when dry air, typically during the winter, dries out nasal passages and makes them more susceptible to bleeding. That's why it's a good idea to run a humidifier while you sleep whenever the weather gets cool enough to trigger your home's heating. If you get a nosebleed, try these measures first:

• Sit straight up and lean forward to take pressure off the blood vessels in your nose and to lessen bleeding.

• With your thumb and index finger, firmly press your nostrils together and hold them closed for 5 to 10 minutes.

• Once the bleed is under control, don't pick your nose or blow it, and don't bend down for several hours. Keep your head above the level of your heart to prevent a re-bleed.

• If you do start bleeding again, blow your nose forcefully. This will clear your nose of blood clots. Then, give it a spray with a nasal product such as Afrin that contains oxymetazoline. Pinch your nose again, and call your doctor. Note: Never use Afrin for more than three days.

Pantry HEALERS

Aloe

Apple cider vinegar

Cayenne pepper

Ice pack

Olive oil

Petroleum jelly

Vitamin E

Water

Witch hazel

kitchen cabinet cures

Sniff a little cayenne. It's been called one of the best remedies for stopping bleeding, including nosebleeds. Cayenne promotes blood clotting and also acts as an analgesic to ease pain. And we have it on a pediatrician's authority that the hot stuff is an excellent remedy for a child's nosebleed, as counterintuitive as this might sound. Here's the recommendation: Put a little pinch of pepper on your open palm and let your child sniff it into his nostril. Be sure to wash your hands afterward so you don't accidentally transfer the pepper to your eyes.

Try a little witch. Dip a cotton swab in witch hazel and gently insert it into the bleeding nostril. Witch hazel is an astringent that will constrict the blood vessels inside the nose to stop the bleeding.

Apply some E. When your nose has stopped bleeding, puncture a vitamin E capsule of any dose size and squeeze out the liquid. Very gently, rub a tiny bit inside your nose to keep it moist.

Squeeze an aloe leaf. The healing, soothing, and moisturizing power of pure aloe gel is a perfect match for healing a wounded nose. Once your nose has stopped bleeding, slit open a small aloe stalk and dip a cotton swab in the gel. Very gently, apply to the inside of the nostril.

Sip some vinegar water. An old Amish trick for stopping a nosebleed calls for stirring 2 tablespoons of apple cider vinegar into a small glass of water. Fans of this remedy swear it never fails.

Put the freeze on it. Put an ice pack on the bridge of your nose or an icy cold, wet washcloth on the back of your neck for 5 minutes. The cold will shrink blood vessels and cut off the bleeding.

Drink up. Prevent future problems by keeping your mucous membranes moist. Drink eight 8-ounce glasses of water every day. Drink more if your urine is dark, which indicates that you could be dehydrated.

Lube your nostrils. On particularly dry days, dab the inside of your nostrils with a bit of petroleum jelly or even a little olive oil to keep them moist.

When to Call THE DOCTOR

Most nosebleeds are harmless. But seek emergency attention if:

• The nosebleed follows a fall, a blow to the head, or a punch in the nose. Your nose could be broken, or you might have a head injury.

• The bleeding lasts longer than 20 minutes or is very heavy.

• You have blurred vision and/or severe pain in or around one eye.

Otherwise, call your doctor if you have frequent nosebleeds, which may be linked to problems like high blood pressure, an infection, or even a tumor. Blood-thinning medications you're taking, such as aspirin or warfarin, could also be a culprit.

poison ivy/oak

So you didn't remember the famous warning: "Leaves of three, let it be." You were out in the woods or in your own backyard, and somehow you came in contact with poison ivy or oak. Now your skin is covered with an itchy, unsightly rash. Must you suffer in silence? The answer, happily, is no. You can walk into your pantry, pull out a few special items, and whip yourself up some rash relief.

first things first

As soon as you've been in contact with poison oak, poison ivy, or sumac, take these five steps immediately. If the resin is left on your skin, it can spread to other parts of the body—and even to other people.

• Use a poison ivy wipe or wash. Formulated to remove urushiol, the toxic oil to which almost everyone is allergic, these products can whisk up to 95 percent of urushiol off the skin, studies show. Brands include Tecnu Outdoor Skin Cleanser and Cortaid Poison Ivy Care wipes.

• No special products? Try rubbing alcohol, a hand sanitizer containing alcohol, or even vodka. It will disperse the urushiol and get it off your skin.

• Rewash with soap or an ivy wash. Washing with soap will remove any urushiol that hasn't attached itself to skin proteins yet. Even if you've taken emergency measures while outdoors, hopping into the shower or washing off your arms and legs in a sink within an hour after exposure can further cut your risk of itchy blisters.

Pantry HEALERS

Ammonia

Apple cider vinegar

Baking soda

Bentonite clay

Hand sanitizer

Lavender
essential oil

Liquid shoe polish

Oatmeal

Peppermint
essential oil

Rubbing alcohol

Salt

Spray deodorant

Vodka

Witch hazel

- Wash your clothes and shoes. Urushiol is an incredibly tenacious substance and will cling to clothes and shoes. Toss your clothes into the washing machine and launder on hot with laundry soap. Scrub shoes with warm water and soap to remove all traces of the oil.

- Raid your bedroom pantry. A prominent college professor wrote that liquid shoe polish is an antidote for poison ivy, because it contains pipe clay that acts like calamine lotion, as well as zinc oxide, a well-known skin-care ingredient. Others claim that spray deodorant can neutralize urushiol, and antiperspirant can provide relief from itching.

- Or raid your cleaning closet. Because you want to wash away the toxic oil, many people swear by household cleaners. Some folk remedies say to mix one part ammonia to 10 parts water and spray on skin that has recently been exposed. Be careful with strong cleaners, particularly if you have sensitive skin or if you have an open wound. And never put commercial cleaners on your face!

kitchen cabinet cures

Slip into an oatmeal bath. Boil ½ to 1 pound oatmeal (not instant or flavored) in 1 to 2 gallons water for 30 minutes, then add to your bathwater. Soak in the tub for as long as you can spare.

Slap on an oatmeal poultice. Cook regular oatmeal according to package directions and let it cool. Then, spread directly on skin, cover with moist gauze or a thin cloth, and let it do its work for up to ½ hour. Commercial oatmeal bath products are also available.

Chill out with vinegar. Mix equal parts of apple cider vinegar with water, and pour into a spray bottle. Chill in the refrigerator. When you need cool relief, spritz the rash liberally with the cold tonic.

Try table salt. Many people swear that the key to poison ivy relief is to wet the skin and then coat it with table salt, with the goal of drying the rash out. Others recommend sprinkling Epsom salts into a bathtub and taking a soak.

Take a tea bath. Throw three to five tea bags into a bathtub, stir it, and then take a pleasant soak. Use black tea, not herbal. The tannic acids in the tea should help relieve the inflammation and the itching.

When to call THE DOCTOR

Generally, the weepy, blistery rash appears from two hours to 14 days after contact with the resin and lasts up to three weeks. Symptoms can include headache and fatigue. If you're in extreme discomfort, or if you have severe blistering, swelling, or redness, call your doctor. You should also alert the doctor if you might have inhaled the smoke of burning poison ivy plants, especially if you become short of breath. Seek medical attention at once if the rash is on your eyes, nose, mouth, throat, or genitals.

poison ivy
mask

Recipe page 309

 **recipes for healing**

Poison Ivy Mask

The key to healing poison ivy is to dry it up. This absorbent coating does just that. We know you probably don't have bentonite clay handy, but it's inexpensive and worth tracking down, especially if you live in an ivy-infested area. It also does double-duty in many do-it-yourself beauty treatments.

½ teaspoon salt
½ cup water
Bentonite clay
12 drops lavender essential oil
12 drops peppermint essential oil (optional)

1. In a small bowl, dissolve the salt in the water and add enough bentonite clay to make a creamy mixture.
2. Stir in the lavender and peppermint essential oils.
3. Spread over the affected area.

Anti-Itch Wrap

Apple cider and witch hazel combine to cool the burning itch, the lavender oil is soothing and healing, and the baking soda neutralizes the acid that causes itch and pain.

¼ cup apple cider vinegar
¼ cup witch hazel
2 cups cold water
10 drops lavender essential oil
2 teaspoons baking soda

1. In a large bowl, mix the vinegar, witch hazel, and water. In a separate small bowl, mix the essential oil with the baking soda. Stir the baking soda mixture into the water mixture.
2. Soak a clean cloth in the cool solution, and wrap it over the itchy area for 20 minutes at a time or until the cloth begins to dry. Keep the solution chilled in the refrigerator for up to two weeks.
3. Repeat up to three times a day.

psoriasis

People who have this puzzling but common skin condition will tell you that it can drive them crazy. But what's really gone crazy are their T-cells. Normally, these cells—think of them as your immune system's soldiers—seek and destroy germs that enter your system. But when you have psoriasis, the T-cells attack healthy skin cells instead. The result is an overproduction of skin cells plus a build-up of dead skin cells that create "plaques" on the skin's surface. What you're left with is red, raised, sometimes scaly-looking patches of skin that may appear and disappear for no apparent reason. Psoriasis is notoriously tough to treat, but if you attack it diligently on all fronts, these kitchen-born remedies may provide some relief.

first things first

Take measures to soothe your skin—and your spirit. The appearance of the unsightly skin plaques can be difficult on the psyche. Take a daily bath to which you've added bath oils, salts, or oatmeal. Use lukewarm, not hot, water and mild, moisturizing soaps. Choose gentle, organic products free of chemicals and preservatives. After bathing, blot skin gently and slather on a heavy moisturizer while skin is still damp. And moisturize skin regularly throughout the day, particularly when the weather is cold and dry.

At night, apply a heavy moisturizer and cover the skin with plastic wrap if you can; leave in place overnight. In the morning, gently wash away the scales when you shower.

Pantry HEALERS

Bath oils

Beeswax

Canned fish (salmon, sardines, herring, mackerel)

Epsom salts

Flaxseed oil

Honey

Lavender essential oil

Oatmeal

Olive oil

Tea tree oil

Turmeric

kitchen cabinet cures

Enrich your bath. Take a good, long soak in warm water, and then add some olive oil or other chemical-free bath oil. Here's why: A long bath can soften scaly patches and soothe itching, but bathing can also dry your skin and make itching worse. So sit in the tub for about 10 minutes, letting your skin get thoroughly soaked, but about 5 minutes before you get out, add a few spoonfuls of oil. That's all it takes to seal the water into your skin. (Be careful getting in and out of the tub, because oil makes the tub slippery.)

Take an oatmeal bath. Oatmeal eases itching and is known for its skin-soothing and moisturizing properties. To use it, put a good-sized handful or two of plain—not instant or flavored—oatmeal in a blender or food processor and grind it until it turns into a fine powder. Then sprinkle it in the water. Or, wrap the ground oatmeal in a couple of thicknesses of cheesecloth (or tie it up a clean piece of pantyhose or knee-high hose) and toss it in the bath, then use the oatmeal bundle to rub over affected skin.

Go to the mineral springs. You can turn your tub into a healing mineral spring simply by adding 1 to 3 cups of Epsom salts. These salts contain magnesium, which helps heal psoriasis; it can remove scales and reduce itching. Also, add a teaspoon of lavender essential oil, which has soothing and healing properties. Try a daily 15-minute soak, and make sure the water is lukewarm, not hot.

Get friendly with canned fish. Just as creamy moisturizers can help relieve itchy skin, the right fats in your diet

Weird & wacky

It may sound crazy to think that something as simple as a bandage could heal something as complicated as psoriasis, but for some lucky folks, that might be all it takes. Back in the 1980s, Ronald N. Shore, a doctor from Johns Hopkins Hospital, discovered that when he covered a spot of psoriasis with a regular adhesive bandage for three weeks, the skin covered by the adhesive—but not by the gauze pad—healed completely. He went on to repeat the treatment on other lesions on his patient's elbows—and these also healed completely. Dr. Shore noted that this trick seems to work best when combined with other psoriasis treatments; it appeared to be effective on its own for only a minority of patients.

When to call THE DOCTOR

If an outbreak covers a wide area of skin, or affects the palms of your hands and soles of your feet, call your doctor for an appointment. You also need a doctor's attention if you see signs of infection, such as pus, a yellow crust on your skin, or a feeling of heat around the area. If your psoriasis is accompanied by joint pain, you might have a condition called psoriatic arthritis that requires a doctor's care. If you develop widespread, pus-filled bumps and a fever, it's an emergency. Call a doctor or head to the emergency room to deal with the infection immediately.

can "moisturize" you from the inside out. Oily fish like canned salmon, mackerel, and herring contain omega-3 fatty acids that help to quell inflammation. One British study compared the effect of eating 6 ounces of white fish (low in omega-3s) daily for six weeks to eating a similar portion of omega-3 rich fish. The oily fish improved the symptoms of psoriasis in patients by 15 percent, but eating the white fish didn't help much at all.

To make a difference, you have to eat a lot of fish—at least three 3- to 4-ounce servings of canned fatty fish per week. Choose salmon over tuna (substitute canned salmon for tuna in any recipe). Or, quickly sauté onions in a little olive oil till limp, add a tin of sardines, stir till warm, spritz generously with lemon, and toss over whole wheat pasta. If you're not much of a fish eater, consider taking fish oil supplements. Very high doses, between 3 and 10 grams a day, have been shown in some studies to ease psoriasis. Talk to your doctor before taking more than 3 grams of fish oil per day.

Spoon on a yellow healer. Studies have linked turmeric, the spice that gives curry its yellow hue (but not its "heat"), to reducing inflammation in a number of conditions, including psoriasis. In a recent study, a researcher at the Uniformed Services University of Health Sciences at Bethesda, Maryland, showed that curcumin, an antioxidant found in turmeric, protects skin by neutralizing free radicals. What's more, curcumin reduces wound-healing time.

Rethink your diet

Physicians who practice natural medicine advise psoriasis sufferers to make dietary tweaks in hopes of foiling this persistent and tenacious condition. Here's what they recommend:

• Nix alcohol, sugars, and inflammatory fats, such as those found in meat, fast foods, processed foods, and dairy products.

• Consider trying a gluten-free diet. Doing so seems to improve the condition for some people. This means eliminating most grain products, including wheat and anything made with wheat flour; rye, semolina, malt, and barley. Instead, choose foods made with rice and rice flour, buckwheat, corn, flax, nuts, potatoes, soy, or millet.

• Check with an allergist to see whether you have food sensitivities or allergies; some experts link these to psoriasis. Common triggers include citrus, milk, corn, and eggs.

How to use: Stir 1 teaspoon turmeric—which has a subtle, citrusy flavor—into rice, vegetables, pasta, or any other cooked foods. To achieve benefits, you need to use turmeric every day.

Tap the tea tree. Rub a few drops of tea tree oil, diluted in a little olive oil, into your psoriasis patches several times a day. This Australian remedy is useful for relieving itch and softening plaques, especially if you have a mild case.

Grind or pour some flax. Grind up a couple of table-spoons of flaxseeds. Flaxseeds are packed with omega-3 fatty acids. They help block a chemical in your body called arachidonic acid, which causes inflammation. Alternately, you can use flaxseed oil as a salad or veggie drizzle.

 recipe for healing

Calming Cream for Psoriasis

This thick, rich ointment can soften psoriasis plaques and help them heal.

   1 ounce beeswax, grated or chopped
   1 ounce extra-virgin olive oil
   1 ounce honey

1. Melt the beeswax in the top of a double boiler set over simmering water.

2. In a separate saucepan, warm the oil, then pour it into the melted wax. Beat until combined.

3. Warm the honey in the saucepan, then slowly stir it into the oil and wax mixture. Remove from the heat and stir until the mixture is cooled and thick.

4. Spoon mixture into a jar and store in a cool, dark place. Makes about one-third cup.

5. Smooth this ointment onto the affected area at night. Cover with plastic wrap, then hold in place firmly but not too tightly with elastic bandages.

shingles

People describe the pain of shingles as being down-right excruciating—more painful than anything they've previously experienced. Shingles is caused by the varicella-zoster virus, which is also responsible for chicken pox. After you've recovered from chicken pox, the virus can lie dormant for decades. Then, for reasons that are unclear, the virus explodes back into activity. Only this time, it emerges as shingles, not chicken pox. The telltale symptoms include intense nerve pain, which may precede a crusty or blistery rash. While kitchen remedies can't cure shingles, they can provide some soothing relief at a time you need it most.

first things first

If you're suffering a shingles attack, you're likely to feel exhausted and weak. That's your body's way of telling you it needs plenty of rest to fight off the virus, so slow down and take it as easy as you can. Cool wet compresses and cool baths may help relieve pain and itching—as will many of the helpful remedies which follow.

To protect others from the virus, wash your hands often, especially if you have an oozing rash. The blisters contain the varicella virus, so you could potentially infect someone with chicken pox. If possible, cover the blisters with an antibiotic ointment and wrap them with gauze. Until your blisters dry and scab over, consider yourself contagious. Avoid contact with anyone who has a weakened immune system, newborns, and women who are pregnant.

kitchen cabinet cures

Befriend the bees. Folk healers suggest that raw honey can relieve shingles pain and speed the healing of the blisters. No studies have investigated this treatment, but we do know that honey helps wounds heal and feels soothing. Use raw honey exclusively for this treatment (find it at the health food store) because many of honey's healing compounds are lost when honey is pasteurized. Slather the honey on the blisters several times a day.

Make an oat rub and bath. Oatmeal contains antioxidants that reduce inflammation, along with compounds that soothe skin and relieve itching. To use, grind a few handfuls of regular oatmeal (not instant or flavored) in a blender or food processor. Separately, stuff a few heaping spoonfuls of unground oatmeal into a piece of clean panty hose or cheesecloth and tie up securely. Toss the ground oatmeal into a tub of lukewarm water. When you get into the tub, wet your oatmeal bundle. Glide it gently over the blisters as you bathe. Soak three times a day if you can—even a 10-minute bath can make you feel better.

...Or an oat paste. Grind up a handful or so of regular (not instant or flavored) oatmeal in the blender or food processor until it becomes a fine powder. Add just enough water to make a paste, and apply directly to the blistered skin. No oatmeal? Try baking soda. To a few spoonfuls of baking soda, add enough water to make a paste and apply to the blisters.

Chill a chamomile compress. This gentle herb has a long, justifiable history of soothing skin problems. It contains compounds that reduce inflammation and abet wound healing. Make an extra-strong tea with four chamomile tea bags to 2 cups of boiled water. Steep, covered, for 20 minutes, then chill in the refrigerator. Separately,

When to call THE DOCTOR

Contact the doctor within 72 hours (sooner is better) if you develop a painful rash—or if you develop pain in the absence of a rash. Starting antiviral drugs immediately can help reduce the severity and duration of an attack and may stave off the chronic pain that sometimes follows a shingles outbreak. Call, too, if you're unable to endure the pain of an outbreak of shingles or if your shingles have disappeared but the pain hasn't. If you get shingles on your nose, forehead, or near your eyes, call your doctor immediately for treatment. Finally, see the doctor immediately if you or someone you're physically close to has a weakened immune system, a chronic illness, HIV/AIDS, or cancer.

Pick up a spicy pain reliever

Capsaicin cream, made from red peppers, may relieve the nerve pain associated with shingles. Though you probably don't normally have this item on your pantry shelf, it's wise to have it in the house if you or a family member is shingle-prone.

Zostrix is a capsaicin cream especially formulated for shingles and other painful conditions. Apply it four to five times a day for up to four weeks. Don't use on open sores—it will burn intensely. Avoid contact with the eyes and nose.

We dug this shingles prevention strategy up from a tome on old healing folklore, but naturally, we don't give it much credence: As legend has it, hanging a turpentine-soaked string around your neck will keep shingles attacks at bay.

brew yourself a hot cup of chamomile tea with one tea bag to 1 cup water, cover and let steep for 10 minutes. Soak gauze pads in the refrigerated tea and apply to the blisters. Rest for 15 minutes or so while the pads are in place and sip your tea.

Say aloe to the blisters. Cut a stalk from an aloe plant, split it open, and scrape the fresh gel directly on blisters. Aloe gel soothes and helps skin heal.

Try crushed aspirin. Aspirin taken internally doesn't appear to provide much relief for the pain of shingles, but there is anecdotal evidence that when applied directly to a rash, it can provide temporary relief. Crush two aspirin into a powder, then mix into 2 tablespoons of rubbing alcohol. Apply directly to the rash, up to three times a day.

Apply vinegar. Another popular home remedy is to dab apple cider vinegar directly from the bottle onto itchy, rashy skin. Let it air dry, and repeat as necessary for relief. Another approach: Mix ½ cup of the vinegar with 2 cups of water, moisten a clean cotton facecloth with the solution, and gently rub the affected area with the towel.

sinusitis

The pressure in your face feels like lots of tiny little people with jackhammers are going at it inside your head. You're stuffed up and you hurt—it actually feels like your entire face is pounding. Welcome to sinusitis, a condition that causes headache, nasal discharge, and cheekbone pain. If allergies, a cold, or the flu have left your sinuses all blocked up, handy kitchen cures can come to the rescue and provide nearly instant relief.

first things first

Before you get to home remedies, tend to the basics to help get past your sinusitis:

• Since you're coping with an infection, you need to rest. So even if the rest of your body feels fine, take it easy. This helps your body fight the infection and will hasten your recovery.

• Drink plenty of fluids—water and especially hot herbal tea. Avoid caffeine and alcohol because they can dehydrate you; alcohol can also worsen the swelling in your sinuses and nose.

• Steams and rinses, detailed in this chapter, help ease pain and facilitate drainage. If you've never done a nasal rinse, it's time to learn how. They really do make a difference.

• Keep that box of tissues nearby and use them. You want to clear out all that is being generated inside your sinuses.

• Use a couple of extra pillows under your head at night to help congestion drain and to ease sinus pain.

Pantry HEALERS

Apple cider vinegar

Baking soda

Eucalyptus
   essential oil

Garlic

Gingerroot

Herbal tea

Honey

Horseradish

Lemon

Peppermint

Sea salt

Thyme

Water

You can usually trump most cases of sinusitis by using home remedies diligently. Call your doctor if your symptoms persist or worsen after a few days or if you have a fever over 100.5°F. See your doctor immediately or seek emergency care if you have these symptoms—they could be signs of a serious infection that needs urgent attention:

- Pain or swelling around your eyes
- A swollen forehead
- Severe headache
- Confusion
- Double vision or other visual abnormalities
- Stiff neck
- Shortness of breath

kitchen cabinet cures

Enjoy a horseradish canapé. This spicy-peppery root is prized for its ability to clear congested sinus passages. To use it, just stir together 1 tablespoon horseradish, 1 teaspoon olive oil, and 1 teaspoon lemon juice. Spread the blend on crackers, and nibble until you feel your sinuses start to drain. Or toss horseradish into some cooked rice or mashed potatoes, or take it straight from the spoon if you can tolerate the heat.

Make a hot ginger compress. Ginger can reduce inflammation and ease pain—these actions, combined with the heat from the wet towel, work wonders on painfully congested sinuses. Here's how: Slice up a 3-inch piece of ginger root. Boil 2 cups of water in a saucepan and add the ginger. Cover and simmer over low heat for 20 minutes. Soak a washcloth in the brew, make sure it's not too hot to burn your skin, then apply to your face for 15 minutes or so. Do this lying on the couch with your head elevated to help your sinuses drain.

Steam with antiseptic herbs. Place 3 teaspoons of dried thyme and 3 teaspoons dried peppermint (or three peppermint tea bags) in a small heatproof bowl and add boiling water. Lean over the bowl, covering your head and the bowl with a thick towel, and inhale for 10 minutes, keeping your face 8 to 10 inches above the water. Repeat two to three times a day, as needed. Thyme is antibacterial, and the menthol in mint is a natural decongestant that eases breathing.

Give your nose a hand

Make like an ancient healer. Acupressure is an ancient Chinese healing art. Think of it as needle-free acupuncture. Use your left thumb and index finger to press the areas next to the inner eyes on both sides of the bridge of your nose. At the same time, use your fingers and the heel of your other hand to grab muscles on both sides of the spine at the back of your neck. Put pressure on all four points for about one minute.

Press out the pain. Weird as it may sound, giving your sinuses a finger massage will increase circulation to the area and help erase the pain. Here's how: Using your index fingers, press hard on the outer edge of your nostrils at the base of the nose. Hold for 30 seconds, release, and repeat three or four times.

Attack with eucalyptus. Eucalyptus essential oil is scientifically proven to kill several of the strains of bacteria that cause respiratory problems like sinus infections. To use, stir 5 drops of pure eucalyptus essential oil into 1 quart of boiling water in a heatproof bowl. Lean over the bowl, covering your head and the bowl with a thick towel, and inhale the steam for 10 to 15 minutes. Repeat three or four times a day while you're fighting the infection.

Sip some vinegar. Mix a teaspoon of apple cider vinegar in a glass of water and drink. This helps sinus drainage.

 recipes for healing

Lemon-Garlic Germ Killer

This natural antibiotic tea tastes way better than it sounds and is a remarkably efficient remedy for chasing away a sinus infection.

> 3 cloves garlic, peeled
> 1 whole lemon, scrubbed and cut into quarters
> ½ cup water
> 1 cup or so boiling water
> 3 tablespoons honey, more or less to taste

1. Toss the garlic, lemon pieces, and ½ cup water into a blender. Blend until the mixture is a smooth mush.
2. Pour the mixture into a clean, heatproof 16-ounce glass jar with a lid.
3. Top the mixture with boiling water; cover and steep for 5 minutes.
4. Pour the tea through a strainer into a large mug.
5. Sweeten to taste with honey and sip the entire cup. Drink this tea—which is actually pretty tasty—two or three times a day to help clear your sinus infection.

Simple Saline Spray

This easy-to-make solution clears your nasal passages and relieves pressure on the sinuses.

> ¼ teaspoon sea salt
> ¼ teaspoon baking soda
> 1 cup boiled water, cooled to a comfortable temperature

1. Add the salt and baking soda to the water and stir until dissolved.
2. To get the solution into your nose, use an ear bulb syringe, a neti pot, or a water pick on the lowest setting (you'll need a special adapter for this). Flush your nasal passages two or three times a day.

sore throat

Pantry HEALERS

Apple cider vinegar

Baking soda

Brown sugar

Cayenne pepper

Chamomile tea

Honey

Hot pepper sauce

Lemon

Marjoram

Peppermint tea

Pickles

Sage

Salt

Tea (green, black, or herbal)

Zinc lozenges

Sometimes, the pain erupts out of nowhere and comes on so suddenly you don't know what hit you. Or, it can start as a little tickle that grows into a fierce, fiery feeling. Either way, a sore throat may be your first signal that you're coming down with a cold or the flu. It can make you feel just plain miserable—you can't really eat, your voice may sound froggy or disappear entirely, and you'll probably feel generally ill and run-down, depending on what's causing the problem. In most cases, all it takes to make you feel better are some soothing remedies, like those that follow. To whip them up, you'll need nothing more exotic than the healing ingredients you keep inside your pantry.

first things first

The minute you feel the slightest tingle of a sore throat coming on, do these things:

• Gargle with warm salt water (see instructions in this chapter) to help ease the pain.

• Get out the zinc lozenges—preferably ones with at least 6 milligrams of zinc gluconate. Have one every two hours. Suck on it until it's gone. Don't chew or swallow.

• Avoid kissing anyone, and don't share glasses or eating utensils. Sore throats and the viruses or bacteria that cause them are highly contagious.

• Wash your hands frequently with soap and water, for the same reason: to prevent spreading the germs to others.

- Use a humidifier if the air in your home tends to be dry.
- Above all, don't smoke or drink alcohol while you're sick, and stay clear of second-hand smoke.

kitchen cabinet cures

Reach for the vinegar. As soon as you feel the prickle of a sore throat, employ germ-busting vinegar to help head off the infection at the pass. Turns out, most germs can't survive in the acidic environment vinegar creates. Just mix ¼ cup apple cider vinegar with ¼ cup warm water and gargle every hour or so.

Try the all-time classic gargle. As we noted above, the first thing most folks reach for when treating a sore throat is salt, and with good reason. Not only is salt mildly antiseptic, it helps dilute mucus and rinses phlegm away. Gargle with ½ teaspoon salt in 8 ounces of warm water three or four times daily. Some experts recommend that alternating a salt gargle with a vinegar gargle every hour or so will boost the germ-killing power of both treatments.

Signal a sage. This aromatic herb contains elements that combat bacteria, viruses, and fungi. Sage is also a mild astringent, so it relieves swollen throat tissue, and the herb can lessen the inflammation that causes throat pain. Leading herbalists deem it an excellent gargle for sore throats. To use, make sage tea with 1 teaspoon dried sage to 1 cup of boiled water. Cover and steep for 15 to 20 minutes, until it's comfortably warm. Gargle as often as necessary.

Imitate Winnie-the-Pooh. Honey has been easing sore throats for who knows how many thousands of years. Even the ancients recognized that honey acts as a mild antiseptic and soothes inflamed, irritated throat tissue. Here are three ways to harness honey's healing power:

- Add 3 teaspoons honey and a squirt of lemon to 1 cup of hot water and drink.
- Make a cup of sage tea (see above) and sweeten liberally with honey.
- Brew green, black, or herbal tea, and add honey and a squeeze of lemon juice.

Caution: Never give honey to babies under one year old.

When to call THE DOCTOR

Home remedies can clear up most sore throats within a day or so. But see a doctor if you have severe pain or pain that lasts longer than a week or if you have a fever above 103°F (101°F for babies six months or younger). If you have strep throat, your doctor will prescribe antibiotics to prevent serious potential consequences, such as rheumatic fever.

Other symptoms that need a doctor's care include:

- Tender or swollen lymph nodes in the neck
- Pus or white patches in the throat
- Skin rashes with a sore throat (could indicate measles, meningitis, scarlet fever, or mononucleosis)
- Ear pain

From Merry Olde England spring some mighty strange sore throat remedies. One—which was actually used widely until the 20th century—called for wrapping your own dirty socks around your throat. Our guess? Since sore throats are so contagious, and in the olden days a signal of potentially lethal diseases, the dirty socks were used to keep loved ones as far away as possible from the patient. But that's just a guess. Another English treatment involved wrapping bacon around the throat before bedtime. Finally, we couldn't resist passing along this Irish gem: To heal a sore throat, simply apply salt herring to the soles of the feet.

Make it better with mint. Paiute medicine men and Chinese healers have something in common: Both rely on mint tea to treat sore throats. That's because mint is laced with compounds that kill inflammation, pain, and germs. In fact, this sprightly tasting herb contains eight anesthetic compounds that can provide quick (but temporary) sore throat relief. To dull sore throat pain, make a strong peppermint tea with two tea bags to 1 cup boiled water. Cover and let cool till it's comfortably warm, then gargle until the entire cup is used up. Do not use peppermint gargle for children under the age of two.

Try marjoram. This green herb is used widely in Europe for remedying several common respiratory and infectious conditions, thanks to its antibacterial and pain-killing properties. A popular cure for sore throats and laryngitis is to gargle with marjoram tea sweetened with honey. Put 1 teaspoon of dried marjoram into 1 cup of boiled water. Let steep for 5 minutes, strain, then stir in a teaspoon of honey. Gargle as needed.

Take some heat. Add a few drops of hot pepper sauce to a cup of salt water (½ teaspoon salt) and gargle. Sounds painful, but the capsaicin in the cayenne will fool your nerve endings into forgetting about the pain. Use this several times a day for a day or two for maximum effectiveness.

Defuse pain with soda. Baking soda, that is. It's mildly antiseptic and soothing. Simply dissolve ½ teaspoon of baking soda in a glass of warm water and gargle a few times a day.

Blame your belly?

If you get more than your share of scratchy throats or if you have a throat irritation that doesn't abate, your problem may be related to GERD, or gastroesophageal reflux disease. When you have GERD, stomach acid backs up and can irritate your throat as well as your esophagus. One tip-off that GERD's the problem: You have no other symptoms of a viral illness. You're not feverish, congested, tired, or achy. Try avoiding foods that make you uncomfortable, and never eat right before going to bed. See your doctor if your problem persists.

spicy honey-vinegar cocktail

Recipe page 324

Sip something sweet. Chamomile fights inflammation and even acts as a mild sedative, which comes in handy when sore throat pain puts you on edge. Make a double-strength tea by steeping four tea bags in 2 cups boiling water, covered, for 10 minutes. Gargle with half of the tea and add a little honey to the rest, then sip the tea.

Try the pickle cure. Most pickles are made either in vinegar or brine—both of which are good for sore throats. So it makes some sense that pickles or pickle juice are popular folk remedies. Many people swear by drinking a few tablespoons of warmed pickle juice, or just munching on a few pickles, as a terrific way to get temporary sore throat relief. But you might want to have food in your belly before drinking pickle juice; otherwise, the vinegar might cause some stomach distress.

recipes for healing

Spicy Honey-Vinegar Cocktail

This concoction's ingredients kill germs, relieve pain, and soothe irritated throat tissues.

   ½ cup apple cider vinegar
   4 tablespoons raw honey
   1 teaspoon cayenne pepper
   ½ cup warm water

1. Blend the vinegar, honey, cayenne pepper, and water together until well mixed.
2. Take a tablespoon or two of the cocktail every three or four hours.

Sweet 'n' Salty Throat Rinse

This old-fashioned throat gargle is mildly antiseptic and very soothing.

   2 heaping tablespoons brown sugar
   ½ teaspoon salt
   ¼ teaspoon baking soda
   1 quart warm water

1. In a jar with a tight-fitting lid, combine the brown sugar, salt, baking soda, and warm water. Shake well before each use.
2. Gargle with up to ½ cup of this mixture as often as needed.

splinters

Almost anything can embed itself in your skin—a needle-sharp piece of wood, a sliver of glass, or a tiny shard of metal. But little slivers can cause a big hurt, especially if they lodge in a sensitive spot, such as under a fingernail. And there's always the possibility of infection if they're not removed carefully and completely. Here's how to use your kitchen pantry to minimize the damage.

Pantry HEALERS

Adhesive tape

Epsom salts

Fenugreek

Honey

Hydrogen peroxide

Olive oil

Vegetable oil

first things first

Even before you get the tweezers out , if you can see that even a tiny bit of the splinter is protruding from the skin, try to remove it using a piece of tape. Just stick adhesive tape (or even duct tape) over the splinter and press down gently so the adhesive catches it. As you lift the tape, the splinter should come away with it. This works well if you have a number of tiny splinters that aren't very deeply embedded.

kitchen cabinet cures

Soak the splinter. If you've acquired a wood splinter, it might pop out on its own if you make it swell up. Add 1 tablespoon of Epsom salts to a cup of warm water, and soak the area of skin where the splinter is buried for 10 or 15 minutes. Do this twice a day. A tiny splinter might swell up so much that it comes right out, or it may swell enough so that you can grab it with tweezers.

When to call
THE DOCTOR

You can usually treat a splinter at home. Most of the time, they'll ease themselves out of your skin naturally. But if it's large or deeply embedded, or if it's underneath your nail or on your face, let a doctor handle it. Also call your doctor if you notice signs of infection: pain, pus, swelling, redness, warmth, or red streaks. Finally, make the call if the splinter is metal and you haven't had a tetanus shot within five years.

Try an Indian remedy. If you have an embedded splinter and some fenugreek, a spice used in making curry, you're in luck. Do this before bedtime: Buzz whole fenugreek seeds in a clean coffee grinder—you want a teaspoon or so (or use 1 teaspoon powdered fenugreek). Add just enough water to make a paste. Apply the paste to the splinter, wrap with gauze, and leave on overnight. In the morning, when you rinse away the paste, the splinter will have surfaced enough so that you can remove it with tape or just scrape it off.

Oil it up. Simply dab some olive or other vegetable oil on the area in which the splinter is embedded. It should slip out pretty easily.

Try honey. Wash the area thoroughly, apply honey over the splinter, then wrap with a clean bandage. Check every couple of hours, adding honey if needed. Many home healers swear it'll draw out the invader.

Bubble it out. Many people swear by hydrogen peroxide for getting splinters out. Just dowse the area with the peroxide; if all goes well, the splinter will "fizz" itself out. If it doesn't work, you've still cleaned the area well.

When all else fails... Make like a medic and use this doctor-approved first-aid approach. Do not try this if the splinter is embedded near the eye or on the face—in that case, see a doctor for removal.

• Wash your hands and the splinter area well with soap and water.

• Wipe a clean, sharp sewing needle with rubbing alcohol (vodka or a soap and water wash works, too).

• Break the skin over the splinter with the needle. Use the tip of the needle to carefully ease the tip of the splinter up and out.

• Now, the splinter should be easy to remove with a piece of tape or tweezers.

• Wash the spot again with soap and water.

• Apply an antibiotic ointment.

stings & bites

It's a jungle out there, and everywhere from the under-brush to under your bed lurk creatures great and small that can sting and bite—often painfully and, rarely, even lethally. Here's how to handle attacks from the various creepy crawlies it may be your misfortune to encounter. Take heart—no matter which critter left its mark on you, you'll be able to find something in your pantry to take out the sting and relieve the itch.

first things first
Start here when you or someone you love has been stung:

• If you've been stung by a honeybee, the creature will die, but she's left you something in her will—a venom sac that will spread more painful, itchy poison if you inadvertently squeeze it while trying to pull it out. Instead of yanking or tweezing, use a credit card from your wallet, a plastic knife from the kitchen, or other straight-edged object to *scrape* the stinger and sac out of the skin.

• Then wash immediately with soap and water. Your spider bite or bee sting needs to stay clean for several days to heal and avoid infection.

• Apply cold compresses. A clean cloth soaked in very cold water will temporarily relieve the pain, swelling, and itch of any insect bite. Apply it 15 minutes off and 15 minutes on. Alternatively, massage the area with an ice cube for 10 minutes.

Pantry HEALERS
Aloe

Apple cider vinegar

Baking soda

Chamomile tea

Cornstarch

Dishwashing liquid

Echinacea root tincture

Lavender essential oil

Meat tenderizer

Peppermint essential oil

Tea bag

Vanilla extract

Witch hazel

When to call THE DOCTOR

If you've been stung by a bee, wasp, or hornet and feel faint, have trouble breathing, have swelling in your mouth or throat, or a rapid pulse, call 911 and get to the emergency room. Those are symptoms of a potentially fatal allergic reaction called anaphylaxis. Also call your doctor if you have a bull's-eye rash, muscle aches, fever, and headache within weeks of a tick bite because you may have Lyme disease.

kitchen cabinet cures

Use some bicarb. Neutralize acidic bee or fire ant venom with that baking soda (bicarbonate of soda) you keep with your baking supplies. Mix just enough of the powder with very cold water to make a paste, and completely cover the bite with the paste.

Pour on the meat tenderizer. The enzyme product you use to make tough cuts of meat chewable is an old home remedy for insect bites and stings. How it works: The enzyme (usually papain, from papaya, or bromelain from pineapples) that breaks down the protein in that shoulder roast zeroes in on the venom (which is also a protein) in the bite, reducing inflammation and pain. Make a paste of one part tenderizer to four parts water and place it on the bite or sting. Leave it on for 30 minutes or less, otherwise it will irritate your skin. (Aluminum chlorohydrate in antiperspirants—*not* deodorants—may also help, but not quite as well.)

Head 'em off at the pass

No one wants to get stung, just like no one wants the flu. But unlike flu germs, things that sting are easy to see—and keep away. Here are a few clever ways to keep bees, mosquitoes, and other similar critters away from you.

Use your baking ingredients. American military health experts recommend combining a couple of teaspoons of ordinary vanilla extract with a cup of water and spritzing yourself with a spray bottle to keep mosquitoes at bay. You may love the smell, but those little buzzers don't. Peppermint oil may also drive them away.

Skip the spirits. Mosquitoes can sense the lactic acid and carbon dioxide we give off from 100 feet away. And they're apparently nature's own breathalyzers, too. Studies have found that mosquitoes make a beeline for you when you've consumed alcohol. So if you're enjoying an outdoor picnic, skip the beer—unless it's root beer.

Try the soap approach. In summer, bees are like us—they are drawn to water to help cool down. If you have a pool, birdbath, or other water source that is drawing lots of bees to your yard, do this: Mix ¼ cup of dishwashing liquid into a quart of water, and pour the solution into an empty spray bottle. Spray any bees that are hovering nearby. The solution will kill the bees quickly without harmful pesticides. Soon enough, the rest of the hive will start avoiding your space.

Stay on the straight and narrow. Ticks love to hide in tall grass and weeds and climb on you as you brush by. If you're walking through a field or the woods, make sure you're wearing long, light-colored pants and a long-sleeved shirt so you can spot the hitchhikers, some of which are smaller than the period at the end of this sentence. Stay toward the center of the trail—ticks don't jump; they can only crawl on you if you get close enough.

Mix up vinegar and cornstarch. Blend a spoonful of cornstarch with enough apple cider vinegar to make a paste and slather it over the bite. This remedy pulls fluid from the itchy bite, which decreases inflammation and the discomfort it causes. If you only have vinegar handy, swipe some all over the bitten area.

Whip on a wet tea bag. The tannic acid in tea can help reduce the swelling around a bite or sting.

Give it some mint. Peppermint essential oil can reduce the pain and swelling of a bee sting. Use a cotton swab to dab the fragrant oil on the site two or three times a day.

Witch for the itch. This is one of the best reasons for keeping witch hazel in the fridge: A few drops of this cool, astringent liquid will bring instant relief to a bug bite or sting.

Dab on some aloe vera. Snap off a stalk-like leaf of this helpful plant, slit it, scrape out the gel, and apply it directly to bites and stings to help relieve pain and inflammation.

Soak in some chamomile. Make a strong chamomile tea with two tea bags to 1 cup boiled water. Cover and steep for 15 minutes. Soak a cotton pad or towel in the tea, then place it over the bite and leave it on for 15 minutes or more.

Bugs in your ears?

If it's just a gnat or a fly, it's annoying, but if it's a yellow jacket, bee, or wasp, it can be downright scary. Here's what *not* to do: Stick your finger in your ear to dislodge the unwelcome visitor. You'll just push the bee in farther, anger it, and you'll probably get stung. Instead, use an insect's natural inclination to go to the light by standing next to a lamp or have someone shine a flashlight into your ear. With any luck, the critter will crawl out. If that doesn't work, place several drops of vegetable oil into the ear to kill the bug, then tilt your head and tug on your ear to allow it to float out.

recipe for healing

Pain-Fighting Bite Treatment

Native Americans boiled up the roots of the wild purple coneflower to treat insect bites and stings—even snakebites. Today, we know it as echinacea, the herb that helps reduce the severity of colds by killing viruses. The plant contains compounds that reduce swelling, prevent infection, and enhance healing. Here's how to use it to take the sting out of stings.

    1 tablespoon echinacea root tincture
    1 tablespoon water
    10 drops lavender essential oil
    1 tablespoon cosmetic clay

Combine the echinacea, water, and lavender, then slowly add it to the clay and blend. Apply the paste to the sting or bite. Store any remainder in an airtight container to prevent it from drying out. If you only have echinacea tincture on hand, just apply several drops of the liquid directly on the bite several times a day.

stress

You can't avoid stress. It's as natural a part of our daily lives as oxygen. And you want a little of it in your life. It can be a positive thing, a challenge that pushes you to excel, keeps you stimulated, boosts your immune system, and adds to your self-esteem and sense of mastery. But if you have a little too much of this good thing, or if stress turns your life upside down, you can be stuck cleaning up the emotional wreckage—anxiety, depression, frequent illnesses, psychological paralysis. Your body will start churning out hormones like cortisol that tell your brain and cardiovascular system that you're under siege 24/7, and that can lead to serious problems, from heart attack to stroke to chronic inflammatory diseases like arthritis. Fortunately, your kitchen cabinet is your doorway to an oasis of calm.

Pantry HEALERS

Almonds

Beans

Chamomile

Chamomile tea

Lavender
 essential oil

Oatmeal

Peanut butter

Peanuts

Raisins

Tea (green or black)

Vitamin C

Wheat germ

first things first

If a feeling of anxiousness lasts for more than a few days, make like a detective and try to figure out what's getting on your nerves. If you can't do it on your own, talk to a friend, a trusted clergyman, or a mental health professional who can look at your situation objectively and help you figure out the root of your distress.

Meanwhile, these strategies are proven to be among the best to help ease your way through turbulent times:

• Take an exercise break. You may not be able to quit your job and move to a desert island, but you can create a little oasis of calm for yourself. When you're feeling crazed, take a walk. Studies show that taking a brisk walk, swimming laps, or doing other vigorous exercise can raise levels of feel-good chemicals called endorphins, help clear your mind, and reduce symptoms of anxiety and depression.

• Get spiritual for 15 minutes every day. Having some spiritual practices—prayer, meditation, even charity work—can help buffer the effects of most of the negatives in your life.

• Stay in touch—physically or virtually, by phone or through social Web sites or text messages—with people who make you feel good and keep you grounded. Having people in your life, studies show, can make you feel secure, happy, and able to handle life's slings and arrows.

kitchen cabinet cures

Pop a C. Make it 1,000 milligrams. A German study subjected 100 people to two of the most stressful things a human can face: public speaking and doing math problems. The group that took a vitamin C tablet had lower levels of cortisol—a hormone you produce in response to tension, fear, and anxiety—and had lower blood pressures than the group that didn't take the vitamin. The vitamin C takers also said they felt less stressed. Studies have shown the vitamin C reduces cortisol in animals subjected to repeated stress.

Have a cuppa. Even though tea contains jitter-causing caffeine, it seems to calm rather than jangle your nerves. And it may not have anything to do with chemistry. Researchers at the City University of London put 42 volunteers to the test: They asked them to fill out two scientifically validated tests that measure stress and anxiety. Then they stressed them out with a timed exercise in which they had to scan a document for the letter "d" and, based on a mark above or below it, either cross it out or pass over it. Afterward, they gave half the group a cup of tea and the other half a glass of water before repeating the tests. Both groups had equal scores before the beverages, but the tea group was far less stressed afterward: They actually experienced a 4 percent drop in anxiety while the water group had a 25 percent increase. The researchers noted that many members of the group reported they used tea to relax and, in fact, the tea group was far chattier after the test than the water group. They concluded that the tea ritual and its social aspects may be the reason it's nature's own Xanax.

Make it green. Green tea is lower in caffeine than most other teas, so you may be able to drink the five cups a day that lowered psychological stress in a large group of Japanese people in a recent study done at Sendai's Tohoku University Graduate School of Medicine. The researchers didn't identify any particular ingredient of green tea that might have been soothing, but animal studies suggest that one compound, EGCG, had both sedative and hypnotic effects that tamp down the body's production of stress chemicals.

Soothe yourself with chamomile. For people with generalized anxiety disorder, feeling stressed is a full-time condition. They constantly worry, suffer from muscle tension, irritability, fatigue, insomnia, and are sometimes easily startled. So if chamomile can help them—and a study found that taking chamomile reduced their symptoms by an astonishing 50 percent—it can certainly ease your everyday tension. Studies suggest it acts as a nerve relaxant. To make the tea, pour 1 cup of boiling water over two chamomile tea bags and let steep, covered, for 10 minutes. Enjoy the sweetly fragrant tea three times a day.

Bathe in chamomile. As you sip that tea, you can soak in the soothing scent of chamomile for a double dose of relaxation. Wrap six tea bags in a piece of cheesecloth or piece of hose, and hold it under the faucet while you fill the tub. Adding a teaspoon of lavender essential oil to your bathwater will plunge you even deeper into serenity.

Rub on a little lavender. It's one of the few essential oils that you can apply directly on your skin. Studies have found that lavender reduces stress, as measured by systolic blood pressure, which rises when you're tense. You can also shake a few drops on a tissue and carry it with you for those unexpected stressful moments that come up at work or when you're in traffic.

Grab a handful of almonds. Or any magnesium-rich food in your kitchen cabinet, including peanuts, instant fortified oatmeal, peanut butter, beans, or raisins. A study of university chemistry students found that test anxiety

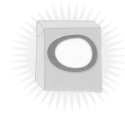

Chamomile is so soothing that some recommend adding it to your bath.

caused them to lose magnesium, a trace mineral that helps relax muscles. Other studies have found that when magnesium levels are depleted, it can worsen stress symptoms. Interrupt this vicious cycle by including one or more of these foods at every meal during tough times.

Dish up some wheat germ. Along with being high in magnesium, wheat germ contains a phytonutrient called octacosanol, which may help improve your body's ability to withstand stress. Add a few spoonfuls to yogurt or cereal every day.

Have a bowl of oats. This traditional remedy is so well-accepted that a British career counseling site encourages nervous job seekers to have a bowl of porridge before they head off to interviews to keep themselves calm. Oats contain a compound called gramine, which has mild sedative properties. They're also packed with complex carbohydrates that may increase the amount of mood-lifting serotonin in your brain.

Avoid high-stress foods. Drinking coffee when you're tense is like trying to put out a house fire with lighter fluid, particularly if you're sensitive to caffeine. Alcohol may seem like a smart idea—after all, it relaxes you—but it increases your adrenal gland's production of stress hormones and interferes with your sleep. Likewise, sugar and refined carbohydrates (cake, cookies, and white bread to you) can heighten anxiety. So don't try to soothe your stress with "comfort foods" that are sweets.

the natural
DOCTOR'S ℞

Do this breathing exercise to alleviate anxiety caused by stress: Breath in through your nose for 4 counts, hold your breath for 7 counts, and then breathe out through your mouth, making a whooshing sound as you do so, for 8 counts. Repeat 4 times and do the exercise twice a day.

sunburn

Pantry HEALERS

Aloe

Apple cider vinegar

Baking soda

Evaporated milk

Green tea

Lavender
  essential oil

Oatmeal

Vitamin C

Vitamin E

White vinegar

Think of sunburn as a bad gift that keeps on giving in all the wrong ways. Not only does it hurt and irritate you for several long days, it also causes permanent damage that can eventually lead to lines and wrinkles, liver spots, and, potentially, skin cancer. All that for a few weeks of tanned skin? Your best bet is to avoid sunburn at all costs: Slather yourself with sunscreen with an SPF factor of at least 15, and wear a hat and protective clothing when you have to be out in the sun. If you do get a burn, your best bet for relief is right in your kitchen.

first things first

When you first realize your skin has sunburn, get indoors fast and take these steps:

• Take an over-the-counter nonsteroidal anti-inflammatory such as ibuprofen (400 milligrams is about right) to block any pain and reduce inflammation.

• Either apply cool compresses, stand in a cool shower, or soak in a cool bath. This will ease the pain and inflammation of a new sunburn.

• Ignore the common advice to grease your skin up. Butter, petroleum jelly, and other greasy ointments prevent heat and sweat from escaping from your pores and are tough to remove from extra-tender skin. Likewise, ignore advice to apply ice; that can further injure already damaged skin.

• Instead, apply thinner, more natural healing ingredients like those described in this chapter.

kitchen cabinet cures

Snip a stalk. It's time again to use that aloe vera plant on your windowsill. You'll get that same soothing relief you get after an oven burn if you apply the aloe gel directly from the plant to your sunburn. In fact, aloe is the main ingredient in many of the pricey sunburn relief products you'll find at the pharmacy. Slit the stalk open with a knife, and scrape out the gel inside. Apply to the sunburn.

Comfort yourself with oatmeal. This breakfast staple also has skin-soothing properties and reduces inflammation. Stuff an old nylon stocking with oats and place under the faucet as you run some cool bathwater. Soak for 15 to 20 minutes and air-dry yourself, so you don't wipe off the healing oats with your towel.

Spritz on some lavender. A French chemist discovered the healing powers of lavender oil in the early 1900s. When he severely burned his hand in a lab accident and plunged it into a vat of lavender essential oil, the oil eased the pain and his burn healed quickly. Mix 1 teaspoon of pure lavender essential oil into about 2 ounces of water in a misting bottle. Shake and mist sunburned skin lightly as often as needed.

You're fried, so try some baking. Baking soda, that is. Bicarbonate of soda helps soothe skin inflammation. Toss a handful into cool bathwater and soak for 20 minutes.

Make like lettuce. Ordinary white vinegar contains acetic acid, a component of aspirin that can help relieve the pain, itching, and inflammation of sunburn. Soak paper towels with vinegar and apply like a compress to painful areas; leave them on until they dry. Be careful around the eyes, because vinegar can sting. Alternatively, pour a cup of white vinegar into tepid bathwater and soak for 20 minutes.

Got canned milk? You don't want to pull milk out of the fridge—too cold! But canned evaporated milk is just cool enough to ease the pain of your burn. Pour some on a clean cloth and apply to areas that hurt. It will provide a protein layer that will continue to soothe your discomfort.

Mix E and C. Taking 2,000 milligrams of vitamin C and 1,000 IU of vitamin E for eight days could help your sunburn heal and potentially reduce your chances for developing skin cancer in the future, say experts.

When to call THE DOCTOR

Most sunburns are first-degree burns—the least serious type—and respond well to home measures. But if your burn blisters, you develop chills or a fever, or the pain is unbearable, call your doctor. If you also have nausea or vomiting, headache, confusion, or fainting, you should go to an emergency room because you may have heat exhaustion or heat stroke.

Weird & wacky

We dug up one old folk remedy for sunburn that made instant sense—it called for having the victim bathe in an "easterly flowing stream." Naturally, the cool water would chill a burn and make the sufferer feel better. But here's one that we're sure won't soothe nearly as well: Having an elderly person "blow" the fire out of your blistered skin. (Unless, of course, it's your granny, and you're under the age of six.)

Go for green tea. Studies suggest that the antioxidant compounds in green tea help prevent sunburn and skin cancer when you apply it to skin or sip it regularly. It doesn't act as a sunblock, but it does protect skin against inflammation caused by the sun's UV rays. You need about 3 milligrams of the green tea compound EGCG per square inch of skin. One cup of brewed green tea contains 20 to 35 milligrams of EGCG, so after you sip a cup, brew a second cup, let it cool, and dab it on skin with a cotton ball after coming in out of the sun.

recipes for healing

Burn-Soothing Bath

Oatmeal is known for its ability to reduce inflammation and soothe irritated skin; baking soda reduces itching and helps skin heal; and milk's protein helps ease the pain.

> 2 to 4 cups oatmeal
> 1 cup baking soda
> 1 cup evaporated (or regular) milk

1. Grind oatmeal in a food processor until fine.

2. Add oatmeal, baking soda, and milk to bathwater, or wrap dry ingredients in cheesecloth or a nylon stocking; hold under the faucet as you run bathwater. Soak for 20 minutes; don't towel dry. Caution: Do not add milk if your skin is blistered.

Aloe-Lavender Gel

This fragrant combination cools the feeling of heat on your skin, reduces swelling and inflammation, and wards off infection.

> 4 tablespoons aloe gel
> 1 teaspoon pure lavender essential oil
> 1 teaspoon apple cider vinegar
> 2 capsules vitamin E, 400 IU

1. Slit a few thick aloe stalks and scrape out enough gel to make 4 tablespoons. If you don't own an aloe plant, buy 100 percent pure aloe vera gel at the health or natural foods store.

2. In a small container, combine the aloe gel, lavender, and vinegar.

3. Pierce the vitamin E capsules with a clean needle and squeeze the contents into the other ingredients. Stir to blend.

4. Gently pat the gel on the sunburned skin. Use as often as needed to ease the discomfort. If you have large areas of sunburn, you might want to double the recipe.

aloe-lavender gel
Recipe page 336

swimmer's ear

Pantry HEALERS

Earplugs

Garlic

Hot towel

Lavender
 essential oil

Olive oil

Rubbing alcohol

White vinegar

All those laps you've been swimming have toned your muscles and built up your endurance. But your ears—ow! Swimmer's ear (otitis externa) is an infection of the skin that lines the ear canal. It's itchy, but so painful you don't dare scratch. It usually occurs when you've been in the water for a long time (and that includes those long, luxurious showers you take). Water trapped in the ear canal breaks down its waterproof coating and makes the lining damp, swollen, and ripe for infection. Even your doctor will recommend some natural ways to heal the hurt—and prevent it, too.

first things first

To prevent swimmer's ear from occurring—or recurring—do these things:

• Consider wearing swimmer's earplugs when you swim or shower.

• After emerging from the pool or shower, turn your head to each side, pulling on your earlobe to encourage any water in your ear canal to run out. You can also use a hairdryer on the lowest setting; direct the air into your ear for about 30 seconds.

• If you sense there's water in your ear, fill the ear canal with rubbing alcohol and follow the instructions above to empty it. Alcohol is drying, plus it will help kill the bacteria and fungi that can cause swimmer's ear. (Don't use it when you have the condition—it'll sting!)

kitchen cabinet cures

Add more fluid. This time, make it white vinegar. This isn't just an old home remedy—it's recommended by doctors as a frontline treatment for this ear infection because the vinegar creates an inhospitable environment for bacteria and fungi. Mix equal parts white vinegar and water and, with a dropper, fill the ear canal with the blend. After five minutes, tilt your head to the side and pull on your earlobe to empty the canal. Do this twice a day until your ear canal is normal.

Kill the itch. Gently rub a few drops of lavender oil blended with a teaspoon of olive oil on your outer ear to relieve that annoying itch. Lavender is also an antibacterial and antifungal.

Treat it with heat. Stuff a small, damp towel loosely into a plastic storage bag with a "zipper" closure. Put the unzipped bag into the microwave and heat for a minute or two. Take it out, test to make sure it's not too hot, then zip it up and place on the sore ear. Keep it on for 20 minutes or so.

When to call THE DOCTOR

Set up an appointment with your doctor if you have one or more of the following symptoms:

- Unbearable pain in your ear
- Persistent, unusual redness in your ear
- Discharge
- Hearing loss
- Symptoms that persist for three days

You might need antibiotic drops or steroids to eradicate an ear infection.

recipes for healing

Swimmer's Ear Preventative

This classic combo helps prevent the growth of bacteria and fungi responsible for swimmer's ear infection.

    1 tablespoon white vinegar
    1 tablespoon rubbing alcohol

Mix the vinegar and alcohol together and pour a teaspoon into each ear. Let it drain. Use before you get into a shower or a swimming pool.

Antibiotic Garlic Oil

Garlic effectively combats all the microbugs that can cause swimmer's ear: bacteria, viruses, and fungi. If someone in your family is prone to the problem, it's a good idea to keep this oil handy.

    3 or 4 peeled cloves of garlic, crushed
    ¼ cup olive oil

1. Soak the crushed garlic in olive oil (make sure the oil completely covers the garlic) for three or four days.
2. When the oil is ready, use a funnel to transfer it to a small bottle. Use an eyedropper to instill a few drops in the painful ear a few times a day.

toothache

Inside every tooth is an exquisitely tender nerve. A toothache is nature's way of telling you that something is rubbing that nerve the wrong way. In many cases, the problem is a cavity. Your tooth's protective outer shell—the enamel—has been eaten away by acid and bacteria, exposing the nerve underneath. Or, the problem may be a cracked tooth—chewing something hard has caused a fracture that exposes the nerve. Or it could be something else: an infection, abscess, or a lost filling or crown. While you wait to get to a dentist to fix the underlying cause, turn to your kitchen pantry to find some relief.

first things first

Take care of your teeth, and you'll never have worry about painful toothaches. The rules haven't changed much for a few decades:

• Before brushing your teeth in the morning, gargle with apple cider vinegar. It helps remove stains, whiten teeth, and kill bacteria in your mouth and gums.

• Brush and floss your teeth in the morning and at night, and if you can, after each meal. If you can't brush after a meal, drink some water, then rinse your mouth with water.

• Brush lighter and longer. Hold your toothbrush like a pencil, brush in a circular motion, and keep going for at least two minutes. Most people brush too hard and too short.

• Visit the dentist at least twice a year.

kitchen cabinet cures

Apply cloves. Your grandma always kept a bottle of oil of cloves around for toothaches. It's a traditional remedy for numbing nerves, and today we know why. The primary chemical compound of this spice, made from the dried bud of an evergreen, is eugenol, a natural anesthetic. But clove oil needs to be used carefully. Pouring the oil on the aching area can actually worsen the pain if you get it on sensitive gum tissue or your tongue. To avoid that, put two drops of clove oil on a cotton ball and place it against the tooth itself until the pain recedes. In a pinch, use a pinch of powdered clove or place a whole clove on the tooth. Chew the whole clove a little to release its oil and keep it in place up to half an hour or until the pain subsides.

Mix ginger and cayenne. Mix equal parts of these two heat-packing spices with enough water to make a paste. Roll a piece of cotton into a tiny ball and stick it in the paste. Then, place the cotton ball on your tooth, carefully avoiding gums and tongue, and leave it there until the pain fades—or as long as you can stand it (the concoction is likely to burn). You can use these spices together or separately—they're both potent painkillers. Ginger and cayenne have been shown to be effective against arthritis pain, and the main chemical component of cayenne—capsaicin—has been found to help block pain messages from reaching the brain.

Plug it up. If a cracked or broken tooth or a cavity is causing your toothache, sealing it will help stop the pain until you can get to the dentist. Sugarless gum will work, as will cooled but still soft candle wax. Some traditional healers also recommend using roasted ginger to both cap the aching tooth and reduce pain. Simply bite down on the cooked ginger.

Shake some salt. A teaspoon of salt dissolved in a cup of boiling water makes a pain-killing mouthwash, which will clean away irritating debris and help reduce swelling. Swish it around for about 30 seconds before spitting it out.

Black bag it. The astringent tannins in strong black tea may help quell pain by reducing swelling. Place a wet tea bag against the affected tooth.

When to call THE DENTIST

Most of us experience one-time pains in our teeth or jaw. Remember them and report them to your dentist on your next visit. But if you have a recurring pain, don't wait: Make an appointment—particularly if the pain is severe, your jaw hurts or throbs (along with your pulse), or you know you've lost a filling or a crown or your tooth is broken.

Weird & wacky

Peanut butter and mustard for toothache? Some natural healers recommend it in an emergency. It's an edible version of a mustard plaster that eases sore muscles. In this case, you coat a chunk of peanut butter with a little powdered mustard, and stick it, mustard-side down, on the tooth. Mustard is a counterirritant, like the capsaicin in peppers, which may interfere with pain messages your body sends to the brain. The peanut butter holds the mustard against the tooth.

ulcers

At one time, stomach ulcers were considered the price you paid for living a hard-charging, stressful life. While stress may indeed play a role, we now know that most ulcers are actually a bacterial infection caused by the ubiquitous germ, *Helicobacter pylori (H. pylori),* which enters your body through food, water, and even kissing. The infection weakens the protective mucous coating of the digestive system; that in turns allows acid to work on the sensitive lining underneath. The two—acid and bacteria—can create an open sore, which is what an ulcer is. Once you're diagnosed, there are plenty of natural remedies that not only soothe your stomach, but also act on the root cause of your tummy troubles.

first things first

In addition to smart medicine and home remedies, part of the plan for managing ulcers is common sense.

• Don't smoke or drink alcohol. Not only do they raise your risk of stomach ulcers, they can also exacerbate your symptoms.

• If your stomach is hurting, hide the hot sauce. Spicy foods don't cause ulcers, but putting a hot pepper on an open wound—whether it's a cut on your skin or an ulcer in your stomach—is painful and counterproductive.

• Avoid ibuprofen, aspirin, and other nonsteroidal anti-inflammatories. One side effect of NSAIDS is stomach bleeding. If you must take them for another condition, talk to your doctor about the possibility of adding an acid reducer to your regimen.

• Limit caffeine intake. Foods that contain caffeine, such as coffee, tea, and chocolate, stimulate acid production in the stomach that can irritate an ulcer.

kitchen cabinet cures

Get some omega-3s. Gastric ulcers have been linked to a deficiency of linoleic acid, an omega-3 fatty acid found in canned fish, fish oil capsules, and flaxseed oil. Flaxseeds pack a double whammy: They create mucilage in the stomach that protects against excess acid, plus they're rich in omega-3s. To ease your ulcers, take a teaspoon of flaxseeds and chew them up thoroughly. You can also find linoleic acid in pumpkin, sunflower, and sesame seeds and oil, as well as in walnuts.

Knock out germs with ginger tea. *H. pylori* hates ginger and the feeling is mutual. In studies, powdered and fresh ginger killed the bacteria responsible for the majority of stomach ulcers. Add a teaspoon of powdered or grated fresh ginger to a cup of boiling water. Allow it to steep, covered, for about 30 minutes. Strain and drink three times a day.

Drink some aloe vera. You apply the gel from this plant on burns and wounds to soothe and heal—and aloe works the same way on wounds inside your body. Studies have found that drinking aloe vera gel reduces inflammation and promotes healing of gastric ulcers. Your Rx: Drink ¼ cup of gel three times a day. That's a large amount to harvest from one plant, so pick up 100 percent pure aloe gel at a good health or natural food store. Read the label carefully: Aloe gel should be the only ingredient. It should not contain aloin, which is aloe sap that has a strong laxative action, or anything else for that matter.

Have an apple. Or a cup of tea. Or even a handful of dried cranberries or cherries a couple of times a day. What these foods have in common are flavonoids, powerful compounds that protect your cells from damage. In a number of studies, a variety of flavonoids helped prevent ulcers from forming when researchers used a chemical to induce them in laboratory animals. Other flavonoid-rich foods

When to call THE DOCTOR

Any ongoing stomach symptom—a burning sensation in your belly, belching, bloating, or pain—as well as blood in your stool or unexplained nausea is good reason for a doctor's visit. More seriously, if you vomit blood (which looks like dark or black coffee grounds or is bright red or maroon), have tarry black stools (which indicates internal bleeding), or feel extreme pain, your ulcer may have perforated—that is, opened a hole all the way through the stomach or duodenum. This development could be life threatening. See a doctor or get to the emergency room immediately.

Weird & wacky

Oddly, no scientific studies have been conducted on this silly piece of folklore. And we're pretty convinced there's no way it could possibly ease an ulcer. But who knows? Maybe old folk healers knew something we don't about the power of this harmless remedy. Here goes: Just before you put on your shoes and socks in the morning, swab the soles of your feet with apple cider vinegar. Let it dry, then don your footwear. Repeat the process before dinner.

include onions and garlic. Several studies suggest that onions and garlic, which are natural antibiotics, may also attack the *H. pylori* bacteria.

Sip some chamomile. This relaxing tea helps reduce the stress that exacerbates ulcers while it calms inflammation and inhibits the growth of *H. pylori*. Brew up a tea with two chamomile tea bags per cup of boiling water. Cover and steep for 10 to 15 minutes before drinking. Have 3 cups a day.

Try this sweet antibiotic. With *H. pylori* becoming increasingly resistant to prescription antibiotics, experts have been looking at natural remedies like honey, a traditional treatment for burns and wounds. In animal studies, honey can reduce the incidence of stomach ulcers by up to 98 percent. Why it may work: When New Zealand researchers tested honey on bacteria taken from gastric ulcers, the bacterial growth was quashed. No one knows how much honey is helpful, so start by eating 2 tablespoons a day as a sweet treat on your morning toast or in oatmeal or other cereal. Keep it up until symptoms disappear.

recipe for healing

Healing Barley Tea

Barley water is a time-honored ulcer treatment, used by physicians and folk healers alike. Add soothing honey to the tea to boost its healing power.

    2 ounces barley
    6 cups water
    2 to 3 teaspoons honey

1. Put the barley and water in a saucepan and bring to a boil. Simmer gently until the liquid is reduced by one-half.

2. Strain and cool the liquid, then add honey to taste. For best results, have 3 cups of barley tea a day.

urinary tract infections

About half of all women will experience a urinary tract infection (UTI) over a lifetime (and women get them 10 times more often than men). UTIs start with a burning sensation when you urinate and can advance to cramps, pain during sexual intercourse, and even fever or chills. About 30 percent of all UTIs go away by themselves; others require antibiotic treatment. If you get frequent infections, use these measures to keep them at bay.

first things first

Better to prevent UTIs than to remedy them. Here are the fundamentals of prevention:

• Drink fluids, and plenty of them, every day. Keep a glass or bottle of water at your side throughout the day, and refill whenever it gets low.

• Wash your vaginal area before and after sexual intercourse and urinate immediately afterward to flush away bacteria that can be pushed up into your urethra.

• Stick with loose-fitting cotton undies and change them frequently. A warm, damp environment is more likely to foster bacterial growth.

• Change into dry clothes immediately after a swim.

• Wipe front to back. The most common cause of UTIs is *E. coli* bacteria, which dwell in feces.

Pantry HEALERS

Blueberry juice
Cranberry juice
Dried cranberries
Green tea
Rice
Vitamin C
Water

• Take showers, not bubble baths. The chemicals in bath salts and gels can irritate the urethra and make it prone to infections.

• Avoid harsh chemicals. Feminine sprays, douches, and deodorants could irritate the urethra, as can some spermicides.

kitchen cabinet cures

Drink berry juice. That popular old cure really does work: Drink three 8-ounce servings of cranberry or blueberry juice when you're experiencing symptoms for quick relief. Make sure to use pure cranberry or blueberry juice rather than juice "cocktails," which contain lots of sugar. Certain antioxidants in cranberries (and blueberries, too) alter antibiotic-resistant bacterial strains so they can't stick to the urinary tract and do their worst. These antioxidants literally cut the "ropes"—called tendrils—that anchor the bacteria to the lining of your urethra and weaken the bacteria cells themselves.

Or munch on some dried cranberries. About ⅓ cup of these dried antioxidants work like cranberry juice to help prevent UTIs, according to a small Harvard study.

Take some C. Most bacteria hate an acidic environment. One of the effects of taking vitamin C is the creation of nitric acid, which is toxic to all kinds of bad bacteria. Naturopathic doctors recommend taking 500 to 2,000 milligrams every two hours for two days, then 500 to 2,000 milligrams three times a day for as long as the infection is symptomatic. Once you've beaten the infection, take 500 to 1,000 milligrams per day to help prevent UTIs from coming back.

Microwave the rice sock. Fill an old sock with plain dry rice, tie it closed, and microwave for about two minutes. Test to make sure it's not too hot, then put the warm sock on your lower abdomen to relieve cramps or pain from a UTI.

Drink green tea. Drink two or three cups of tea daily. Green tea contains antioxidants that one recent study found can reduce bladder inflammation.

varicose veins

When your legs look like a road map, all you want to do is keep them covered. But varicose veins are more than a cosmetic issue: These gnarled blue veins just below the skin can throb, ache, itch, and cause blood clotting and water retention. Occasionally, they can rupture, triggering internal bleeding that can leave your legs discolored; ulcers may also form. Your doctor has a myriad of treatments, up to and including surgery, but try some of these home remedies first.

first things first

Our kitchen cabinet cures work, but start with these basic lifestyle adjustments to stop the situation from worsening:

• If you have varicose veins or even a family history of them, avoid prolonged standing. If you must be on your feet all day, be sure to take frequent breaks where you can sit down and elevate your legs.

• Put in 20 to 30 minutes of aerobic exercise every day. A daily walk is best since you pump blood back to your heart every time you contract your leg muscles.

• Periodically during the day, walk around to help get blood flowing. Sitting in one position too long when you have varicose veins encourages blood to pool and puts you at greater risk of a clot.

• While standing, raise yourself onto the balls of your feet and then lower your heel back down. Do this calf exercise

Pantry HEALERS

Apple cider vinegar

Bran

Canned beans

Dried blueberries

Dried cranberries

Dried strawberries

Epsom salts

High-fiber cereal

Lavender
  essential oil

Oatmeal

Olive oil

Peppermint
  essential oil

Rosemary

Rosemary
  essential oil

Witch hazel

When to call THE DOCTOR

Varicose veins tend to worsen over time, so consult your doctor when you first notice them (they often arrive when you're pregnant). Call if the pain gets worse and doesn't improve with simple home measures or if you develop an ulcer (an open wound) on your leg. Also call if your leg swells, develops lumps, or turns red (which could be a sign of a clot), or if a vein ruptures (the skin around the vein will be bruised and discolored). If you develop itching and a cord-like swelling, consider it a medical emergency: It could be a potentially lethal pulmonary embolism.

for 10 minutes several times a day to squeeze the blood vessels in your legs to force blood upward.

• Don't cross your legs. Doing so puts pressure on your engorged veins and prevents blood from pumping back to the heart.

kitchen cabinet cures

Keep a fiber shelf. Move canned beans, oatmeal, bran, and other high-fiber cereal to one shelf in the pantry and have a few servings from it every day. Fiber will help prevent constipation, and straining can cramp blood flow and put serious pressure on your veins.

Try the witch's brew. The astringent tannins in witch hazel can temporarily relieve the pain of varicose veins. Best way to use it: Refrigerate the witch hazel for extra relief. Then soak a clean dishtowel, cheesecloth, or similar material in the chilled brew. Lie down with your legs elevated, and drape the wet cloth over the affected area. Leave it on until the cloth dries; repeat as often as needed.

Snack on dried berries. An antioxidant compound in blueberries, cranberries, and strawberries seems to have antiangiogenic properties, meaning it prevents the growth of blood vessels. That's a vitally important quality for fighting cancer: Preventing a tumor from developing a blood supply will actually starve it to death. It may also help prevent varicose veins, according to a study at Creighton University Medical Center, which looked at a product containing berry extracts.

Sprinkle and brew rosemary. This savory herb contains a compound that strengthens blood capillaries. In fact, that compound, called diosmin, is used synthetically in drugs prescribed for varicose veins, hemorrhoids (varicose veins in the anal area), and chronic venous insufficiency, a condition in which the veins in your legs have trouble pumping blood back to the heart. To use the natural stuff, add dried or fresh rosemary to food as frequently as you can—it's particularly tasty in chicken, lamb, and bean dishes. You can also get rosemary's healthy vein benefits by making a tea. Just add a teaspoon of dried rosemary to 1 cup of boiling water. Cover and steep for 15 to 20 minutes; drink two cups a day. Don't drink rosemary tea if you're pregnant.

Try the vinegar treatment. This folk remedy for varicose veins may require more patience and time than you're willing to give it. But at the very least, elevating your legs for 30 minutes twice a day will go a long way toward easing your vein problem. Morning and night, wrap your legs in cloths you've soaked in apple cider vinegar. Elevate your legs and rest for 30 minutes. Keep the treatments up regularly for six weeks. Some healers also recommend drinking a glass of water to which you've added a teaspoon or two of apple cider vinegar at the end of each treatment.

 recipes for healing

Healing Leg Soak

This bathtub recipe, along with the bath itself and a relaxing rest afterward, brings several proven remedies together into one wonderful treatment.

> 2 teaspoons dried rosemary
> 1 cup water
> ½ cup Epsom salts
> ½ cup witch hazel

1. Add the rosemary to the cup of water in a small saucepan; bring to a boil. Cover and steep for 20 minutes.

2. Fill the bathtub half full with hot water and add the Epsom salts and witch hazel. Filter the rosemary out of the tea and add the tea to the bathwater as well.

3. Get in the tub and soak for 15 to 20 minutes. When you get out, lie down with your legs elevated for at least 30 minutes.

Healthy Leg Rub

Rosemary helps strengthen blood capillaries, and peppermint and lavender essential oils can help ease the pain of varicose veins.

> 10 drops rosemary essential oil
> 10 drops peppermint essential oil
> 10 drops lavender pure essential oil
> 2 tablespoons olive oil

Mix the rosemary, peppermint, and lavender oils with the olive oil and gently rub the fragrant blend on your legs. Use light pressure on the veins that bulge. It's best if you elevate the legs and stroke upward toward the heart. After your rubdown, continue to rest with your legs elevated. Don't wash off the oil.

warts

They're linked in lore and old wives' tales to toads, witches, and magic, and people have used everything from snails to grasshopper spittle to get rid of them. But there's nothing whatsoever weird about warts. They're caused by common viruses—one of the 70 types known as the human papillomavirus (HPV). These can produce the little cauliflower-like sprout on the side of your finger, the painful pad on the bottom of your foot (plantar wart), and the symptomless genital condition that is the leading risk factor for cervical cancer. Your own immune system is your best defense against warts—it will vanquish 65 percent of most warts within two years, even if you do nothing. But they're unsightly, tend to spread (they're contagious!), and sometimes hurt, so it's smart to take these simple at-home measures to make them disappear—like magic.

first things first

Warts may seem strange, but that doesn't mean you need strange methods to remedy them. Start with the common-sense basics:

• Put down the scissors. Tempting though it may be to snip off an ugly wart, you're asking for trouble—pain and infection.

• Consider a store-bought wart removal product. As long as your wart isn't in a sensitive area (on the face or genitals), over-the-counter products have a good track record of successfully eradicating the problem.

• Plantar warts, which occur on the soles of your feet, can be very painful. Cut a piece of moleskin or purchase a special adhesive cushion at the drugstore to provide some padding until the wart is gone.

kitchen cabinet cures

Try a garlic patch. Garlic acts as an antiviral, but its caustic effects can potentially make warts blister and fall off naturally in a week. Just cut a peeled clove in half and rub it on the wart, cut side down. Repeat daily as needed for seven days.

Spice your food with garlic as well. Many studies have linked garlic to reduced risk of cancer—the ultimate enemy you want your immune system to fight. Why it might be effective against warts: Compounds in garlic have been shown in lab studies to fight viruses and stop them from replicating inside infected cells.

Use the banana peel trick. Some practitioners recommend taping a piece of banana peel—gooey side down—against the wart; change it daily until the wart disappears. Theories abound as to why this works: The irritation stimulates the immune system; the potassium in the banana peel helps reduce a deficiency (some believe warts are sign of a potassium shortage); the peel taped tightly to skin deprives the wart of oxygen. The truth is, no one really knows why it works, but there's considerable anecdotal evidence that it does.

Choose oats for breakfast and barley for lunch. These whole grains contain a special kind of fiber, beta-glucan, that boosts the immune system by mobilizing white blood cells and natural killer cells. There's scientific evidence that beta-glucan can even thwart tumors.

Yes, reach for the duct tape. A well-run study found that duct tape worked better than cryotherapy (freezing) on warts. Subsequent studies failed to achieve the same great results, but experts still recommend "duct tape therapy," particularly for those who are doctor- and medical-procedure–shy. Here's how to do it: Using rubber-backed duct tape (the kind used in the original study), cover the warts for six days. Then, soak the warts in warm water and rub them gently with an emery board or pumice stone. In the original study, the researchers had patients do this for as long as two

When to call
THE DOCTOR

If you have genital warts, see your gynecologist; never attempt to treat these with home remedies. The virus that causes them is linked to cervical cancer.

For warts on other parts of your body, try simple remedies first, but if they don't work, make an appointment with a dermatologist. Another reason to call your dermatologist: You're over 45 and a wart suddenly appears out of nowhere. To be on the safe side, schedule a skin cancer check.

Also, have your doc take a look if a wart is red, swollen, or pus-filled—it could be an infection. If you get a lot of warts, you may have an immune system problem and should have it checked out. Finally, if you have diabetes or an immune system dysfunction, always have your physician examine any new warts.

months until the warts finally disappeared. Theoretically, the duct tape works by irritating the wart and causing the immune system to sit up, take notice, and attack it. But, in reality, no one really knows why it worked.

Add dried mushrooms to your soup. Delectable fungi such as shiitake, maitake, and morels—found in many dried mushroom mixes—contain 300 compounds, including beta-glucan, that rev up infection-fighting white blood cells.

Have a sprinkle of wheat germ. Top your morning oatmeal with this tiny, nutty part of the wheat seed, which is a powerhouse of immune-boosting nutrients, including vitamin E, the B vitamins, magnesium, potassium, iron, and zinc.

Make pumpkin muffins. Canned pumpkin is an intense source of vitamin A, which helps regulate the immune system and helps specific immune cells called lymphocytes fight off infections more effectively.

recipe for healing

Immune-Boosting Mushroom Barley Soup

This tasty potage combines many of the pantry ingredients known to beef up your immune system—which better enables your body to fend off warts.

2–3 ounces packaged dried mixed mushrooms
2 tablespoons olive oil
1 cup chopped onion
½ cup chopped celery
1 cup chopped, sliced, or diced carrots
2 teaspoons minced garlic
5 cups canned low-sodium chicken broth
¾ cup barley
Salt and pepper, to taste

1. To reconstitute the mushrooms, place them in a bowl and cover with boiling water (or other liquid). Allow to soak, covered, until tender. Save liquid to add to soup.

2. Place olive oil in a soup pot, add onion and celery, and sauté over medium heat until the onion is translucent, about 6 to 8 minutes. Add the carrots and mushrooms and sauté for another 6 to 8 minutes. Stir in the garlic, mushroom soaking liquid, chicken broth, and barley. Bring to a boil, then reduce heat and simmer until the barley and vegetables are tender. Season with salt and pepper to taste.

yeast infections

Yeast infections, also called candidiasis, aren't just a girl thing. Even though vaginal yeast infections are one of the top reasons women see their doctors, the fungus that causes the infection can populate your mouth (where it's called thrush), your esophagus (esophagitis), your skin, and even your bloodstream (where a yeast infection can be life threatening). It's also a common cause of a baby's diaper rash and can be passed back and forth between mother and child during breastfeeding. You'll want to see your doctor before treating any kind of yeast infection at home, but mild cases of thrush and vaginal infections do respond to natural remedies like these.

first things first

If you have a vaginal yeast infection, these simple measures will bring you a world of relief and may help prevent a recurrence.

• Go fragrance free. Perfumed powders, intimate fragrance products, soap, bath products, and even toilet paper can irritate already sensitive tissue.

• Skip the skin-tight jeans or workout outfits. Like other fungi, yeast loves a nice warm, moist environment, so you need to give yourself a little ventilation. Wear roomy cotton undies, skirts, and loose-fitting slacks if you have or are prone to yeast infections.

• Sleep naked. From the waist down, at least.

Pantry HEALERS

Cinnamon sticks

Garlic

Lavender
  essential oil

Salt

Tea tree oil

Vinegar

Yogurt

When to call
THE DOCTOR

Vaginal infections cause a burning itch and discharge; oral thrush shows up as a white, itchy mouth rash and is sometimes the result of a depressed immune system. You should contact your doctor if:

• You're experiencing these symptoms for the first time.

• Your discharge is bloody or foul-smelling.

• You feel pain during urination or intercourse.

• Your symptoms don't go away after five days of treatment.

• You have more than three to five yeast infections a year (a diabetes symptom).

• You have discharge and a rash, especially during your period. These may signal toxic shock syndrome.

• You're pregnant.

• Your baby develops a bright red diaper rash on his bottom that doesn't clear up with the usual creams; it could be a yeast infection.

• Don't lounge around in a wet swimsuit. In fact, after removing your suit, use a hair dryer set on low to dry your vaginal area.

• Avoid hot tubs. Hot, moist...you know yeast is lurking in there.

• Eat yogurt. Studies have found that the beneficial bacteria in yogurt and other fermented milk products is effective against the yeast fungus. If you're taking antibiotics, which can destroy the good bacteria, eat yogurt containing *Lactobacillus acidophilus* or *bifidobacterium* to help replenish these *Candida* fighters.

• Avoid sugar and yeasty foods. They simply feed *Candida*, encouraging its growth.

kitchen cabinet cures

Use a warm saltwater rinse. For thrush, stir half a teaspoon of salt into a cup of warm water and swish it around in your mouth for a minute before spitting it out. For vaginal or skin infections, sprinkle a cup of sea salt into a tub of warm water and stir till dissolved. Soak for 20 minutes every day. The salt will not only speed healing, it will reduce the pain and itching.

Have some cinnamon tea. Cinnamon and yeast go great together when you're making buns, but this delicious spice has it in for yeast infections. It's a powerful antifungal that's been shown to be effective even against the nasty, drug-resistant yeast *Candida albicans*. Make a batch of tea by breaking 8 to 10 whole cinnamon sticks into 4 cups of boiling water and allowing it to simmer, covered (covering medicinal brews preserves their medicinal oils), for 15 minutes. Take the pan off the burner and allow the tea to steep, covered, for about 45 minutes. You can drink some of the tea and use the rest as a douche or to swab onto skin infections.

Try a vinegar douche. Add 2 tablespoons of vinegar to a quart of water and use as a douche twice a day for two consecutive days. The vinegar creates an inhospitable environment for the fungus. But it also makes the living difficult for beneficial bacteria, too, so don't use this home remedy for more than two days.

Eat garlic. This traditional antifungal is best eaten raw. If that sounds like something you won't relish, hide it: Chop up two cloves and sprinkle it on salads and in sauces every day. You can also mince a couple of cloves into a spoonful of honey or applesauce and swallow right off the spoon.

Treat with yogurt. Yes, eating yogurt may help prevent yeast infections. And some folk healers say that applying yogurt containing *Lactobacillus acidophilus* directly to the infection may help remedy the situation. They claim the bacteria in the yogurt produces lactic acid, which reduces the pH level in the vagina, making it less hospitable to the *Candida*. Just be sure to use plain, unsweetened yogurt, since yeast feeds on sugars. The method is simple: Dip a tampon into yogurt and insert into the vagina for 30 minutes. Repeat two or three times a day.

recipe for healing

Tea Tree-Lavender Yeast Treatment

Studies have found that tea tree oil disrupts the membranes of yeast cells, and lavender kills Candida *in a test tube. Mix them together and yeast doesn't have a chance. Tea tree oil is toxic when swallowed so don't use this to treat oral infections.*

> 5 drops tea tree essential oil
> 5 drops lavender essential oil
> Distilled water

Mix the tea tree and lavender oils with a few drops of distilled water. Using a cotton swab, dab the blend on the affected parts of the body.

practical home healing

Tips and lists to help you get started

Reading practical advice makes us all feel good. There are so many positive messages: that we *can* succeed; that it doesn't take decades of experience to solve problems well; that simplicity and frugality remain valuable, viable traits. Clever advice inspires, motivates, makes us smarter. And not least of all, clever, new ideas are entertaining merely to know and share!

We hope that reading all the clever cures in this book has brought you many such feel-good moments. The question—the crucial, fundamental question—is whether you're prepared to act on the advice. And therein lies the rub. It's one thing to agree in your mind to advice; it's another thing to convince the rest of you to actually follow it.

So in this final section of *Kitchen Cures*, we want to help you take action. Not by mindless cheerleading, but rather by making it as easy as possible. Here are specific things you can do, starting the very next time you walk into your kitchen, to become an even better home healer. From what to stock in your pantry to how to store a healing concoction you just whipped up, here are resources, checklists, and tips for putting into action all the great advice you've read so far.

the healthy home pantry

You need just two things to be a successful home remedy specialist: a well-stocked pantry and a willingness to use what's stocked. In this chapter, we'll tell you exactly what items to have on hand so that you'll be prepared to act the minute you or a family member needs a healing remedy.

1 Purge the bad stuff

All the home-remedy advice in the world won't help if your pantry is packed with unhealthy food. Say it out loud: Sugary treats, processed snacks, candy, and similar products are no longer welcome here! Then grab an empty box for food to be given away and a garbage can for open packages to be tossed, and start sorting, using the following tips:

Lose the bad sugars. Sugar comes in many forms, but no matter what it's called, factory-sweetened foods should be eaten as little as possible. Though it's fine to occasionally use products that contain a little honey, maple syrup, or even white sugar for that matter, toss anything that contains corn syrup or high-fructose corn syrup within the first four ingredients. These calorie-dense, nutritionally empty sweeteners may be much worse for you than white sugar.

A shocking number of foods and drinks are thick with it, including seemingly healthy items like fruit juices, premade spaghetti sauces, and even bread. So check labels closely.

Toss the toxic fats. Get rid of anything in your pantry that lists "partially hydrogenated oil" on the label, and don't buy any products with labels listing anything partially hydrogenated. Eating these fats, called trans fats, is like putting cement in your arteries—there's no such thing as a "healthy amount" of them. These fats raise your bad (LDL) cholesterol and lower your good (HDL) cholesterol. Eating foods containing trans fats increases your risk for developing heart disease, stroke, and type 2 diabetes.

Dump products with chemical ingredients. A laundry list of chemicals means that a food product has been processed beyond recognition. Products that contain more ingredients than you can count, especially those with lots of unpronounceable chemicals, should be purged from the pantry.

Sniff your spices. If you've had that jar of thyme on your shelf for years, it's probably lost its zing—along with its medicinal properties. Take a few minutes, open each herb or spice jar, and give it the nose test. If you don't smell the herb's natural, pungent aroma when you open the bottle, it's probably lost its essential healing (and culinary) power. Toss it and replace with a fresh product. In general, most herbs, properly stored in a cool, dry, dark pantry can last a year or two. Whole spices, such as cinnamon sticks, black pepper, and whole cloves, can last a year or so longer.

Sack the loser cereals. Here's what a serving of nutritious cereal (about 1 cup) looks like. Get rid of those that fall short of these recommendations.

- 120 calories or less
- 2 grams or more protein
- 5 grams fiber (more is better)
- 8 grams (or less) sugar, unless it's an otherwise healthy cereal containing dried fruit
- 3 grams or less fat; no trans fat. If an otherwise healthy cereal contains nuts, it's fine if the fat content is a little higher.
- 10 to 25 percent of the daily value for key vitamins and minerals (e.g., iron, folate, B_6, and B_{12}).

Check for expiration dates. Though not all outdated pantry items are unhealthy, there's a good chance they've lost their nutritional value and should be discarded.

Banish sugary drinks. If you could do just one thing to improve your family's health, strictly limiting their intake of sugary drinks, including sodas and fruity drinks, would be it. That's because these beverages are the number one source of added sugars in the typical Western diet, according to a recently issued scientific statement from the American Heart Association. In America, the typical adult consumes a whopping 29.8 teaspoons of sugar a day, nearly half of which comes from soda and sweetened beverages.

The report links drinking these to a higher body weight and lower intake of essential nutrients—not to mention metabolic abnormalities (think diabetes) and a destructive impact on heart health, among other concerns.

Get wise to "natural." Some food marketers list terms like "natural" or "healthy" on product labels. That's meaningless, because there are no standards governing the use of the word. If you're interested in "natural" products, skip the promotional messages and read the nutrition label to make sure the product is free of chemical ingredients.

Organize, then shop

It may sound obvious, but when you shop with a list organized by the layout of your store, it speeds and simplifies your trip. A list also helps you resist impulse purchases that jack up your bill (and may be less nutritious than what's on your list).

If you can, avoid shopping with little kids, especially when you're in a hurry. Colorfully packaged cereals and junk foods are designed to inspire desire in children, and it can be hard to resist your kids' pleas. Take them along only when you have plenty of time and energy. Make sure they're well-fed and rested, and use the opportunity to teach them about reading labels and selecting healthy products over less nutritious ones.

You, too, should be well-fed before you shop. Walking through the grocery store when you're starving makes you want to buy everything in sight. If you don't have time to eat a full meal, at least munch an apple and drink a large glass of water before heading into the store.

2 Stock the good stuff

Once you've gone through the pantry and tossed out the stuff that's not so good for you and your family, check to see which of these items you already have on your shelves. Then shop as needed for the staples you'll want to have on hand to make home remedies—and healthful meals—for your family. For a truly healthy pantry, you should have many of the following ingredients.

Canned or dry legumes and vegetables

Beans: cannellini, kidney, chickpeas (garbanzos), pinto, black, and other varieties
Carrots
Corn
Leafy greens such as spinach and collards
Lentils
Sauerkraut
Split peas
Tomatoes, whole, crushed, pureed

Cereals and whole grains

Bulgur
Cereal, high-fiber, low-sugar
Barley, regular and quick-cooking
Oat bran
Oats, rolled and steel-cut
Quinoa
Wheat bran, unprocessed
Wheat germ
Whole-wheat couscous
Whole-wheat flour
Whole-wheat pasta

Condiments

Capers
Horseradish
Hot pepper sauce
Mustard
Sea salt
Salsa
Tamari or soy sauce

Dried fruit

Apricots
Blueberries
Cherries
Cranberries
Dates
Figs
Prunes
Raisins

Fish (canned)

Anchovies
Caviar, red and black (salmon and lumpfish)
Chunk light tuna
Herring
Sardines, packed in sardine oil
Wild Alaskan salmon
Mackerel

Groceries

Baking soda
Borax
Broth, low-sodium, preferably organic (available in cans or cartons): chicken, vegetable, and beef
Brown sugar
Chocolate, dark (65 percent cacao or higher)
Coffee
Cocoa powder
Cornstarch
Lemons
Limes
Mushrooms, dried
Onions
Granulated sugar
Plastic storage bags, assorted sizes
Tea bags: Black, chamomile, green, peppermint, rooibus

Health food and drug store items

Almond oil
Avocado oil
Beeswax
Cosmetic clay
Epsom salts
Essential oils (see page 368)
Honey, flavored and raw (health food stores typically offer more varieties than supermarkets)
Jojoba oil
Rubbing alcohol
Vegetable glycerin
Witch hazel

Herbs and spices

Aloe plant, potted (for your windowsill)
Black pepper
Caraway seeds
Cayenne pepper, ground
Cinnamon, ground
Cloves, whole
Coriander, ground
Cumin
Dill seed
Fennel seed
Fenugreek seed

Garlic, fresh
Ginger: fresh root, powdered root, crystallized slices
Horseradish
Lemon balm plant, potted (windowsill or garden)
Mint plant, potted (windowsill or garden)
Mustard (powder, such as Coleman's)
Mustard seed, brown or yellow
Nutmeg
Oregano
Peppermint
Rosemary
Sage
Thyme
Turmeric, ground
Wasabi

Juices

Blueberry juice (100 percent pure, unsweetened)
Cranberry (100 percent pure, unsweetened)

Grape (100 percent pure, unsweetened)
Tomato juice, low-sodium
Vegetable cocktail (100 percent vegetable juice, no sugar, low-sodium)

Oils and shortenings

Canola oil
Grapeseed oil (subs in recipes for olive oil, good for high-temperature cooking)
Virgin olive oil (use for cooking)
Extra-virgin olive oil (look for the words "cold-pressed" on the label for the best quality; use for dressings)
Toasted sesame oil and light sesame oil
Walnut oil (nice for salads)
Flaxseed oil (Buy refrigerated oils from good health or natural food stores and keep refrigerated. Never heat. Use

it frequently because it's highly perishable. Discard if it develops an off odor.)

Nuts and seeds

Almonds
Brazil nuts
Flaxseeds
Pecans
Pistachios
Sesame seeds
Sunflower seeds
Walnuts

Vinegar

Apple cider vinegar
Distilled white vinegar
Wine vinegar

Spirits (optional)

Dark rum
Red wine
Vodka

Storage tip for nuts

Nuts and seeds spoil quickly. Store them in airtight containers and use within a month or two. Flaxseeds have an especially short shelf life. If nuts lose their nutty flavor or have an off taste, discard them and replenish your supply with fresh nuts.

the healthy shopper

Having a shopping list is a huge help in making your grocery choices smarter and healthier, and we hope the pantry guide on the previous pages helps you organize your needs. To go the next step, here are tips for knowing what to do when standing in the grocery aisle, staring at a bewildering array of seemingly similar products.

1 Shop for fresh foods first, not last.

That usually means starting in the produce section and working your way around the perimeter of the store to buy meats, seafood, dairy and fresh baked goods. Only when you've picked up all your perishable goods should you dip into the aisles for the canned and boxed foods you need to fill your pantry and round out your meals. Make this a habit, and you'll find that your cart increasingly contains healthy foods in their more natural state.

2 Choose brown grains, not white.

This holds true for products in several aisles of the grocery store: pasta, bread, crackers, rice, flour, and even the cooking-grains section. Here's why: When grains are processed and milled (giving them their white color), the most nutritious parts are stripped away. For example, when whole-wheat grain is milled into white flour, the grain's germ and bran are discarded. The germ contains concentrated nutrients; the bran, the grain's outer "skin," contains most of the grain's fiber. A similar process removes the bran and germ from rice grains to produce white rice, making brown rice the more nutritious choice.

Look for whole-wheat grain pastas and couscous, mixes that contain barley, instant brown rice, and even whole-grain crackers. Other excellent whole grains include barley, buckwheat, bulgur, oatmeal, wild rice, and popcorn.

3 Choose brown sweeteners, not white.

By white sweetener, we mean refined sugar. By brown, we mean honey, maple syrup, and agave nectar. Now, we have to be honest: In terms of nutrition, *no* sweetener is all that good for you. But refined sugar is definitely the worst—it metabolizes extremely fast, causing fast blood-sugar surges that are bad for your health in so many ways. Plus refined sugar has no useful nutrients; it's pure, empty calories. And oddly enough, sugar isn't all that sweet— you need a lot of it in comparison with some other sweeteners. In contrast, honey, maple syrup and agave nectar all are straight from nature, and so contain far more minerals and nutrients than sugar. Plus, they are often sweeter in flavor, so you need less in your food or drink. If you wish to go the artificial sweetener route, we recommend two: xylitol and stevia. They are the healthiest, and have far less effect on blood sugar than other sweeteners.

4 Take your time in the bread section.

It's tricky, because there's little correlation between the color of the bread and what's in it. Some brown-colored "wheat" breads are made from refined flour, but colored with molasses; some whitish breads are made from whole wheat. What to do: Pick only breads in which "whole grain" is listed as the first ingredient—whole wheat, white whole wheat, whole oats or rye, for example. Also look for 3 grams of fiber or more per serving. If the first ingredient on the list is simply "wheat flour," then it's made from the same wheat as white bread—which means, stripped of fiber and nutrients.

5 Pick the right olive oil.

You want two types in your kitchen: a large container of virgin olive oil for cooking, and a small bottle of a high-quality extra-virgin olive oil for dressings and medicinal recipes.

6 Choose prepared foods with short ingredient lists.

You don't have to cut out prepared foods entirely. Just remember: The shorter and more natural-sounding the ingredients are, the healthier the food usually is. Of course, if the top ingredients are sugar and butter, put the item back on the shelf. And watch the sodium content: Even otherwise healthy processed foods can contain a day's worth of sodium. Avoid products that have more than 500 milligrams of sodium per serving.

7 Stock dried mushrooms.

Delectable dried mushrooms make a scrumptious, meaty addition to soups, stews, sauces, and egg dishes. They keep forever on your pantry shelf and offer a surprising powerhouse of benefits, depending on the species. Generally speaking, mushrooms are excellent sources of vitamin D, B vitamins, selenium, and tryptophan. Many contain compounds that help protect you against viral infections, and some mushrooms even appear to have anticancer actions. Look for dried mushroom blends that combine a few varieties—shiitake, maitake, oyster, crimini, button, portabella, and morels—to get the most nutritional bang for your buck.

8 Buy healthy add-ins for plain cereals.

Fiber-rich cereals such as bran flakes can, frankly, be a little boring. The best breakfast-cereal strategy is to buy unsweetened cereals and then add in your favorite flavors. That helps you bypass all the empty sugary calories—and lets you enjoy the cereal more. For ease, keep a wide-mouth, well-sealed jar on your counter with shelf-stable ingredients for quick mix-ins. Keep a scoop and ziplock bags handy, and you've got a handy, nutritious meal or snack for home or on the go. Stock these wise pantry shelf add-ins:

- Raisins
- Dried berries
- Almond slivers
- Pumpkin seeds
- Walnuts

the home remedy chef

If you can make a salad dressing, you can make a skin cream or cough remedy. It doesn't take any special skill or know-how to make home remedies that really work. But just like making a cake, you don't want to stray from the recipes. Here's some additional guidance for remedy-making success.

Have the right tools

The basic gear. As with cooking, there's more to making home remedies than just having the ingredients. Here's a comprehensive list of the equipment you would use if you were to make all the remedies in this book:

- Glass, stainless steel, or enameled double boiler
- Set of nonreactive mixing bowls
- Stainless steel or ceramic funnel
- Stainless steel measuring and stirring spoons
- Wooden stirring and mashing spoons
- Stainless steel, glass, or ceramic lemon squeezer or reamer
- Tea kettle
- Ceramic tea bowls and cups
- Tea strainer
- Candy thermometer (for cough drops)
- Kitchen knives
- Coffee or spice grinder, reserved for home remedy use
- Blender
- Large plastic basin, for soaking feet
- Large bowl, for facial steams

- Neti pot for sinus rinsing, available at health food stores
- Grater, reserved for grating beeswax (it's almost impossible to clean wax from a grater)
- Cheesecloth for making poultices and bath "tea bags"
- An ace bandage or two, for holding poultices in place
- Supply of pint and quart canning jars
- Aromatherapy diffuser, available at health food stores

Choose nonreactive equipment. This will protect your health and beauty preparations from chemical reactions that can affect the color and fragrance of your remedies. That means avoiding uncoated aluminum, iron, or copper cookware.

Yes, they can serve double duty. Most of the equipment mentioned above might already be in your kitchen. Yes, you can use the same stuff for cooking as you do making home remedies. Just be sure that everything has been cleaned very well and is completely dry before starting.

Remedy making and storing advice

Select safe storage jars and dispensers. Look for small opaque jars with wide mouths and tight-fitting lids for storing your beauty creams or skin ointments. Because your home remedies don't contain preservatives, they need to be kept away from light and air. Any tinted or colored glass—amber, white, or blue—protects creams from light. Keeping a cream in a small container that it fills almost completely also protects it from air. In fact, when you use up half a jar of cream, decant the remaining cream into a smaller jar to protect it further. Tight-fitting lids are important to keep out air and prevent evaporation. Cork lids are too porous to be safe.

Also be on the lookout for spray bottles and pint-size bottles with tight lids for mouthwashes and spritzes you'll be making. You can probably recycle these from your regular kitchen and bathroom supplies. Before using storage jars, sterilize them in the dishwasher or scrub them well with soap and hot water, rinse thoroughly, and let them air-dry.

Work on a protected surface. While none of the ingredients in home-remedy recipes is all that strong, some could discolor or harm certain countertop materials. For this reason, we recommend creating your remedies on a large, washable cutting board. Choose boards made from high-density polypropylene, which is antimicrobial, nonporous, and nonabsorbent. Only work on it when it's completely dry.

Put bottle tops back on right away! You don't want bottles of hydrogen peroxide, rubbing alcohol, or essential oils left unopen in a work area. First, they evaporate fast. Second, they spill. The moment you've poured out what you need, put the top back on, tightly.

Be a wise hoarder. Most of the home remedy recipes in this book are for products that are intended to be used immediately or within a few days, so if you store a remedy at all, the safest place is in the refrigerator. You can keep some ointments and other remedies for longer; each recipe will advise you.

Don't forget the label! If you are making one of the recipes that can be safely stored, be sure to label each new jar or bottle as soon as you fill it. The label should give the product's name and the date on which it was prepared. If you're planning to give a homemade beauty product as a gift, list its ingredients as well (you don't want to inadvertently cause an allergic reaction). Labeling is crucial, because many of these preparations look alike in the bottle, and it's easy to forget what you made and when.

Use a permanent marker. When making labels, use a permanent waterproof marker, and consider covering the label with clear package tape. This will keep labels from smearing and becoming illegible—especially good for potions that contain oil.

Make tea ice cubes. Next time you brew up a strong medicinal tea, especially one that you're likely to use frequently triple or even quadruple the recipe. Use what you need now, then let the rest cool to room temperature. Pour the tea into ice cube trays or single-serving containers, label clearly with the tea name and date, then freeze. Once the cubes are frozen, you can pop them into a freezer bag (don't forget to label it, too) for easier storage. Next time you need some tea, open your freezer and heat it up. Tip: Calming lemon balm tea ice cubes are extra-refreshing to use in regular iced tea.

a greener, cleaner home

If you think it's rewarding to make your own home remedies, just wait until you start whipping up your own home cleaning products. You'll be impressed with how effectively these simple formulas—several of which use healing ingredients mentioned throughout this book—remove dirt and kill germs. And you'll be tickled to see how much money you'll save in the process. Here's another thing that will make you smile: You won't be polluting your indoor atmosphere with potentially harmful chemicals, and you won't be exposing your family to the toxins found in many commercial cleaning products.

The five magic ingredients

You've read about these ingredients (with the exception of borax) elsewhere in this book, and here, you'll discover that they do double duty as simple home cleansers. How do we know they work? Simple: They've cleaned untold millions of homes over the decades, particularly in the days before fancy, chemical commercial cleaners ever graced store shelves. Plus, there's science to support them: Their chemical properties and pH levels (that is, alkalinity or acidity) neutralize germs and break down grease and dirt. With these five simple ingredients, you can safely clean and shine pretty much your entire home.

- Baking soda
- Borax
- Lemon juice
- White vinegar
- Tea tree essential oil

Borax, the one ingredient on the list that isn't detailed elsewhere in this book, is a natural mineral made of sodium, boron, oxygen, and water. It has properties that make it a terrific natural cleanser. It disinfects and acts as a natural laundry booster, fungicide, and multipurpose cleaner. Don't mistake borax for boric acid, by the way—they are different and not interchangeable.

Though borax is natural, it's not entirely without risks—like many natural substances, it can be toxic if ingested. Store it out of children's reach, don't use it around food, and just to be on the extra safe side, use borax in a well-ventilated area or wear a face mask when cleaning with it.

As for making the recipes below, this helpful note: The amounts are flexible. Since every cleaning situation is different, you may need to use a little more or a little less of a particular ingredient to get the job done.

recipes for home cleaning

All-Purpose Surface Cleaner

1 teaspoon borax
½ cup white vinegar
3 tablespoons fresh lemon juice
1½ cups water

Add the borax, vinegar, lemon, and water to a bowl and stir well until the borax is completely dissolved. Use a funnel to pour the solution into a spray bottle and use freely to clean kitchen surfaces. If you double or triple the recipe, you can also use this to mop kitchen and bathroom floors. In all cases, rinse thoroughly.

No-Scratch Pot Scrubber

¼ cup baking soda
White vinegar

Put the baking soda in a bowl, and add just enough white vinegar to make a thick, spreadable paste. (When you add the vinegar to the baking soda, the mixture will bubble.) Use with a plastic scrubbing sponge to clean pots and pans; the mixture won't scratch no-stick finishes.

Glass Cleaner

1 cup water
1 cup white vinegar

Combine the water and vinegar in a spray bottle and use to clean and shine any glass surface. To make the glass extra-shiny, use newspaper instead of paper towels.

Bathroom Tile Mold-and-Mildew Spray

¼ cup borax
2 cups hot water
¼ teaspoon tea tree essential oil
5 to 10 drops thyme essential oil

Stir the borax into the hot water in a bowl until it's completely dissolved. Add the tea tree and thyme essential oils and pour the mixture into a spray bottle. Spritz on the mold-darkened grout and scrub with a stiff brush. Depending on how badly the grout is mildewed and how long you've had the problem, you may need to use some elbow grease and repeat the treatment a couple of times. Once you've gotten rid of the mold, spray the solution on the tiles after every shower to keep mildew at bay. Note: The borax may make the tub or shower slippery, so rinse the surfaces thoroughly and be careful getting in and out.

all about essential oils

Essential oils capture both the fragrance and complex healing chemicals contained in certain medicinal plants. Here's what you need to know about them. When inhaled, these concentrated essences pass directly to nerve centers in our brain, where they produce a wide range of responses. Essential oils can help relieve anxiety and depression, tame our physical reactions to stress, induce sleep, and enhance energy. Research shows that the scents of certain herbs—such as lavender, bergamot, marjoram, and sandalwood—actually alter brain waves, helping to induce relaxation and sleep. When used topically or in steam inhalations, essential oils help ease pain, clear up skin problems, relieve congestion, and treat fungal, viral, and bacterial infections.

Though the word "oil" is part of their name, essential oils are very different than oils you use for cooking. Cooking oils, like olive or canola oil, come mostly from seeds or nuts. But essential oils are highly concentrated volatile distillations of leaves and flowers. They vaporize easily, and they don't leave a greasy stain like cooking oils do. In fact, they don't even feel oily. They are called "essential" because they capture most of the chemical compounds that give a plant its unique fragrant and medicinal qualities.

Because essential oils are highly concentrated, you must dilute them in a "carrier oil," such as olive, almond, sesame, or jojoba oil, before you can apply them to your skin. One notable exception is lavender essential oil, which is gentle enough to be directly applied.

Though essential oils are expensive, most recipes in this book call for just a few drops. Most of the essential oils we recommend will cost under $20 for a bottle that should last you a year or two, depending on how often you use it.

Shopping and storage tips

To make sure you purchase high-quality 100 percent pure essential oils, buy them at a reputable health food store or online.

Many essential oils can be stored for years without losing their potency. Keep them in dark bottles, tightly sealed, preferably in a cool place and always away from sunlight. Never consume essential oils; most are toxic when ingested. Store them securely, and keep them well out of children's reach.

If you're interested in exploring aroma-therapy—the healing art of using aromas to stimulate health—consider consulting an aromatherapist for guidance. You should be able to find a qualified practitioner at a good local day spa. Be sure she has a state license to perform the services she offers, such as massage or beauty services. As of yet, no states have a licensure process for aromatherapists.

20 top healing oils

1 Basil
Latin name: Ocimum basilicum
Properties: Antiseptic, eases muscle spasms, expels digestive gas, calms nerves, eases PMS symptoms
Uses: Headaches, bronchitis, colds, coughs, cosmetic applications
Cautions: Avoid during pregnancy

2 Bergamot
Latin name: Citrus bergamia
Properties: Pain reliever, antibacterial, eases muscle cramps, deodorant, antidepressant
Uses: Eczema, depression, anxiety, acne, bad breath, colds, bronchitis, insect repellent
Cautions: Don't use on skin exposed to sun; may irritate sensitive skin

3 Chamomile
Latin name: Anthemis nobilis
Properties: Pain reliever, antidepressant, anti-inflammatory, antiseptic, sedative
Uses: Skin problems, stress, arthritis, bursitis, blisters, wounds, menopause, PMS
Cautions: Avoid in first trimester of pregnancy

4 Clove bud
Latin name: Syzygium aromaticum
Properties: Pain reliever, especially for oral problems
Uses: Tooth pain, gum problems
Cautions: Avoid during pregnancy

5 Cypress
Latin name: Cupressus sempervirens
Properties: Antiseptic, eases muscle spasms, astringent, deodorant, decongestant
Uses: Asthma, coughs, bruises, sinusitis, insect repellent, stress

Cautions: Avoid during pregnancy or if you have high blood pressure

6 Eucalyptus
Latin name: Eucalyptus globulus
Properties: Pain reliever, decongestant, expectorant, antiviral, antibacterial, antifungal
Uses: Asthma, coughs, bronchitis, arthritis, headache, wounds, fever, insect repellent
Cautions: Dilute before using on skin; avoid if you have epilepsy or high blood pressure

7 Fir, White
Latin name: Abies alba
Properties: Antiseptic, anti-inflammatory, expectorant
Uses: Coughs, colds, muscle aches
Cautions: Do not use on skin if bottle has been stored over one year

8 Geranium
Latin name: Pelargonium graveolens
Properties: Pain reliever, anti-inflammatory, antiseptic, antidepressant, deodorant, insect repellent
Uses: Menopause, menstrual problems, breast tenderness, stress, PMS, anxiety
Cautions: Avoid in early pregnancy; overuse may cause insomnia

9 Ginger
Latin name: Zingiber officinale
Properties: Antiseptic, relieves muscle spasms, expels digestive gas, pain reliever, anti-inflammatory
Uses: Congestion, coughs, colds, headaches, fever, arthritis, nausea
Cautions: May irritate sensitive skin

10 Grapefruit
Latin name: Citrus paradisi
Properties: Antidepressant, antiseptic, astringent
Uses: **Acne, oily skin, muscle stiffness, headache, stress, fatigue**
Cautions: Don't expose treated skin to sun

11 Lavender
Latin name: Lavendula officinalis, L. angustifolia
Properties: Antiseptic, antidepressant, antiviral, sedative, relieves muscle spasms, astringent
Uses: **Skin problems, arthritis, pain, gout, stress, anxiety, insomnia**
Cautions: Avoid if you have extremely low blood pressure

12 Lemon
Latin name: Citrus limonum
Properties: Antiseptic, eases muscle spasms, astringent, kills bacteria, antifungal, insect repellent, antiviral
Uses: **Acne, boils, exfoliant, oily skin, fever, PMS, painful joints, depression fatigue**
Cautions: Don't expose treated skin to sun; may irritate sensitive skin

13 Lemon balm
Latin name: (Melissa) Melissa officinalis
Properties: Antiviral (effective against herpes); antifungal, relieves muscle spasms, sedative
Uses: **Cold sores, depression, stress, athlete's foot**
Cautions: Lemon balm is expensive to produce; bargain brands may be blended with cheaper oils

14 Myrrh
Latin name: Commiphora myrrha
Properties: Anti-inflammatory, antifungal, kills germs, astringent, expectorant
Uses: **Wounds, athlete's foot, mouth ulcers, sore throat, gum problems, laryngitis**
Cautions: Avoid during pregnancy

15 Peppermint
Latin name: Mentha piperita
Properties: Pain reliever, antiseptic, relieves muscle spasms, astringent, expels digestive gas, eases stomach pain, decongestant, antifungal
Uses: **Headache, fever, colds, sinusitis, nausea, muscle spasms, ringworm, bad breath, lethargy, depression**

Cautions: May irritate skin; do not use on damaged or broken skin

16 Rosemary
Latin name: Rosmarinus officinalis
Properties: Pain reliever, antiseptic, eases muscle spasms, decongestant, stimulant
Uses: **Fatigue, asthma, bronchitis, cramps, muscle soreness, arthritis, headache, memory booster, oily hair, dandruff, stress, depression**
Cautions: Avoid if you have high blood pressure or a history of epilepsy; do not use on broken or damaged skin

17 Sage, Clary
Latin name: Salvia sclarea
Properties: Antidepressant, deodorant, relaxes cramps
Uses: **PMS and menopause symptoms, skin toner, acne, dandruff, depression, stress, migraine, fatigue**
Cautions: Do not confuse with garden sage (*Salvia officinalis*); overuse may cause headaches

18 Tea tree
Latin name: Melaleuca alternifolia
Properties: Antibiotic, antibacterial, antiviral, decongestant
Uses: **Cuts, abrasions, insect bites, mouth ulcers, cold sores, herpes, chicken pox, colds, bronchitis, acne, athlete's foot, nail fungus, ringworm, dandruff**
Cautions: Possible irritant to sensitive skin

19 Thyme
Latin name: Thymus vulgaris
Properties: Antibacterial, pain reliever
Uses: **Arthritis, skin problems, wounds, acne, colds, sinus infections**
Cautions: Avoid red thyme oils; thyme essential oil should be a pale yellow color

20 Ylang-ylang
Latin name: Cananga odorata
Properties: Antiseptic, antidepressant, sedative
Uses: **Anxiety, stress, acne, insomnia, depression, PMS**
Cautions: Avoid use on damaged or sensitive skin

index

C